NEW YORK CITY

Orange Line 4

für Klasse 8

Das Lehrbuch versteht sich als Gesamtangebot. Welche Texte und Aufgaben verpflichtend sind, wird durch die schulinternen Curricula festgelegt.

Zusatzmaterial für Schülerinnen und Schüler:
Orange Line 4 Workbook mit Audio-CD und Übungssoftware (ISBN 978-3-12-548084-1)
Orange Line 4 Workbook mit Audio-CD (ISBN 978-3-12-548284-5)
Orange Line 4 Vokabellernheft (ISBN 978-3-12-548094-0)
Orange Line 4 Vokabeltraining aktiv (ISBN 978-3-12-548244-9)
Orange Line 4 Grammatiktraining aktiv (ISBN 978-3-12-548304-1)
Orange Line 4 Klassenarbeitstraining aktiv (ISBN 978-3-12-548104-6)

1. Auflage 1 5 4 3 2 1 | 21 20 19 18 17

Alle Drucke dieser Auflage sind unverändert und können im Unterricht nebeneinander verwendet werden.
Die letzte Zahl bezeichnet das Jahr des Druckes.

Herausgeber: Dr. Frank Haß, Kirchberg
Autorinnen und Autoren: Chris Caridia, London sowie
Jo Cummins, London; Wolfgang Hamm, Marktredwitz; Dr. Andrea Jessen, Tamm; Leonie Pohl, Gütersloh; Nadine Uesbeck, Dortmund; Anna Zagermann, Hattingen; Konstanze Zander, Großenehrich
Beratung: Brunhilde Biek, Leonberg; Karin Braun, Dortmund; Wilma Brings, Bedburg; Amanda Chisnell, Lollar; Sara Conway, Stuttgart; Ulf Degen, Braunschweig; Tanja Frank, Ulm; Sandra Haberland, Recklinghausen; Wolfgang Hamm, Marktredwitz; Ulrike Heringhaus, Altheim; Michael Herrmann, Ludwigsfelde; Christa Kathmann-Fuhrmann, Bonn; Dr. Margitta Kuty, Greifswald-Eldna; Grit Machut, Berlin; Michael Meisenzahl, Karlstadt; Beatrix Pierce, Eppingen; Annegret Preker-Franke, Bielefeld; Dr. Hubert Schwandt, Parchen; Christian Straukamp, Nordhorn; Ines van Hove, Oldenburg; Dieter Vilimek, Helmstadt-Bargen

Redaktion: André Schmitt; Joanne Popp; Birgit Piefke-Wagner, Korntal-Münchingen
Herstellung: Ulrike Wursthorn

Umschlaggestaltung und Gestaltungskonzept: know idea, Freiburg; Koma Amok, Stuttgart
Umschlagfoto: Getty Images (Derek Von Briesen), München; plainpicture GmbH (BHarman), Hamburg
Illustrationen: Marek Blaha, Offenbach; Kirill Chudinskiy, Köln sowie
Friederike Ablang, Berlin; Iris Blanck, Hamburg; Martina Burghardt-Vollhardt, Kamenz; Udo Clormann, Wiesbaden; Thorsten Droessler, Leipzig; Andreas Florian, Lübeck; Anke Fröhlich, Leipzig; Carolin Görtler, Immenstadt im Allgäu; Josef Hammen, Trierweiler; Christian Hansen, Berlin; Rob Harvey, Cirencester, GB; Carmen Hochmann, Bielefeld; Martin Hoffmann, Stuttgart; Yvonne Hoppe-Engbring, Steinfurt; Steffen Jähde, Sundhagen; Klett Archiv, Stuttgart; Hendrik Kranenberg, Drolshagen; Jeongsook Lee, Köln; Katja Leuschner, Halle; Helga Merkle, Albershausen; Lutz-Erich Müller, Leipzig; Axel Nicolai, Brauweiler; David Norman, Meerbusch; Liliane Oser, Hamburg; Sven Palmowski, Barcelona, Spain; Katja Rau, Fellbach; Anja Rieger, Berlin; Annika Sauerborn, Mainz; Sandra Schmidt, Berlin; Carolin Ina Schröter, Berlin; Friederike Schumann, Berlin; Birgit Tanck, Hamburg; Inge Voets, Berlin; Sylvia Wolf, Wiesbaden; Katrin Wolff, Wiesbaden; Steffen Wolff, Brohl-Lützing; Dorothee Wolters, Köln

Satz: Satzkiste GmbH, Stuttgart
Reproduktion: Schwabenrepro GmbH, Stuttgart
Druck: Mohn Media Mohndruck GmbH, Gütersloh

Printed in Germany
ISBN 978-3-12-548074-2 (fester Einband)
ISBN 978-3-12-548274-6 (flexibler Einband)

9 783125 480742 9 783125 482746

L = Listening S = Speaking R = Reading W = Writing V = Viewing I = Intercultural

L = Listening S = Speaking R = Reading W = Writing V = Viewing I = Intercultural

L = Listening S = Speaking R = Reading W = Writing V = Viewing I = Intercultural

So lernst du mit Orange Line

Hier zeige ich dir, wie du dich in deinem Buch gut zurechtfindest. Das Buch hat fünf Units (Kapitel). Jede Unit ist gleich aufgebaut.

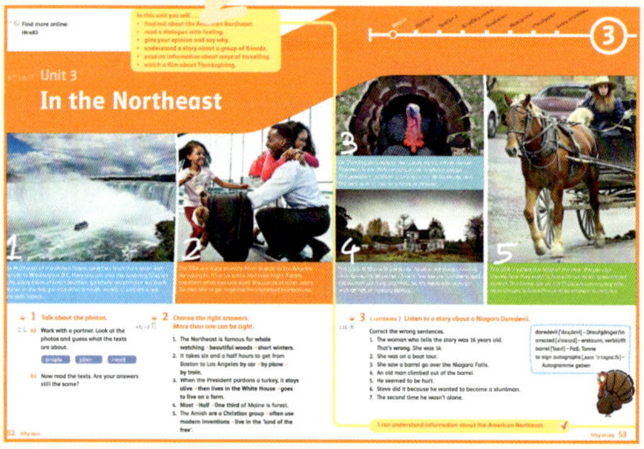

Way in

Hier steigst du in das neue Thema ein. Dazu gibt es auch einen kurzen Film.

Im gelben Kasten siehst du, was du in der *Unit* lernst.

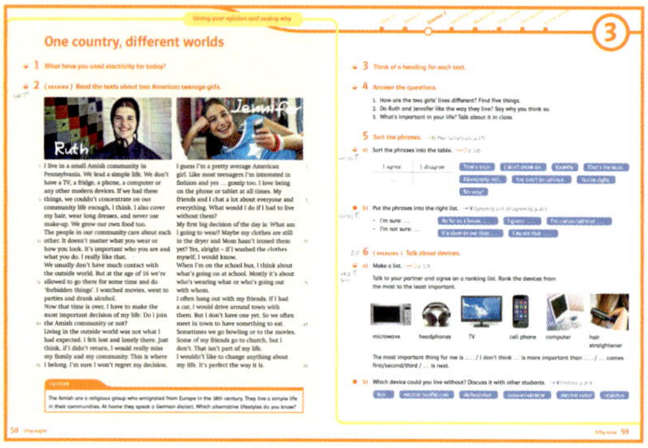

Stations

In jeder *Unit* gibt es zwei *Stations*, in denen du viele neue Dinge lernst. Diese Symbole zeigen dir, wie schwer die Übung ist und ob es im Anhang eine leichtere Variante gibt:

◒ → ○ p. 132, ●

In der *Your turn*-Aufgabe kannst du zeigen, dass du alles verstanden hast, und deine eigenen Ideen einbringen.

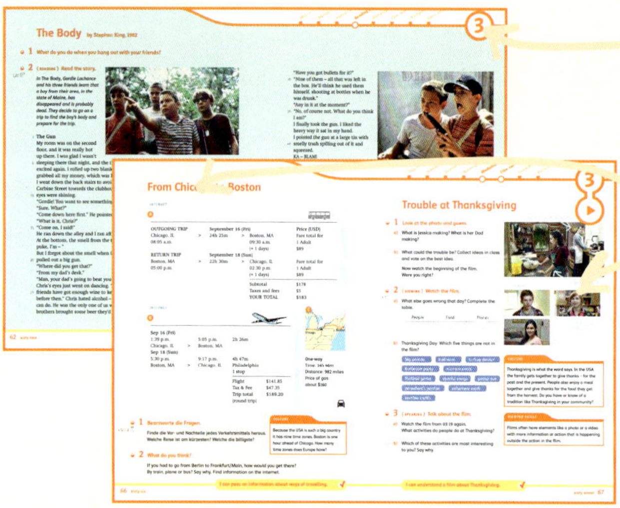

Reading corner

In der *Reading corner* gibt es verschiedene Geschichten und Sachtexte.

Mediation/Film corner

Auf der linken Seite geht es darum, englische Informationen auf Deutsch weiterzugeben oder umgekehrt.

In der *Film corner* geht es um einen englischen Film.

Checkpoint

Auf dieser Seite kannst du überprüfen, ob du in der *Unit* alles verstanden hast. In der *Checklist* sind alle Lernziele noch einmal aufgelistet.

Die Abschluss-Aufgabe (*task*) sollt ihr zu zweit oder in der Gruppe lösen.

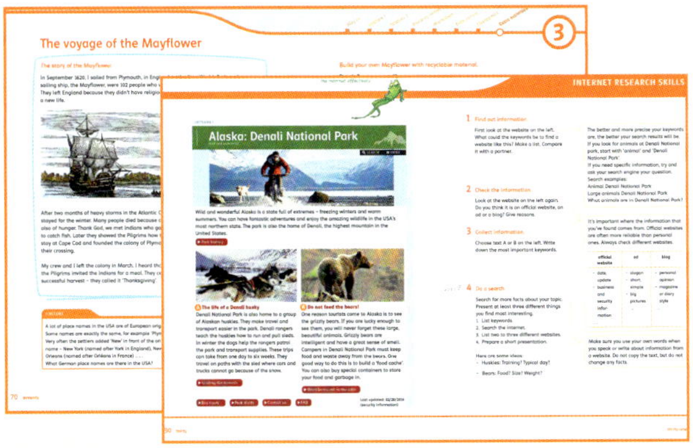

Extra activities

Hier findest du zwei Seiten mit besonderen Aktivitäten, z. B. einem Spiel.

Skills

Auf einige *Units* folgt eine Doppelseite, auf der du eine bestimmte Fertigkeit (*skill*) besonders trainieren kannst, also z. B. das Lesen, Schreiben, Sprechen oder Wörterbucharbeit.

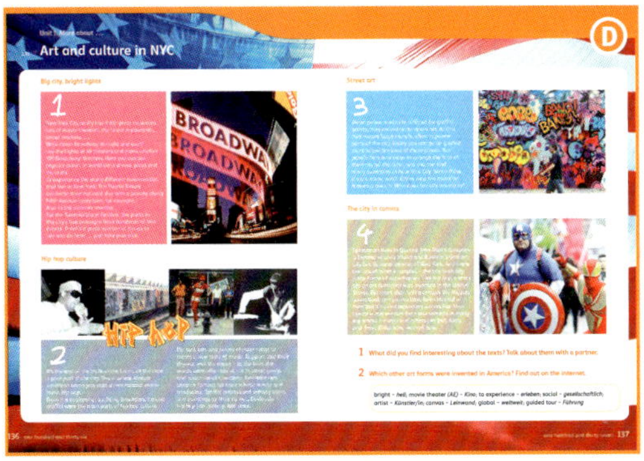

More about

Hier findest du interessante weiterführende Informationen zur Region der Unit.

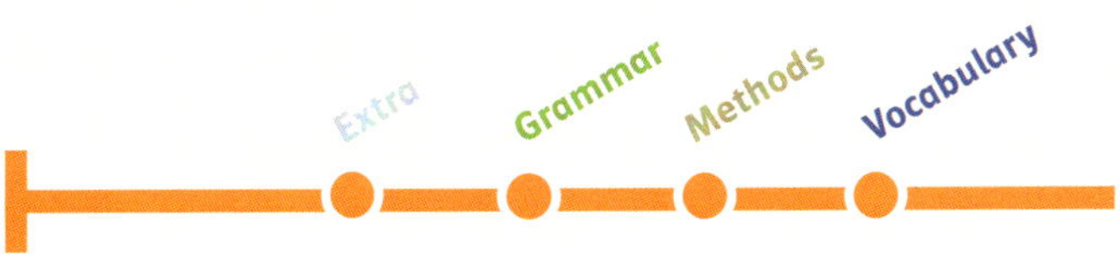

Im Anschluss an die fünf *Units* gibt es noch weitere nützliche Seiten:

Extra: Hier erwarten dich weitere Lesetexte und vieles mehr.

Grammar: Hier findest du alle Regeln und Erklärungen zur Grammatik sowie weitere Übungen.

Methods: Manche Übungen könnt ihr auf eine bestimmte Art und Weise bearbeiten.
Das erkennt ihr an diesem Symbol: → M
Wie es genau funktioniert, kannst du hier nachlesen.

Vocabulary: Im *Vocabulary* findest du alle neuen Wörter in der Reihenfolge, in der sie in der *Unit* auftauchen, und die wichtigsten Arbeitsanweisungen.
Im *Dictionary* sind die Wörter noch einmal alphabetisch aufgelistet: zuerst Englisch-Deutsch und dann Deutsch-Englisch.

Am Schluss des Buches findest du noch
- Sätze, die du im Unterricht sagen kannst, z. B. bei der Gruppenarbeit
- eine Liste mit den unregelmäßigen Verben.

Symbol	Erklärung
○ ◒ ●	leicht/mittel/schwer (Niveaudifferenzierung)
✿	individualisierende Aufgabe (natürliche Differenzierung)
→ ○ p. 131	Verweis auf leichtere Parallelübung auf der *Diff corner*-Seite
OR	Aufgabe zur Auswahl (Wahldifferenzierung)
	Entwicklung von Schlüsselkompetenzen
P	Hier entsteht ein Produkt für das Portfolio.
4/1	Verweis auf eine Übung im *Workbook*
→ G6, p. 165	Verweis auf den Grammatikanhang (*Grammar*)
→ M	Verweis auf die Methodenseite (*Methods*)
→ V	Verweis zum Wortfeld im Vokabular (*Vocabulary*)
	Partnerarbeit
	Gruppenarbeit
	Verweis auf die Lehrer-CD (Audio)
	Verweis auf die Lehrer-DVD (Film)
Find more online:	Code auf www.klett.de eingeben und Zusatzinformationen erhalten

Zoom in – The USA

Every year in fall the New England states shine in bright colors.

1

Denali (Mt. McKinley) is the highest mountain in Alaska and North America (6,190 m).

4

flag

rose

bald eagle

Name:	United States of America
Population:	≈ 321,400,000 (July 2015)
Area (total):	≈ 9,800,000 km² (≈ 3,600,000 sq.mi.) (3rd largest country in the world)
Currency:	US dollar
Capital:	Washington D.C.
States:	50
Time zones:	9
Major rivers:	Mississippi, Missouri, Colorado
Mountains:	Rocky Mountains, Appalachian Mountains

The Midwest is a huge open area with lots of corn and soybean fields.

2

Hawaii is a surfer's paradise with perfect waves and white and black beaches.

3

Most parts of the Rocky Mountains are protected. Lots of tourists enjoy the beautiful landscape.

5

In some parts of the American south there are swamps where alligators live.

6

1 Look at the photos and read the texts.

Which parts of the USA would you like to visit? Say why.

2 Look at the map at the back of the book. Find the answers.

1. Name the countries that are north and south of the USA.
2. Name the oceans that are east and west of the USA.
3. Name the sea that's south of the states of Louisiana, Mississippi and Alabama.
4. Name the state that's in the Pacific Ocean, southwest of California.
5. Name the state that's to the northwest of Canada.
6. Find out the distances from north to south and east to west.

3 Look at the photos and choose one of the places.

Find out more about it on the internet. Present some interesting facts to the class.

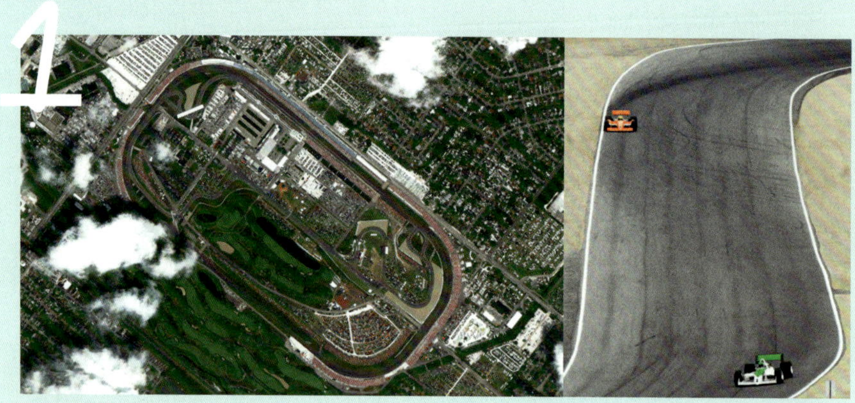

1. Indiana: Indy 500
2. Kentucky: Fort Knox
3. Pennsylvania: Declaration of Independence
4. Washington: Space Needle, Seattle

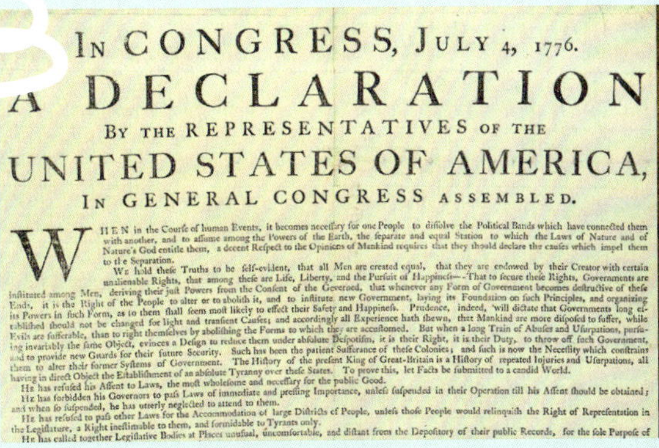

IN CONGRESS, JULY 4, 1776.

A DECLARATION

BY THE REPRESENTATIVES OF THE

UNITED STATES OF AMERICA,

IN GENERAL CONGRESS ASSEMBLED.

WHEN in the Course of human Events, it becomes necessary for one People to dissolve the Political Bands which have connected them with another, and to assume among the Powers of the Earth, the separate and equal Station to which the Laws of Nature and of Nature's God entitle them, a decent Respect to the Opinions of Mankind requires that they should declare the causes which impel them to the Separation.

We hold these Truths to be self-evident, that all Men are created equal, that they are endowed by their Creator with certain unalienable Rights, that among these are Life, Liberty, and the Pursuit of Happiness—That to secure these Rights, Governments are instituted among Men, deriving their just Powers from the Consent of the Governed, that whenever any Form of Government becomes destructive of these Ends, it is the Right of the People to alter or to abolish it, and to institute new Government, laying its Foundation on such Principles, and organizing its Powers in such Form, as to them shall seem most likely to effect their Safety and Happiness. Prudence, indeed, will dictate that Governments long established should not be changed for light and transient Causes; and accordingly all Experience hath shewn, that Mankind are more disposed to suffer, while Evils are sufferable, than to right themselves by abolishing the Forms to which they are accustomed. But when a long Train of Abuses and Usurpations, pursuing invariably the same Object, evinces a Design to reduce them under absolute Despotism, it is their Right, it is their Duty, to throw off such Government, and to provide new Guards for their future Security. Such has been the patient Sufferance of these Colonies; and such is now the Necessity which constrains them to alter their former Systems of Government. The History of the present King of Great-Britain is a History of repeated Injuries and Usurpations, all having in direct Object the Establishment of an absolute Tyranny over these States. To prove this, let Facts be submitted to a candid World.

He has refused his Assent to Laws, the most wholesome and necessary for the public Good.

He has forbidden his Governors to pass Laws of immediate and pressing Importance, unless suspended in their Operation till his Assent should be obtained; and when so suspended, he has utterly neglected to attend to them.

He has refused to pass other Laws for the Accommodation of large Districts of People, unless those People would relinquish the Right of Representation in the Legislature, a Right inestimable to them, and formidable to Tyrants only.

He has called together Legislative Bodies at Places unusual, uncomfortable, and distant from the Depository of their public Records, for the sole Purpose of

5. North Dakota: Sitting Bull
6. Alabama: US Space & Rocket Center, Huntsville
7. Colorado: Mesa Verde
8. Nevada: Las Vegas
9. New Mexico: Very Large Array

Find more online:
i8ce82

In this unit you will ...
- find out about New York City.
- present interesting places in a city.
- write an article about a person.
- read a text about the history of immigration to the USA.
- pass on information about how to become a citizen.
- watch a film about sights in New York City.

1 1,1

Unit 1
Gateway NYC

New York City (NYC) is the biggest city in the United States. Over eight and a half million people live in its five boroughs: The Bronx, Brooklyn, Queens, Manhattan and Staten Island. The city's nickname is the 'Big Apple'.

One building stands out in the New York City skyline: One World Trade Center is the tallest building in the USA. It is 400 feet higher than the old World Trade Center, which it replaced after the attacks on September 11, 2001.

1 Look at the photos.

a) What do you know about New York City? The photos can help you.

b) Read the texts. Then match them with these phrases.

tallest building in the USA
sports in the USA
a symbol of American independence
American culture
the Big Apple

2/1-2

2 Correct the wrong sentences.

1. There are eight boroughs and eight and a half million people in New York City.
2. One World Trade Center is taller than the building which it replaced.
3. People in New York aren't very interested in baseball.
4. Important cultural movements started in New York.
5. The Statue of Liberty was made in the USA.

Baseball is one of the most popular sports in the USA, and New Yorkers especially love it. Some players of the sport are among the biggest and best-paid stars in the country.

New York is an important center for music, theater, dance and art. It's home to some of the world's finest art collections and to many modern American cultural movements, like hip hop and street art.

The Statue of Liberty was a present from France to celebrate 100 years of American independence. They sent it in pieces across the Atlantic. It opened in 1886. For immigrants it became a symbol of hope for their new life.

3 (LISTENING) Listen to a guided tour of One World Trade Center.

1,2

Answer the questions.

1. What happened on September 11, 2001?
2. How many people saw the events on TV?
3. How tall is One World Trade Center?
4. How long does it take to travel to the top?
5. What do visitors watch in the elevators?
6. Where does the electricity for the lights in the tower come from?
7. Why is the new One World Trade Center located on the grounds of the World Trade Center?

billion ['bɪliən] – Milliarde
event [ɪ'vent] – Ereignis
elevator ['elɪveɪtə] – Aufzug, Lift
top [tɒp] – Spitze
grounds [graʊndz] – Gelände, Gebiet

I can understand information about New York City. ✓

A taxi ride in NYC

1 (READING) Read the text.

1,3
3/1

David Singh: A traffic jam! It's always bad on the Brooklyn Bridge during rush hour. And last Monday they started roadwork here too. Don't even ask me what it's like in the winters. Two years ago we had so much snow that I didn't get into the city at all on some days! I live in Queens, but I like to work in downtown Manhattan, because that's where the money is!

Anyway, you can get a very good look at the New York skyline from here. I never get tired of it – let me tell you about the landmarks. That's One World Trade Center there. Those skyscrapers over there are on Wall Street, the financial center of the world. Can you see the Empire State Building in the distance? They built it in the early 1930s. With its 102 stories it was the tallest building in the world back then.

Rockefeller Center is just a few blocks away. You should go up there while you're here, the view of Manhattan from the top is really something.

How long are you here for, anyway? If you only have one day, I say: buy a bagel and a coffee early in the morning and go for a walk in Central Park. There are trees, lakes, playgrounds, a zoo and lots more.

After that check out the Metropolitan Museum of Art. It only had a collection of 174 pieces of art when it opened in the 19th century, but today it's huge.

Next, take the subway at 86th Street and Lexington Avenue to Grand Central Station. When you're in there, look up. Fun fact: the star signs on the ceiling aren't correct. Why did no one notice when they put them up there? I've no idea.

Around the corner there's a hot dog cart. It belongs to my friend Nick. Remember the name – he does the best hot dogs in New York! In the afternoon you should go shopping and finish the day with a Broadway show. Just make sure you walk far enough to get to Times Square too. At last, the lights are green again. Now, let's get moving.

2 Describe the situation. → M Think-pair-share, p. 179

Where is David Singh? Who is he talking to? What is he talking about?

CULTURE

You can't get lost in Manhattan if you look at the street names: 'avenues' go from north to south and 'streets' go from east to west. Where do the streets get their names from where you live?

David Singh

3 Right or wrong? Cite the sentence from the text. → M Peer correction, p. 177

1. The traffic on the Brooklyn Bridge is bad during rush hour.
   That's **right**. ***(lines 1–2)*** *"It's always bad on the Brooklyn Bridge during rush hour."*
2. David lives in downtown Manhattan.
3. In the 1920s the Empire State Building was the tallest building in the world.
4. There's a zoo in Central Park.
5. The Metropolitan Museum of Art had 102 pieces of art when it opened.
6. David thinks that you can buy the best hot dogs in New York from a hot dog cart.

4 Work with the city words.

a) Find the odd one out. → ○ p. 116

3/2

1. public transport • shopping mall • rush hour • traffic jam
2. skyline • skyscraper • subway • tower
3. intersection • campsite • roadwork • road sign
4. sightseeing • sidewalk • tourist • visitor

b) Match the words with their definitions. → V City words, p. 185

3/3

parking lot | commuter | construction site | suburbs

1. a place where they are building something
2. people live here, away from the city center
3. you can leave your car here
4. a person who travels to work every day

5 (SPEAKING) Talk about the city.

a) Present what is in the photo. → ○ p. 116

3/4
4/5a)

Have a good look at …
On the corner there is …
Over there …
Right ahead …
Have you noticed …?
In the distance you can just see …

b) Show a visitor places in your town: → V City guide, p. 191

4/5b)-6

Don't miss … | Make sure you visit … | I'd like to point out … | Down there is …

CULTURE

Some everyday words are different in British (BE) and American (AE) English: *underground* – *subway*; *car park* – *parking lot*; *town centre* – *downtown*; *crossroads* – *intersection*; *lift* – *elevator*. Some are different in spelling: *centre* – *center*; *theatre* – *theater*; *colour* – *color*, *favourite* – *favorite*, *licence* – *license* or different in pronunciation: *tomato* [tə'mɑːtəʊ] – [tə'meɪtəʊ]. You can find more examples on pages 182-221.

Language → G1, p. 160

Last Monday they started roadwork here.
Two years ago we had so much snow that I didn't get into the city at all on some days.
Why did no one notice that?

What tense is this? When do you use it?

5/7

6 Complete the sentences. → M Bus stop, p. 174

1. The island of Manhattan —— the Native Americans until 1626. (belong to)
2. The Brooklyn Bridge —— on May 24, 1883. (open)
3. The Statute of Liberty —— a present from France. (be)
4. More than 40,000 people —— Rockefeller Center. (work on)
5. In the 1980s Central Park —— a very safe place. (not be)
6. Grand Central Station —— its new name 'Grand Central Terminal' in 1913. (get)
7. Two years ago the traffic in New York —— because of heavy snow. (not move)

7 (WRITING) Tell the taxi driver's story.

5/8a)

a) Make sentences in the simple past. The words below can help you. → ○ p. 116

airport · passenger · get in · traffic jam · talk · arrive
leave · saxophone · find · run · hotel · give back

Last winter a passenger got in my taxi at John F. Kennedy Airport. …

5/8b)

b) Write an ending for the story.

Here's one idea:

8 (SPEAKING) What did they do at One World Trade Center yesterday?

a) Ask and answer questions about the people in the picture. → ○ p. 117

5/9
6/10

drink | eat | look at | sit | talk to
wear | phone | stand | feel | ...

A: What did Henry eat? – B: He ate a sandwich.
B: Did Susan take photos? – A: No, she didn't. She ...

b) Now Partner B closes his or her book. Partner A asks questions. Then take turns.

6/11

A: Did Lisa eat a burger? – B: No, she didn't. Henry did.
A: Where did Scott stand? – B: Scott ...

9 (YOUR TURN) New York City landmarks → V City guide, p. 191

Choose one of the five boroughs of New York. Then look at the map at the front of the book and pick three landmarks. Find out information about them in the library or on the internet:

- What is special about them?
- Who built them?
- When did they open?
- ...

Imagine you are a New York taxi driver: Present the landmarks of your borough to a tourist. → M Tip top, p. 179

STUDY SKILLS

You will often find too much information about a topic. So focus your search on the few facts which you need for this presentation.

I can present interesting places in a city. ✓

Living the dream?

1 (READING) Read the interview with José Blanco.

1,4 7/1

Interviewer: Hello José. Can I ask you a few questions for our magazine, please?

José: Hi. Sure, go ahead.

Interviewer: You're new on the baseball team. Are you happy with your season so far?

José: We won the first three matches, so I can't complain, really.

Interviewer: You're one of many players from Latin America in the league. When did you immigrate to the United States from Cuba?

José: I arrived with my mom and sisters when I was ten. That was twelve years ago. My dad had arrived in New York two years before I came.

Interviewer: That was a big decision for your parents. They left their home and moved to a strange place.

José: Yes, but they were very poor in Cuba. My father had been unemployed for a long time. Above all they wanted to give me and my sisters the best chances in life.

Interviewer: What were the first years like?

José: My parents had problems because they hadn't learned English in school. But there's a strong community of Cubans here, and they all help each other. So my parents opened a small shop and sold goods to other immigrants.

Interviewer: And how did you feel in your new home? Had you ever seen skyscrapers before?

José: No, I hadn't. It was exciting. But later I was homesick. I missed all my friends. But my parents had given up a lot for me. After I had stopped counting the weeks, I slowly got used to it.

Interviewer: And when did you begin your baseball career?

José: As a child in Cuba I always played a lot of sports. But I hadn't taken any sports seriously before I was about 15. From then on I really wanted to be successful. I think people who leave their own culture and language are usually motivated and ambitious. I was the star of the baseball team in high school, and after that my career just took off.

Interviewer: Well you have certainly been successful!

José: Yes, I have been very lucky. For most people it is much harder. This country has given me a great opportunity. My story really is an example of the American Dream come true.

Interviewer: What about your plans for the future?

José: I am a US citizen now and my home is here. But I still have contact with Cuba, and I plan to help develop tourism there.

Interviewer: José, thank you for your time.

2 Work with the text.

a) Complete the sentences. → ○ p. 118 → M Peer correction, p. 177

1. José was ten years old when …
2. His parents decided to immigrate because …
3. They opened a shop for other immigrants because …
4. In the beginning, José felt … but later …
5. As a successful player, now José feels …
6. José is a US citizen but he also …

b) Explain what José means by 'the American Dream come true' (*lines 51/52*).

3 (LISTENING) Listen to the interview with Angela.

1,5

Take notes about …
1. Angela's home country
2. reasons why she came to New York
3. her new life (good and bad things)
4. her situation now
5. her dream

STUDY SKILLS

Make your notes as short as possible. Use keywords only. You don't need to write full length words – write 'Am.' for 'American', for example. You can use symbols, like '+' for good things and '–' for bad things.

4 Imagine you want to leave your country.

a) Use these phrases to describe your thoughts, hopes and wishes. → ○ p. 119

7/2

have many opportunities | feel foreign | get used to | emigrate from ✓ | immigrate to

1. I want to **emigrate from this country.**

2. Maybe I could …

3. I hope I won't …

4. I will probably …

5. I'm sure I can …

b) Make your own thought bubbles with these words. You can draw pictures or write sentences.
→ V Going to a new country, p. 186

7/3
7/4

succeed in | fail at | get support from | adapt to | cross the border

5 (SONG) Empire State of Mind (Part II) Broken Down

1,6

Listen to the song. What can you find out about New York?

Ooooh, New York!
Ooooh, New York!

Grew up in a town that is famous as a place of movie scenes.
Noise is always loud, there are sirens all around and the streets are mean.
If I can make it here, I can make it anywhere, that's what they say.
Seeing my face in lights or my name in marquees found down on Broadway.
Even if it ain't all it seems, I got a pocketful of dreams.

Language detectives → G2, p. 161

After I had stopped counting the weeks, I slowly got used to it.
But I hadn't taken any sports seriously before I was about 15.
Had you ever seen skyscrapers before you went to New York? – No, I hadn't.

The simple past and past perfect describe events in the past.
Which event happened first? Which tense do you use for it?
Which word(s) tell(s) you which event happened first?

6 Complete José's sentences with the past perfect.

8/5-7

1. After my dad had lived (live) in New York for two years, we joined him.
2. After I —— (be) in school for a year, I started to play baseball.
3. Everything was new for me. But I —— (see) yellow taxis in movies before.
4. My grandma —— (die) a few weeks before I left for the USA.
5. I —— (never visit) the USA before I came to live here.
6. José —— (not speak) English very often before he moved to New York.

7 (WRITING) Write about one of Angela's days.

a) Make sentences with the simple past and the past perfect. → ○ p. 119

9/8

After …

buy a present

take the subway

visit Ellis Island

Before …

order a milkshake

put on their fan shirts

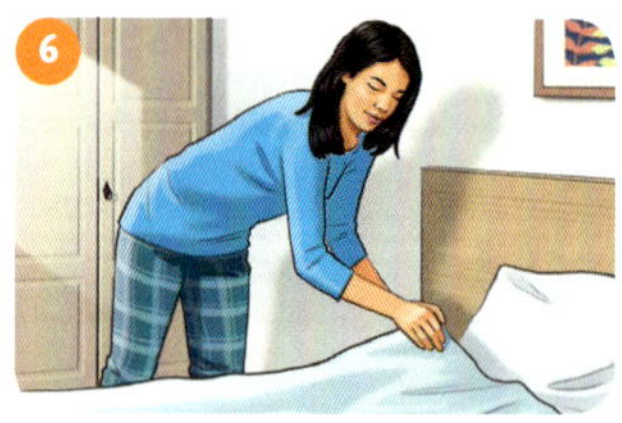

watch a TV show

1. After Pablo had invited Angela to his party, she bought a present.

b) Make more sentences about Angela.

9/9

1. before • go to work • call Pablo • and • ask him about the party
2. after • leave the house • go back • and • close the windows
3. after • arrive home • feel very tired • and • take a hot shower

8 (SPEAKING) Ask and answer questions.

a) What had or hadn't José done before his first important baseball game last summer? Ask questions and answer them. → ○ p. 120

9/10

1. Interviewer: Had you played every day last summer before your first big game?
   José: Yes, I had.

1 play every day ✓
2 buy new sports shoes
3 order tickets for his friends ✓
4 phone his dad ✓
5 eat a small meal
6 go to bed early

b) What would you ask Angela? Here are some ideas:

Before you left the Philippines, …

ask friends for advice? | plan a party? | be to the USA? | … ?

9 (YOUR TURN) A magazine article → V Presenting personal information, p. 192 → M Writers' conference, p. 179

10/11
11/1-2

Use the information on page 18 to write an article about José
or
the information from Ex. 3 on page 19 to write about Angela.
You can start like this …

A Cuban-American success story
José Blanco is a baseball player with a big future – that's what half of our readers tell us.
José immigrated to the USA with his parents when …

WRITING SKILLS

First, collect the facts that you would like to write about.
Give your text a structure:
Write …
- … a short introduction to say who the person is;
- … the main part with more details about the person;
- … an interesting ending.

Then find a headline for your article.
Finally, check what you have written. Use the checklist on page 181.

I can write an article about a person. ✓

Ellis Island – a symbol of immigration

1 **Think of reasons why people leave their home country.** → M Think-pair-share, p. 179

2 **(READING) Read the text.**

1,7

The United States is a country of immigrants. A visit to the Immigration Museum on Ellis Island brings this dry statement to life. Between 1892 and 1954 Ellis Island was the most important gateway for twelve million new immigrants. Today more than half of the American people are their descendants. In the Family History Center visitors can search millions of ships' passenger lists and find out more about their personal family story.
Families often saved money for the father or the oldest son to make the journey alone. Later, when they had a home and a job, they sent for the whole family. Statistics show that many of those who arrived hadn't paid for their tickets themselves or had to work off their tickets.

The voyage on steamships took seven to 21 days. But conditions were very hard on board. Immigrants were poor, so they traveled third class. Here they stayed in a crowded and dirty space at the bottom of the ship. There was bad food and very little deck area to get fresh air. Many passengers were sick for the whole crossing. So at the end of the long trip, the majority were not in a good physical or mental state.
However, their journey was not over after the sea crossing. Before they could leave the ship, doctors came on board to check for dangerous diseases. After this inspection, the ship moved slowly into the harbor.
The first thing that the arrivals saw was the huge Statue of Liberty. "No one spoke a word," said one Polish immigrant. "She was like a goddess, a symbol of the big, powerful country which was our future home."
After the ship had docked in Manhattan, they went to Ellis Island on a small boat. Here they had medical inspections and personal interviews, which were often very unpleasant. If the doctors found certain diseases or the immigrants were too weak to work, they sent them back to their home countries. About two percent had to return. A minority of about 20 percent stayed on the island for days or sometimes weeks for more checks, but the rest were free to go after a few hours. The immigrants' journey to the USA, which had begun months or years before, was now over. Finally they were in the 'land of opportunity'. But they still had a long way ahead of them to find out if they could make it there.

CULTURE

Everyone who is born in the United States is an American citizen and can have an American passport. What is the situation in your country?

READING SKILLS

When you read a pie chart, look at the title, keys and labels first. Then look at the different parts of the chart and look at their sizes.

Immigration to the USA

From the 1840s to the 1890s most immigrants to the USA came from Britain, Ireland, Scandinavia and Germany. Between the 1890s and the 1920s the majority of immigrants came from Italy, Greece, Eastern Europe, Russia and Turkey. They came for religious or political freedom, or to find work and escape poverty.

Immigration to the USA today: 2013

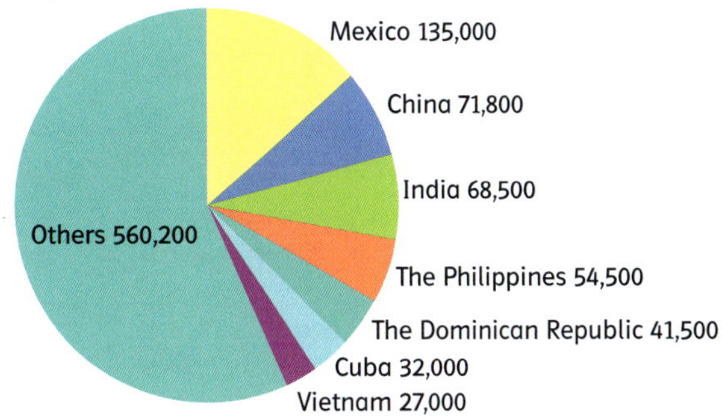

Source: Department of Homeland Security

3 Answer the questions about Ellis Island.

1. How many immigrants arrived between 1892 and 1954?
2. How many weeks did the sea crossing take?
3. What were the conditions on the ships like?
4. What checks were there on board?
5. Where did the ships dock?
6. How many immigrants couldn't stay in the USA?
7. Why could these people not stay?

4 Find the facts in the box.

a) Why did people immigrate to the USA?

b) What does the pie chart tell you about immigration to the USA in 2013?

5 Choose one of these tasks.

a) Work with a partner. Prepare an interview with an immigrant who has just arrived. Here are some questions:

13/2-3
13/4

- Where are you from?
- Why did you choose this country?
- What was the journey like?
- What are your plans for the future?
- ...

Present your interview to the class. → M Dramatic reading, p. 175

OR

b) What country would you like to immigrate to? What do you like about the country? What don't you like?

Give a short presentation to the class.
→ M 1-minute-presentation, p. 174

I can understand a text about the history of immigration to the USA. ✓

How to become a US citizen

How do I apply for US citizenship?

- be age 18 or older
- be a permanent resident for a certain amount of time (usually 5 years or 3 years)
- be a person of good moral character
- have a basic knowledge of US government
- be able to read, write and speak basic English
  There are exceptions to this rule for someone who:
  - is 55 years old and has been a permanent resident for at least 15 years;
  - is 50 years old and has been a permanent resident for at least 20 years;
  - has a permanent physical or mental impairment that makes the individual unable to fulfill these requirements.

Sample test questions:

1. What did the Declaration of Independence do?
2. What is the name of the President of the United States now?
3. In what month do we vote for President?
4. What is one reason colonists came to America?
5. What group of people was taken to America and sold as slaves?
6. There were 13 original states. Name three.
7. Name one Native American tribe in the United States.
8. What ocean is on the West Coast of the United States?
9. Why does the flag have 50 stars?
10. Name two national US holidays.

CULTURE

To become a US citizen you must take a test. It's an oral exam in which an officer will ask you ten out of 100 questions. You must answer six out of these ten correctly. There is also an English test. Is there a test like that in your country?

You can find the answers on page 314.

1 Fasse die wichtigsten Punkte zusammen.

14/1-2

Was sind die Voraussetzungen, um die amerikanische Staatsbürgerschaft anzunehmen?
- Wie alt muss man sein?
- Was muss man können und wissen? Gib Beispiele.
- Welche Ausnahmen gibt es?

2 Find the information on the internet.

What does an immigrant to Germany have to do to become a citizen? Present your results.

I can pass on information about how to become a citizen. ✓

New York City, here we come!

1 Talk about New York City.

What do you already know about New York City? Make a mind map of buildings and places in the city.

the Brooklyn Bridge
NYC
buildings
places

CULTURE

Central Park lies in the heart of Manhattan. It has a zoo, seven lakes, an ice rink, baseball fields and lots more. Did you know that the New York Marathon ends in Central Park? Where's the nearest park to where you live? What can you do there?

2 (VIEWING) Watch the film.

2

a) Name the sights that Wesley and Jessica show to Ronan. Put them in the right order.

A

B

C

D

b) Match the facts with the pictures.

1. It's between Manhattan and Brooklyn. There were once elephants here.
2. It's not far from Little Italy and there isn't only one of these in NYC.
3. It has names on a 'Wall of Honor'. Maybe Ronan's great-grandparents were here.
4. There are no elevators here. In summer it can get very hot inside.

3 (SPEAKING) Talk about the film.

a) Watch the film again and write four details of special interest to you. Say why.

b) Where would you like to go in New York City? Why? Tell your partner.

VIEWING SKILLS

When you watch a film the people and the story are important, but so is the setting and what you can see in the background.
Choose a sequence from the film. Turn the sound off. What's happening in the background?

I can understand a film about sights in New York City. ✓

Checklist

I can understand information about New York City. ✓

15

I can present interesting places in a city. ✓

Over there you can see .... • In the distance there is .... • You must visit .... • Don't miss .... • Can you see the ... ?

15

I can write an article about a person. ✓

They left their home. • It was exciting. • I was homesick. • I missed .... • I have contact with .... • ... get used to ...

16

I can understand a text about the history of immigration to the USA. ✓

16

I can pass on information about how to become a citizen. ✓

17

I can understand a film about sights in New York City. ✓

(TASK) A city profile

Work in groups of three students. Each group chooses an American city and finds out some basic facts about it and its population. Each group makes a poster and compares the city with another one.

Step 1

Get into groups. Choose an American city.

Choose one of America's big cities like Los Angeles. Look at the map at the back of the book to find an interesting place.

Step 2

Find the basic facts and some photos.

City: Los Angeles (Nickname: City of Angels)
Location: in the state of California
Landmarks: Hollywood sign; Venice Beach
History: first belonged to Spain; became part of Mexico in 1821; the USA bought California in 1847

Step 3

Find statistical data.

Find data on the internet for these questions:

1. What's the total population of the city that you chose?
2. What are the sizes of the different age groups?
3. Which ethnic groups are part of the city's population? How many people are in each one?

STUDY SKILLS

Check official government websites to find out correct statistical data. You can find data for US cities on the website of the US Census Bureau.

Step 4

Make charts.

Make two different charts. Remember that every chart must have a title, labels and a key. Your charts should take up about 50 percent of your poster.

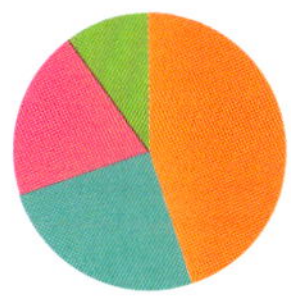

A

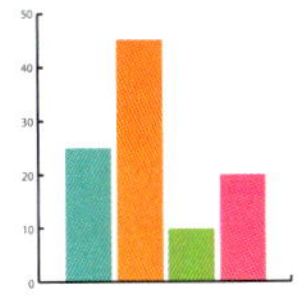

B

STUDY SKILLS

You can make bar charts or pie charts with the help of a computer programme. They're simple and look nice and clear.

Step 5

Write a short text for each chart.

This text should explain the most important information.

most · the majority · the minority · half of · two-thirds · the total number

Step 6

Finish your poster.

Arrange your photos, charts and texts.
Can you read everything from two metres away?
Did you cite your sources?

STUDY SKILLS

Check if your poster is eye-catching.
Is it neatly done and well-organized?

Step 7

Put up your poster.

→ M Gallery walk, p. 175

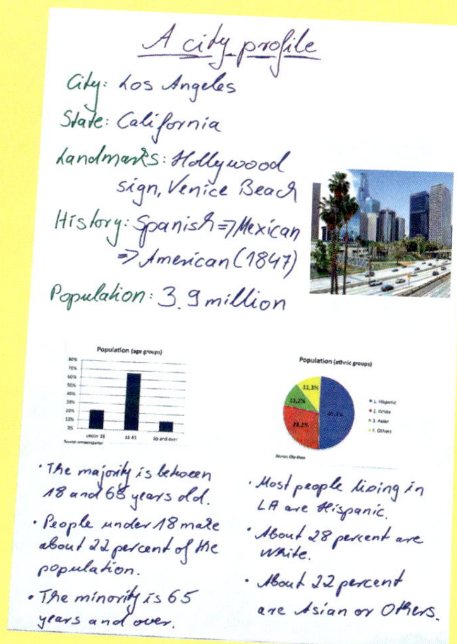

Step 8

Choose one of the other groups' cities and compare it with your city.

Is it bigger? Smaller?
Are there any other differences?
...

0.7 = zero point seven

Make your own street art

Five steps to turn your school yard into an American Dream art gallery

You need:

a piece of paper

pens

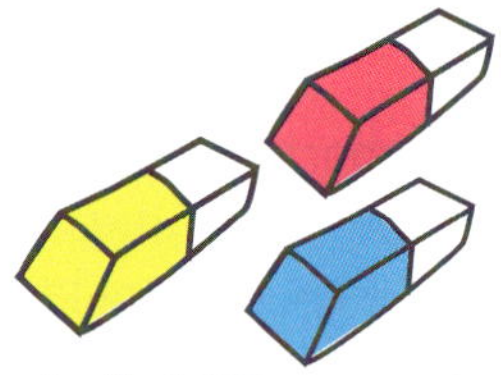

chalk (different colours)

1 Find out about the American Dream.

The American Dream

The basic idea of the American Dream is that you can be anything you want – you only have to work hard enough. Typical dreams are, for example, the dream of being happy, rich or famous. Other people dream of a house for their family or want to have a life which is better than their parents' life. Millions of immigrants have come to the United States searching for a country where their dreams can come true. Critics say that the American Dream does not exist in reality because it isn't for everyone.

2 What do you (not) like about the American Dream?

3 Turn your idea into a piece of street art.

Choose one aspect of the American Dream.
You can write words or sentences and/or draw pictures.
Decide the style of your piece of street art.

Here are some ideas:

1

2

3

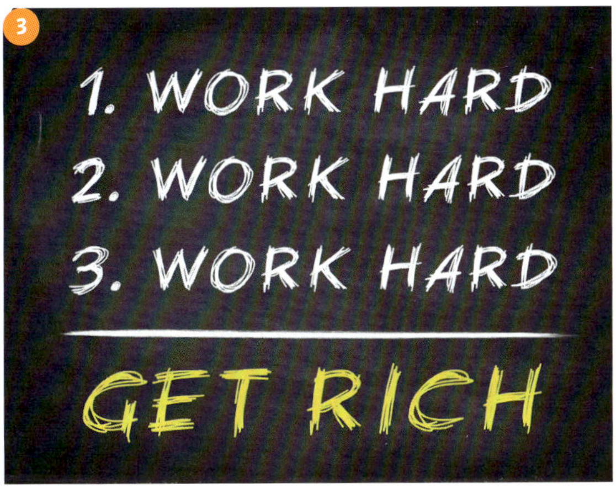

4

4 **Make a draft for your street art on a piece of paper.**

5 **Draw your street art in the schoolyard with chalk.**

You'd better take a photo of your street art before the rain washes it away!

Here you can learn how to use the internet effectively.

Alaska: Denali National Park

wild and wonderful

SEARCH ≡ MENU

Wild and wonderful Alaska is a state full of extremes – freezing winters and warm summers. You can have fantastic adventures and enjoy the amazing wildlife in the USA's most northern state. The park is also the home of Denali, the highest mountain in the United States.

▶ Park history

A The life of a Denali husky

Denali National Park is also home to a group of Alaskan huskies. They make travel and transport easier in the park. Denali rangers teach the huskies how to run and pull sleds. In winter the dogs help the rangers patrol the park and transport supplies. These trips can take from one day to six weeks. They travel on paths with the sled where cars and trucks cannot go because of the snow.

▶ Visiting the kennels

B Do not feed the bears!

One reason tourists come to Alaska is to see the grizzly bears. If you are lucky enough to see them, you will never forget these large, beautiful animals. Grizzly bears are intelligent and have a great sense of smell. Campers in Denali National Park must keep food and waste away from the bears. One good way to do this is to build a 'food cache'. You can also buy special containers to store your food and garbage in.

▶ What bears eat in the wild

▶ Bus tours ▶ Park alerts ▶ Contact us ▶ FAQ

Last updated: 02/20/2016
(security information)

1 Find out information.

First look at the website on the left. What could the keywords be to find a website like this? Make a list. Compare it with a partner.

The better and more precise your keywords are, the better your search results will be. If you look for animals at Denali National park, start with 'animal' and 'Denali National Park'.
If you need specific information, try and ask your search engine your question.
Search examples:
Animal Denali National Park
Large animals Denali National Park
What animals are in Denali National Park?

2 Check the information.

Look at the website on the left again. Do you think it is an official website, an ad or a blog? Give reasons.

It's important where the information that you've found comes from. Official websites are often more reliable than personal ones. Always check different websites.

official website	**ad**	**blog**
– date, update – business and security infor-mation …	– slogan – short, simple – big pictures …	– personal opinion – magazine or diary style …

3 Collect information.

Choose text A or B on the left. Write down the most important keywords.

21/1-3

4 Do a search.

Search for more facts about your topic. Present at least three different things you find most interesting.
1. List keywords.
2. Search the internet.
3. List two to three different websites.
4. Prepare a short presentation.

Here are some ideas:
- Huskies: Training? Typical day?
- Bears: Food? Size? Weight?

Make sure you use your own words when you speak or write about information from a website. Do not copy the text, but do not change any facts.

Find more online:
i8ce82

In this unit you will ...
- find out about life in the Midwest.
- compare school life in the USA and Germany.
- talk about student jobs.
- read a comic strip about high school life.
- pass on information about how to get a driver's license.
- watch a film about someone's first day at a new school.

3 1,8

Unit 2

Teens in the Midwest

The American Midwest is best known for its huge areas of flat farmland and small towns. Here the summers are very hot and the winters are very cold. In the tornado alley area there are terrifying storms.

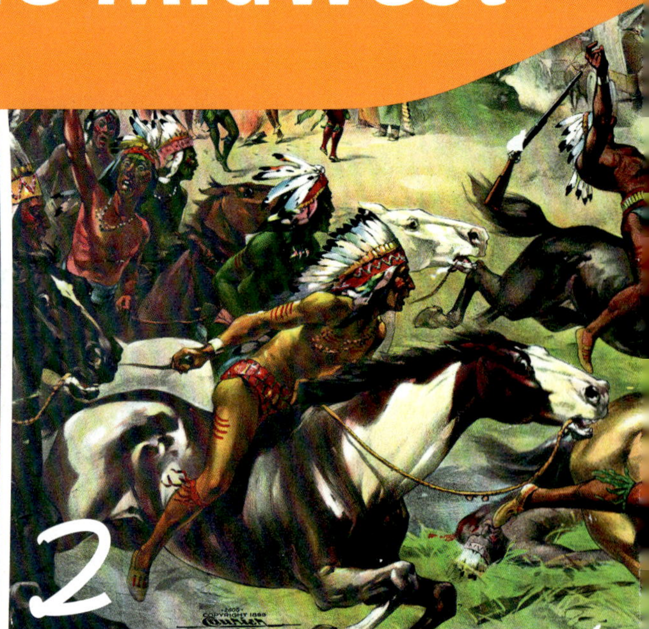

In the 1840s more and more European settlers moved west. They were looking for land and gold. The government forced the Native Americans who lived there to sell their land and move to reservations.

1 (SPEAKING) **Talk about the photos.**

a) Which photos are about the same topic? What are the other photos about?

b) Which photo would you like to know more about? Say why.

→ M Round robin, p. 178

22/1-2

2 **Read the texts and answer the questions.**

1. What is the Midwest famous for?
2. Why did the government force the Native Americans to move to reservations?
3. How do high school students earn some extra money?
4. What is special about American high schools?
5. What happens at Homecoming?

High school students in the USA often do part-time jobs. They can work in stores, help clearing the tables in restaurants or serve ice cream in cafés if they are over 14 years old.

American high schools are usually big. There can be over 2,000 students in a school. Students are 15 to 18 years old when they go to high school. They can get grades from A (very good) to F. The schedule for the students is almost the same every day.

At the start of the new school year former students return to their high schools to celebrate Homecoming. There's a football game and a dance in the evening. Students vote for a Homecoming King and Queen.

3 (LISTENING) Listen to a radio report about a tornado.

1,9

Choose the right answer.

1. Warren's job is to
   present new songs • report on storms • make coffee.
2. Most cars are driving
   away from the storm • 150 miles per hour • west.
3. Warren asks if we can hear the
   wind • traffic • things flying around.
4. The situation is dangerous so people should
   drive away • hurry to a safe place • wait for help.
5. Warren sees some people who
   are crossing the road • are leaving a store • are taking photos.

storm chaser ['stɔ:m ˌtʃeɪsə] – Sturmjäger/in
to report (on) [rɪ'pɔ:t] – berichten (über)
to drive [draɪv] – fahren
direction [dɪ'rekʃn] – Richtung
cloud [klaʊd] – Wolke
to tear up ['teər‿ʌp] – kaputt machen, zerreißen

I can understand information about life in the Midwest. ✓

A student exchange

1 Describe the pictures. What's unusual or new to you?

A

B

C

D

E

2 (READING) Read Luise's report.

1,10

"Oh shoot! I'll be stuck in the middle of nowhere." That's what I thought when I learned that I would go to South Dakota for my exchange year in the USA. But after my year there I can now tell you that it was the best time ever.

In the first couple of weeks it felt like living in a movie. It all seemed so familiar from what I had seen on TV. My American school was huge. Teachers usually stay in their classrooms, and students go to them for each lesson. Because of that we weren't allowed to keep things in the classrooms. We had to put our stuff into our lockers, instead. It took a while to get used to it, but after two weeks I was able to find the way to the different classrooms by myself.

Every day school started at 8:00 with a morning message from the principal and the Pledge of Allegiance. Everyone stood and promised to be true to the United States. That was pretty strange.

After that the first class started at 8:30. I was a 'freshman'. I had to take Math, English, Science and History. But I was also able to choose 'electives' like Astronomy and Journalism. There were lots of interesting options to choose from. We also had six study hall periods a week, where you could do your homework or study. You weren't allowed to talk there.

School rules were strict. Much stricter than I was used to, really. You had to get a hall pass from the teacher to go to the bathroom, for example. Another rule at my school: We weren't allowed to wear short skirts.

Classes ended at 3:30 p.m. After that there were many extracurricular activities. I wanted to join the cheerleaders. There was a lot of competition for places, but exchange students were allowed to try too, so I did. And I actually got a place on the cheerleading squad, which was awesome!

My host family was great too. They even took me on a trip to the east coast, so that I was able to see the Atlantic. Anyway, my exchange year was a blast, even in the middle of nowhere.

CULTURE

Parents are allowed to teach their children of all ages at home and not send them to school. But only a very small number of students (about 3%) is homeschooled. Is there homeschooling in Germany?

3 Take notes about these things at Luise's high school. → M Think-pair-share, p. 179

1. school times
2. before class
3. subjects and electives
4. rules
5. after school

	Monday	Tuesday	Wednesday	Thursday	Friday
1	English	English	English	English	English
2	Math	Math	Math	Math	Math
3	Science	Science	Science	Science	Science
4	History	History	History	History	History
5	Journalism	Journalism	Journalism	Journalism	Journalism
6	Astronomy	Astronomy	Astronomy	Astronomy	Astronomy

4 What do these words mean? → M Peer correction, p. 177

a) Match the word with the right definition. → ○ p. 120

23/1-2a)

grade · class · pledge · detention · schedule · locker

1. a lesson or course
2. a list of classes and times in a school
3. it tells you how well you did in a test
4. when you promise to do something
5. when a student must stay at school after classes
6. where students keep their things

b) Complete the sentences with the right words. Use a dictionary. → V At American schools, p. 194

23/2b)

campus · core subject · vacation · recess

1. The students played cards during ___ .
2. The school has 2,000 students and a large ___ .
3. This is not an 'elective', it's a ___ .
4. What did you do on your summer ___ ?

5 (SPEAKING) Describe a school day.

23/3
24/4

a) Describe a day at an American high school. Use the photos on the left and your notes from Ex. 3 for help.

- school bus
- lockers
- lunch
- pledge
- classes
- extracurricular activities

In the morning, most students go to school by …

SPEAKING SKILLS

Use words to connect events that follow each other. Use words like *then*, *after that*, *next*, *finally*.

b) Describe a typical day at your school.

6 (SONG) Cool kids

1,11

Listen to the song. How does the singer describe the 'cool kids'?

She sees them walking in a straight line,
that's not really her style.
And they all got the same heartbeat,
but hers is falling behind.
Nothing in this world could
ever bring them down.
Yeah, they're invincible, and she's just in the
background.

And she says,

I wish that I could be like the cool kids,
'cause all the cool kids, they seem to fit in.
I wish that I could be like the cool kids,
like the cool kids.

Language detectives → G3, p. 162

I was able to choose 'electives'.
Exchange students were allowed to try too.
We weren't allowed to keep things in the classrooms.
I had to take Math, English, Science and History.

Which word do we use for must in the simple past here? And for can?
What is the difference between be allowed to and be able to?

7 (SPEAKING) Talk about school rules.

24/5

a) What was Luise (not) allowed to wear at high school? Use these verbs.

come to school with | wear | put on

INTERNET

High School Dress Code

Dos

Don'ts

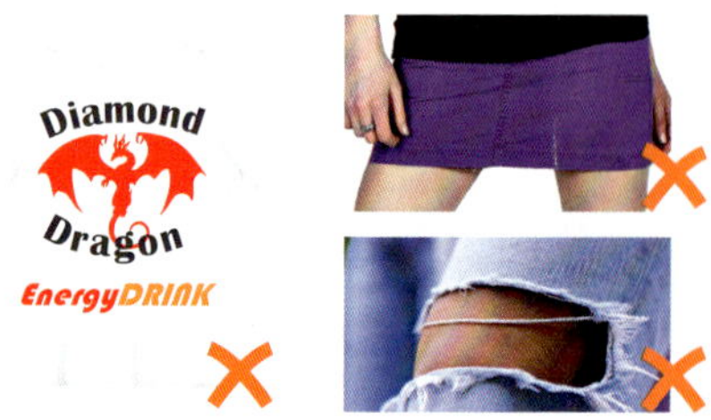

1. She was allowed to wear jeans.

b) What are you allowed to do at school? What aren't you allowed to do?

8 (WRITING) Find out about other exchange students in the USA.

24/6
25/7

a) Make sentences. Use (not) be allowed to and (not) be able to. → ○ p. 120

	Aileen	Jannik
During the exchange	+ wear jeans at school – bring any boys to her bedroom + stay up until 10 p.m. during the week	– wear jeans at school – bring any girls to his bedroom + stay up until 10 p.m. during the week
After the exchange	+ get used to her old life easily + speak English a lot better – keep in touch with all her American friends	– get used to his old life easily + speak English a lot better + help students from other countries

1. During the exchange Aileen was allowed to … but Jannik … 2. She … and he … 3. They …

25/8

b) Find someone who has been to another school.
Ask what he or she was (not) allowed to/able to do.

9 Complete the sentences about Luise and the cheerleading squad.

25/9

1. When Luise joined the cheerleading squad she had to • **didn't have to** learn new dance moves.
2. A week before it started she **had to** • **didn't have to** get the right clothes.
3. She was fit, so she **had to** • **didn't have to** be afraid.
4. For the first practice she **had to** • **didn't have to** be there 15 minutes early.
5. During her first practice the squad **had to** • **didn't have to** shout really loudly.
6. She was very good at it, so she **had to** • **didn't have to** worry.

10 Make a dialogue.

a) Complete the dialogue. Then act it with a partner. → ○ p. 121

26/10

Sarah: How was your host family in America last year? Did you have to (have to) do jobs around the house?
Luise: No, —— (not have to). —— (able to) decide when I wanted to help in the house.
Sarah: —— (allowed to) stay up late? —— (have to) be in bed at a certain time?
Luise: During the week —— (have to) be in bed at 9. On weekends —— (able to) go to bed later.
Sarah: —— (able to) travel around with the family?
Luise: Yes, —— (able to). But I —— (not allow) to travel alone.

b) When was the last time you had a guest at your home? Talk about the things that he or she had to do, was(n't) allowed to do or was(n't) able to do.

26/11

11 (YOUR TURN) A comparison → V Comparing schools, p. 199 → M Writers' conference, p. 179

a) Look at this station again and collect information about American and German schools.

b) Compare American schools to German schools. Give your opinion: Would you like to go to an American school? Say why (not).

WRITING SKILLS

This is how you can compare two things:
1. Introduce your topic.
2. Give your facts for both sides in the main part. Focus on five aspects that you want to compare.
3. Give your opinion at the end.

You can start like this:
There are many students like Luise who go to an American high school for one year. What is different from schools in Germany?

I would like to compare … to … .
In American high schools …
However, in German schools …
For … this is the same.
But … is different.
Finally …

I can compare school life in the USA and Germany. ✓

A lesson outside school

1 Have you ever tried to earn some extra money? What did you do?

2 (READING) Read the story.

1,12
27/1

INTERNET

Student Jobs

JIMMY'S SPORTING GOODS Lincoln, NE

Job title: Sales associate

Job type: Part-time (weekends)

Education: High school

Bring your love of sports to Jimmy's.

Like a lot of American teenagers 16-year-old Michael Adams badly needed money. His allowance just wasn't enough. He wanted to get his driver's license soon, he needed new clothes, and he had a new girlfriend who he wanted to impress.

So when he read the advert for a student job in a sports store, he thought, "That's the perfect one for me. It will never be boring, with all the customers." He didn't waste any time and applied for the job.

The job interview was tough. The manager asked lots of tricky questions. "How will you react if you see someone steal something?" or "What will you do if a customer complains?" Luckily, Michael was well prepared, and they offered him the job. Ten hours a week and the minimum wage was OK for him.

The staff was helpful and cooperative. One of his co-workers said, "If you have any questions, I'll help you." At first everything was new and exciting. After two weeks, however, Michael learned that jobs have their good and bad sides. There were days when there wasn't much to do. He folded every pair of pants twice, dusted every shelf, and sorted the shirts – the blue ones on the right, the green ones on the left. Then on other days he was so busy that he didn't know what to do first.

One Saturday two students from his school came into the store. As soon as they saw him, they started teasing him. "Your job is so lame! You'll miss all the fun if you work here every weekend. Just look at your clothes. If you wear a uniform like that, you won't be one of the cool kids, ever."

Michael got angry. They were such pinheads! He got into a big argument with them, and in the end he threw them out of the store.

Later that day his manager called him into his office. "I can understand your reaction," he said. "But such behavior is very bad. What will our customers think if the staff behaves like that? Be more responsible. If this happens again, you'll lose your job. Now please go back to work."

3 Find the information in the text. → M Think-pair-share, p. 179

Find …

1. the reasons why Michael wanted a job.
2. the things that the manager asked about.
3. Michael's working hours and pay.
4. the things that Michael learned at work.
5. the reason why Michael got angry.

4 What do you think?

a) What do you think about what Michael's manager says at the end? → ○ p. 121

I think he's right/wrong because …

b) Explain the title of the story.

5 (LISTENING) Listen to Marie on her first day at work at Fruit4U.

1,13

Answer the questions.

1. Who is Stacey?
2. What does Marie have to learn about?
3. What are Marie's working hours?
4. How long is Marie's lunch break?
5. What's her wage?
6. How can she get a bonus?

6 Practise words to describe people at work.

Which of the words have parts that you already know?

a) Put the words into groups. → ○ p. 121

27/2

bossy · unmotivated · cooperative · responsible · lazy · helpful · hard-working · disorganized

strength (+)	weakness (–)
cooperative	…

b) Make pairs of opposites. → V Describing people, p. 196

27/3

confident · generous · polite · rude · stubborn · selfish · willing · shy

7 (SPEAKING) Describe the most … job.

28/4-5

What jobs do you know? Make a list in two minutes. Then decide which job is the …

most dangerous · most exciting · most boring · best-paying

Present your results to the class. Give reasons.

I think being a/an … is the … job because …

CULTURE

Most of the time Americans don't use cash. They use credit cards instead. You can even pay for a single bagel with your credit card.

Language → G4, p. 163

If you have any questions, I'll help you.
If you wear a uniform like that, you won't be one of the cool kids.
What will our customers think if the staff behaves like that?

These sentences have two parts. Which part is the condition? Which part is the consequence? What are the tenses in each part?

8 What does Marie think after her first day at work? Complete the sentences.

28/6 → M Bus stop, p. 174

1. If I watch everything that Linda does, I'll learn (learn) quickly.
2. I'm really happy that I got the job. I —— (not complain) if I have to cut fruit all day.
3. Will I get fed up if a customer —— (get) unfriendly? I hope I'll stay polite.
4. The manager will give me a bonus if I —— (do) well. I hope I will.
5. What —— (happen) if I get sick? I need the money.
6. If my friends —— (work) every weekend too, we won't be able to go out any more.

9 (WRITING) What will happen if ...?

a) Look at the pictures. Make sentences. → ○ p. 122

29/7-8

1. find student job • earn money

2. need help • ask co-worker

3. be late • lose job

4. steal T-shirt • catch her

5. complain • get new one

6. buy two • get one free

1. If Michael finds a student job, he'll earn some money.

b) What will happen if ...

29/9

- Michael • get sick
- he • need change
- he • buy something from the store
- he • leave early
- computer • not work
- somebody • look for boss

1. If Michael is sick, he'll stay at home.

Language detectives → G5, p. 164

He read the advert for a student job. "That's the perfect one for me."
He sorted the shirts – the blue ones on the right, the green ones on the left.

Why do you use one and ones here?

10 Complete the sentences.

a) Use one or ones. → ○ p. 122

30/10-11

1. I really like this rain jacket. This one suits me perfectly.
2. We have lots of helmets. The best —— are over there.
3. Is there a restroom near the store? – Yes, there's —— over there.
4. This beach towel is a bit dirty. Do you have a clean —— ?
5. How about these pants? – No, I prefer the —— that I tried on before.
6. I need some new sport sunglasses. My old —— are broken.

b) Make questions with Which one/ones ...?

30/12

1. These are all the sports shoes that we have in our store. (you / like / ?)
2. Here I have a white pair of sports shoes and a black pair. (you / prefer / ?)
3. We have that pair in different sizes. (you / need / ?)

Use 'ones' to replace plural nouns like 'sunglasses' and 'pants'.

11 (YOUR TURN) A job for me → V Jobs, p. 200

31/1-2

Which student job would you like to do? Choose one and talk about it.

- Why did you choose the job?
- Why will you be good at it (and not so good at the others)?
- How will your life change if you take the job?

I chose / didn't choose ... because ....
Another reason why ....
I like to work ....
I'm a ... person, so a job like this ....
People say that I ....
I'm very / quite / not good at ....
If I earn money, I'll be able to ....
If I work in my free time, I won't be able to ....
I will probably feel ....

JOBS FOR TEENS

Paperboy/girl
- work early in the morning
- every day (even on Sundays)
- earn $40 per week

Dog walker
- work near your home
- be outside (also when the weather is bad)
- earn $10 per hour

Babysitter
- take care of kids in their homes
- work mostly in the evenings
- earn $12 per hour

I can talk about student jobs.

A first date

1 **Which stereotypes of American high school characters do you know from movies and TV shows?** → M Placemat, p. 177

2 **(READING) Read the comic strip.**

1,14

1. Dylan often thought about Abby. He really liked her. But he was too shy to ask her out on a date.

2. One day his books fell out of his locker right when Abby showed up. With Scott in tow, of course. How embarrassing.

3. A few days later they had lunch together. Dylan helped Abby with her Science project. They didn't notice Scott and his football friends.

4. When Dylan went to the gym, the boys attacked him. Scott pushed him really hard and Dylan couldn't do anything about it.

3 **Work with the text.**

a) Did you like the story? Do you think it would happen like this in real life?

b) Answer the questions.

1. Why didn't Dylan ask Abby out on a date?
2. What did Scott think of Dylan?
3. What did Dylan do at lunch?
4. Why did Scott and his friends attack Dylan?
5. How did Dylan feel before and during the Homecoming party?
6. How did Abby's dad react at the end?

5. A few days later Dylan asked Abby, “So, are you coming to the dance with me?” And she said yes. He was very nervous when he picked her up.

6. The party was great. Everybody enjoyed the music and dancing. There was a big surprise that evening. Dylan and Abby were so proud.

7. At the end of the evening Dylan took Abby home. There it was, the perfect moment. But …

4 (SPEAKING) Retell the story.

a) Take notes. Don’t write more than two or three notes for each picture.

b) Tell the story in your own words.

A boy called Dylan and his friends …

First … | Then … | After that … | In the end …

STUDY SKILLS

When you retell a story from a comic strip, also use the information from the pictures. They sometimes offer more interesting details for your story-telling.

5 Choose one of these tasks. → M Tip top, p. 179

32/5
33/2-3

a) Do Dylan and Abby stay together? What happens next? Write the last paragraph.

OR

b) Draw two or three more pictures. Show how you think the story continues.

Add speech bubbles and short descriptions to each one.

I can understand a comic strip about high school life. ✓

How to get your driver's license

Classroom Driver Ed

Length: 9 weeks

Classroom driver education is a course available to all students who will reach the age of 15 years before the last day of instruction and who have successfully completed eight out of ten courses in 8th grade. The course introduces students to basic skills of driving.
To take the written and the practical driving test, please contact your local driving school.

DRIVER EDUCATION APPROVAL FORM

Name and Address of Driver Training School:

Sally's Driving School Inc., 524 Bird Highway, Park Ridge 60068 IL

Student's Full Name: (last) Jenkins (first) Caitlin (middle) Amy

Street Address: 1815, Baxendale Road

City or Town: Chicago ZIP Code: 60004 IL

Caitlin A. Jenkins	12/16/2016	Steve M. Jenkins
Signature of Student	Date	Signature of Parent

CULTURE

US citizens don't have an ID card, so they can use their driver's license as an ID card. After five years they have to get a new one (but they don't need to take the test again).

1 Berichte darüber, wie man in den USA den Führerschein macht.

34/1

2 Pass on the information in a conversation about how to get a driver's license.

34/2

If you don't know a certain word, think of a different way to say it.

A: Stimmt es, dass man in Illinois den Führerschein schon mit 15 machen kann? Das geht bei uns ja erst viel später …

You: Is it true that …? In Germany …

B: Really? At what age can you get your driver's license in Germany?

You: …

A: Eigentlich mit 18. Aber in Ausnahmefällen geht's auch schon mit 17, dann muss aber eine weitere Person mit Führerschein mitfahren.

You: …

B: So, do you need a parent's signature for that too?

You: …

A: Ich denke schon. Muss man in den USA eigentlich auch eine theoretische und eine praktische Prüfung ablegen?

You: …

I can pass on information about how to get a driver's license. ✓

The new kid at school

1 Talk about a new school.

a) What would you show a new kid at your school?

b) How would you feel if you were the 'new kid' at school?

What could be positive about it?
What could be difficult?

2 (VIEWING) Watch the film.

4

a) Watch the film until 02:48. Right or wrong? Correct the wrong sentences.

1. A buddy is a teacher's favourite student.
2. CJ and Ronan are in the same homeroom.
3. Ruby has had seven detentions this year.
4. They have Math first period.
5. All students must say the Pledge of Allegiance.

b) Watch the film from 02:48 to the end. Name the places Ronan and CJ go to and say one sentence about what they do there.

c) Which words are they?
Watch the film again to check your answers.

1. ['lɒkə]
2. ['həʊmru:m]
3. ['pɪəriəd]
4. [dɪ'tenʃn]
5. [pledʒ]

3 (WRITING) Write about the film.

Write Ronan's e-mail to Roy, his best friend at his old school, to tell him about his first day at the new school.

CULTURE

Many schools in the USA start the day with the Pledge of Allegiance: Students stand and look at the US flag, with a hand on their heart, and swear to be true to the nation and God.
Do you think a pledge is a good idea? Why or why not?

VIEWING SKILLS

Most film scenes start with an 'establishing shot'. This is the first shot of a scene that shows the time of day, where the action will take place, who it's about etc.
Look at the first establishing shot in the film. What do you learn from it (at least three things)?

I can understand a film about someone's first day at a new school.

Checklist

I can understand information about life in the Midwest. ✓

35

I can compare school life in the USA and Germany. ✓

In American high schools .... • However, in German schools .... • Most students go to school by .... • School rules ... stricter. • ... is the same. • But ... is different.

35

I can talk about student jobs. ✓

I like to work .... • I'm very/quite/not good at .... • If I earn money, I'll be able to .... • If I work in my free time, I won't be able to ....

36

I can understand a comic strip about high school life. ✓

36

I can pass on information about how to get a driver's license. ✓

37

I can understand a film about someone's first day at a new school. ✓

❀ (TASK) A speech

Every year your class elects a class president. You would like to be the next one. Give a 1-minute speech. Then answer your classmates' questions.

Step 1

Collect ideas.

What's important for you and your class?
(atmosphere, relationships, ...)

What topics interest you?
(field trips, projects, ...)

What are you good at?
(listening to ..., talking to ..., ...)

What will you do if your class elects you?
(try to paint the classroom in a new colour, have a party every month, ...)

Step 2

Structure and write your speech.

→ M 1-minute-presentation, p. 174

1. Think about how to address your listeners.
2. Say that you would like to be the next class president. Use one paragraph for each topic to tell your listeners why you are the right person for the job.
3. Think of an ending.

WRITING SKILLS

A speech has similar features to most written texts: an introduction, a main part and an ending.

Step 3

Practise your speech.

→ M Read and look up, p. 178

Find different partners.

Practise your speech in front of them.
Read your speech a couple of times.
Then make notes and repeat your speech again and again.

SPEAKING SKILLS

To get elected, you must convince your classmates. Make them listen to you. You can also repeat things that are important to you. Don't speak too quickly or too slowly. Just speak naturally.

Step 4

Give your speech.

- Stand straight and try to relax.
- Look at your listeners from time to time. Eye contact is important.
- Don't make hectic movements. They can distract your listeners.
- Speak loudly and clearly.

Dear class,
Next Friday will be a big day for all of us. We're going to elect our class president. …
I think our class is already a really good team.
If you elect me, I'll … . I'll listen and … .
If you have any problems, I am sure … .
I promise … because I am hard-working and motivated.
You think classes could be more fun? You think we should have …? Come and talk to me. I'll try to talk to the staff and the principal.
Thanks for listening. I'll be happy to answer your questions now.

Step 5

Answer your listeners' questions.

Answer the questions politely. If you didn't understand the question, ask the person to repeat it.

High school electives

In American high schools you can choose from a number of electives, depending on your interests. They also look great on your CV. Some courses offer extra credits for your graduation.

INTERNET

< 1 > Home < 2 > About < 3 > News <4 > Courses

COURSE #	DESCRIPTION	CORE SUBJECT OR ELECTIVE	OTHER INFORMATION
A022	**Astronomy**	**Elective**	

Length: 2 semesters
Credits: 2
Open to Grades: 10–12
Prerequisite: Algebra, Science

This course introduces students to our solar system, planets and galaxies. Topics include the history of astronomy, its impact on society, and the methods and tools that scientists use to locate objects in the night sky. Students are required to attend some observations in the early morning or in the evening.

COURSE #	DESCRIPTION	CORE SUBJECT OR ELECTIVE	OTHER INFORMATION
B005	**Introduction to Welding Technology**	**Elective**	**$20 Lab Fee**

Length: 2 semesters
Credits: 2
Open to Grades: 9–12
Prerequisite: –

This course introduces students to the process of making things out of metal. Students learn about different forms of metal and also how to cut and join metals. This course also makes students familiar with required safety measures. Students create individual projects as well as complete projects for school.

C011	Journalism	Elective

Length: 1 semester
Credits: 1
Open to Grades: 9–12
Prerequisite: –

This course introduces students to the fundamentals of journalism. Topics include writing, editing, layout and graphic design. Students learn different styles of journalistic writing such as news, interviews, features, sports, book and movie reviews, and blogs. They contribute articles to the school's yearbook and online newspaper. Students are required to work in teams, be ready to write articles in their free time and have to meet deadlines.

1 Which elective would you choose? Say why.

2 Think of electives for your school and write a course description.

You can think of anything you like!

- Collect ideas in groups.
- Write a course description.
  Say what the course is about, what students can learn there and what they have to do. Write about 50 words.
- Present your course descriptions in class.
- Vote in class to find the most popular elective.

STUDY SKILLS

Use a computer programme to format your text. Here are some ideas:
- Choose a font and use a font size between 10 and 14 points.
- Use a bold font or a colour for the heading.
- Use the word counter and spell checker.
- You can insert text boxes to structure your page.
- You can find a photo on the internet and download it to make your text look interesting.
- You can choose a background colour.

Here you can learn how to prepare and give a presentation.

American football

A

- Super Bowl: most famous sporting event
- first Sunday in February
- famous sporting event on TV
- unofficial national holiday
- final match of the season
- game first played in USA in 1869

B

C

- team of supporters
- motivate players and spectators
- today: 95% girls
- dance, jump, yell, do stunts
- 1–3 minutes per performance (= routine)

D

- pass the ball by throwing and kicking
- allowed: running with the ball, hands
- aim: take the ball as far as possible into the other team's half
- score: touchdown, field goal

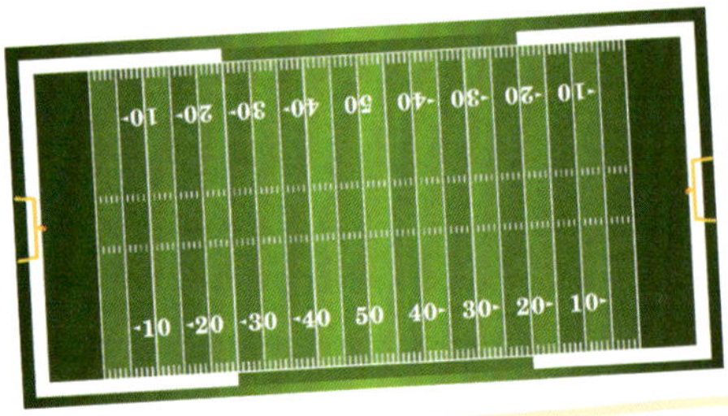

E

F

- team sport
- each team: 11 players on the field
- one game: 60 minutes (plus pauses)
- 4 quarters (one quarter = 15 minutes)

1 Organize the cards on the left.

a) Give each card and each photo a heading.
You can start like this:
- General facts
- ...

b) Put the information cards and the photos in a suitable order.

Look up new words. Make sure you understand and pronounce them correctly. Think about how to explain them to your classmates. Use photos or sketches.

2 Prepare your presentation about American football.

a) Prepare your poster, transparency or computer presentation.

Check that your presentation is complete:
- a big headline
- no spelling mistakes
- photos

b) Use the prompt cards from page 50 or prepare your own prompt cards.

Your prompt cards need to have:
- short notes
- an explanation of new words

3 Practise your presentation.

You can practise your presentation in front of the mirror or with family and friends.

1. Give a general introduction.
2. Present the different aspects of your information.
3. End your presentation: Emphasize the most important facts and come to a conclusion.

Helpful phrases for the beginning are:
My presentation is about ....
First, I'd like to talk about ....

This is how you go to the next aspect of your presentation:
Now I'm going to talk about ...
My next topic is ...
Second, ... Finally, ...

Thank the audience for their attention and ask if there are any questions:
That's the end of my presentation.
Thank you for listening. Do you have any questions?

41/1-5

4 Give your presentation.

Look at your audience while speaking. Speak slowly, loudly and clearly. Show special facts on your poster or transparency. Watch the time.

Find more online:
i8ce82

In this unit you will ...
- find out about the American Northeast.
- read a dialogue with feeling.
- give your opinion and say why.
- understand a story about a group of friends.
- pass on information about ways of travelling.
- watch a film about Thanksgiving.

5 1,15

Unit 3

In the Northeast

The Northeast of the United States stretches from the border with Canada to Washington, D.C. Here you can visit the amazing Niagara Falls, enjoy miles of clean beaches, go whale watching or eat fresh lobster. In the fall you can drive through woods of beautiful red and gold leaves.

The USA is a huge country. From Boston to Los Angel
for example, it's a six and a half hour flight. Family
members often live and work thousands of miles ap
So they like to get together for important celebratio

1 Talk about the photos.

a) Work with a partner. Look at the photos and guess what the texts are about.

people | place | event

b) Now read the texts. Are your answers still the same?

2 Choose the right answers. More than one can be right.

44/1-2

1. The Northeast is famous for **whale watching** • **beautiful woods** • **short winters.**
2. It takes six and a half hours to get from Boston to Los Angeles **by car** • **by plane** • **by train.**
3. When the President pardons a turkey, it **stays alive** • **then lives in the White House** • **goes to live on a farm.**
4. **Most** • **Half** • **One third** of Maine is forest.
5. The Amish **are a Christian group** • **often use modern inventions** • **live in the 'land of the free'.**

3

On Thanksgiving almost everybody eats a turkey dinner. However, in the 20th century, a new tradition began. The president 'pardons' a turkey in the White House and the bird goes to live on a farm in Virginia.

4

The state of Maine is a favorite location for creepy movies and novels. It's 90 percent forest, few people live there, and the winters are long and dark. So it's especially popular with writers of mystery stories.

5

The USA is called the 'land of the free'. People can choose how they want to live without much government control. The Amish are an old Christian community who have chosen to live without most modern inventions.

3 (LISTENING) Listen to a story about a Niagara Daredevil.

1,16

Correct the wrong sentences.

1. The woman who tells the story was 16 years old.
   That's **wrong**. She was 14.
2. She was on a boat tour.
3. She saw a barrel go over the Niagara Falls.
4. An old man climbed out of the barrel.
5. He seemed to be hurt.
6. Steve did it because he wanted to become a stuntman.
7. The second time he wasn't alone.

daredevil ['deəˌdevl] – Draufgänger/in
amazed [ə'meɪzd] – erstaunt; verblüfft
barrel ['bærl] – Faß; Tonne
to sign autographs [ˌsaɪn 'ɔːtəgrɑːfs] – Autogramme geben

I can understand information about the American Northeast.

A family Thanksgiving

1 What is the biggest celebration that your family has? → M Round robin, p. 178

2 (READING) Read the dialogue.

1,17 45/1

The Miller family from Boston are getting ready for Thanksgiving dinner. Julia is in the kitchen. Her husband Mark, their teenage son Jacob and Grandma Brenda are in the living room.

Grandma: Last year we had such a terrible storm. I got stuck in my car for over two hours. Do you remember?

Mark: Yes, that's right. Did you have a hard time again yesterday, when you drove here? *(The doorbell rings. Mark opens the door. It's their elderly neighbor.)*

Robert: Happy Thanksgiving, Mark!

Mark: You too, Robert. How are you?

Robert: Great, thanks. Brr. It's freezing outside, isn't it?

Mark: Come on in then. I'm so glad you could make it. *(They enter the living room.)* Grandma, this is Robert. He's our new neighbor. He doesn't have family here, so we've invited him to join us. Robert, this is Brenda.

Robert: Nice to meet you, Brenda. You came all the way from Miami, didn't you? Do you always come by car?

Grandma: Yes, always. Please have a seat. When did you move here? And where do you originally come from?

Mark: *(shouting across the room)* Jacob, why don't you say hello? You can't spend all your time playing with your phone.

Jacob: What's up, Robert?

Robert: How's it going? Are you enjoying the holiday? Do you like turkey?

Jacob: Not really. I'm a vegetarian, so I won't eat any.

Julia: *(coming out of the kitchen)* You always used to eat everything. *(She notices the new guest.)* Oh, hi Robert.

Robert: Hey Julia. Thanks so much for inviting me. I've brought you a little something. You eat chocolates, don't you? *(He gives her a box as a present.)*

Mark: OK everybody. I'm making a video of today. First, will you all answer this Thanksgiving question: 'What do you feel thankful for?' Julia, you go first, please. *(He starts filming.)*

Julia: Me? Well, err, most of all I am thankful for my husband and my two lovely children who … *(Mark's phone rings.)*

Mark: That's probably your second lovely child and her new boyfriend who are on their way here. Hello Lily. … Oh, no! *(to the others)* Their plane from Washington, D.C. had engine trouble, and they had to land in New York. *(to Lily)* So when does your plane arrive, later today or tomorrow? … OK. … Will you call us again when you know more? I promise we'll save some turkey for you!

CULTURE

'Small talk' is important in the USA when you meet new people. It's friendly conversation about simple, everyday things.

Language tip → G 6, p. 165

You eat chocolates, **don't you**?
You came all the way from Miami, **didn't you**?

3 Find out about the Miller family's Thanksgiving. → M Peer correction, p. 177

a) Who is it? → ○ p. 123

1. Who got stuck in her car last year?
   That's **Brenda**.
2. … is not a member of the Miller family?
3. … used to eat turkey, but not any more?
4. … gets a present?
5. … is making a video?
6. … landed in New York?

b) What is the 'Thanksgiving question'? How would *you* answer it?

1,18

4 (LISTENING) Listen to Lily introduce her boyfriend Evan the next day.

a) Listen to the conversation. Match the questions and answers. → ○ p. 124

45/2

1. How are you doing?
2. So what have you been up to?
3. How about going for a walk?
4. How is she?
5. Can I help with anything?

A Let's do it.
B No, thanks, it's all organized.
C Not much.
D Everything is fine, thanks.
E She's good, thanks.

b) Listen again. Which other small talk phrases can you understand?
Take notes.

- What's …?
- We've heard …
- How are …?

LISTENING SKILLS

Don't worry if you don't understand everything. Keep calm and go on listening. You'll probably understand more the second time.

5 (SPEAKING) Make small talk.

45/3

a) Copy the table. Fill in the phrases from the text on page 54 and Ex. 4. → V Small talk, p. 202

Saying 'How are you?'	*Saying 'I'm fine.'*	*Talking about everyday things.*

b) Use the phrases from a) to have small talk conversations. → M Milling around, p. 176

6 (SOUNDS) Listen, read and say.

1,19

1. Do you like turkey? ↗
2. Yes, I love turkey. ↘
3. I've lived in Boston for five years. ↘
4. Have you invited the neighbors? ↗
5. Did you come by car? ↗
6. No, I flew from Miami. ↘

Language → G7, p. 166

Do you like turkey?
Did you have a hard time yesterday?
Will you call again later?
Where do you come from?

How do you make questions about the present, past and future? What are the signal words?

7 Make questions in the right tense.

46/4-5

1. Do you usually prefer turkey or ham? (prefer)
2. ___ your mum ___ at 6:30 a.m. to have breakfast every day? (get up)
3. ___ your dad always ___ a football game on Thanksgiving? (watch)
4. ___ you ___ the snowstorm on the news yesterday? (see)
5. ___ you ___ by plane last year? (travel)
6. ___ you ___ me how to make a great cake like this tomorrow? (teach)
7. ___ Grandma ___ with you next Thanksgiving? (stay)

8 (SPEAKING) Ask questions about holidays.

a) Interview your partner. → p. 124

47/6

1. Which • holidays • your family • celebrate?
2. When • *(name of holiday)* • usually • start?
3. Who • your family • invite • every time?
4. What • you • always • eat?
5. What • you • like • about • last *(name of holiday)*?
6. How many • guests • your family • invite • last time?
7. Who • you • talk to • last *(name of holiday)*?
8. Where • *(name of holiday)* • take place • next year?

GRAMMAR → G7, p. 166

Who did you invite?
Who did you talk to?

b) Think of more questions like these that Grandma asks at a family party.

9 (WRITING) Write Jacob's questions to his grandma.

a) What did Jacob ask his grandma? Write his questions for the underlined answers. → p. 125

47/7

what? · where? · when? · who? · why?

E-MAIL

Dear Jacob,
Yes, it's true, it will be my 65th birthday soon! I'm planning (1) a big family celebration. I will have it (2) at my house in Miami. It will take place (3) on May 1. I will invite (4) everybody who can come to Miami. And of course you can ask your new girlfriend to come too. Yes, I already know about her. That's because (5) your dad told me about her.
Much love,
Grandma

(1) What are you planning for your birthday?

b) Read Grandma's e-mail again and write three more of Jacob's questions.

48/8

10 (YOUR TURN) A holiday dialogue → M Dramatic reading, p. 175

48/9

a) Work in groups of five. Each of you chooses a role from the dialogue on page 54.

b) Read the notes and prepare your role.

c) Read the dialogue as your character.

d) Give feedback to the other groups.

READING SKILLS

When you read the dialogue, use your voice to express your character's emotions.
For example, read faster when he or she gets excited.

I can read a dialogue with feeling. ✓

One country, different worlds

1 What have you used electricity for today?

2 (READING) Read the texts about two American teenage girls.

1,20

I live in a small Amish community in Pennsylvania. We lead a simple life. We don't have a TV, a fridge, a phone, a computer or any other modern devices. If we had these things, we couldn't concentrate on our community life enough, I think. I also cover my hair, wear long dresses, and never use make-up. We grow our own food too.

The people in our community care about each other. It doesn't matter what you wear or how you look. It's important who you are and what you do. I really like that.

We usually don't have much contact with the outside world. But at the age of 16 we're allowed to go there for some time and do 'forbidden things'. I watched movies, went to parties and drank alcohol.

Now that time is over, I have to make the most important decision of my life: Do I join the Amish community or not?

Living in the outside world was not what I had expected. I felt lost and lonely there. Just think, if I didn't return, I would really miss my family and my community. This is where I belong. I'm sure I won't regret my decision.

I guess I'm a pretty average American girl. Like most teenagers I'm interested in fashion and yes … gossip too. I love being on the phone or tablet at all times. My friends and I chat a lot about everyone and everything. What would I do if I had to live without them?

My first big decision of the day is: What am I going to wear? Maybe my clothes are still in the dryer and Mom hasn't ironed them yet? Yes, alright – if I washed the clothes myself, I would know.

When I'm on the school bus, I think about what's going on at school. Mostly it's about who's wearing what or who's going out with whom.

I often hang out with my friends. If I had a car, I would drive around town with them. But I don't have one yet. So we often meet in town to have something to eat. Sometimes we go bowling or to the movies. Some of my friends go to church, but I don't. That isn't part of my life.

I wouldn't like to change anything about my life. It's perfect the way it is.

CULTURE

The Amish are a religious group who emigrated from Europe in the 18th century. They live a simple life in their communities. At home they speak a German dialect. Which alternative lifestyles do you know?

3 Think of a heading for each text.

4 Answer the questions.

1. How are the two girls' lives different? Find five things.
2. Do Ruth and Jennifer like the way they live? Say why you think so.
3. What's important in your life? Talk about it in class.

5 Sort the phrases. → M Peer correction, p. 177

a) Sort the phrases into the table. → ○ p. 125

49/1a)

I agree:	I disagree:
...	...

That's true. | I don't think so. | Exactly. | That's for sure. | Absolutely not. | You can't be serious. | You're right. | No way!

b) Put the phrases into the right list. → V Agreeing and disagreeing, p. 203

49/1b)

- I'm sure: ...
- I'm not sure: ...

As far as I know, ... | I guess ... | I'm convinced that ... | It's clear to me that ... | I doubt that ...

6 (SPEAKING) Talk about devices.

a) Make a list. → ○ p. 126

49/2
50/3

Talk to your partner and agree on a ranking list. Rank the devices from the most to the least important.

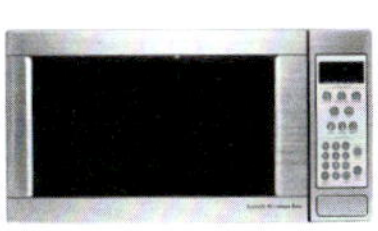
microwave

headphones

TV

cell phone

computer

hair straightener

The most important thing for me is .... / I don't think ... is more important than .... / ... comes first/second/third / ... is next.

b) Which device could you live without? Discuss it with other students. → V Devices, p. 203

fan | electric toothbrush | dishwasher | vacuum cleaner | electric razor | radiator

Language → G8, p. 167

Jennifer: If I had a car, I would drive around town with my friends.
Ruth: If I didn't return, I would miss my family.
Jennifer: What would I do if I had to live without them?

What are the verb tenses in each part of these sentences? Read the 'if' parts of the sentences. Will Ruth or Jennifer probably do or probably not do these things?

50/4-5

7 Complete the sentences. → M Bus stop, p. 174

1. If Jennifer met Ruth, they would compare their different lives. (meet, compare)
2. If Ruth — with Jennifer, Jennifer — bowling with her. (stay, go)
3. If Ruth — how to use a tablet, Jennifer — her. (not know, help)
4. Ruth — Jennifer how to grow her own food if she — Ruth's family. (show, visit)
5. Jennifer — about her clothes if she — with the Amish. (not worry, live)
6. Jennifer — phone her friends if she — to talk to them. (not be able to, want)

8 What would make Jennifer's life easier?

51/6

a) Look at the pictures. Complete the sentences. → ○ p. 126

1. Jennifer would be less worried in the morning if ....

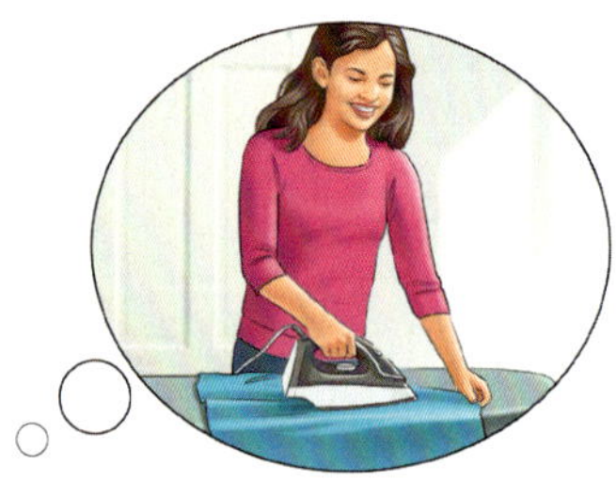

2. Her T-shirt would look much nicer if ....

3. She wouldn't feel so tired in the morning if ....

4. She would hear what her dad said if ....

5. She wouldn't get cold if ....

6. It would be healthier if ....

1. Jennifer would be less worried in the morning if she chose her clothes in the evening.

b) What would make your life easier? Make sentences.

9 (SPEAKING) What would you do if …? → M Round robin, p. 178

a) Answer the questions. Then ask your partner. → ○ p. 127

51/7

What would you do if you …

1. were president of the United States for a day?
2. were a superhero?
3. could stop time?
4. had a million dollars?
5. knew the answers to your next English test before the test?
6. didn't have the money to buy a ticket for the bus home?

b) Make more questions for your partner.

51/8

meet an alien · have no brothers/sisters · be a teacher · …

10 (YOUR TURN) Giving your opinion → V Giving opinions, p. 207

a) Could you live without electricity? Why (not)?
Write a short text. Give three reasons.

52/9
53/1

(1) The question is "Could I live …?"
(2) I could (not) live without electricity
(3) because … • I also think that … • Another reason is …
(4) For example, … • If I only had / If I had no …
(5) So all in all …

WRITING SKILLS

First mention your topic (1). Then give a short statement of your position (2). After that explain why (3) and give examples (4). Finish with a short conclusion of your arguments (5).

b) Work in groups of three. One of you reads his or her text to the others. The other two comment on the positions and reasons in the text. Then take turns.

I (don't) agree with you. / I think you're right/wrong there. / That's true. / I don't think so because … . / …

I can give my opinion and say why. ✓

The Body by Stephen King, 1982

1 **What do you do when you hang out with your friends?**

2 **(READING) Read the story.**

1,21

In The Body, *Gordie Lachance and his three friends learn that a boy from their area, in the state of Maine, has disappeared and is probably dead. They decide to go on a trip to find the boy's body and prepare for the trip.*

The Gun

My room was on the second floor, and it was really hot up there. I was glad I wasn't sleeping there that night, and the thought of where we were going made me excited again. I rolled up two blankets and tied an old belt around them. I grabbed all my money, which was less than a dollar. Then I was ready to go. I went down the back stairs to avoid meeting my dad. I was walking up Carbine Street towards the clubhouse when Chris caught up with me. His eyes were shining.

"Gordie! You want to see something?"

"Sure. What?"

"Come down here first." He pointed down an alley between two shops.

"What is it, Chris?"

"Come on, I said!"

He ran down the alley and I ran after him.

At the bottom, the smell from the trash was terrible. "Chris, I'm going to puke, I'm – "

But I forgot about the smell when Chris put his hand into his backpack and pulled out a big gun.

"Where did you get that?"

"From my dad's desk."

"Man, your dad's going to beat you when he finds out."

Chris's eyes just went on dancing. "He isn't going to find out. He and his friends have got enough wine to keep them drunk for a week. I'll put it back before then." Chris hated alcohol – he'd already seen too much of what it can do. He was the only one of us who didn't have a drink when the DeSpain brothers brought some beer they'd stolen from their father.

"Have you got bullets for it?"

"Nine of them – all that was left in the box. He'll think he used them himself, shooting at bottles when he was drunk."

"Any in it at the moment?"

"No, of course not. What do you think I am?"

I finally took the gun. I liked the heavy way it sat in my hand.

I pointed the gun at a large tin with smelly trash spilling out of it and squeezed.

KA – BLAM!

The gun jumped in my hand. Fire shot from the end. It felt as if my wrist was broken. My heart was in my mouth. A big hole appeared in the tin – it was the work of an evil magician.

"Wow!" I screamed.

Chris was laughing wildly; I couldn't tell if he was amused or scared.

"You did it, you did it! Gordie Lachance is shooting Castle Rock to pieces. Be careful, everyone! Here comes Gordie!"

"Shut up! Let's go!" I screamed, and grabbed him by the shirt.

I gave the gun to Chris and he pushed it into his backpack as we ran up the alley. When we reached Carbine Street we slowed to a walk, so that no one would notice us if they had heard the noise of the gun. Chris was still laughing.

"Man, it's a pity you couldn't see your face. Oh, man, that was really great."

"You knew there was a bullet in it, didn't you? That was a mean trick, Chris, really."

"I didn't know, Gordie, honestly. I just took it out of my dad's desk. He always takes the bullets out of it. I guess he was too drunk to remember last time."

Chris looked as innocent as a baby, but when we got to the clubhouse we found Vern and Teddy waiting, and he started to laugh again. He told them the whole story, and after everyone had had a good laugh Teddy asked Chris, "What do you think we need a gun for?"

"Nothing, really," Chris said. "Except we might see a wild animal. And anyway, it's frightening out in the forest at night." Everyone agreed with that. Chris was the strongest and bravest guy of us all, and he could say things like that.

"Did you put your tent up in the field?" Teddy asked Vern.

"Yeah, and I put two lamps in it and turned them on, so it'll look as if we're there after dark."

"Hey, man, great!" I said, and slapped Vern on the back. For him, that was real thinking. He grinned.

"So let's go," Teddy said. "It's nearly twelve already."

Chris stood up and we gathered round him.

"We'll walk across Beeman's field," he said, "and then we'll get to the railway tracks and just walk across the bridge into Harlow."

"How far is it, do you think?" Teddy asked.

"I don't know," said Chris. "Harlow's big. We're going to have to walk at least twenty miles. Does that sound right to you, Gordie?"

"Yeah. Maybe more – thirty miles."

"Come on, you guys," Chris said, and picked up his backpack, blankets and water bottle.

CULTURE

In the USA, about 30,000 people die every year in gun attacks. But the law clearly says that Americans have the right to carry guns. And many believe that they need guns to protect themselves.
Who is allowed to carry a gun in Germany? What's your opinion?

3 Did you like the story? Say why or why not.

4 Work with the story.

a) Put the sentences in the right order and say what happened.

A Chris showed Gordie his father's gun.
B They walked to the clubhouse.
C Chris told the others what had happened.
D They left before twelve.
E Chris thought it was very funny.
F Gordie got ready to leave home.
G Gordie shot a hole in the tin.
H Gordie met Chris in Carbine Street.

b) Who is the narrator of the story? How do you know? Find sentences in the text that tell you.

c) Do you think this chapter is near the beginning or the end of the story? Why?

5 Find out about the characters.

a) What do you know about Chris and Gordie? Match these adjectives with the characters.

1. Gordie seems to be … because …
2. Chris seems to be … because …

brave | crazy | excited | strong | worried | scared | amused

b) Look at these lines to find out if you were right.

Gordie: *lines 4–6; 19–23; 43–46*
Chris: *lines 24–26; 52–55; 64–66*

c) Exchange your answers with your partner.

d) Discuss with your partner:

The text says: "Chris looked as innocent as a baby." (*line 60*)
Do you think Chris knew about the bullet in the gun? Why (not)?

STUDY SKILLS

The narrator can use adjectives to say what a character is like ("The boy was quiet."), or he or she can describe the character's behaviour ("The boy listened to his friends but he never talked much.").

6 Choose one of these tasks.

54/1
5/2-4

a) How could the story continue? Write a summary with your ideas. Use the simple present.
→ M Writers' conference, p. 179

The boys walk … | Then they find … | Suddenly … | They start to feel … | After a long time … | In the end … | Their parents are …

Find out on the internet what really happens in the story *The Body* by Stephen King.

OR

b) Work in groups of four.

1. Take notes about something really exciting that you did together with your friends.
2. Talk about the stories in your group.
3. Choose the best story and tell it to the class.

When I was … | I always wanted to … | One day I … | I was afraid to tell … | I didn't expect …

I can understand a story about a group of friends. ✓

From Chicago to Boston

INTERNET

A

OUTGOING TRIP		**September 16 (Fri)**			**Price (USD)**
Chicago, IL 08:05 a.m.	>	24h 25m	>	Boston, MA 09:30 a.m. (+ 1 days)	Fare total for 1 Adult $89
RETURN TRIP		**September 18 (Sun)**			
Boston, MA 05:00 p.m.	>	22h 30m	>	Chicago, IL 02:30 p.m. (+ 1 days)	Fare total for 1 Adult $89
				Subtotal	$178
				Taxes and fees	$5
				YOUR TOTAL	**$183**

INTERNET

B

Sep 16 (Fri)				
1:39 p.m. Chicago, IL	>	5:05 p.m. Boston, MA	2h 26m	
Sep 18 (Sun)				
5:30 p.m. Boston, MA	>	9:17 p.m. Chicago, IL	4h 47m Philadelphia 1 stop	
			Flight	$141.85
			Tax & Fee	$47.35
			Trip total (round trip)	**$189.20**

C

One-way
Time: 14h 46m
Distance: 982 miles
Price of gas:
about $160

1 Beantworte die Fragen.

65/1-2

Finde die Vor- und Nachteile jedes Verkehrsmittels heraus. Welche Reise ist am kürzesten? Welche die billigste?

CULTURE

Because the USA is such a big country it has nine time zones. Boston is one hour ahead of Chicago. How many time zones does Europe have?

2 What do you think?

If you had to go from Berlin to Frankfurt/Main, how would you get there? By train, plane or bus? Say why. Find information on the internet.

I can pass on information about ways of travelling. ✓

Trouble at Thanksgiving

1 Look at the photo and guess.

a) What is Jessica making? What is her Dad making?

b) What could the trouble be? Collect ideas in class and vote on the best idea.

Now watch the beginning of the film.
Were you right?

2 (VIEWING) Watch the film.

6

a) What else goes wrong that day? Complete the table.

People	*Food*	*Places*
…	…	…

b) Thanksgiving Day: Which five things are not in the film?

big parade · balloons · turkey dinner · barbecue party · nice presents · football game · special songs · pecan pie · president's pardon · volunteer work · terrible traffic

CULTURE

Thanksgiving is what the word says. In the USA the family gets together to give thanks – for the past and the present. People also enjoy a meal together and give thanks for the food they get from the harvest. Do you have or know of a tradition like Thanksgiving in your community?

3 (SPEAKING) Talk about the film.

a) Watch the film from 03:19 again.
What activities do people do at Thanksgiving?

b) Which of these activities are most interesting to you? Say why.

VIEWING SKILLS

Films often have elements like a photo or a video with more information or action that is happening outside the action in the film.

I can understand a film about Thanksgiving. ✓

Checklist

I can understand information about the American Northeast. ✓

57

I can read a dialogue with feeling. ✓

What's up? • How's it going? • I'm glad you could make it. • What have you been up to? • Are you enjoying …?

57

I can give my opinion and say why. ✓

I really like that. • I wouldn't change … • I don't think so. • That's for sure. • Absolutely not. • That's true. • I couldn't live without …

58

I can understand a story about a group of friends. ✓

58

I can pass on information about ways of travelling. ✓

59

I can understand a film about Thanksgiving. ✓

(TASK) A talk show

"Living without your phone for one day – piece of cake or total nightmare?" Organize a 5 to 10-minute talk show. At the end make a decision if you want to live without your phone for one day. Do more than one show for practice and for fun.

Step 1

Brainstorm ideas. → M Think-pair-share, p. 179

Collect arguments for both sides:
What's good about a day without a phone? What isn't?

Step 2

Get into groups: 'piece of cake', 'total nightmare' or 'hosts'.

It's always easier to present your own opinion. However, you sometimes have to take a different perspective. Think of that when you make groups.

A host loves talking, keeps the show running, is well-informed and has to be very flexible.

Step 3

Prepare for the show.

Guests

1. Decide on three to four arguments.
2. Explain your arguments, give reasons and examples.
3. Decide who is going to present which argument in the show.
4. Write your arguments on cards (keywords only).
5. Practise your talk.

1. parents control us
2. out with friends
3. phone rings > Mum
4. annoying situation

Hosts

1. Think of introductions for the show and the guests.
2. Think of questions that you can ask your guests. Write them on cards.
3. Think of ways to react: What will you say if your guests stop talking or nobody has any questions?
4. Practise.

Welcome to today's talk show. / Our topic today is … / David, what do you think about …? / That's all for today. Thank you for coming.

Step 4

Set the scene and act the show.

1. Prepare the classroom for the show: Arrange the tables and chairs.
2. Decide which groups are going to be in the first show.
3. Decide who is going to be the host.
4. Act the show.

SPEAKING SKILLS

Don't forget to say your opinion first. Address the audience directly to catch their attention. Speak fluently but do not speak too fast.

Step 5

Make a decision.

What does your class think? Should you live without phones for one day?

Step 6

Do more shows for practice and for fun.

The voyage of the Mayflower

The story of the Mayflower

In September 1620, I sailed from Plymouth, in England, to the New World. On board my sailing ship, the Mayflower, were 102 people who were later to be known as the Pilgrims. They left England because they didn't have religious freedom and they wanted to start a new life.

After two months of heavy storms in the Atlantic Ocean, we landed at Cape Cod where we stayed for the winter. Many people died because of the cold, hard winter, diseases and also of hunger. Thank God, we met Indians who gave us food, showed us how to hunt and to catch fish. Later they showed the Pilgrims how to grow corn. The Pilgrims decided to stay at Cape Cod and founded the colony of Plymouth, named after the starting point of their crossing.

My crew and I left the colony in March. I heard that after the first year in the New World, the Pilgrims invited the Indians for a meal. They celebrated a festival to say thanks for the successful harvest – they called it 'Thanksgiving'.

CULTURE

A lot of place names in the USA are of European origin. Some names are exactly the same, for example 'Plymouth'. Very often the settlers added 'New' in front of the original name – New York (named after York in England), New Orleans (named after Orléans in France) … .
What German place names are there in the USA?

Build your own Mayflower with recyclable material.

Step 1: Prepare yourself.
You can recycle lots of everyday things to build your own Mayflower: You can choose things from this material list (or your own ideas) in steps 2 to 4 below.

an empty tea light

walnut shells

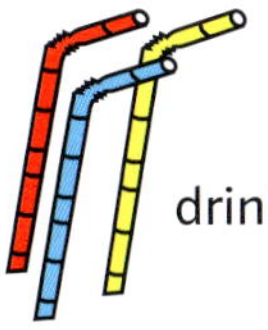
drinking straws

an empty yogurt pot
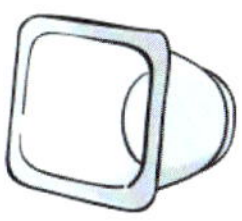

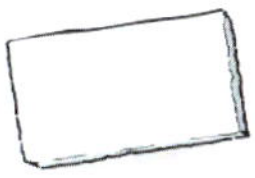
polystyrene

plastic bags

toothpicks

the lid of a jam jar

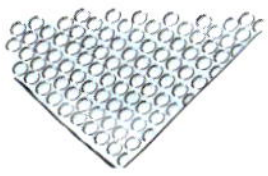
bubble wrap

You also need:

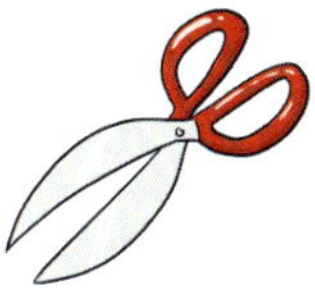
scissors

tape

glue stick

waterproof felt-tips

coloured paper

Step 2: Build and design the body of the ship.
- Choose a material that floats.
- Make the body of the ship.
- Use things like coloured paper and waterproof felt tips to decorate your Mayflower.

Step 3: Make the sails.
- Make the masts and sails and fix them to your Mayflower.

Step 4: Add the crew and passengers.
- Make the Pilgrims, Christopher Jones (Master of the Mayflower) and his crew.
- Put them on your Mayflower.

Whose ship arrives first?

Step 5: Start the journey.
- Fill a big plastic box or a sink with water to make your Atlantic Ocean.
- Put your Mayflower in the water.
- Blow the sails of your Mayflower to make it cross your Atlantic Ocean.

Here you can learn how to write a summary.

1,22

Healthy and active at Thanksgiving?

headline

written by Pam Warner
(published 07/12/16 in Health & Style)

author, date, source

introduction

What is your Thanksgiving like? Turkey and pumpkin pie? American football on the sofa? In the last couple of years a new trend has become popular in the USA: More people like to eat better quality food and live a more active life.

main part

It is slowly going out of fashion to live off convenience and frozen food. A number of people shop for organic food at special supermarkets instead. In some states farmers' markets offer a great variety of fresh vegetables and fruit from the region. "There are also dairy products, bread and meat without chemical additives at these markets. Organic food is not only much healthier but it tastes a lot better as well," explains Emma from Boston. So how about some healthy recipes for Thanksgiving? Maybe pumpkin soup or mashed sweet potatoes? A roast turkey breast or a turkey roulade filled with apples and cranberries is delicious too.

But there's more to a healthy lifestyle than just food. A lot of trend sports show that you can have fun, spend time with friends and stay fit at the same time.
Have you found the right sport for you yet? If not, here is a suggestion: How about standup paddleboarding? If you like water, that's the ideal kind of sport for you. You stand on the board and you use a paddle to move through the water. Don't worry, you don't have to travel to the sea. A lot of clubs offer standup paddleboarding on lakes and rivers.

Of course living healthy also means avoiding alcohol and drugs. Finn, a fitness instructor from Cleveland, says: "Drinking too much alcohol isn't good for your health. Most alcoholic drinks have a lot of calories and negative effects on your fitness too. So why not try a smoothie instead?" Drugs are even worse. You can easily get addicted, and they often cause problems with your family or at school.

conclusion

To sum up, you can say that organic food together with doing sports is a great way to stay fit. You don't have to do without your favorite meals. Just changing your lifestyle a bit will make you a much happier person.

1 Read the text and take notes.

Find the most important keywords in each paragraph and make a list. Look at the examples in the introduction and the first paragraph on the left.

> Don't give any examples, numbers, comparisons, quotes or direct speech. They're not really necessary for your summary.

2 Write a summary of the text.

Use your notes to write your summary.

> A general rule says that a summary can be up to one third of the original text. It can be shorter though too. Remember to use your own words.

1. Start with the introduction. Name the title, the author and where the text comes from. Don't forget to say what the text is about.

> The article "…" was written by … on … .
> The text/article/story is about … . It explains …/describes …/deals with …

2. Now summarise each paragraph of the main part in a few sentences. Use your notes to help you.

> Always use the simple present to write a summary. Use your own words:
> Pam Warner talks about organic food and farmers' markets. She explains what these markets offer. …
> First/Second/Third …/Then/After that …

3. Write a conclusion. Say what you think about the article.

> To sum up, I can say … .
> In general the article explains … .
> I think … .
> In my opinion … .

3/1-5

3 Check your summary.

Read your text again and check:
- Spelling (all words correct?)
- Grammar (correct tense?)
- Style (linking words?)
- Content (the most important information?)

The checklist on page 181 can help you.

Find more online:
i8ce82

In this unit you will ...
- find out about California and the West.
- design an ad.
- talk about trends.
- understand a text about the Gold Rush.
- pass on information about child labour.
- watch a film about jobs and careers.

7 2,1

Unit 4
California dreams

California is the most densely populated state in the USA. With its 840 miles of coast, California has something for everyone – from giant redwood trees in the north to sunny beaches in the south. People live a relaxed outdoor lifestyle here. They especially enjoy beach sports like surfing and beach volleyball.

You can take a ride on one of the old-fashioned cable cars which go up and down the many hills in San Francisco. Or visit the largest Chinatown outside of Asia. In San Francisc you are never far from water. The Golden Gate Bridge is th city's famous landmark.

1 What do you know about California?

a) Before you read, look at the photos and start a mind map with a partner.

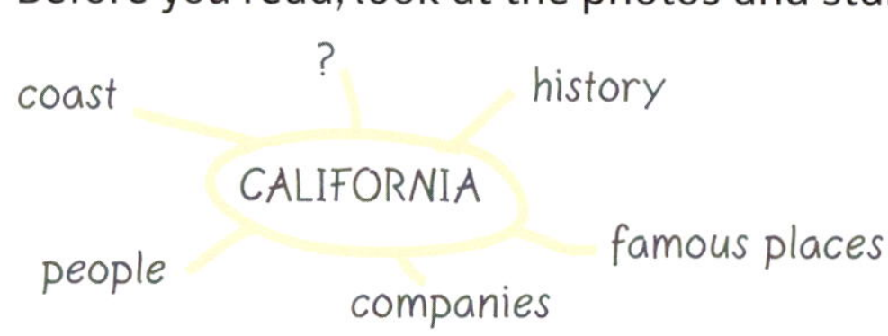

b) Now tell the class what you already know.

2 Read the texts and add more information about California to your mind map.

70/1-2

In 1849 the California Gold Rush started. Hundreds of thousands of people moved to the west, hoping to find gold and get rich. California's nickname, 'The Golden State', comes from that time.

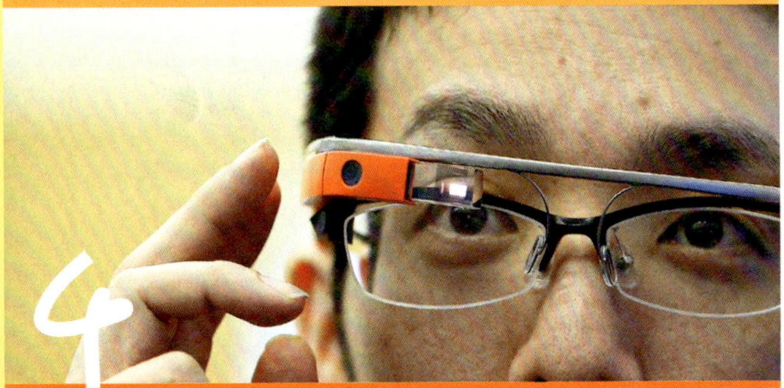

A great number of modern high-tech companies have settled in Silicon Valley near San Francisco. Some of them have developed into the world's largest companies.

Hollywood is the capital of the world's movie industry. Just say the name and people think of the glamour and excitement of the show-business world. You can visit the movie studios there and see the Walk of Fame.

3 (LISTENING) **Listen to the information and take notes.**

2,2
70/3

The Golden Gate Bridge

1. length of the bridge: …
2. Joseph Strauss
3. building the bridge
4. accidents
5. colour and painting
6. traffic on the bridge

bay [beɪ] – Bucht
architect [ˈɑːkɪtekt] – Architekt/in
safety net [ˈseɪfti ˌnet] – Sicherheitsnetz
fog [fɒg] – Nebel
to rust [rʌst] – rosten
lane [leɪn] – Fahrspur

I can understand information about California and the West. ✓

Enjoy the sunny west!

71/1 **1 Describe the photos in the ads.**

In photo 1 I can see … .
He is standing next to … .
There is also a … .

STUDY SKILLS

When you describe a picture, start with your first impression. Then describe it in detail. Say what the people in the picture are doing at the moment.

1

2

3

You'll love Yosemite Family Adventures

4

A day trip to the redwood forest

Stroll through the ancient giant redwood forest – among the oldest and tallest trees on earth.

5

2,3 **2 (LISTENING) Listen to a conversation about an ad.**

a) Answer the questions. → p. 127

1. Who is talking to whom?
2. Which of the ads in exercise 1 are they talking about?
3. What do they say about the ad?

interesting | boring | not special | great

b) Take notes about Daniel's dream.

3 (SPEAKING) What do you think of the ads? → M Think-pair-share, p. 179

a) Use these words to talk about the ads. → ○ p. 128

71/2

catchy | (not) informative | clear | funny | (un)appealing | fascinating

I think ad number 2 looks … .

b) Match each word with one of the ads. Does your partner agree? → V Adjectives for ads, p. 209

71/3

spectacular | pointless | unusual | dull

4 (SPEAKING) What makes a good ad?

72/4

a) Rank ads 1–5 from best to worst.

b) Give reasons for your choice. Say something about …

The layout and design:
appealing/simple/boring/…

The headline or slogan:
funny/catchy/too long/…

Text with a message:
informative/too long/clear/…

A: The layout of number … is simple and appealing.
B: Yes, I agree. And the headline is quite …

5 (SONG) Surfin' U.S.A.

2,4

Listen to the song. What does the song sound like? How does it make you feel?

If everybody had an ocean
Across the U.S.A.
Then everybody'd be surfing
Like Californ-i-a

You'd see 'em wearin' their baggies
Huarache sandals, too
A bushy, bushy blond hairdo
Surfin' U.S.A.

You'd catch 'em surfin' at Del Mar
Ventura County Line
Santa Cruz and Trestles
Australia's Narrabeen

All over Manhattan
And down Doheny way
Everybody's gone surfin'
Surfin' U.S.A.

Language → G9, p. 168

A surfer is standing next to a small bus.
At the moment he's looking at his phone.

I never go in the water.
Summers here are always terrible.

When do you use the present progressive? When do you use the simple present?
What's special about verbs like 'running' and 'coming'?

6 What are the people in the ads doing? Make sentences.

72/5

INTERNET

1. A boy is riding a mountain bike.

carry | sit | walk
ride ✓ | run | hold

7 (WRITING) Simple present or present progressive?

a) Complete the e-mail. → ○ p. 128

73/6-8

E-MAIL

Hi Becky,
At the moment I am sitting (sit) in the sun next to the swimming pool. Our new life in California is a dream! I ___ only ___ (joke). My life here in California isn't much different from what it was like in the Midwest. Every day I ___ (get up), ___ (go) to school, ___ (do) my homework and ___ (go) to bed.
But some things are different. For example, it ___ (not rain) much. It's always warm. We usually ___ (spend) weekends at the beach. At the moment I ___ (learn) how to surf.
What ___ you ___ (do) right now? I miss you.
Sandy

b) Write a short answer to Sandy's e-mail. Use the simple present and present progressive.

74/9

Hi Sandy,
Great to hear from you. I often think about the fun times we had together. Right now I'm waiting for a call from …

Language → G10, p. 169

I'm a terrible swimmer.
It would be nice to sit quietly on the beach.

Which is the adjective and which is the adverb in these sentences?
How can you usually tell an adverb from an adjective?

8 Read the advertising text about a helicopter tour. Choose: Adjective or adverb?

/10-11

Our Grand Canyon Helicopter Tour is a **fantastic** · **fantastically** experience. Fly **comfortable** · **comfortably** in a modern helicopter. The flight leaves at 9:30 every day. We will fly you there **quick** · **quickly** and you will land at 10 o'clock. Our pilots know the area very **good** · **well**. After a **delicious** · **deliciously** picnic, they will **happy** · **happily** answer any questions you have. This **fascinating** · **fascinatingly** tour lasts about three hours. Find out for yourself: The Grand Canyon looks **good** · **well** in photos, but it looks even better from the air.

GRAMMAR → G10, p. 169

to feel sad
to look happy
to seem easy

9 (YOUR TURN) Making an ad → V Talking about a region, p. 215

a) In groups of four make an ad about a state or region in Germany.

1. Decide on a region.
2. Collect ideas. → M Placemat, p. 177
3. Make a quick draft of the layout.
4. Divide the tasks:
   - find pictures or make drawings (two students)
   - write the text (two students)

Use the ads on page 76 as examples. Don't write too much!
A slogan plus two or three sentences is enough.

b) Present your work to the class. Which ad is the most appealing, which one is the most informative? Say why.

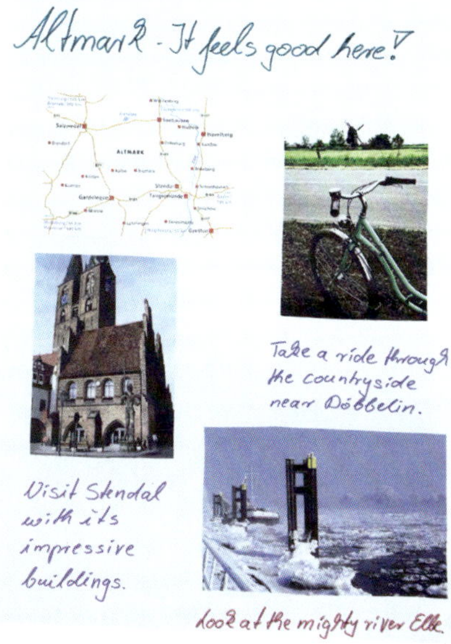

STUDY SKILLS

When you design an ad, first decide who it is for. Is it for children or for adults, for example?
Next choose a picture or photo which speaks for itself. The text should be short and simple, and the message clear. Talk directly to the reader; use questions and imperatives.
You can use a slogan maker on the internet.

I can design an ad. ✓

Made in California

1 How often do you go online? How many text messages do you send in a day? Which websites do you use the most? → M Round robin, p. 178

2 (READING) Read the blog of a Californian teenager.

2,5

BLOG

A quick look back

Thursday, March 16, 2017

My state, California, has always welcomed new ideas and innovations – just think of the high-tech companies in Silicon Valley or the movie and gaming industries.

The internet is one of these innovations. The World Wide Web started in the early 1990s, so it's been around for almost 30 years. And it has really changed the world. The social media sites that we use every day came with it. Companies from California started this trend. Today almost everyone uses social media. I've had an account since I was 13. Why have they been so successful? Well, that's easy: you can post your photos, share your thoughts and keep in touch with friends. Most of the time you don't even have to look for information. News, gossip and cat pics will find you. We should give that a big 'like', don't you think?

Online videos have become extremely popular too. And they've had a huge impact on our lives. Basically there is something for everybody. Of course there are tons of funny clips, but I like the tutorials best. You can find videos on how to do almost anything there, from guitar lessons to make-up tips. People mostly check out video clips online or stream their favorite shows. Nobody watches much TV any more.

Mobile devices like smartphones and tablets became the next big thing. They have strongly influenced how we communicate. I don't even have a radio, write letters or use a map any more. Instead, I use my smartphone. And I'm pretty sure it's the same for most people.

I've been thinking about all this for the last few days, so I decided to do a small survey of my friends. What I've found is that more than 90 percent of them go online daily, and half of them are online almost all the time. Most use several different social media sites at the same time. Some say it's difficult for them to stop using social media. They get messages every minute of the day and feel that they have to answer right away. Others are worried about cyberbullying because if somebody writes bad things about you online, a lot of people can read it. It looks like we haven't really found any good answers yet.

Posted by Derek Lee at 8:51 a.m. 2 comments: Links to this post

CULTURE

In the USA kids can join most social networks from the age of 13 if their parents allow it. What is it like in your country?

3 Put the headings in the right order.

A. A survey
B. Instead of TV
C. A place for new ideas
D. The impact of smartphones
E. A successful social media company

4 Work with the text.

a) Complete the sentences. → ◯ p. 129

1. The blogger lives in …
2. The World Wide Web started …
3. The blogger's favourite video clips are …
4. He doesn't watch …
5. People use mobile devices to …
6. Half of the blogger's friends …

b) Go through the text and find …

1. two new things that began in California.
2. two reasons why social media became popular.
3. two problems that people have with social media.

5 (LISTENING) Listen to the survey and complete the sentence.

2,6
75/1

outdated | in fashion | popular | latest thing | out of fashion | trendy

1. Yeah, it's the — .
2. I read on the internet that it's very — .
3. Didn't it become — in Europe first?
4. I know that jumping fitness is — .
5. I think it will soon go — again.
6. I don't think it will be — so soon.

6 (SPEAKING) Explain the meaning of the words.

a) Explain these social media words and expressions to your partner. → ◯ p. 130

75/2a)
75/3

(dis)like | friend request | post | share | unfriend

When you 'like' something, you tell people that you've enjoyed what they posted.

b) Explain three more words to a partner.
Use a dictionary. → V Social media, p. 210

75/2b)

follower | subscribe | trending

7 (SPEAKING) Say what the cartoon is about.

Language → G11, p. 170

The internet has changed the world.
Smartphones have influenced how we communicate.
We haven't found answers for these problems yet.

What is the tense in these sentences? How do you form it? When do you use it?

8 What have they (not) done? → M Bus stop, p. 174

76/4

1. Derek • just • make • coffee

2. Linda • already • start • computer

3. already • read • his e-mail

4. not finish • her blog • yet

5. not see • each other • in real life • yet

6. just • meet • first time

1. Derek has just made a coffee.

9 Say for how long or since when.

GRAMMAR → G11, p. 170

since 10 o'clock
for an hour

a) Choose for or since. → ○ p. 130

76/5

1. I've had my smartphone **for** • **since** more than three years.
2. Millions of people have seen the cat pics **for** • **since** Tuesday.
3. More than 5,000 people have watched that tutorial **for** • **since** May.
4. He hasn't answered his e-mails **for** • **since** five days.
5. Have you posted a new comment **for** • **since** last week?
6. How long has Silicon Valley been home to high-tech companies **for** • **since**?

b) Make sentences with for or since.

76/6

1. I sent Linda a message 20 minutes ago. She didn't answer.
2. She couldn't live without the internet. She started using it when she was five.
3. I know Derek. We met online six months ago.

1. Linda hasn't answered for 20 minutes.

10 Complete the survey questions and answers.

a) Use the simple past or the present perfect to complete the sentences. → ○ p. 131

7/7-8

1. Interviewer: How much did you spend (spend) on food and clothes last month?
   Person A: I'm not sure how much, but it ___ (be) a lot of money.
2. Interviewer: ___ you ___ (buy) a book or a magazine this week?
   Person B: I usually read everything online. But I ___ (get) a magazine two days ago for my mom.
3. Interviewer: Where ___ you ___ (meet) your friends the last time?
   Person C: In school. But we ___ (decide) to meet at the café around the corner today. I'm going there now.
4. Interviewer: ___ you ever ___ (use) tutorial videos to learn how to do something?
   Person D: Yes, sure. I ___ (learn) to play the guitar that way.
5. Interviewer: ___ you ___ (find) any new music videos that you liked in the last few weeks?
   Person E: Let me think for a second. Yesterday I ___ (see) one that I really enjoyed.

b) Make more sentences from the survey.

78/9

1. I • yet • that movie • not see
2. I • my first • get • tablet • in 2013
3. you • know • invent • 30 years ago • who • the internet?
4. I • that question • not think • about • yet

11 (YOUR TURN) Talking about trends → V Giving opinions, p. 207

a) *Hot* or *not*? What do you think? Sort these trends into the table:

78/10
9/1-2

- selfies
- torn jeans
- veganism

hot	not

b) Think of more trends and put them in the table.

c) Work with a partner. Exchange your tables. Give your opinion: Do you agree with your partner's table?

Do you know …? / Is the trend *hot* or *not*? / What do you think about …? / Have you tried it? / Has it had an impact on your life? / …

I can talk about trends. ✓

Gold rush! → M Jigsaw, p. 176

1 (READING) **Home group: Find two partners. Each of you chooses one of the texts (A, B or C). Read your text and answer the questions.**

2 **Expert group: Find students who have read the same text. Compare your answers with theirs.**

STUDY SKILLS

When you work on different texts in different groups, make sure to pass on your answers to the other groups. Ask yourselves: Which pieces of information and which words do the other groups need to understand your text?

2,7

Text A: A newspaper report

California Star

December 6, 1848

GOLD! GOLD! GOLD! Found in California

Washington. What people have known for months is now official. Yesterday the President of the United States confirmed the discovery of gold in California. The race for gold has just begun. Who will be the winner? It all began in Coloma, 40 miles east of Sacramento, in January this year when one of Mr. Sutter's workers found gold. Mr. Sutter, a German-Swiss immigrant and businessman, wanted to keep the gold a secret because he didn't want to give up his farming plans.

At the same time he tried to buy more land and become the official landowner. He didn't allow his workers to talk about the gold, but the news got out slowly. Sutter's biggest problem now is that he has to prove that he officially owns the land.

At first most local people didn't believe it. Then in May, the news reached San Francisco, and half of the city's population left to look for gold in the American River. Men simply gave up their jobs and set off to the West where they hoped to become rich easily. You have probably heard stories about men who left everything behind.

Landowners in the West now worry that gold fever will increase even more and the problems will get bigger. We will keep you informed and will tell you more in our next edition.

1. When did the President confirm the discovery of gold?
2. Who is Mr Sutter?
3. How did Sutter react when he learned about the gold?
4. What didn't Sutter allow his workers to do?
5. What did a lot of people do when they heard about the gold?
6. What are landowners in the West worried about?
7. When will there be more news?

2,8 **Text B: A letter from a gold hunter**

February 15, 1850
San Francisco

Dear Maddy,

It's been weeks since I left you, my beloved wife. Finally, I've found the time to rest and send you the news that you were probably desperately waiting for.

I arrived safely. There were heavy storms when we crossed the sea to Panama and lots of rain when we went through the jungle. A lot of men got sick, and some died – it got worse on the last ship to San Francisco. Sometimes I wanted to give up, but then I thought of you and our children. Ninety days after I had left you in New York, we sailed into San Francisco Bay. Our spirits were high, and the weather was finally great.

However, it took another week to get to the place where we hired horses and wagons. At night we slept under the stars. On the way we passed a place called 'Hangtown' – because they had hanged three men for stealing there. A few days later we arrived at our camp in the wilderness.

I've made friends with some of the other men, who came from all over the country. We often sit around the fire at night, tell stories and sing. All of us still dream of making a fortune and then returning home to our families. Sometimes there are fights in the camps. But don't worry, Maddy, I'm OK.

Digging for gold isn't easy, but I get better at it every day. Can you imagine how happy I was when I found my first little piece of shiny gold? Some days are better than others, but my love for you keeps me going. Once, I got terribly sick. I hadn't eaten or slept much, and had worked in ice-cold water for hours. Luckily, the fever was gone after a week.

My thoughts and prayers are with you, Maddy. Take good care of our children. Write soon.

Your loving husband,
Edward

1. Who is writing to whom?
2. How did Edward travel to San Francisco?
3. How many days was the total journey?
4. How did the men feel when they reached San Francisco Bay?
5. What problems did Edward have on his journey?
6. How is life in the camp?
7. What does Edward say about his job?

2,9

Text C: An encyclopedia entry

A history of California and the Gold Rush

News of the discovery of gold in California in 1848 caused huge excitement in America and abroad. Thousands of gold hunters made the journey there from all over the world, and in 1849 the Gold Rush started.

By 1852 there was no more 'surface' gold, and gold became difficult and expensive to find. But great numbers of immigrants continued to arrive. Before the Gold Rush, not even 1,000 non-native people lived in California. Ten years later the population was nearly 400,000. San Francisco went from a small village of 500 people to a boomtown of 150,000 in a few years. Many other new towns sprang up for the new arrivals.

Because of these events, California quickly became the 31st state of the United States in 1850. The money from the gold also helped to build transport links with the rest of the country: in 1869 the First Transcontinental Railway to San Francisco opened.

However, the impact on the Native American population was terrible. The immigrants either killed them or made them their slaves. Thousands died, and in 1870 the native population was only 20 percent of what it had been before the Gold Rush.

The boom years did not last long. When there was no more gold, there was no more work. So people moved away and left empty towns behind them. Some of these 'ghost towns' are still there today. The town of Bodie, for example, once had 8,000 inhabitants. The houses have not changed since then, and visitors can walk through the town and step back in time.

1. How did people feel when they learned about the discovery of gold in 1848?
2. What happened until 1852?
3. How much did the population grow after 1848?
4. Where did the money from the gold go?
5. What was the impact of the Gold Rush on the Native Americans?
6. Why are there ghost towns in the region?
7. What can you do and see in Bodie?

CULTURE

The Gold Rush has become a symbol of the 'California Dream': if you take risks in a place of new beginnings, you can get rich in a short period of time. Would you work such long hours and live in terrible places for a chance to become rich?

3 Meet your home group again: Present what you have found out about your text to the group. Take notes about the other texts.

Text A/B/C is a … | It's about … | The writer is … | The most important pieces of information from the text are …

4 Do a quiz in class.

Each expert writes one true or false statement about his or her text.
Read the statement to the class. Is it true or false?

5 Choose one of these tasks.

80/1
31/2-5

a) Do an interview: It's 1848. One of you is a reporter for the *California Star*. Your partner is a gold hunter who has just found a lot of gold.

Reporter: Prepare questions with *where, when, what, who, how long, how much.*
Gold hunter: Prepare your story and your plans for the future. Make notes to answer the reporter's questions.

OR

b) Make a timeline about the history of the Gold Rush. Collect information from the texts.

- 1848 – events in January, May, December
- 1849 – Gold Rush
- 1850 – California
- 1852 – …
- 1858 – population
- 1869 – …
- 1870 – Native Americans

I can understand a text about the Gold Rush. ✓

Too young to work?

Many big farms in California employ children, mostly from Latin America, to pick fruit or vegetables.
Children have to help their parents earn their living because migrant parents often don't have enough income.
It is difficult for them to get a better job because many of them don't have many qualifications or can hardly speak English. Some are even in the USA illegally.
All laborers have the legal right to take breaks and get water to drink in the state of California. But in reality things are different. Fresno Weekly Magazine talked to Matteo (12) and his brother Ramon (14) from Sacramento, who have been working on different farms.
Fresno Weekly: What are the working conditions like for you?
Matteo: We have to get up at 4:30 in the morning. Buses drive us to the fields, where we work all day in the heat. We sometimes work more than ten hours a day and only earn the minimum wage or even less. The long hours in the fields make you tired.
Fresno Weekly: Ramon, how long have you been working in the fields?
Ramon: Since I was ten, just like my Dad.
Fresno Weekly: Do you have any health problems?
Ramon: Yes, because of the pesticides I always have difficulty breathing and I have a constant headache out there. But that's not all. Some people get injured working with the large machines.
A federal law from 1938 allows farm owners to employ children from the age of twelve on big farms and even younger children on small farms. From the age of 14 teenagers can do farm work without their parents' consent. Officially, they are only allowed to work outside school hours, but some of them don't even finish high school. There are no statistics about how many children spend their days as farm helpers, but the estimate is about half a million. All recent attempts to change the law have failed.

CULTURE

Almost half of the USA's fruit, vegetables and nuts come from Central Valley, California. High temperatures of up to 100 °F (almost 40 °C) and little rain are ideal conditions for growing them. But the working conditions are hard.

1 Beantworte die Fragen.

82/1

1. In welchem Bereich arbeiten Kinder in Kalifornien? Warum?
2. Was sagen Matteo und Ramon über die Arbeitsbedingungen?
3. Wie sind die gesetzlichen Bestimmungen?

2 Are teenagers allowed to work as farm helpers in your country?

Search the internet for information about working regulations for teenagers in Germany.

I can pass on information about child labour.

Talking about jobs

1 Talk about the ad on the right.

a) Which question in the ad is the most important to you? Why?

b) Would the job interest you? Give reasons.

2 (VIEWING) Watch the film.

8

a) Watch the film until 02:08. Jessica, Wesley or Ronan: Who …

1. helps neighbours in their gardens?
2. walks the neighbours' dogs?
3. works as a waitress?
4. helps students with their homework?
5. puts groceries in bags for customers?

b) Watch the film from 02:08 to the end.

1. What does Wesley want to be?
2. What animals would Jessica like to work with?
3. Where would Ronan like to work?

CULTURE

The Rocky Mountains (the Rockies) lie in the west of Canada and the USA. They're popular for climbing, camping, hiking and skiing. Parts of the Rockies are in national parks. Find the Rockies on the map at the back of your book. Which mountains do you know?

3 (SPEAKING) Talk about the film.

a) Choose one of the jobs from the film.
Find 2–3 reasons why you'd like this job.

b) You partner argues against it.

I don't think so. No, that's …!
Really? But you'll have to …

I'd love/My big dream is to become a …
I'd like to work with …

at the weekends/after school/on Saturdays
out in the country/in the city
at a computer/outside/alone/… all day
famous/interesting/rich/boring/hard work/ …

VIEWING SKILLS

In a film you can see people or things moving – or the camera can move instead (e.g. by panning or coming nearer). This can give the film more drama and make it more interesting. Watch the second half of the film again. What is moving – the actors, the camera or both?

I can understand a film about jobs and careers. ✓

Checklist

I can understand information about California and the West. ✓

83

I can design an ad. ✓

The ad looks spectacular. • Its layout is simple and … . • The headline is funny. • In the picture there is …

83

I can talk about trends. ✓

Almost everyone uses it. • It has had a huge impact. • … isn't trendy/popular/ … • It's out of fashion. • Have you tried it?

84

I can understand a text about the Gold Rush. ✓

84

I can pass on information about child labour. ✓

85

I can understand a film about jobs and careers. ✓

(TASK) A blog

Write a blog about a trend that you like. Add pictures. Share your blog with others. Which trends do you find interesting? Which ones not? Why?

Step 1

Collect ideas.

Work with a partner.
Make a mind map of trends.

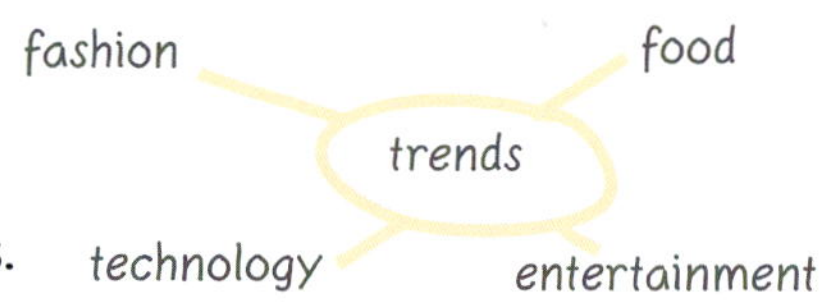

Step 2

Choose your topic.

Decide which trend you would like to write about.
Collect words and phrases.

- It's a kind of …
- You can use it for/when …
- It comes from …

Step 3

Collect information.

- Say where you learned about the trend.
- Say what you like about it.
- Say where the trend comes from.
- Talk about the trend. What is it? What's special about it?
- Say which people like this trend.

WRITING SKILLS

In a blog you give your personal opinion. So don't forget to say what you think.

Step 4

Write your draft and check it.

Check the content and spelling. Use the checklist on page 181.

BLOG

Have you ever heard of bento boxes? No? Well, I hadn't either until a friend of mine introduced them to me. Let me tell you: If you like being creative, try out this fun-filled way of organizing food. I think it's awesome. My little brothers and sisters love it. And it's great for parties too.
I once made a box as a present. It was a blast.
Bento originally comes from Japan and usually means 'home-packed meal'. But you can also buy boxes in supermarkets or at train stations. Bentos have been around since the fifth century. Modern bento boxes are made of plastic or metal. In Japanese restaurants you may get traditional boxes that are made of bamboo. In a traditional box you will find rice, fish or meat and vegetables.

Not that cool, you say? Just you wait and see ...
Here's mine ...

You can make your own bento easily. Just follow these simple steps:
- The food must be easy to eat.
- You must be able to eat it with your fingers.
- Your food must be cut into small pieces.
- Your food must be nice to look at.

Comment:
September 7, 2016
cookie: AWESOME. What a great idea! ...

Step 5

Share your blog with others. → M Gallery walk, p. 175

Read at least three more blogs.
Which one do you find the most interesting? Why?

Step 6

Comment on a blog.

Choose one blog. Discuss it and write a short comment.

Get to the mountain of nuggets

1 Make a set of cards with your partner.

You need:

paper

scissors

a pen

1. Fold the sheet of paper in half four times.

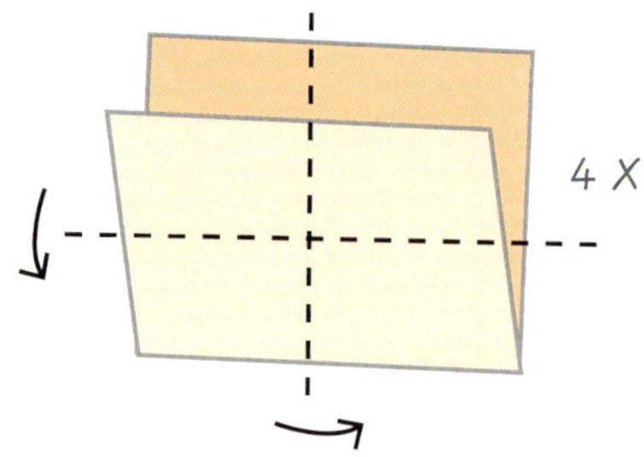

2. Cut along the lines so you have 16 playing cards.

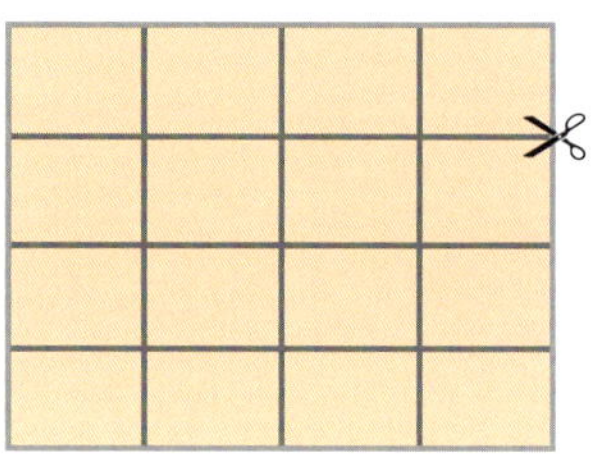

3. Write twelve questions about California on the playing cards. Write the answer in small letters upside down at the bottom of each card.

   Look at Unit 4 for help.

   You need the four empty cards for the next step.

2 Prepare the game.

1. Swap your set of cards with another pair.
2. Put the cards upside down in the middle of the table.
3. Draw a picture of yourself on an empty playing card.
4. Draw a huge mountain of nuggets on another empty card.
5. Put the two cards on the table in front of you.
6. Put the picture of yourself on the left and the mountain of nuggets on the right. Leave enough space for four more cards in between.

3 Play the game.

1. Pick a card from the pile in the middle of the table and read the question to your partner.
2. If your partner answers the question correctly, he or she can put the card next to his or her picture. If he or she is wrong, put the card to one side. It is now out of the game.
3. Take turns.
4. If you answer four questions correctly and get to your mountain of nuggets card, you win and become the richest boy or girl California has ever seen.

Swap your set of cards with another pair and play another round with their set of cards if you finish your game before others in class.

Here you can learn how to keep a conversation going.

2,10

A podcast interview

Wow, that sounds cool!

Isn't that the same every year?

No way!? That's amazing!

That doesn't sound like much fun.

Tell me more.

Is that really interesting?

Thanks so much.

I can imagine that.

I have to interrupt here.

1 Look at the photos on the left.

a) Talk about the photos with a partner. How do the people feel in each photo?

> You can tell how people are feeling when you look at their faces (e.g. a smile) and body language (e.g. crossed arms).

b) Listen to the interviews.
1. Which interview matches which photo?
2. Which interview is the better one?

2 Listen to the interviews again.

Match the sentences from page 94 with the interviews.

> The tone of the voices and the way the people speak also tell you a lot about the situation.

Interview A
- showing interest
- sounding surprised
- saying thank you

Interview B
- sounding bored
- interrupting

88/1
/2-4

3 Interview your partner about the last movie that he or she saw.

a) Work in pairs. Decide who will ask the questions and who will answer.

> Make notes first. Write down everything that comes to your mind when you want to talk about the movie. Answer the Wh-questions (Who? What? When? Where? Why? How did you like it?).

b) Think of some questions and answers together.

> When you prepare your interview, don't forget to use the phrases from interview A too.

c) Act the interview.

> Remember to use facial expressions, body language and tone of voice to show your interest in what your partner has to say when you act your interview.

Find more online: i8ce82

9 2,11

In this unit you will ...
- find out about the southern states of the USA.
- talk about multicultural influences in everyday life.
- report to others about free-time activities.
- read a report about discrimination.
- pass on information about customs.
- watch a film about summer holidays.

Unit 5
Southern life

1 The Southern Appalachian Mountains, the Gulf Coast beaches, the Florida swamps and the wide Mississippi River – the South has many exciting destinations for fans of the outdoors.

2 Until the 1950s African Americans in the South had few rights and there was a lot of discrimination. The Civil Righ Movement was a peaceful protest movement which force the government to change the laws.

1 Talk about the photos.

a) Which picture do you find the most appealing? Why?

b) Match the headings with the photos.

- The southern way of life
- Slaves in the fields
- Styles of American music
- The outdoors
- Protest!

92/1

2 Read and say why ...

1. ... outdoor fans visit the South.
2. ... the Civil Rights Movement began.
3. ... the first settlers brought in slaves.
4. ... people feel proud to be Southerners.
5. ... the South is an important region for music.

In the 18th century, people from France, England, Scotland and Ireland came to the South. Soon after, they brought in African slaves to work on their plantations.

More than other regions of the United States, the South has its own lifestyle, with its own culture and customs. People here are proud to be both Americans and Southerners.

Several styles of music have their roots in the South. Gospel music, the blues and later rock 'n' roll originated here. New Orleans is alive with jazz, and Nashville is the home of country music.

3 (LISTENING) **Listen to the online radio broadcast about Taylor Swift.**

2,12
92/2

Complete the sentences.

1. First a country singer, Taylor Swift became one of the biggest … .
2. She started taking song-writing lessons at the age of … .
3. When she was 14, her family moved to … .
4. Her song "Tim McGraw" was a … hit.
5. She has had hits on both charts, … and … .
6. She is successful because she comes across as … .

business ['bɪznɪs] – Geschäft
to release [rɪ'li:s] – veröffentlichen
copy ['kɒpi] – Exemplar
celebrity [sə'lebrəti] – Prominente/r; berühmte Person

I can understand information about the southern states of the USA. ✓

Living together

1 (READING) Read the text.

2,13
93/1

Rich food, rich culture

by Anna Williams

The South is famous for its great food. If you look at the history of famous southern dishes, you can follow the story of the people who settled in the region. So I went on a trip down there, and here's what I found out.

In the beginning there was the food of the Native Americans. Then new dishes were brought in by European settlers. The slaves from West Africa had a big influence on southern food too.

The delicious southern fried chicken is a good example. It was introduced by people from Scotland. The dish is made with chicken, flour and different spices – some from West Africa. First the spices are mixed with the flour. The chicken pieces are washed and dried and then covered in the flour. After that, you fry them in oil.

In the city of New Orleans, different cultures and traditions come together. The city was founded by the French in 1718; then it came under Spanish rule. New Orleans was the most important cotton and slave market in the South until the middle of the 19th century. Later it became the country's biggest immigration port after New York, and thousands of German, Irish and Italian immigrants passed through it. In the late 20th century large numbers of Vietnamese people arrived.

When you walk through the streets of New Orleans today, you can take in its own special identity. It's very much a multi-cultural city, and you can experience it best at the famous Mardi Gras carnival and the jazz festivals.

New Orleans

But living together does not come without its problems. The different groups living in the South often need to compromise.

The debate about the Confederate flag is one of these cases. I talked to a number of people about it. For many white people in the South this historic flag is a symbol of pride, while others just tolerate it. But most African Americans disagree – for them it is a symbol of racism.

The flag flew over the South Carolina State House for years until it was removed in 2015. After the media reported on a number of killings of black teenagers, protesters confronted the state government, and they had to find a solution. Many big stores have also now stopped selling the flag.

But with all these problems, the rich multicultural life of the South still attracts lots of visitors – like myself.

CULTURE

The Confederate flag was used by the South in the American Civil War, which was fought because the North wanted to abolish slavery, but the South didn't. Today it is seen as a controversial symbol by many people.

2 Answer the questions.

a) Answer these questions about the text.

1. Who had an influence on Southern food?
2. What has the port of New Orleans been in its history?
3. In which ways is New Orleans a multicultural city?
4. Why do many African Americans not like the Confederate flag?

b) What can Southern dishes tell you about the history of the region?

3 What's the nationality?

a) Match the nationalities with the flags. → ○ p. 131

93/2

Chinese · Greek · Italian · Russian · Polish · Turkish

1. 中国

2. Россия

3. Polska

4. Ελλάδα

5. Türkiye

6. Italia

b) Which is typical? Match the food with the nationality. → V Nationalities, p. 217

paella

cheese

sushi

Japanese · Spanish · Swiss

4 Work with words to talk about conflicts and solutions.

a) Complete the sentences. → ○ p. 132

93/3a)
94/4

1. The protesters had a different opinion. They disagreed with the government.
2. It was very hard for them to see the Confederate flag on the State House. They …
3. At first the government did nothing against the protests. It …
4. After that the government didn't want to allow the protests any more. It tried to …
5. Then the government agreed to talk to the leaders of the protests to …
6. But the protesters didn't like the government's ideas for a solution. They …

ban · couldn't stand · tolerated · didn't accept · disagreed ✓ · find a solution

b) Sort the words into the table. → V Conflicts and solutions, p. 217

93/3b)

appreciate · reject · resent · respect

positive	negative
…	…

Language detectives → G12, p. 171

The dish is made with chicken.
Chicken pieces are washed. Then they are dried.

When do you use the passive?
How do you form it?

94/5

5 Complete the sentences with the passive forms.

1. Pork —— (use) in many southern dishes.
2. Southern food —— (eat) across the USA.
3. Vegetables and meat —— (keep) in the fridge.
4. All these dishes —— (make) with rice.
5. The chicken and rice —— (not cook) for a very long time.
6. Rice —— (not grow) in many US states.

94/6

6 (SPEAKING) Describe how southern fried chicken is cooked.

spices and flour • mix

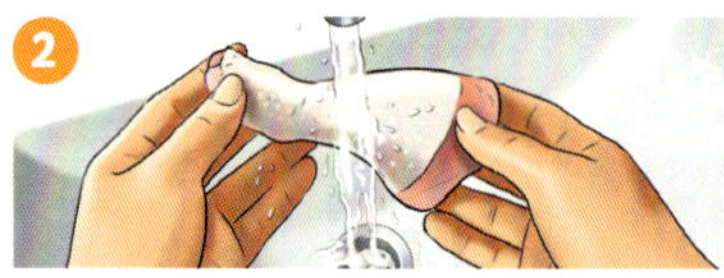
chicken pieces • wash

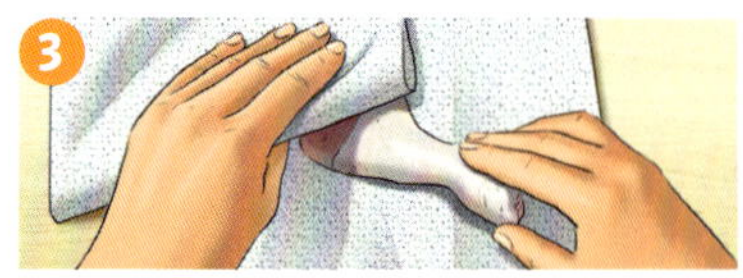
chicken pieces • dry

cover in • flour

put in • hot oil

fry • until golden

1. First the spices and flour are mixed.

7 (WRITING) Make passive sentences.

95/7

a) Change the sentences to passive sentences. Begin with the underlined words. → ○ p. 132

1. In a multicultural society people do not accept <u>racism</u>.
2. These societies welcome <u>people from other countries</u>.
3. People speak <u>more than one language</u> in multicultural societies.
4. In some schools they teach <u>lessons in different languages</u>.
5. They organize <u>special lessons</u> for people who are new.
6. Restaurants here serve <u>dishes from all around the world</u>.

1. Racism is not accepted in a multicultural society.

95/8

b) Change these sentences to passive sentences.

1. The government supports the idea of a multicultural society.
2. A small minority doesn't respect immigrants from other cultures.
3. Visitors appreciate the rich cultural life of New Orleans.

If you want to say who does something in a passive sentence, add 'by + …'

8 Make passive sentences in the simple past.

a) Complete the information about the city of Raleigh. → M Bus stop, p. 174 → ○ p. 133

-10a)

The city of Raleigh (1) was founded (found) in the 18th century as the state capital of North Carolina. Before that, there was no town in the place that (2) —— (choose) for Raleigh. It is an example of a city that (3) —— (plan) from the beginning. The city (4) —— (give) the name of Sir Walter Raleigh, an English adventurer, soldier and writer. The streets (5) —— (build) in a special way, so that they look like a grid. During the 1960s Raleigh grew fast because people (6) —— (attract) by the new jobs in the Research Triangle Park near the city. The tallest skyscraper in the city, the PNC Plaza, (7) —— (not complete) until 2008.

GRAMMAR → G12, p. 171

The city was founded by the French.

New foods were brought here by the slaves.

b) Complete the sentences with more information.

/10b)

sell | **make** | **change** | **open** | **not finish**

1. The land for the city —— to the state by a local plantation owner in the 1780s.
2. The famous Executive Mansion —— only with materials from the state of North Carolina.
3. The South's first African-American college —— in Raleigh in 1865.
4. Work on the first airport of the city, Curtiss-Wright Flying Field, —— until 1929.
5. During the 1960s the state laws —— so that the majority of black people could vote again.

9 (YOUR TURN) Different cultures where I live → V Talking about culture, p. 222

96/11

What is the influence of other cultures where you live? Prepare a short presentation.
→ M Tip top, p. 179

• Describe where you live.	I live in … It's a place where … /
• Say what multicultural influences you find in:	There are many Turkish / Chinese / … there.
– shops	Most of the …
– restaurants	When you look around, you see …
– signs	The … is written in …
– music	People like to buy / go to … because …
• Choose a dish or a piece of music from another culture and describe it.	'Paella' is a famous … dish. It's usually made …. But often other things are added, like ….

STUDY SKILLS

If you don't know a word, look it up in a dictionary. If a word is difficult to translate, try to explain it in English. Sometimes you can use a picture to explain a word.

I can talk about multicultural influences in everyday life. ✓

A trip to Florida

1 Look at the websites. Which trip would you like to go on? Why?

INTERNET

Be there for the most important race in the NASCAR calendar!

Daytona 500 race packages

Our race packages include:

- excellent Daytona 500 race tickets
- a choice of hotels, breakfast included
- transfer to the race track by deluxe bus
- an informative booklet with all details

INTERNET

Go deep into the Florida Everglades!

Airboat rides, alligators, wildlife show

- hotel pick-up
- exciting 30-minute boat tour (with lots of 360-degree turns!)
- alligator, snake and wildlife show
- jungle trail through the swamps

... are all included in the price.

2 (READING) Read the friends' dialogue. → M Dramatic reading, p. 175

2,14 97/1

Anna: ... so Dad can take us to Daytona or to the Everglades. He says that he needs an answer today. These are the websites that he's found.

Matt: Well, for me it's clear. I'd like to go to the race. It's the biggest NASCAR event of the year. And I'm sure we will get great seats.

Anna: That's not my idea of fun. All those crowds of noisy people! I prefer the Everglades. I've never seen an alligator in the wild.

Matt: Why do you want to spend the day walking around in the heat?

Anna: What does Ethan think?

Ethan *is speech impaired. He can hear, but he uses sign language to speak. Matt understands sign language and translates for Anna.*

Matt: Ethan says that he doesn't like crowds much either.

Anna: There you are. He wants to see the alligators too.

Ethan *makes more signs.*

Matt: I'm sorry, I didn't get that, Ethan. Can you please repeat it? *Ethan repeats it.* I see. But he also says that he has always wanted to watch a NASCAR race.

Anna: Oh, no! So I'm outnumbered.

Ethan *makes signs.*

Matt: I'm sorry, I didn't catch that, Ethan. *Ethan repeats it.* Oh, right. He says the jungle trail sounds really interesting too. He'd like to see big snakes. He wants to know if your dad can drive us to the Everglades another time. Maybe next month? Then we could see both.

Anna: Hmm. He said that we could only go to one place. But I can ask him again tonight.

3 Take notes about the places.

a) Where do Anna, Ethan and Matt want to go?

b) Copy and complete the table.

	for	against
Daytona		
Everglades		

2,15 **4** (LISTENING) **Listen to the text about a visit to an alligator farm.**

a) Read notes A–C. Which one is correct? → p. 133
97/2

A
- boat ride
- trainer fed alligators
- trainer put hand in alligator's mouth
- photo of Ethan with snake

B
- boat ride
- trainer fed snakes
- trainer put hand in alligator's mouth
- photo of Anna with alligator

C
- boat ride
- trainer fed alligators and snakes
- trainer had fight with snake
- photo of Matt with snake

b) Answer the questions.

1. Why did Matt feel a bit sick?
2. What did Ethan think was the best part of the day?
3. What did Matt think was cool?

5 **Say that you understand or don't understand.**

a) Put the phrases into two groups. → p. 134
97/3a)

Could you please explain? | I get it. | I know what you mean. | I see. | I'm sorry, but I didn't catch that. | Excuse me?

Saying "I understand": ...   Saying "I don't understand": ...

b) Match the phrases with the definitions. → V Understanding things, p. 219
97/3b)

Please repeat that. | Absolutely! | What do you mean by '...'?

1. Ask somebody to explain a word.
2. Ask somebody to say something again.
3. Tell somebody that you strongly agree with them.

SPEAKING SKILLS

If you don't understand something, never just say "Huh?" or "What?" It's rude.

6 **Use sign language.**

Look at the signs. Then close your books and practise them with a partner.

yes   no   please   thank you

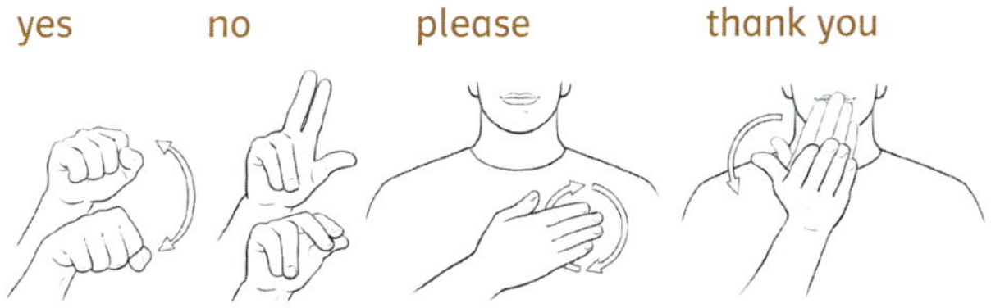

STUDY SKILLS

When you connect certain gestures with certain words, it makes it easier to remember them.

Language detectives → G13, p. 172

Dad says he needs an answer today.
Ethan says that he doesn't like crowds much either.
He wants to know if your dad can drive us to the Everglades.

These sentences report what Dad and Ethan said. What did they actually say (for example: Dad: "I need … .")? Which words have changed?

7 Report what other people say. → M Peer correction, p. 177

a) Report what Anna says. → ○ p. 134

98/4-5

1. "I love the warm weather in Florida."
2. "We just wear T-shirts."
3. "We often go to the beach."
4. "I don't have time to take lots of photos."
5. "I don't like the thousands of insects."
6. "I'm having a great time."

Pronouns and verbs change in reported speech:
I → he/she
I love → he/she loves
we → they

1. Anna says (that) she loves the warm weather in Florida.

b) Play the game: Your teacher gives a sentence to the first student in your group. He or she whispers the sentence to the next person and so on. Is the sentence still the same at the end?

Teacher: "I don't want to be alone with an alligator."
Student 1: He/She says …

8 Report the questions in the speech bubbles.

98/6

She asks if he watches …
He wants to know how much a ticket …

9 (WRITING) Report the statements with the simple past.

a) Report what the animal trainer said. → ○ p. 135

9/7-8

Al Lane, the animal trainer, talked about an exciting day at Florida Alligator Farm: "Most days I get up at 6 a.m. I have breakfast. Then I clean the alligator cage. I also count them and I check the gates. I don't feed them until 10 o'clock. There are only 19 in the cage, not 20. I have no idea where the other one is!"

GRAMMAR → G14, p. 173

"I live in Florida."	–	He said (that) he lived in Florida.
"We love NASCAR races."	–	They told me (that) they loved NASCAR races.

Al Lane said that most days he got up at 6 a.m. He said …
He told the reporter that …

b) Report other things that Al said to the reporter.

100/9

1. "We don't get a lot of visitors any more."
2. "Most tourists go to my brother's farm."
3. "My daughter doesn't like alligators."
4. "But she still often visits me."

1. Al said that …

10 (YOUR TURN) Information for a day trip → V A day trip, p. 223

00/10
1/1-2

Tell an English-speaking friend about Berlin Zoo.

Can you tell me where it is?
– The website says it's in the centre of Berlin.

What animals can you see there?
– It says here …

Which activities can you do there?
What are the opening times?
Where can we buy tickets?
… ?

STUDY SKILLS

It's not necessary to translate word-for-word. You only need to pass on the most important pieces of information. Use your own words.

INTERNET

Herzlich willkommen im Zoo Berlin!
Besuchen Sie den ersten Zoo Deutschlands im Zentrum Berlins. Unter unseren über 17.000 Zoo-Tieren finden Sie Elefanten, Schlangen, Tiger, Gorillas, Flamingos und viele mehr.

» Erleben Sie die Fütterungen und Tiershows.
» Gehen Sie auf Nachtsafari im Nachttierhaus.
» Feiern Sie Kindergeburtstage bei uns.
» Nehmen Sie am Fotospaziergang teil.

Öffnungszeiten
Heute, 2.6.2018, 9:00 – 18:30 Uhr
Jetzt Online Ticket kaufen!

I can report to others about free-time activities. ✓

The girl who fought segregation

1 If you know something is wrong or unfair, what do you do about it?

2 (READING) Read the report.

2,16

Claudette Colvin, 2016

Montgomery, Alabama, is a nice, small southern town. But in the 1950s people's lives there were completely segregated. Black people had to go to separate movie theaters. They weren't allowed to try on clothes in stores. On buses, the seats in the front were for whites, and people of color sat at the back.

Claudette Colvin was an African-American teenager in Montgomery at the time. She strongly believed that segregation was unjust and unfair. On March 2, 1955, Claudette was on a bus with three other girls. They were sitting in the middle of the bus on the last seats that were allowed for people of color. More and more white people got on downtown, and the bus was soon full. When this happened, the rule was that people of color moved to the back of the bus and gave up their seats to whites. The bus driver looked in his mirror and saw the situation. He told the girls that they had to move. Three of them got up and went to the back. But Claudette didn't move.

CULTURE

The Ku Klux Klan is a secret organization of white Americans who hate people of other races and religions. In the 1950s and 60s they often attacked or killed African Americans and members of the Civil Rights Movement. Are there groups like that in your country?

3 Find the information.

1. Where did Claudette sit on the bus?
2. When did the bus get full?
3. Why did her father not sleep that night?
4. Why did Claudette lose a lot of friends?
5. When did she move to New York?
6. What did Rosa Parks do?

4 Read the text again and explain. → M 1-minute-presentation, p. 174

a) Make notes about these things.

Segregation | What Claudette did | The result of her protest

b) Explain why Claudette didn't give up her seat on that bus.

5 What message does Claudette's story have? What do you think?

READING SKILLS

Most texts have a main theme or statement. It's important to find and understand it. You often find it in the headline, the first paragraph or the ending. So read them carefully. The main theme is usually supported by examples. Can you find them in this text?

The bus driver called the police. A police officer got on the bus and confronted Claudette. Claudette refused to move. She said that she always paid her fare like other people, and she said it was her right to sit there. In the end, they had to drag her off the bus because she refused to stand up. She was arrested and taken to jail. Her parents brought her home later in the day, but her father was awake all night with his shotgun because he was afraid of an attack by the Ku Klux Klan.

The next week she had problems in school too. Some students were impressed by her courage. Many others, on the other hand, felt that her action made things more difficult for African Americans. Claudette lost a lot of friends: their parents told her friends that Claudette was crazy and that they had to stay away from her.

But although Claudette's personal life became very difficult, her protest was a success. A year later she was the star witness in the court case which ended segregation on all public transport in the state of Alabama. However, with the reputation she had, it was very difficult for her to find work. So in that same year she left Montgomery and moved to New York.

Claudette's story has been forgotten by most people. Instead, the fight against segregation on buses is linked with the name of Rosa Parks, a woman who did exactly the same thing on a bus nine months later. When she was asked about this, Claudette said that she wasn't bothered that her name wasn't known.

There were hundreds of brave people like Claudette who fought to end segregation. You never see their names or their faces, but they played an important role in the long fight to abolish an unjust system. Their courage will always be remembered.

6 Choose one of these tasks.

102/1
103/2-4

a) Search the internet for information about these people who fought for their rights:
- Rosa Parks
- Martin Luther King
- Malcolm X
- Mahatma Gandhi
- Malala Yousafzai

Choose one and write a short biography of him or her. Add pictures.

→ M Gallery walk, p. 175

OR

b) A quote:

"It is the greatest mistake to do nothing because you can only do a little. Do what you can."
– Sydney Smith

Explain the meaning of this quote. Then discuss: Do you agree? Say why or why not.

I can understand a report about discrimination.

Going out in style

INTERNET

The 'jazz funeral' came from Africa with the slaves about 400 years ago. In the beginning it was called 'funeral with music'. People celebrated the end of slavery for the dead person and wanted to help them find their way to heaven. It was first used mainly for poorer African Americans and later also for musicians. In the mid 20th century it developed into a widely accepted form of funeral.

When the parade is on its way to the church, the brass band usually plays some call-and-response-style music. Like in a dialogue, some musicians play a part and others respond. That shows that everybody has an equal right to take part. On the way to the cemetery the band plays mostly slow and sad songs. But on the way back you can hear joyful music. One of the most famous songs is "When the Saints Go Marching In". At this stage people from the streets are allowed to join in the parade.

One of the biggest jazz funerals in New Orleans took place on August 29, 2006 for the 1,700 victims of Hurricane Katrina. The communities remembered the people who lost their lives during the natural disaster a year earlier. That shows how much the jazz funeral has become a symbol of the way in which people here deal with the death of loved ones and still celebrate life.

1 Beantworte die Fragen.

104/1-2

1. Was feierten die Menschen bei einer Jazz Beerdigung?
2. Was macht einen 'call-and-response-style' aus?
3. Welche Art Musik wird vor und nach der Beerdigung gespielt?
4. An welches Ereignis und an wen erinnerte die Jazz Beerdigung am 29. August 2006?

2 Which funeral traditions do you know in your country or in other countries?

I can pass on information about customs.

The great outdoors?

1 Talk about the summer holidays.

a) Do you prefer outdoor or indoor activities in your free time?

b) What's your favourite activity? Why?

CULTURE

In the USA school vacation lasts 8–12 weeks and children often go to a camp for some of that time. Some camps have a theme like horse riding or another sport or computer games. Do you have a summer camp in your area? Would you like to go to one?

2 (VIEWING) Watch the film.

10

a) Match the statements with the right scene.

1. "I got the job interview at Silverley!"
2. "That was last year. I'm 16 now!"
3. "That's for really young kids …"
4. "Very reliable. You can trust her."

A

B

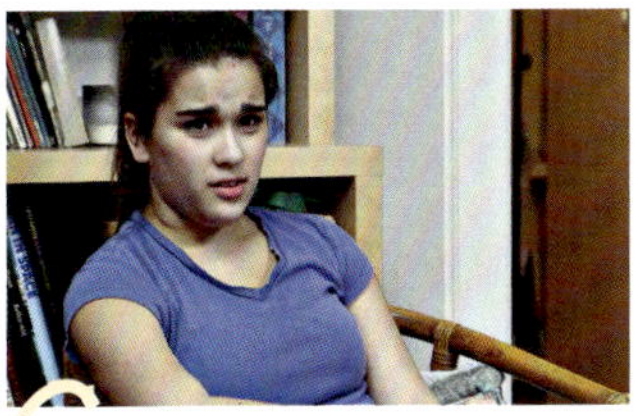
C

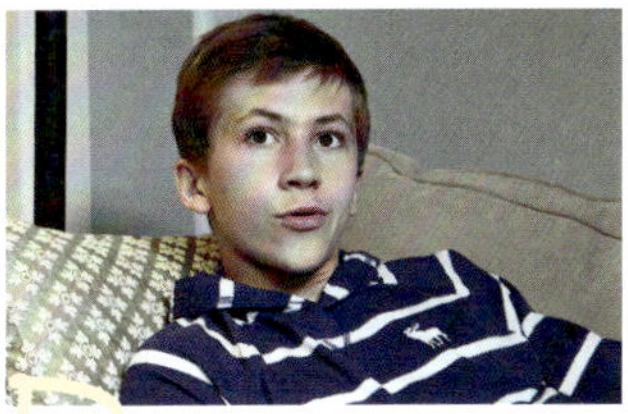
D

b) Watch from 01:31 to 01:55. Make notes about five of the activities there.

Which one of them would you like to try? Give your reasons.

3 (SPEAKING) Talk about the film.

Watch the sequence at Silverley again (from 03:17). Practise an interview for a job.

A: So do you have experience in …
B: Well, I've worked / helped / done …
A: As a … you will … / To be honest, you won't …
B: Oh! OK, I …
A: Excellent! You've got the job!
B: Oh, …

VIEWING SKILLS

Pay attention to how the actor doing the interview makes the candidate feel comfortable, e.g. by smiling.
In what other ways can an actor interact with a partner?

I can understand a film about summer holidays. ✓

Checklist

I can understand information about the southern states of the USA. ✓

105

I can talk about multicultural influences in everyday life. ✓

… had a big influence on … . • … living together is … • When you look around, you see … • … is a famous dish from …

105

I can report to others about free-time activities. ✓

He says that he needs … • What does … think? • I'm afraid I didn't get that. • He wants to know if …

106

I can understand a report about discrimination. ✓

106

I can pass on information about customs. ✓

107

I can understand a film about summer holidays. ✓

(TASK) A feature story

Imagine you are a reporter. Choose a topic. Then choose a place, watch the people there and take notes. Write a feature story. Make a wall newspaper in class.

Early birds
by Mika Hensing
May 13, 2016 — *headline, writer, date*

It's still dark. I can see hardly any people on the street. However, the smell of fresh bread is in the air. And at the bright baker's stall there's a crowd of people in a long line. They are all waiting their turn. (*describing the scene*) Some are looking at their phones. Some are counting their money; others are talking to each other. (*describing details*) Almost everyone looks tired except the saleswoman who … . I feel … . (*describing emotions*) Bakers usually get up at … . (*background information*) "I come here every day," a woman says … . (*direct speech*)

Step 1

Look for an interesting place to go.

You can go to the campus, a bus stop, the park or any other place where you can watch other people. Find other students who chose the same place.

Step 2

Take notes about the scene at your place.

What do you see, hear, smell, feel?
What other details are important to describe the atmosphere?
Take photos too. If you take photos of single people or small groups, you have to ask them if that's OK.

Step 3

Find facts about your place.

You can find facts on location or on the internet. If you choose a bus stop, for example, you can find out how many buses there are every day and where they go.

Step 4

Use your notes to write a draft.

- Find a catchy headline, an interesting opening and an appealing photo.
- Describe the scene, the people and the atmosphere.
- Name the place and give interesting facts and details.
- Say what is special about the place or the people.

WRITING SKILLS

Use adjectives, adverbs and direct speech to make your text more lively.

Step 5

Check your draft. → M Writers' conference, p. 179

WRITING SKILLS

Use a list to check your draft:
- Do you have a headline, an opening sentence and a photo? ✓
- Do you give your name and the date? ✓
- Do you present the place and its people in detail? ✓
- Have you checked the spelling of difficult words with a dictionary? ✓
- Are your sentences grammatically correct? ✓

Ask classmates if you need help.

Step 6

Make a wall newspaper in class. Find the most interesting feature story. → M Gallery walk, p. 175

Read the headlines, the first lines and look at the photos. Vote for the best headline, the most interesting first line and the most interesting photo. Read these three feature stories in class.

Recipes from the South

Po Boy Sandwich (serves 4)

The Po Boy Sandwich is a recipe from New Orleans. It's made with fresh French bread and a wide variety of fillings. You can make a perfect Po Boy Sandwich to your own choice and taste!

You need:
1 fresh French baguette bread
(about 14 ounces or 20 inches long)

Filling of your choice

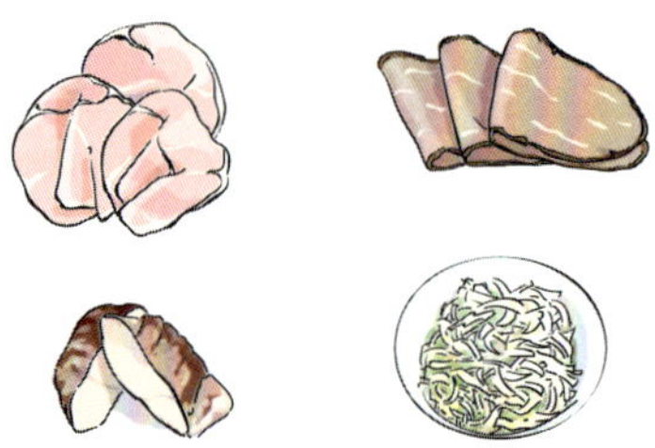

ham, roast beef or chicken breast, coleslaw

smoked tofu, lettuce and tomatoes, onion rings or coleslaw

shrimps in cocktail sauce and tomatoes, shredded lettuce

Sauce

hot BBQ sauce, salsa or mayonnaise

Extras

gherkins or mixed pickles, grated cheese

Serve with

French fries, crisps or nachos

Preparation:

1. Cut the bread into 4 pieces.
2. Cut each piece in half.
3. Spread the sauce on one half.
4. Next choose the fillings of your choice.
5. Add extras to your taste.
6. Put the two halves together.
7. Serve the sandwich with French fries, crisps or nachos.

Enjoy your sandwich!

CULTURE

In the USA they use imperial units for measuring weight, distance or volume:
1 ounce = 28.35 g
1 inch = 2.54 cm
1 cup = 24 ml

Louisiana Sweet tea (makes 4 glasses)

You need:

4 cups of water

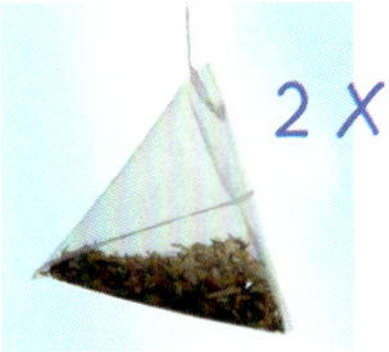

2 breakfast tea bags

1 peppermint tea bag

3–5 tablespoons of sugar

juice of one lemon

crushed ice and slices of lemon

Preparation:

1. Boil the water.

2. Put all the tea bags into the boiling water. Brewing time: 5–6 min.

3. Add the sugar and the juice. Stir it well.

4. Cool it down.

5. You can serve it with crushed ice or slices of lemon.

Here you can learn how to write an essay.

2,17

The man who became a hero

by Chris Rice

When I met Leo Turino for the first time, I could not believe that he was a hero. But on October 4 this small, ordinary, middle-aged man saved four people's lives in Spartanburg during the South Carolina floods of 2016.

I talked to him about it – about his fears and worries. Here is what he said:

"You know, almost every day you read about people who pull others from fires, stop violent crimes or dive into dangerous waters to rescue people. I always asked myself what I would do or how I would react. Would I step back or take action?

When the flood hit our city, we were all in shock. The water quickly flooded all the streets and most of the houses. The state's Emergency Management Division released a statement later that morning via social media: 'Stay. Where. You. Are. Dangerous flooding conditions throughout the state for most of the day.'

I was lucky to have a small motorboat. So I grabbed my wife and my two kids and set off to the city hall. We passed by a woman with her baby and two little kids who were desperately calling for help from the top of their car. The water was still rising. We could hear the baby crying, but our boat was full. My head was buzzing, but in such situations you don't think, you just react. There was no time to wait. Their lives were in danger. We managed to save everyone and to find shelter with all the other people.

It was only afterwards that I had time to think. So many things can go wrong in a situation like that. Your own boat can sink, and you can drown. If you're unlucky, you try to help somebody and end up dead yourself. Maybe it's better to just stand by and call for help?

BUT … I couldn't let this family die. I have a family too. And I don't think I could take it if something happened to them. So I just had to help. I would have done the same for everyone else too. People like me are not exceptionally brave or strong, though."

As you can see real heroes are among us and they do exist. It can be your neighbor, your best friend or small kids. Even you could be one. When they are in difficult situations, they just do what is needed. Give them thanks because they inspire us with their heroism.

1 Prepare your essay.

Read the article on the left. What do you think? Would you risk your life to save others?

1. Think of dangerous situations where people need help.
2. Choose one of these situations and describe it.
3. Now think. Would you help and act like a hero in a situation like this? Collect pro and contra arguments.
4. Number your arguments. The most important one comes last.

Put your arguments in a table.

Pro (yes)	**Contra** (no)
...	...

To make your essay more exciting finish with your strongest argument.

2 Write your essay.

111/1-4

a) Introduction
Introduce the topic in one or two sentences. Make readers curious and tell them what you'll be discussing.

b) Body
1. Give your personal opinion first. Do you agree with the question or not?
2. Structure your arguments.
- Start with the weakest argument, finish with the strongest.
- Write in paragraphs and connect the paragraphs.

c) Conclusion
- Sum up your opinion and the most important points.
- Don't give any new arguments.

Here are some helpful phrases for your introduction:
Many people believe that ...
Nowadays ...

Here are some helpful phrases for the body of your essay:
In my opinion ...
First (of all), second, ...
To start/begin with ..., the next point is ...,
Finally ...
On the one hand ... on the other hand ...
However, ...
Because of ..., that's why ..., ...

Here are some helpful phrases for the conclusion of your essay:
After all ... / To sum up I can say ...
All in all ... / In conclusion ...

Diff corner

Unit 1, p.15

4 Work with the city words.

Find the odd one out.

1. shopping mall • rush hour • traffic jam
2. skyscraper • subway • tower
3. intersection • campsite • road sign
4. sightseeing • sidewalk • tourist

Unit 1, p.15

5 (SPEAKING) Talk about the city.

Present what is in the photo.

Have a good look at ...
On the corner there is ...
Over there ...
Right ahead ...
Have you noticed ...?
In the distance you can just see ...

intersection • (traffic) lights • taxi • hot dog cart • skyscraper • building • van • bike • people • ...

Unit 1, p.16

7 (WRITING) Tell the taxi driver's story.

Make sentences in the simple past.

passenger • get in at airport

be in traffic jam

talk to

arrive at hotel • leave the saxophone • find saxophone

run

give back

1. Last winter a passenger got in my taxi at John F. Kennedy Airport.
2. There was a lot of snow and we …

Unit 1, p.17

8 (SPEAKING) What did they do at One World Trade Center yesterday?

Ask and answer questions about the people in the picture.

A: What did Henry eat?
B: He ate a sandwich.

B: Did Susan take photos?
A: No, she didn't. She called somebody on the phone.

What did Where did Who did Did	+ Donald Lisa Scott Nancy Frank Steve Amy Susan Linda Henry	+ drink eat look at sit talk to wear call stand feel	+ …?

Unit 1, p. 18

2 Work with the text.

1,4

Interviewer: Hello José. Can I ask you a few questions for our magazine, please?

José: Hi. Sure, go ahead.

Interviewer: You're new on the baseball team. Are you happy with your season so far?

José: We won the first three matches, so I can't complain, really.

Interviewer: You're one of many players from Latin America in the league. When did you immigrate to the United States from Cuba?

José: I arrived with my mom and sisters when I was ten. That was 12 years ago. My dad had arrived in New York two years before I came.

Interviewer: That was a big decision for your parents. They left their home and moved to a strange place.

José: Yes, but they were very poor in Cuba. My father had been unemployed for a long time. Above all they wanted to give me and my sisters the best chances in life.

Interviewer: What were the first years like?

José: My parents had problems because they hadn't learned English in school. But there's a strong community of Cubans here, and they all help each other. So my parents opened a small shop and sold goods to other immigrants.

Interviewer: And how did you feel in your new home? Had you ever seen skyscrapers before?

José: No, I hadn't. It was exciting. But later I was homesick. I missed all my friends. But my parents had given up a lot for me. After I had stopped counting the weeks, I slowly got used to it.

Interviewer: And when did you begin your baseball career?

José: As a child in Cuba I always played a lot of sports. But I hadn't taken any sports seriously before I was about 15. From then on I really wanted to be successful. I think people who leave their own culture and language are usually motivated and ambitious. I was the star of the baseball team in high school, and after that my career just took off.

Interviewer: Well you have certainly been successful!

José: Yes, I have been very lucky. For most people it is much harder. This country has given me a great opportunity. My story really is an example of the American Dream come true.

Interviewer: What about your plans for the future?

José: I am a US citizen now and my home is here. But I still have contact with Cuba, and I plan to help develop tourism there.

Interviewer: José, thank you for your time.

Complete the sentences.

1. José was ten years old when …
2. His parents decided to immigrate because …
3. They opened a shop for other immigrants because …
4. In the beginning, José felt … but later …
5. As a successful player, now José feels …
6. José is a US citizen but he also …

Unit 1, p. 19

○ 4 Imagine you want to leave your country.

Describe your thoughts, hopes and wishes.

have many opportunities | get used to | feel foreign | emigrate from ✓ | immigrate to

1. I want to emigrate from this country.
2. Maybe I could — the USA.
3. I hope I won't — and lonely.
4. I will probably — in the USA.
5. I'm sure I can — my new life soon.

Unit 1, p. 20

○ 7 (WRITING) Write about one of Angela's days.

Complete the sentences with the simple past and the past perfect.

eat pizza | invite to a party | go to bed | buy tickets | go to the stadium | walk through the park

After …

buy a present

take the subway

visit Ellis Island

Before …

order a milkshake

put on their fan shirts

watch a TV show

Unit 1, p. 21

8 (SPEAKING) Ask and answer questions.

What had or hadn't José done before his first important baseball game last summer? Ask questions and answer them.

1. Interviewer: Had you played every day last summer before your first big game?
   José: Yes, I had.
2. Interviewer: Had you …?
   José: Yes, I had. / No, I hadn't.
   …

1 played every day ✓
2 bought new sports shoes
3 ordered tickets for his friends ✓
4 phoned his dad ✓
5 eaten a small meal
6 went to bed early

Unit 2, p. 35

4 What do these words mean?

Choose the right word.

1. a lesson or course
   grade • class • locker
2. a list of classes and times in a school
   schedule • pledge • class
3. it tells you how well you did in a test
   class • detention • grade
4. when you promise to do something
   locker • pledge • schedule
5. when a student must stay after classes
   class • detention • locker
6. where students keep their things
   class • schedule • locker

Unit 2, p. 36

8 (WRITING) Find out about other exchange students in the USA.

Make sentences. Use (not) be allowed to and (not) be able to.

During the exchange: (not) allowed to	Aileen	Jannik
wear jeans at school	+	–
bring any boys/girls to the bedroom	–	–
stay up until 10 p.m. during the week	+	+
After the exchange: (not) be able to		
get used to the old life easily	+	–
speak English a lot better	+	+
keep in touch with all her American friends	–	
help students from other countries		+

Unit 2, p. 37

10 Complete the dialogue. Then act it with a partner.

Sarah: How was your host family in America last year? Did you have to (have to) do jobs around the house?
Luise: No, — (not have to). — (able to) decide when I wanted to help in the house.
Sarah: — (allowed to) stay up late? — (have to) be in bed at a certain time?
Luise: During the week — (have to) be in bed at 9. On weekends — (able to) go to bed later.
Sarah: — (able to) travel around with the family?
Luise: Yes, — (able to). But I — (not allow) to travel alone.

Was she allowed to go?
Were you able to choose?
Did you have to go?
When did you have to go?

Unit 2, p. 39

4 What do you think?

What do you think about what Michael's manager says at the end?

I think he's right / I think he's wrong	because	it's important to be polite.
		Michael should really think of the other customers.
		it's part of such a job to deal with difficult customers.
		Michael didn't start the argument.
		the two students weren't polite either.
		the two students were teasing Michael.

Unit 2, p. 39

6 Practise words to describe people at work.

Put the words into groups.

strength (+)	weakness (–)
cooperative	...y
...e	u...
h...	l...
...g	...d

bossy · unmotivated · cooperative ✓ · responsible · lazy · helpful · hard-working · disorganized

Unit 2, p. 40

○ 9 (WRITING) What will happen if ...?

Look at the pictures. Make sentences.

complain | find ✓ | buy | steal | will (3x)

1. If Michael finds a student job, he ___ earn some money.

2. If he needs help, he ___ ask his co-workers.

3. If he is late, he ___ lose his job.

4. If the girl ___ the T-shirt, Michael will catch her.

5. If the man ___, he'll get a new one.

6. If the woman ___ two pairs, she'll get one free.

Unit 2, p. 39

○ 10 Complete the sentences.

Use 'ones' to replace plural nouns like 'sunglasses' and 'pants'.

Use one or ones.

1. I really like this rain jacket. This one fits me perfectly.
2. We have lots of helmets. The best ___ are over there.
3. Is there a restroom near the store? – Yes, there's ___ over there.
4. This beach towel is a bit dirty. Do you have a clean ___ ?
5. How about these pants? – No, I prefer the ___ that I tried on before.
6. I need some new sport sunglasses. My old ___ are broken.

Unit 3, p. 55

3 Find out about the Miller family's Thanksgiving.

1,17

The Miller family from Boston are getting ready for Thanksgiving dinner. Julia is in the kitchen. Her husband Mark, their teenage son Jacob and Grandma Brenda are in the living room.

Grandma: Last year we had such a terrible storm. I got stuck in my car for over two hours. Do you remember?
Mark: Yes, that's right. Did you have a hard time again yesterday, when you drove here? *(The doorbell rings. Mark opens the door. It's their elderly neighbor.)*
Robert: Happy Thanksgiving, Mark!
Mark: You too, Robert. How are you?
Robert: Great, thanks. Brr. It's freezing outside, isn't it?
Mark: Come on in then. I'm so glad you could make it. *(They enter the living room.)* Grandma, this is Robert. He's our new neighbor. He doesn't have family here, so we've invited him to join us. Robert, this is Brenda.
Robert: Nice to meet you, Brenda. You came all the way from Miami, didn't you? Do you always come by car?
Grandma: Yes, always. Please have a seat. When did you move here? And where do you originally come from?
Mark: *(shouting across the room)* Jacob, why don't you say hello? You can't spend all your time playing with your phone.
Jacob: What's up Robert?
Robert: How's it going? Are you enjoying the holiday? Do you like turkey?
Jacob: Not really. I'm a vegetarian, so I won't eat any.
Julia: *(coming out of the kitchen)* You always used to eat everything. *(She notices the new guest.)* Oh, hi Robert.
Robert: Hey Julia. Thanks so much for inviting me. I've brought you a little something. You eat chocolates, don't you? *(He gives her a box as a present.)*
Mark: OK everybody. I'm making a video of today. First, will you all answer this Thanksgiving question: 'What do you feel thankful for?' Julia, you go first, please. *(He starts filming.)*
Julia: Me? Well, err, most of all I am thankful for my husband and my two lovely children who … *(Mark's phone rings.)*
Mark: That's probably your second lovely child and her new boyfriend who are on their way here. Hello Lily. … Oh, no! *(to the others)* Their plane from Washington, D.C. had engine trouble, and they had to land in New York. *(to Lily)* So when does your plane arrive, later today or tomorrow? … OK. … Will you call us again when you know more? I promise we'll save some turkey for you!

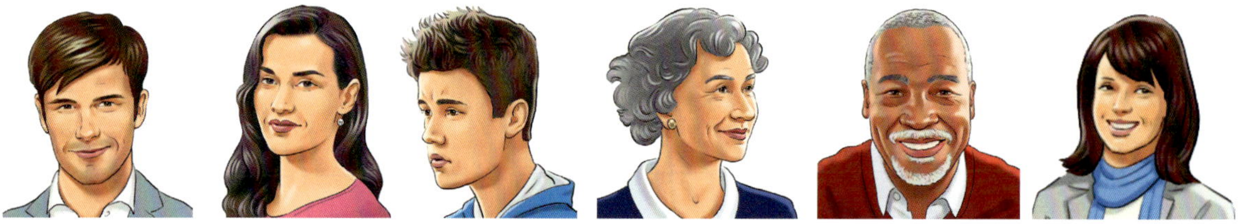

Mark Julia Jacob Brenda Robert Lily

Who is it?

1. Who got stuck in her car last year?
   That's **Brenda**.
2. ... is not a member of the Miller family?
3. ... used to eat turkey, but not any more?
4. ... gets a present?
5. ... is making a video?
6. ... landed in New York?

Unit 3, p. 55

4 (LISTENING) Listen to Lily introduce her boyfriend Evan the next day.

1,18

Listen to the conversation. Match the questions and answers.

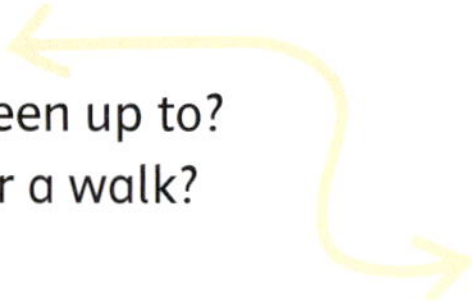

1. Dad: How are you doing?
2. Evan: So what have you been up to?
3. Evan: How about going for a walk?
4. Dad: How is she?
5. Evan: Can I help with anything?

A Lily: Let's do it.
B Dad: No, thanks, it's all organized.
C Dad: Not much.
D Lily: Everything is fine, thanks.
E Evan: She's good, thanks.

Unit 3, p. 56

8 (SPEAKING) Ask questions about holidays.

Interview your partner. Choose do, does, did or will.

1. Which holidays **will** • **does** your family celebrate?
2. When **does** • **will** *(name of holiday)* usually start?
3. Who **does** • **will** your family invite every time?
4. What **do** • **will** you always eat?
5. What **will** • **did** you like about last *(name of holiday)*?
6. How many guests **do** • **did** your family invite last time?
7. Who **did** • **will** you talk to last *(name of holiday)*?
8. Where **did** • **will** *(name of holiday)* take place next year?

GRAMMAR → G7, p. 166

Who did you invite?
Who did you talk to?

D

Unit 3, p. 57

9 (WRITING) Write Jacob's questions for the underlined answers.

What did Jacob ask his grandma? Match his questions with the underlined answers.

E-MAIL

Dear Jacob,
Yes, it's true, it will be my 65th birthday soon! I'm planning (1) a big family celebration. I will have it (2) at my house in Miami. It will take place (3) on May 1. I will invite (4) everybody who can come to Miami. And of course you can ask your new girlfriend to come too. Yes, I already know about her. That's because (5) your dad told me about her.
Much love,
Grandma

A What are you planning for your birthday? (1)
B Who will you invite?
C When will it take place?
D Why do you know about her?
E Where will you have your birthday party?

Unit 3, p. 59

5 Sort the phrases.

Sort the phrases into the table.

I agree	I disagree
Exactly.	Absolutely — .
That's true.	You can't be — .
That's for — .	No — !
You're — .	I don't think — .

not · right · serious · so · sure · true ✓ · way

Unit 3, p. 59

○ 6 (SPEAKING) Talk about devices.

Make a list.

microwave

headphones

TV

cell phone

computer

hair straightener

The most important thing for me **is my cell phone/are my headphones/is my computer/** . . . . • I think/don't think … are more important than . . . . • For me … comes first/second/third. • … are next. • I very often use … • I couldn't live without … • I don't really need …

Unit 3, p. 60

○ 8 What would make Jennifer's life easier?

Look at the pictures. Complete the sentences.

wear | iron | chose ✓ | have | walk | go | not listen

1. Jennifer would be less worried in the morning if she chose her clothes in the evening.

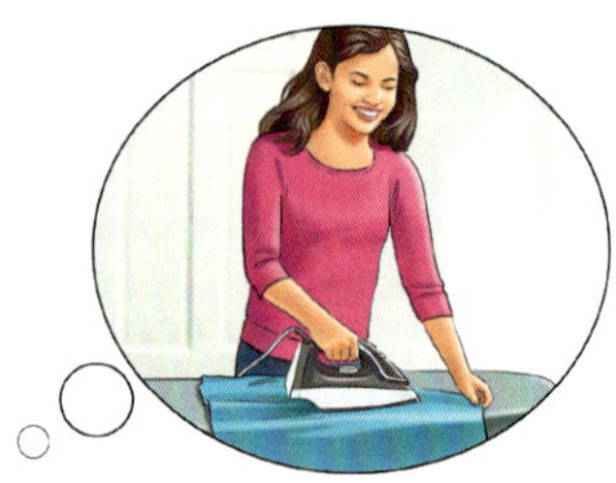

2. Her T-shirt would look much nicer if she —— it in the morning.

3. She wouldn't feel so tired in the morning if she —— to bed early.

4. She would hear what her dad said if she —— to music.

5. She wouldn't be cold if she —— a warm coat.

6. It would be healthier if she —— to school.

D

Unit 3, p. 61

9 (SPEAKING) What would you do if . . .?

Answer the question. Then ask your partner.

What would you do if you . . .

1. were president of the United States for a day?
2. were a superhero?
3. could stop time?
4. had a million dollars?
5. knew the answers to your next English test before the test?
6. didn't have the money to buy a ticket for the bus home?

Unit 4, p. 76

2 (LISTENING) Listen to a conversation about an ad.

2,3

Answer the questions.

1. Daniel is talking to — and — .
2. They are talking about ad number — .
3. Daniel and — like the ad, — doesn't. Daniel thinks . . . . / One girl says . . . . / It's great/ boring/interesting/not special . . . .

Unit 4, p. 77

3 (SPEAKING) What do you think of the ads?

Talk about the ads.

catchy | (not) informative | clear | funny | (un)appealing | fascinating

Ad number 1 is/isn't … . / I think ad number 2 looks/doesn't look … . / But number 3 looks … . / And 4 is … . / However, I find ad 5 … .

Unit 4, p. 78

7 (WRITING) Simple present or present progressive?

Choose the correct verb form to complete the e-mail.

E-MAIL

Hi Becky,
At the moment I **am sitting** • **sit** in the sun next to the swimming pool. Our new life in California is a dream! I **am** only **joking** • only **joke**. My life here in California isn't much different from what it was like in the Midwest. Every day I **am getting up** • **get up**, **am going** • **go** to school, **am doing** • **do** my homework and **am going** • **go** to bed.
But some things are different. For example, **it isn't raining** • **doesn't rain** much. It's always warm. We usually **are spending** • **spend** weekends at the beach. At the moment I **am learning** • **learn** how to surf.
What **are you doing** • **do you do** right now? I miss you.
Sandy

Unit 4, p. 81

4 Work with the text.

2,5

BLOG

A quick look back

Thursday, March 6, 2017

My state, California, has always welcomed new ideas and innovations – just think of the high-tech companies in Silicon Valley or the movie and gaming industries.
The internet is one of these innovations. The World Wide Web started in the early 1990s, so it's been around for almost 30 years. And it has really changed the world. The social media sites that we use every day came with it. Companies from California started this trend. Today almost everyone uses social media. I've had an account since I was 13. Why have they been so successful? Well, that's easy: you can post your photos, share your thoughts and keep in touch with friends. Most of the time you don't even have to look for information. News, gossip and cat pics will find you. We should give that a big 'like', don't you think?
Online videos have become extremely popular too. And they've had a huge impact on our lives. Basically there is something for everybody. Of course there are tons of funny clips, but I like the tutorials best. You can find videos on how to do almost anything there, from guitar lessons to make-up tips. People mostly check out video clips online or stream their favorite shows. Nobody watches much TV any more.
Mobile devices like smartphones and tablets became the next big thing. They have strongly influenced how we communicate. I don't even have a radio, write letters or use a map any more. Instead, I use my smartphone. And I'm pretty sure it's the same for most people.
I've been thinking about all this for the last few days, so I decided to do a small survey of my friends. What I've found is that more than 90 percent of them go online daily, and half of them are online almost all the time. Most use several different social media sites at the same time. Some say it's difficult for them to stop using social media. They get messages every minute of the day and feel that they have to answer right away. Others are worried about cyberbullying because if somebody writes bad things about you online, a lot of people can read it. It looks like we haven't really found any good answers yet.

Posted by Derek Lee at 8:51 a.m. 2 comments: Links to this post

Complete the sentences.

1. The blogger lives in …
2. The World Wide Web started …
3. The blogger's favourite video clips are …
4. He doesn't watch …
5. People use mobile devices to …
6. Half of the blogger's friends …

Unit 4, p. 81

6 Explain the meaning of the words.

Match the sentence parts.

1. When you 'like' something,
2. When you 'dislike' something,
3. When you make a 'friend request',
4. When you 'post' something,
5. When you 'share' something,
6. When you 'unfriend' somebody,

a) you send it to people who will probably find it interesting.
b) you tell people that you've enjoyed what they posted.
c) you put it on social media so that other people can see or read it.
d) you don't want to be friends with him or her.
e) you tell people that you haven't enjoyed what they posted.
f) you ask somebody to be your friend.

Unit 4, p. 82

9 Say for how long or since when.

Complete the sentences with for or since.

1. I've had my smartphone **for** • **since** more than three years.
2. Millions of people have seen the cat pics **for** • **since** Tuesday.
3. More than 5,000 people have watched that tutorial **for** • **since** May.
4. He hasn't answered his e-mails **for** • **since** five days.
5. Have you posted a new comment **for** • **since** last week?
6. How long has Silicon Valley been home to high-tech companies **for** • **since**?

Unit 4, p. 83

10 Complete the survey questions and answers.

Use the simple past or the present perfect to complete the sentences.

1. Interviewer: How much **did you spend** • **have you spent** on food and clothes last month?
   Person A: I'm not sure how much, but it **was** • **has been** a lot of money.
2. Interviewer: **Did you buy** • **Have you bought** a book or a magazine this week?
   Person B: I **usually** read everything online. But I **got** • **have got** a magazine two days ago for my mom.
3. Interviewer: Where **did you meet** • **have you met** your friends the last time?
   Person C: In school. But we **decided** • **have decided** to meet at the café around the corner today. I'm going there now.
4. Interviewer: **Did you** ever **use** • **Have you** ever **used** tutorial videos to learn how to do something?
   Person D: Yes, sure. I **learnt** • **have learnt** to play the guitar that way.
5. Interviewer: **Did you find** • **Have you found** any new music videos that you liked in the last few weeks?
   Person E: Let me think for a second. Yesterday I **saw** • **have seen** one that I really enjoyed.

Unit 5, p. 99

3 What's the nationality?

Match the nationality with the flag.

Chinese | Greek | Italian | Russian | Polish | Turkish

1. 中国 (China)

2. Россия (Russia)

3. Polska (Poland)

4. Ελλάδα (Greece)

5. Türkiye (Turkey)

6. Italia (Italy)

Unit 5, p.99

○ 4 Work with words to talk about conflicts and solutions.

Match the sentences which have the same meaning.

1. The protesters had a different opinion.
2. It was very hard for them to see the Confederate flag on the State House.
3. At first the government did nothing against the protests.
4. After that the government didn't want to allow the protests any more.
5. Then the government agreed to talk to the leaders of the protests to …
6. But the protesters didn't like the government's ideas for a solution.

a) find a solution.
b) It tried to ban the protests.
c) They didn't accept the ideas.
d) They disagreed with the government.
e) They couldn't stand it.
f) It tolerated the protests.

Unit 5, p.100

○ 7 (WRITING) Make passive sentences.

Change the sentences to passive sentences.

1. In a multicultural society ~~people~~ do not accept racism.

   Racism is not accepted in a multicultural society.

2. ~~These societies~~ welcome people from other countries.

   People from other countries are —— .

3. ~~People~~ speak more than one language in multicultural societies.

   More than one language —— in multicultural societies.

4. In some schools they teach lessons in different languages.

   Lessons in different languages …

5. They organize special lessons for people who are new.

   Special lessons …

6. Restaurants here serve dishes from all around the world.

   Dishes from all around the world …

If you want to say who does something in a passive sentence, add 'by + …'

Unit 5, p.101

8 Make passive sentences in the simple past.

Complete the information about the city of Raleigh.

were attracted | were built | was chosen | was not completed | was founded ✓ | was given | was planned

The city of Raleigh (1) was founded (found) in the 18th century as the state capital of North Carolina. Before that, there was no town in the place that (2) — (choose) for Raleigh. It is an example of a city that (3) — (plan) from the beginning. The city (4) — (give) the name of Sir Walter Raleigh, an English adventurer, soldier and writer. The streets (5) — (build) in a special way, so that they look like a grid. During the 1960s Raleigh grew fast because people (6) — (attract) by the new jobs in the Research Triangle Park near the city. The tallest skyscraper in the city, the PNC Plaza, (7) — (not complete) until 2008.

GRAMMAR → G12, p. 171

The city was founded by the French.

New foods were brought here by the slaves.

Unit 5, p.103

4 (LISTENING) Listen to the visit to an alligator farm.

2,15

Read notes A–C. Which one is correct?

A
- boat ride
- trainer fed **alligators**
- trainer put hand in **alligator's mouth**
- photo of **Ethan** with **snake**

B
- boat ride
- trainer fed **snakes**
- trainer put hand in **alligator's mouth**
- photo of **Anna** with **alligator**

C
- boat ride
- trainer fed **alligators and snakes**
- trainer had **fight with snake**
- photo of **Matt** with **snake**

Unit 5, p.103

5 Say that you understand or don't understand.

Copy the table and complete the phrases.

Saying "I understand":	Saying "I don't understand":
I get it.	Could you please — ?
I know what — .	I'm sorry, but I didn't — .
I — .	— ?

catch that. | explain? | get ✓ | Excuse me? | see. | you mean.

Unit 5, p.104

7 Report what other people say.

Report what Anna says.

she doesn't have | she's having | they go | she loves ✓ | they wear | she doesn't like

1. "I love the warm weather in Florida."
2. "We just wear T-shirts."
3. "We often go to the beach."
4. "I don't have time to take lots of photos."
5. "I don't like the thousands of insects."
6. "I'm having a great time."

Pronouns and verbs change in reported speech:
I → he/she
I love → he/she loves
we → they

1. Anna says (that) she loves the warm weather in Florida.

Unit 5, p.105

○ 9 (WRITING) Report the statements with the simple past.

Report what the animal trainer said.

Direct speech	Reported speech
Al Lane, the animal trainer, talked about his work:	
"Most days I get up at 6 a.m.	Al Lane said that most days he got up at 6 a.m.
I have breakfast.	He said that he ___ breakfast.
Then I clean the alligator cage.	He told the reporter that he ___ the alligator cage.
I also count them and I check the gates.	Then he said that he ___ them and he ___ the gates.
I don't feed them until 10 o'clock.	He said he ___ them until 10 o'clock.
There are only 19 in the cage, not 20.	He said that there ___ only 19 in the cage, not 20.
I have no idea where the other one is!"	He told the reporter that he ___ where the other one ___ !

GRAMMAR → G14, p.173

"I live in Florida."	–	He said (that) he lived in Florida.
"We love NASCAR races."	–	They told me (that) they loved NASCAR races.

2,18 Art and culture in NYC

Big city, bright lights

1

New York City really has it all: great museums, lots of movie theaters, the finest restaurants, street markets, …
Walk down Broadway at night and you'll see the lights of 40 theaters and many smaller 'Off-Broadway' theaters. Here you can see popular actors in world-class shows, plays and musicals.
Or experience the many different communities that live in New York. The Puerto Ricans celebrate their national day with a parade along Fifth Avenue every June, for example.
Also in the summer months:
For the SummerStage Festival, the parks in the city's five boroughs have hundreds of free events. There's a great number of things to see and do here … just take your pick.

Hip hop culture

2

It's the end of the 1960s in the Bronx, at the time a poor part of the city. This is where African-American teenagers start a new cultural movement, hip hop.
From the beginning rap, DJing, breakdancing and graffiti were the main parts of hip hop culture. DJs took bits and pieces of older songs to create a new style of music. Rappers said their rhymes over the music – at the time the words were often about life in street gangs and about social questions. Breakdancers became famous for their robotic moves and headspins. Graffiti artists used subway trains and buildings as their canvas. Obviously, hip hop has gone global since.

D

Street art

3

When police made life difficult for graffiti artists, they moved on to street art. At first that meant large murals, often in poorer parts of the city. Today you can go on guided tours to see the best of these pieces. But people find new ways to change the face of their city all the time, and you can find many examples in New York City. Some think it's art, some don't. Either way, the question it always asks is: Who does the city belong to?

The city in comics

4

Spiderman lives in Queens, Iron Man's company is located in Long Island and Batman's Gotham City is a fictional version of New York. And there are lots of other examples – the city basically is the home of superheroes. Like hip hop, comics are an art form that was invented in the United States. For more than half a century the biggest comic book companies have been located in New York City and legendary writers like Stan Lee (you can see him for a few seconds in many superhero movies) and artists like Jack Kirby and Steve Ditko have worked here.

1 What did you find interesting about the texts? Talk about them with a partner.

2 Which other art forms were invented in America? Find out on the internet.

bright – *hell*; movie theater *(AE)* – *Kino*; to experience – *erleben*; social – *gesellschaftlich*; artist – *Künstler/in*; canvas – *Leinwand*; global – *weltweit*; guided tour – *Führung*

2,19 Native Americans then and now

Christopher Columbus didn't discover America!

The history of Native Americans in our country is fascinating and tragic. When Europeans made first contact with them around 1500, about ten million people lived in North America. They had come from Siberia to Alaska in about 10,000 BC and migrated south. Over time they adapted to the environment. They spoke different languages and had many different lifestyles. The ones in the cold north were hunters and fishermen. In forest areas, they built houses made of wood and built canoes. Others lived in villages by rivers and were farmers and traders. On the Great Plains, on the other hand, tribes lived in tepees and hunted buffalo with bows and spears. They moved from place to place and carried their tepees.

"I was born on the prairie where the wind blew free and there was nothing to break the light of the sun. [...] I want to die there and not within walls. I know every stream and every wood between the Rio Grande and the Arkansas. [...] So, why do you ask us to leave the rivers and the sun and the wind and live in houses? Do not ask us to give up the buffalo for the sheep."

Chief Ten Bears in 1867

The Europeans arrive

From the 17th century, the impact of large numbers of European settlers on Native Americans was terrible. Firstly, they brought illnesses which killed thousands. Then, when more people arrived, they wanted land, and the tribes had to leave their traditional farming and hunting lands. The settlers pushed them further and further away from the coast, until in the 1830s a number of large tribes had to move west of the Mississippi River. On this terrible journey hundreds died of cold, hunger and illness.
On the Great Plains, however, the story was different. The tribes had got horses from the Europeans, so they were able to hunt buffalo more easily. They didn't want to give up their freedom and their hunting lands, and they often attacked settlers who crossed the plains. Many bloody battles followed. But by 1900 most tribes had to go and live on reservations. In 1924, after they had fought in the First World War, Native Americans became full American citizens.

Native Americans today

Today only a minority of the five million Native Americans live on reservations. Some reservations make money from the casino business, but most of them are poor and there's a lot of unemployment. However, among younger people today, both on and off the reservations, there's a new interest in their Native American culture. Alaqua (16), for example, lives in Oklahoma and he is typical of this new generation: "The government took my grandad away from his parents and sent him to boarding school, together with thousands of others. They didn't let him learn about his language or culture there. So my dad never learned anything either. We lost a lot of things in that period.
Even in school today nobody teaches us about the thousands of years of our history before the Europeans arrived. But many of us want to change this situation. My history is part of me. I feel like we Native Americans are picking up the pieces of our culture and moving forward. I want to help rebuild things."

By Pat Smith
September 15, 2016
Junior History Magazine

1 **What did you already know about Native Americans? What didn't you know? Talk with a partner.**

2 **Read the text again. In your opinion, which historical facts does Alaqua want Native Americans to learn about? Say why you think they are important.**

tragic – *tragisch;* BC (= before Christ) – *vor Christus;* environment – *Umwelt, Umgebung;* hunter – *Jäger/in;* fisherman – *Fischer;* trader – *Händler/in;* Great Plains – *Flachland in den USA;* tribe – *(Volks-)Stamm;* impact – *Einfluss, Auswirkung;* further – *weiter;* to attack – *angreifen;* boarding school – *Internat*

2,20 Holidays in the USA

JANUARY Martin Luther King Day

1

I have a dream

This day marks the birthday of the civil rights activist. Matrin Luther King lived at a time when African Americans did not have the same rights as white Americans. He used peaceful ways to protest against this situation and to change it. He also was a great public speaker. His 'I have a dream' speech is famous. Martin Luther King was assassinated in 1968.

FEBRUARY Presidents' Day

2

This holiday celebrates the birthdays of two great presidents – George Washington and Abraham Lincoln. Washington led the American army which defeated Great Britain. He became the first American president in 1789 and one of the 'founding fathers' of the new country. In 1865, after the terrible Civil War (1861–1865), Lincoln ended slavery in the United States. He was assassinated in the same year.

MAY Memorial Day

3

This is a day when people remember all the soldiers who have died for their country since the Civil War. Flags fly at half-mast and many people visit cemeteries. Others see it as a day to relax with family and friends. People often think of Memorial Day as the start of the summer.

D

JULY Independence Day

4

The Fourth of July celebrates the USA's independence from Great Britain. That is the day in 1776 when the 13 American states signed the Declaration of Independence, which became a famous document in the history of democracy. People dress in red, white and blue – the color of the flag. They have picnics or barbecues and there are fantastic firework shows all across the country.

OCTOBER Columbus Day

5

Christopher Columbus first saw America on October 12, 1492. Many communities organize parades and dinners in memory of the event. However, some people don't like this holiday because Columbus didn't actually discover America. But the day also remembers a man of ideas, dreams and great ambition who was successful. That is something most Americans understand very well.

NOVEMBER Thanksgiving

6

The history of Thanksgiving began in 1621 when, after the harvest, the Pilgrim settlers celebrated their first year in their new country. They invited some local Native Americans to share their meal. More than any other holiday, this is a family day. A traditional Thanksgiving dinner has turkey, cranberry sauce, and pumpkin pie for dessert. Big football games are usually a major part of the day too.

1 What celebration would you like to take part in? Why? Talk with a partner.

2 Choose an important holiday in your country and write a short text about it. Why do you celebrate it and how do you celebrate it?

civil rights – *Bürgerrechte;* was assassinated – *wurde ermordert;* to defeat – *schlagen;* founding father – *Gründervater;* civil war – *Bürgerkrieg;* slavery – *Sklaverei;* in memory of – *in Erinnerung an;* harvest – *Ernte*

Unit 4, More about ...

2,21 Hollywood

The movie industry

1

Since the silent movies of the early 20th century, Hollywood has been the centre of the movie industry. The famous sign was originally an ad from 1923 which read HOLLYWOODLAND. They changed it to HOLLYWOOD in 1949. Today the sign is so well-known all over the world that the police need to protect it with cameras and alarms.

Movie classics

2

The 1930s was the Golden Age of Hollywood. It began with the introduction of sound into movies. New types of movies appeared, such as musicals, documentaries, westerns, action and horror movies. *Snow White and the Seven Dwarfs* (1937), *Gone with the Wind* (1939) and *The Wizard of Oz* (1939) are just three examples of the hundreds of movies that came out every year. *Gone with the Wind* is still the most successful film ever made. In the 1970s, Hollywood found new markets for younger audiences with high-action movies and lots of special effects, such as *Jaws* and *Star Wars*. In the 21st century, the search for the successful blockbuster has continued with movies like *Avatar*, *The Hobbit* and *Jurassic World*.

"And the Oscar goes to ... "

3

The highest honor in the movie business is an Oscar or Academy Award. The ceremony has taken place every year since 1929. Millions of people around the world watch the stars arrive and walk the Red Carpet into the theater in Hollywood. There are many different categories of awards, but the most famous are Best Picture, Best Actor and Best Director. A winner's name is secret until the last minute, when the presenter opens an envelope on stage.

D

Walk of Fame

4

The Walk of Fame – a boulevard about two kilometers long – remembers famous or important people in the entertainment industry. On the sidewalk, in pink stars are the names of more than 2,500 actors, musicians, directors, authors and many others from the past and present. Every year they add new names. The Walk attracts millions of tourists every year, and many of them enjoy looking for 'their' star.

Hollywood or Bollywood

5

Hollywood may be famous, but the biggest film industry in the world is actually located in India. 'Bollywood' is its nickname.
Here's the difference:

- Bollywood makes way more films. But Hollywood spends more and earns more.
- One Bollywood movie has action, drama, romance and comedy. In Hollywood you need to see four movies for that.
- Hollywood movies with music are called musicals. All Bollywood films have music and dance.
- Hollywood movies are shorter (2 hours) than Bollywood movies (3 hours), which have a short break in the middle.

1 What did you find interesting? What did you already know? Talk with a partner.

2 You are a tourist in Hollywood for one day. Make a schedule for your day. Use the internet and add details not in the text or different places.

honor (AE) – *Ehre;* audience – *Publikum;* entertainment – *Unterhaltung;* envelope – *Umschlag;* to attract – *anziehen*

Unit 5, More about ...

2,22 Life in the South

Plantation houses

1

When Louisiana and other territories were bought by the United States from the French in 1803, rich Anglo-American landowners moved there. They built large houses on their sugar, cotton and tobacco plantations to show their great wealth. Oak Alley Plantation was built by slaves on a sugar plantation and was completed in 1839. Since the Civil War it has had many different owners. Today the house is open to the public. Movies have been filmed there, and many weddings have been celebrated there.

Paddle steamers

2

The Mississippi, the longest river in the USA, begins near the Canadian border and flows into the Gulf of Mexico near New Orleans. It is nearly 4,000 miles long.
In the 19th century, before the development of railroads, paddle steamers were the most popular way to transport people and goods up and down the river. Because of their paddle-wheels, they could go far up the river, even when the water level was very low.
Later boats there also were 'showboats', on which passengers could enjoy music and theater on the journey. Today there are many modern riverboats for tourists to explore the Mississippi.

D

Fishing in the Florida Keys

3

In the Florida Keys you can find all kinds of fishing, for beginners or for expert fishermen. If you love the sea and fishing, there's no place like it. Here you can find some of the best fishing guides and captains in the world. And when you return to the harbor, take your fish back to one of the local restaurants and a great meal will be prepared for you.

Line dance

4

Line dancing as we know it today goes back to the 1970s. Its origins, however, lie in the different folk dances of 18th and 19th century Europe. What is line dance? A group of people dance in one or more lines. They all face the same direction and they all do the same steps at the same time. Each dance has its own style. People can dance to country and western music but also to rock and pop. Even the internet sensation video "Gangnam Style" had elements of line dancing in it.

1 Read the texts and ask your partner four questions about them.

2 Make a poster and prepare a short presentation for the class. Draw a map of the southern states, mark the places and events in the texts with a short note about them. Include pictures too.

territory – *Gebiet*; to show off – *angeben*; to destroy – *zerstören*; public – *Öffentlichkeit*; paddle steamer – *Raddampfer*; origin – *Ursprung*

Extra

When the earth shakes

1 What's an earthquake?

Every day there are minor or major earthquakes[1] around the world. The ground shakes for seconds or sometimes even minutes. Earthquakes can occur at any time and we don't notice most of them. You can't tell when or where they will happen. In the USA the West Coast is most at risk[2] because of its special geological structure. However, there can be earthquakes in the Midwest or on the East Coast too.

2 What causes an earthquake?

The earth's crust consists[3] of about 20 different (tectonic) plates which slowly move. The place where two plates meet is called a fault line[4]. Each plate rubs[5] against another one. This puts both plates under stress. When the force[6] gets too strong, it comes apart with a jerk[7]. The released energy makes the earth move in waves.

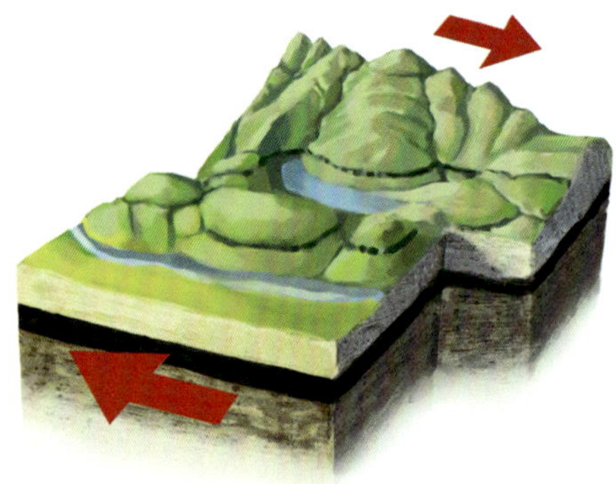

3 What can earthquakes do?

Major earthquakes can cause many problems. Buildings or bridges can collapse[8] or pipelines burst[9]. There can be mudslides[10], fires or tsunamis too. A large number of people can be hurt or even die during an earthquake.

1 earthquake ['ɜ:θkweɪk] – *Erdbeben*; 2 be at risk [rɪsk] – *einem Risiko ausgesetzt sein*; 3 consist of [kən'sɪst‿əv] – *bestehen aus*; 4 fault line ['fɔ:lt,laɪn] – *Verwerfungs-, Bruchlinie*; 5 rub [rʌb] – *reiben*; 6 force [fɔ:s] – *Kraft, Stärke*; 7 jerk [dʒɜ:k] – *Ruck*; 8 collapse [kə'læps] – *zusammenbrechen*; 9 burst [bɜ:st] – *platzen*; 10 mudslide ['mʌdslaɪd] – *Schlammlawine*

4 How are earthquakes measured?

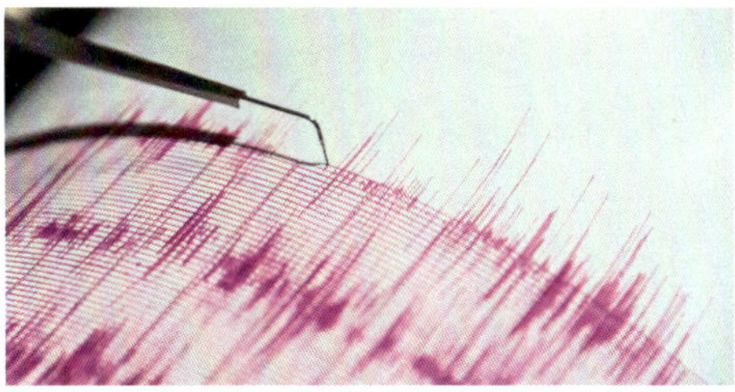

Scientists[1] record earthquakes with the help of a special instrument – the seismograph. It measures[2] the magnitude of an earthquake.
The Richter scale shows how destructive[3] earthquakes can be:

The Richter scale

0 – 1.9	only recorded by seismograph; not felt
2.0 – 2.9	objects may swing; hardly any damage
3.0 – 3.9	comparable to a passing truck
4.0 – 4.9	may break windows; smaller objects may fall
5.0 – 5.9	loose objects may fall from walls; furniture moves
6.0 – 6.9	damage to buildings
7.0 – 7.9	major ground breaks; buildings destroyed in large numbers
8.0 – 8.9	bridges and most houses destroyed
9.0 and over	total devastation

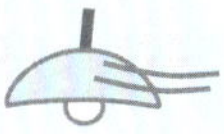

5 Find out about recent earthquakes worldwide.

Search the internet for 'map of latest earthquakes'. Where did the last earthquakes happen?

6 Earthquake facts – What do you find most interesting?

Animals seem to sense[4] an earthquake is going to happen. No one knows how they do it.

An earthquake on the moon is called a moonquake. But they happen less and are smaller than earthquakes on earth.

There are about 500,000 earthquakes in the world each year. 100 of them cause heavy damage[5].

Because of the earth's movements, San Francisco and Los Angeles will meet in a few million years.

In Japanese mythology, it's a giant fish which makes the earth move.

1 scientist ['saɪəntɪst] – *Wissenschaftler/-in*; 2 measure ['meʒə] – *messen*; 3 destructive [dɪ'strʌktɪv] – *zerstörerisch*; 4 sense [sens] – *spüren, fühlen*; 5 damage ['dæmɪdʒ] – *Schaden*

Static electricity

1 Are you 'electrified'?

Have you ever …

- ☐ … rubbed[1] a balloon on your hair and made it stand on end[2]?
- ☐ … touched a person or a metal object and felt an electric shock[3]?
- ☐ … taken off a pullover and it made your hair crackle[4]?
- ☐ … felt like your clothes were clinging[5] to you?

All of these situations happen because of static[6] electricity. Sometimes your hair does funny things. Sometimes you may feel a small electric shock. It doesn't hurt badly but it's a strange feeling. The most spectacular example of static electricity is lightning[7].

2 Why does static electricity happen?

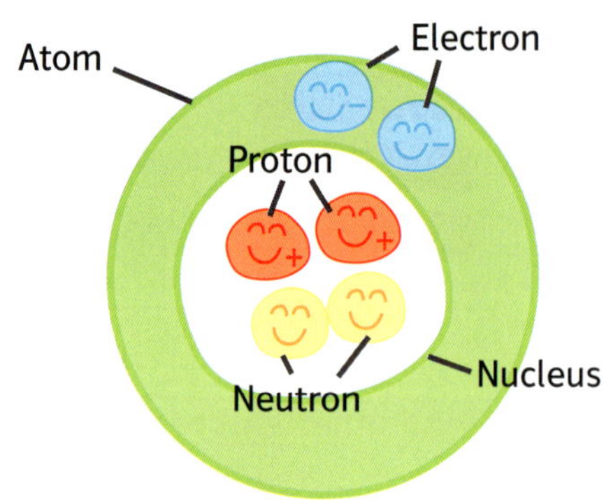

Static electricity happens because everything is made of atoms. Atoms are tiny particles that are so small we can't see them. Inside of atoms are protons, neutrons and electrons. Protons, neutrons and electrons are very different from each other. Protons have a positive charge[8] (+). Neutrons have no charge. Electrons have a negative charge (–). Protons and neutrons make the center of the atom, the nucleus. The electrons move around this center.

Usually atoms have no charge, because there are as many electrons as protons. But some electrons can move between atoms. This happens when two atoms come in contact or rub against each other. If electrons move from one atom to another, the charge of the atom changes. If there are more protons than electrons in an atom, the atom has a positive charge. If there are more electrons than protons, it has a negative charge.

If two atoms that have the same charge meet, they move away from each other. If two atoms have different charges, they move towards each other.

1 rub [rʌb] – *reiben;* 2 stand on end [stænd‿ɒn‿end] – *zu Berge stehen;* 3 electric shock [ɪ'lektrɪk ʃɒk] – *elektrischer Schock;* 4 crackle ['krækl] – *knistern;* 5 cling [klɪŋ] – *sich festhalten, klammern, hängenbleiben;* 6 static ['stætɪk] – *statisch;* 7 lightning ['laɪtnɪŋ] – *Blitz;* 8 charge [tʃɑ:dʒ] – *Ladung*

3 Why does your hair stand on end?

When two objects with different charges touch[1] or rub against each other, the charges react and we sometimes see sparks[2] or feel an electric shock. When you rub a balloon on your hair, for example, electrons move from your hair to the balloon. The balloon then has more negative charge and the tips[3] of your hair have more positive charge. That's why your hair moves towards the negative charge of the balloon and away from all the other positively charged hair – suddenly your hair stands on end!

4 Some experiments

a) You need these materials:

balloons

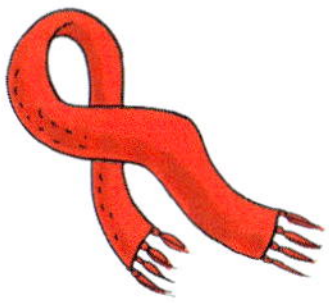
a wool scarf

pieces of paper

an empty can[4]

a string[5]

b) Try these experiments and write what happens.

1. Rub a balloon with a wool scarf. Hold it against a wall and let go[6].
2. Rub a balloon with a wool scarf. Hold the balloon over some small pieces of paper (e.g. confetti).
3. Put an empty can on the floor or a table. Rub a balloon with a wool scarf. Hold the balloon in front of the can without touching it.
4. Cut a piece of string (~70 cm). Tie a balloon to each end of the string. Rub both balloons with a wool scarf and then hold up the middle of the string so that the balloons hang down.

1 touch [tʌtʃ] – *berühren, antippen*; 2 spark [spɑːk] – *Funke*; 3 tip [tɪp] – *Spitze*; 4 can [kæn] – *Dose, Getränkedose*; 5 string [strɪŋ] – *Schnur, Bindfaden*; 6 let go [ˌlet ˈɡəʊ] – *loslassen*

2,23

The Absolutely True Diary of a Part-Time Indian by S. Alexie (2007)

This is the diary of Arnold 'Junior' Spirit. He is small, very skinny[1], wears big glasses and has a stutter[2] and a lisp[3]. He is also really intelligent and he loves to draw cartoons. This is a cartoon Arnold 'Junior' drew of himself:

Arnold 'Junior' Spirit is a Spokane[4] Indian. He lives in Wellpinit, a small town on an Indian reservation. He calls it the "rez". A lot of people there are very poor and never leave the rez.

One day, Arnold 'Junior' decides that he has to change his life. He doesn't want to be poor all his life and he wants to see the world. So Arnold 'Junior' decides to go to school in Reardan, a little town outside the reservation. At Reardan High School, all the kids are white, rich and amazing. Arnold is scared, because he will be the only Indian at this school. But he also knows that it is his only chance to make his life better. That's how Arnold 'Junior' becomes a part-time Indian: He goes to school in Reardan where everyone calls him Arnold, but he lives on the reservation with his family where everyone calls him Junior.

This is his diary entry from his first day at the new school:

The next morning, Dad drove me the twenty-two miles to Reardan.

"I'm scared," I said.

"I'm scared, too," Dad said.

He hugged[5] me. "You don't have to do this," he said. "You can always go back to the rez school."

"No," I said. "I have to do this."

1 skinny ['skɪni] – *dünn, mager;* 2 stutter ['stʌtə] – *Stottern;* 3 lisp [lɪsp] – *Lispeln;* 4 Spokane [spəʊ'kan] – *„Kinder der Sonne" oder „Sonnenvolk", ein Indianerstamm im Nordwesten der USA (Bundesstaat Washington);* 5 hug sb [hʌg] – *jmd. umarmen*

"Just remember this," my father said. "Those white people aren't better than you."

But he was so wrong. And he knew he was wrong. He was the loser Indian father of a loser Indian son living in a world built for winners.

But he loved me so much. He hugged me again.

"This is a great thing," he said. "You're so brave. You're a warrior[1]."

It was the best thing he could have said.

"Hey, here's some lunch money," he said and gave me a dollar.

We were poor enough to get free lunch, but I didn't want to be the only Indian and the only one who needed charity[2].

"Thanks, Dad," I said.

"I love you," he said.

"I love you, too."

I felt stronger so I stepped out of the car and walked to the door. It was locked[3].

I watched my father drive away.

24 I stood alone at the door for a few very long minutes. It was still early.

Then the white kids began arriving for school. They surrounded[4] me. Most of the kids were my size or smaller, but there were ten or twelve monster dudes[5]. Giant white guys. They looked like men, not boys. They had to be seniors[6]. Some of them looked like they had to shave[7] two or three times a day.

They stared[8] at me, the Indian boy. Those white kids couldn't believe their eyes. They stared at me like I was a UFO. What was I doing at Reardan, whose mascot[9] was an Indian, thereby making me the only other Indian in town?

So what was I doing in racist[10] Reardan, where more than half of every graduating[11] class went to college? Nobody in my family had ever gone near a college.

Reardan was the opposite of the rez. It was the opposite of my family. It was the opposite of me. I didn't deserve to be there. I knew it; all of those kids knew it. Indians don't deserve anything.

1 warrior [ˈwɒriə] – *Krieger/-in;* 2 charity [ˈtʃærɪti] – *Almosen, Wohltätigkeit;* 3 locked [lɒkt] – *abgeschlossen;* 4 surround [səˈraʊnd] – *umgeben, umringen;* 5 dude [duːd] – *Mann (ugs.);* 6 senior [ˈsiːniə] – *Schüler/-in im letzten Schuljahr;* 7 shave [ʃeɪv] – *sich rasieren;* 8 stare [steə] – *starren;* 9 mascot [ˈmæskɒt] – *Maskottchen;* 10 racist [ˈreɪsɪst] – *rassistisch;* 11 graduating [ˈgrædyueɪtɪŋ] – *Abschluss*

So, feeling worthless[1] and stupid[2], I just waited. And pretty soon, a janitor[3] opened the door and all of the other kids strolled inside.

"Okay," I said to myself. "Here I go."

I walked into the school, made my way to the office, and told them who I was. "Oh, you're the one from the reservation," the secretary said.

"Yeah," I said.

I couldn't tell if she thought the reservation was a good or bad thing.

"My name is Melinda," she said. "Welcome to Reardan High School. Here's your schedule and a Student ID. We've got you assigned[4] to Mr. Grant for homeroom[5]. You better hustle[6] on down there. You're late."

"Ah, where is that?" I asked.

"We've only got one hallway here," she said and smiled. She had red hair and green eyes. "It's all the way down on the left."

I shoved[7] the paperwork into my backpack and hustled down to my homeroom. I paused a second at the door and then walked inside.

2,25 Everybody, all of the students and the teacher, stopped to stare at me.

They stared hard.

Like I was bad weather.

"Take your seat," the teacher said. He was a muscular[8] guy. He had to be a football coach.

I sat down in the back and tried to ignore[9] all the stares and whispers[10], until a blond girl leaned[11] over toward me.

Penelope!

Yes, there are places left in the world where people are named Penelope!

"What's your name?" Penelope asked.

"Junior," I said.

She laughed and told her girlfriend at the next desk that my name was Junior. They both laughed.

1 worthless ['wɜ:θləs] – *wertlos;* 2 stupid ['stju:pɪd] – *blöd, dumm;* 3 janitor ['dʒænɪtə] – *Hausmeister/-in;*
4 assigned to [ə'saɪnd] – *zugeordnet;* 5 homeroom ['həʊmru:m] – *Zimmer des/der Klassenlehrers/-in;*
6 hustle ['hʌsl] – *hier: schnell dorthin gehen;* 7 shove [ʃʌv] – *hineinstecken, hineinstopfen;* 8 muscular ['mʌskjələ] – *muskulär;*
9 ignore [ɪg'nɔ:] – *ignorieren;* 10 whisper ['wɪspə] – *Geflüster;* 11 lean over toward sb [li:n'əʊvə] – *sich zu jmd. rüberbeugen*

Word spread[1] around the room and pretty soon everybody was laughing.

They were laughing at *my name*.

I had no idea that Junior was a weird[2] name. It's a normal name on my rez, on any rez. You walk into any trading post[3] on any rez in the United States and shout, "Hey, Junior!" and seventeen guys will turn around. And three women. But there were no other people named Junior in Reardan, so I was being laughed at because I was the only one who had that silly name.

And then I felt smaller because the teacher was taking roll[4] and he called out my *name* name.

"Arnold Spirit," the teacher said. No, he yelled[5] it.

He was so big and muscular that his whisper was probably a scream.

"Here," I said as quietly as possible. My whisper was only a whisper.

"Speak up," the teacher said.

"Here," I said.

"My name is Mr. Grant," he said.

"I'm here, Mr. Grant."

He moved on to other students, but Penelope leaned over toward me again, but she wasn't laughing at all. She was mad[6] now.

"I thought you said your name was Junior," Penelope said.

She *accused*[7] me of telling her my *real* name. Well, okay, it wasn't completely my real name. My full name is Arnold Spirit Jr. But nobody calls me that. Everybody calls me Junior. Well, every other *Indian* calls me Junior.

"My name is Junior," I said. "And my name is Arnold. It's Junior and Arnold. I'm both."

I felt like two different people inside of one body. No, I felt like a magician[8] cutting myself in half, with Junior living on the north side of the Spokane River[9] and Arnold living on the south.

"Where are you from?" she asked.

She was so pretty and her eyes were so blue. I was suddenly aware[10] that she was the prettiest girl I had ever seen. She was movie star pretty.

"Hey," she said. "I asked you where you're from."

Wow, she was tough.

"Wellpinit," I said. "Up on the rez, I mean, the reservation."

"Oh," she said. "That's why you talk so funny."

And yes, I had that stutter and lisp, but I also had that singsong reservation accent that made everything I said sound like a bad poem.

Man, I was freaked[11]. I didn't say another word for six days.

---

1 word spread [wɜːd‿spred] – *es sprach sich herum;* 2 weird [wɪəd] – *komisch;* 3 trading post ['treɪdɪŋ‿peʊst] – *Laden, Handelsposten;* 4 take roll [teɪk‿rəʊl] – *die Anwesenheitsliste durchgehen;* 5 yell [jel] – *brüllen, schreien;*
6 mad [mæd] – *wütend;* 7 accuse sb of sth [ə'kjuːz] – *jmd. beschuldigen;* 8 magician [mə'ʤɪʃn] – *Magier, Zauberer;*
9 Spokane River [spəʊ'kan 'rɪvə] – *Name eines Flusses;* 10 be aware of sth [bi‿ə'weə] – *sich etw. bewusst sein;* 11 freaked [friːkt] – *total erschrocken*

2,26

Deep water by C. Gardiner (2009)

Henry Jackson is sixteen years old and he lives with his grandmother in Arkanaw, a small town in Nebraska. Their house is outside of town; near a dam[1] and a lake that were built some years ago. Every day when Henry comes home, his grandmother tells him to not go to The Lake. It is dangerous and people die there. That's why Henry is afraid of deep[2] water and he still cannot swim. Henry's best friend is Alice. She is a great swimmer and Henry likes her a lot.

One day Alice tells him that she is going to have a picnic and go swimming with some friends. Henry doesn't go because he hates swimming. But later in the evening he realizes[3] that Alice and the other kids from his class probably went to The Lake. Some strange things have been happening at The Lake and Henry is afraid that something bad will happen, so he quickly leaves the house to go find Alice …

Henry ran into the woods at the back of the house. It was nearly night and the moon was just rising. Now Henry was glad that he was a good runner. No other kid in the school could have got through the woods so fast. He wished he had Alice's cell phone number. Then he could call her and warn her. But then what could he say – 'don't swim in The Lake! There's something evil[4] there'? She wouldn't believe him and he would just look stupid[5].

He had to go to The Lake. Grandma's worries[6] weren't important. His friend Alice, the girl he liked more than anyone else in the whole school, was in danger[7]. He had to help her.

The moon was up as Henry burst[8] out of the woods. He heard kids laughing. He could see the dam wall not far away. The surface[9] of The Lake was shining in the moonlight. Everything looked calm[10].

The whole class was there with their picnic baskets. But they were over on the other side of The Lake. Henry shouted, "Alice!" She looked up and saw him.

She waved to him and shouted something. But she was too far away so he couldn't hear her. He shouted again, "Don't go swimming, it's dangerous!"

Alice shook[11] her head to show that she didn't understand what he was saying.

Henry looked around quickly. There was a path all along The Lake. But it was a long way to the other side. Even at his fastest, it'd take time to get to Alice. He was tired from his run through the woods but he had to try.

"Oh, Alice – please, please don't go swimming before I get there," Henry said softly to himself.

1 dam [dæm] – *Damm, Staumauer;* 2 deep [di:p] – *tief;* 3 realize ['rɪəlaɪz] – *erkennen, realisieren;* 4 evil ['i:vl] – *böse, schlecht;* 5 stupid ['stju:pɪd] – *dumm, blöd;* 6 worry ['wʌri] – *Sorge;* 7 danger ['deɪndʒə] – *Gefahr;* 8 burst out of [bɜ:st] – *herausstürzen;* 9 surface ['sɜ:fɪs] – *Oberfläche;* 10 calm [kɑ:m] – *ruhig, friedlich;* 11 shake [ʃeɪk] – *schütteln*

His legs hurt badly, he was out of breath and his heart was beating fast. But he started to run along the path round The Lake, towards Alice.

27 Then Matt jumped. Henry heard the splash as Matt went under the water. Henry ran faster. He was afraid that Matt would just disappear, that something would grab his foot and pull him down.

But then Matt's head came up again. He was laughing as he shook the water out of his hair.

Henry shouted but the kids paid no attention[1]. He was still a long way away. Most of the other kids followed Matt into the water. Henry could see their heads as they splashed each other. Alice stood at the waterside. She didn't go in right away. She was watching Henry racing[2] round the path.

Henry ran on although it was getting hard to breathe. He waved and waved, trying to get the kids' attention. Then Alice went into the water. Henry almost fell to the ground. "Alice! No!" Henry was shouting as loudly as he could.

Suddenly something started moving towards the swimmers. It was big and black, like a shadow[3], moving smoothly[4] just under the surface of the water. The kids couldn't see it.

They were busy with their game. They were playing with a ball, throwing it and trying to catch it before it hit the water.

Alice started to swim towards Henry and away from the other kids. Henry could not run another step. He could hardly get his breath. He fell down onto his knees.

Then Chet threw the ball up high into the air instead of throwing it to the next kid. He laughed loudly and he looked over at Henry. So Henry could see how surprised Chet was as something pulled him under the water. His head went down so fast that he didn't even have time to shout. His mouth was wide open as he went under.

The ball that Chet had thrown was still up in the air. At that same moment every other kid disappeared under the water. Every head just went down without making any waves in the water. Except Alice. She was quite a bit away. She was moving fast towards Henry and didn't notice anything behind her.

The surface of the water was smooth again. The Lake was quiet. The black shadow was gone and the kids were gone. It all happened in just a few seconds. The ball landed back on the surface of the water with a splash.

Alice heard the splash. She looked back. The ball floated[5] on the water.

1 pay attention to sth [ˌpeɪ‿əˈtenʃn] – *seine Aufmerksamkeit auf etw. richten;* 2 race [reɪs] – *(sehr schnell) rennen;* 3 shadow [ˈʃædəʊ] – *Schatten;* 4 smooth [smuːð] – *geschmeidig, gleichmäßig;* 5 float [fləʊt] – *gleiten, treiben*

There was nothing else, no kids anywhere. She turned round and started to swim faster and faster towards Henry.

Henry stood up again. The dark water of The Lake came right up to the path. He wanted to save Alice. But he was afraid of the black shadow in the water. She was still swimming fast towards him.

Something moved on the other side of The Lake, where the picnic baskets were. Henry didn't want to look but he could not control his eyes. He saw a tall, thin[1] man standing there.

2,28 "Henry!" Alice screamed, and he tore[2] his eyes away from the man. She was much nearer Henry now but still too far for him to reach her. He put one foot into the water. It was very cold. It was like putting his foot into ice. He stepped in a bit deeper. Alice swam closer[3].

Behind her Henry saw the black shadow in the water again. It was coming very close to her. Henry went into the water as fast as he could. The water was up to his knees.

The black shadow was right at Alice's feet. Her hand came towards him, her fingers just touched his fingers – then a shout came from the other side of The Lake.

"Henry! Henry!" That was Grandma's voice!

Henry automatically looked up towards her. And then suddenly he couldn't feel Alice's hand any more. He looked back at The Lake.

Alice was gone.

"Sheriff!" It was Grandma's voice. "Please, help him!"

Henry looked towards her. Sheriff Anders, the chief of police in Arkanaw, was with Grandma and she wanted him to go into The Lake after her grandson[4]. Henry hurried out of the water and raced back round the path.

"Sheriff Anders!" He was still running as he shouted. "You have to call for help! The kids in my class were swimming in The Lake. Then they all went under the water! They'll drown[5] if we don't get help! Please …"

"All right, Henry, just stay calm," said the Sheriff. "Show me where the kids were swimming."

Henry pointed out at The Lake. There was nothing to see. The ball was gone. There were no waves. The surface of the water was completely smooth.

"Henry, are you sure you didn't just see some big fish?" asked Sheriff Anders.

1 thin [θɪn] – *dünn;* 2 tear one's eyes away [teə] – *die Augen losreißen;* 3 close [kləʊs] – *nah;*
4 grandson ['græn,sʌn] – *Enkel;* 5 drown [draʊn] – *ertrinken*

"Nobody's that mad[1] to swim here. Everyone knows it's too dangerous."

"Just listen to me!" shouted Henry. "They were all here, all the kids from my class! And they went swimming and then they all just disappeared. And there was a man over there, where they left their picnic stuff."

"All right, Henry. Show me where the picnic stuff is," said the Sheriff.

Henry pointed to the other side of The Lake, where the tall man had stood. The Sheriff hurried away to check.

As soon as they were alone, Grandma shouted, "Henry, have you gone crazy? How many times do I have to tell you to stay away from The Lake!"

"Don't you understand?" he answered. "Something terrible happened! Those kids all disappeared!"

"Henry, why don't you listen to me? I knew you'd come here. So I called the Sheriff."

Henry was angry. "Well, he doesn't believe me. He thinks I'm nuts[2]. But something in the water pulled them all under, Alice as well …"

Grandma sounded very strict. "Henry. You mustn't say that again or people really will think you're crazy. Just stay away from The Lake and forget what you saw!"

Sheriff Anders came back round the path. He spoke kindly to Henry. "There's no sign of a picnic and no clothes left around. The water here is very cold. I think you just had a bad shock. Why don't I give you both a ride[3] home?"

Grandma put her arm round Henry's shoulders[4]. They walked over to the car. Henry said nothing. He sat in the back seat. He was thinking hard.

Maybe it was some sort of dream?

No, he was sure the events at The Lake were real.

He almost had Alice's hand in his and he let her drown!

What happened? Was it just a dream or is there a terrible mystery?

1 mad [mæd] – *verrückt;* 2 be nuts [nʌts] – *verrückt sein;* 3 give sb a ride [ˌɡɪv‿ə ˈraɪd] – *jdn. (im Auto) mitnehmen;* 4 shoulder [ˈʃəʊldə] – *Schulter*

Grammar

G2

Mit G sind die Grammatikkapitel gekennzeichnet und der Reihe nach durchnummeriert. Eine Übersicht über alle Themen in diesem Band findest du auf der nächsten Seite.

Language tip G6

Die Seiten kennzeichnen zusätzliche Grammatikkapitel. Du kannst dir die neuen Formen dort wie neue Vokabeln merken oder – wenn du es genau wissen willst – ein paar Regeln dazu lernen.

Hier stehen Besonderheiten und Tipps.

(TEST YOURSELF)

Hier kannst du üben.
Die Lösungen findest du auf S. 311.

(FÜR PROFIS)

Hier findest du knifflige Extras zum Thema.

R = Revision (Wiederholung)

Unit 1 Unit 2 Unit 3 Unit 4 Unit 5

G

Unit 1

G1 R: Die einfache Vergangenheit

Revision: The simple past

Um über Dinge zu sprechen, die in der Vergangenheit passiert und vorbei sind, verwendest du die einfache Vergangenheit (**simple past**).

Signalwörter	
yesterday	gestern
last year	letztes Jahr
a week ago	vor einer Woche
in 2015	(im Jahr) 2015

Das **simple past** bildest du so:
Hänge die Endung **-ed** an das Verb.
Achte auf unregelmäßige Verben, z. B. have → **had**; do → **did**; get → **got**; build → **built**; go → **went** etc.

Eine Liste der unregelmäßigen Verben findest du ab Seite 226.

They **started** roadwork last Monday.	Sie begannen am letzten Montag mit Straßenarbeiten.
Two years ago they **had** a lot of snow in New York.	Vor zwei Jahren hatten sie in New York viel Schnee.

Um zu sagen, was in der Vergangenheit nicht passiert ist, setzt du **didn't** (= did not) vor das Verb.

David **didn't get** into the city.	David kam nicht in die Stadt.

Und so kannst du im **simple past** Fragen stellen:

Did you **have** a good time in New York?	Yes, I **did**.	No, I **didn't**.
When **did** your friend **visit** Manhattan?	Last weekend.	

Aussagen und Verneinungen mit **be** bildest du so:

I **was** in New York.	Ich war in New York.
I **wasn't** in Washington.	Ich war nicht in Washington.
The Statue of Liberty **was** a present from France. It **wasn't** a present from Germany.	Die Freiheitsstatue war ein Geschenk von Frankreich. Sie war kein Geschenk von Deutschland.
We **were** in New York, but we **weren't** in Brooklyn.	Wir waren in New York, aber wir waren nicht in Brooklyn.

Fragen mit **be** bildest du so:

Were you at the zoo in Central Park?	Yes, I **was**.	No, I **wasn't**.
What **was** special in New York?	The Brooklyn Bridge.	

(TEST YOURSELF) Put the verbs in the simple past.

1. Tom ___ (have) a great time in NYC last summer.
2. He ___ (like) the New York skyline.
3. We ___ (not take) a taxi.
4. What ___ you ___ (do) in Manhattan?
5. ___ (be) you in the USA last year?
6. I ___ (not be) in Chicago.

G2 Die Vorvergangenheit

The past perfect

After I had built my new house, I felt much better.

Um über Ereignisse zu sprechen, die noch **vor** einem vergangenen Ereignis stattfanden, verwendest du die Vorvergangenheit, das **past perfect: had / hadn't + 3. Form** des Verbs (past participle).

Signalwörter	
after	nachdem
before	bevor

Bei den meisten Verben hängst du für die 3. Form ein **-ed** an das Verb: visit → visit**ed**
Achte auf unregelmäßige Verben, z. B. go → **gone**; see → **seen**; be → **been** etc.

Eine Liste der unregelmäßigen Verben findest du ab Seite 224.

Was in der Vergangenheit weiter zurückliegt, wird mit dem **past perfect** ausgedrückt!

She wasn't at home. She **had gone** to Tim's (house).	Sie war nicht zu Hause. Sie war zu Tim gegangen.
After I **had been** in NYC for two months, I moved to Chicago.	Nachdem ich zwei Monate in NYC gewesen war, zog ich nach Chicago um.
I **hadn't seen** skyscrapers before I went to New York.	Ich hatte noch keine Wolkenkratzer gesehen, bevor ich nach New York ging.

Und so kannst du im **past perfect** Fragen stellen:

Had you ever **been** to the USA before you left Cuba?	Yes, I **had**.	No, I **hadn't**.
Which countries **had** you **visited** before you went to the USA?	I **hadn't visited** any other countries at all.	

(TEST YOURSELF) Put the verbs in the past perfect.

1. After I — (leave) the shop, I lost my shopping bag.
2. I couldn't go to the swimming pool because I — (not do) my homework.
3. When I arrived, the concert — already — (start).
4. What — you — (do) before you phoned me?
5. My grandad didn't want to move because he — (live) in Cuba all his life.
6. Yesterday I saw an animal which I — (not see) before.

Unit 2

G3 Modale Hilfsverben und ihre Ersatzformen

Modal auxiliaries and their substitutes

I'm lucky. I didn't have to book a holiday, I only had to swim to this lovely rock.

Modale Hilfsverben kannst du nur im **simple present** verwenden. Für alle anderen Zeiten, benötigst du **Ersatzformen**. Ausnahme **can**: Für **can** kannst du im **simple past** auch **could** verwenden.

Mit **can/could** und der Ersatzform **be able to** sagst du, was du tun **kannst** (Fähigkeit).

Simple present	Simple past
Kim **can/is able to** speak English. Kim **kann** Englisch sprechen. **Can/Is** he **able to** speak English? **Kann** er Englisch sprechen?	Kim **could/was able to** understand it. Kim **konnte** es verstehen. **Could** he/**Was** he **able to** speak English? **Konnte** er Englisch sprechen?

Mit **can/could** und der Ersatzform **be allowed to** sagst du, was du tun **darfst** (Erlaubnis).

She **can't/isn't allowed to** use her phone. Sie **darf** ihr Handy **nicht** benutzen. **Can** you/**Are** you **allowed to** wear jeans? **Darfst** du Jeans tragen?	She **couldn't/wasn't allowed to** use it. Sie **durfte** es **nicht** benutzen. **Could** you/**Were** you **allowed to** wear jeans? **Durftest** du Jeans tragen?

Mit **must** und der Ersatzform **have to** sagst du, was du tun **musst** (Verpflichtung).

Sarah **must** take English and History. Sarah **muss** Englisch und Geschichte nehmen. We **don't have to** worry. Wir **müssen** uns **keine** Sorgen machen. **Must** you help your parents? **Musst** du deinen Eltern helfen?	Sarah **had to** take Biology too. Sarah **musste** auch Biologie nehmen. We **didn't have to** worry. Wir **mussten** uns **keine** Sorgen machen. **Did** you **have to** help in the house? **Musstest** du im Haus helfen?

Bei **must** musst du die Ersatzform schon in **verneinten Sätzen** im **simple present** benutzen!

(TEST YOURSELF) Use the correct forms in the simple past.

1. When Luise was in the USA, she —— (not can) keep her things in the classrooms.
2. She —— (must) put her books into lockers.
3. She —— (can) travel around in the USA.
4. She —— (not must) take lessons in basketball.
5. The students —— (can) wear jeans.
6. When she was ten, she —— (not can) dance like she dances today.

G4 R: Bedingungssätze Typ I

Revision: If-clauses type I

Um Bedingungen und Folgen auszudrücken, benutzt man **if**-Sätze.
Dabei steht im **if-Satz** das **simple present**, im Hauptsatz das **will-future**.
Geht der **if**-Satz voran, steht am Ende des **if**-Satzes ein Komma.

Bedingung (condition)	Folge (consequence)	
If Michael **finds** a job,	he **will earn** some money.	Wenn Michael einen Job findet, wird er etwas Geld verdienen.
If you **don't work** well,	you **won't get** a bonus.	Wenn du nicht gut arbeitest, bekommst du keine Prämie.

Bedingungssätze können auch mit dem Hauptsatz beginnen. Dann entfällt das Komma.

Folge (consequence)	Bedingung (condition)	
You **will be** late	if you **walk.**	Du wirst zu spät kommen, wenn du zu Fuß gehst.
You **won't be** successful	if you **don't work** more carefully.	Du wirst nicht erfolgreich sein, wenn du nicht sorgfältiger arbeitest.

Das **will-future** drückt allgemein Zukünftiges aus. Im **if**-Satz steht nie **will** oder **won't**!

Für das **will-future** kannst du im Deutschen die Zukunft oder die Gegenwart benutzen. Beides ist richtig. Vergleiche:

He will earn some money.	Er wird etwas Geld verdienen. Er verdient etwas Geld.

(TEST YOURSELF) Complete the sentences.

1. If you ___ (need) me, I ___ (help) you.
2. If you ___ (not phone) me, I ___ (be) sad.
3. If she ___ (not come) on time, she ___ (lose) her job.
4. Matt ___ (not find) a job if he ___ (not read) the adverts.
5. I ___ (talk) to Sue if I ___ (meet) her.
6. You ___ (not sleep) well if you always ___ (read) scary stories.

(FÜR PROFIS)

Im Deutschen können **if** (falls, wenn) und **when** (dann, wenn) mit wenn übersetzt werden.
Im Englischen kommt es darauf an, welche **Absicht** du ausdrücken möchtest.

If I go shopping, I'll get you a T-shirt.
(Ich weiß noch nicht, **ob** ich einkaufen gehe. Aber **falls** ich gehe, dann kaufe ich dir ein T-Shirt. Es ist nicht sicher und nur eine Möglichkeit.)

When I go shopping, I'll get you a T-shirt.
(Ich gehe auf jeden Fall einkaufen. Das weiß ich schon sicher. Ich weiß nur noch nicht, **wann**. Aber dann kaufe ich dir ein T-Shirt. Es ist sicher und nur eine Frage des Zeitpunkts.)

G5 Stützwort one / ones

One / ones

Which cave is better?
The right one or the left one?

Um eine unnötige Wiederholung von Nomen zu vermeiden, kannst du sie durch **one** (Einzahl) und **ones** (Mehrzahl) ersetzen. **One** / **ones** werden nicht übersetzt. Sie stehen oft nach einem Adjektiv. Auch nach der Steigerungsform eines Adjektivs kommt **one** oder **ones** häufig vor.

Who are those boys over there? The tall ~~boy~~ **one** is Jim and the short ~~boy~~ **one** is Tim.	Wer sind diese Jungs dort drüben? Der große ~~Junge~~ ist Jim und der kleine ~~Junge~~ ist Tim.
Which towels did you buy? – The cheaper **ones.**	Welche Handtücher hast du gekauft? – Die billigeren.
Which books do you prefer? – Exciting **ones.**	Welche Bücher bevorzugst du? – Spannende.

One oder **ones** stehen auch oft nach Fragen mit **which.**

You can borrow my CDs. **Which ones** would you like?	Du kannst dir meine CDs ausleihen. **Welche** möchtest du?
There are lots of nice T-shirts here. **Which one** do you like best?	Es gibt hier viele schöne T-Shirts. **Welches** gefällt dir am besten?

(TEST YOURSELF) **Use one or ones.**

1. You should try on some shoes. What about these black ___?
2. The short skirt is much nicer than the long ___.
3. The new computers are much better than the old ___.
4. I like these sunglasses. – Yes, they are nice. Which ___ would you like to buy?
5. I've missed my bus. Now I have to wait for the next ___.
6. That shop doesn't look very good. – You're right. Let's look for another ___.

(FÜR PROFIS)

Auch nach **the**, **this**, **that** und **these**, **those** kann one oder ones stehen.

Look at these beautiful dresses. **These ones** here are really cheap. I like **this one**, **the one** with the flowers.	Schau dir diese schönen Kleider an. **Diese** hier sind wirklich günstig. Ich mag **dieses**, **das** mit den Blumen.

G

Language tip

G6 Bestätigungsfragen

Question tags

You didn't eat the turkey, did you?

Um ein Gespräch nicht abreißen zu lassen, kannst du eine Bestätigungsfrage (question tag) benutzen. Im Deutschen sagt man dafür Ausdrücke wie **nicht wahr?**, **nicht?**, **oder?**
Für negative **question tags** benutzt du immer Kurzformen.
Alle **question tags** werden mit einem Komma vom Aussagesatz abgetrennt.

Ist der Aussagesatz positiv +, so wird die Bestätigungsfrage negativ −.

Aussagesatz +	Question tag −
It's cold,	**isn't** it?
You **are** fifteen,	**aren't** you?
She **can** play the guitar,	**can't** she?
Robert **was** in Boston,	**wasn't** he?
You **were** in New York,	**weren't** you?

Ist der Aussagesatz negativ −, so wird die Bestätigungsfrage positiv +.

Aussagesatz −	Question tag +
Your shirt **isn't** new,	**is** it?
You **weren't** in the USA last year,	**were** you?

Bei Vollverben musst du **do**, **does**, **did** oder **don't**, **doesn't**, **didn't** benutzen:

You **like** chocolates,	**don't** you?
Julia **wants** to go to Miami,	**doesn't** she?
You **met Brenda**,	**didn't** you?
You **don't like** turkey,	**do** you?
Nick **doesn't drink** coke,	**does** he?
Robert **didn't see** the Niagara Falls,	**did** he?

(TEST YOURSELF) Use the correct question tags.

1. You are from Boston, —— ?
2. The USA is a huge country, —— ?
3. You were in Chicago last year, —— ?
4. You like Thanksgiving, —— ?
5. You enjoyed your holiday, —— ?
6. Jacob doesn't eat meat, —— ?

G7 R: Fragen

Revision: Questions / questions with who

So bildest du unterschiedliche Fragen mit Vollverben, z. B. like, go etc.:

Fragen, auf die man mit yes oder no antwortet (Ja/Nein-Fragen)
– Fragen im **simple present** beginnst du mit **do** oder **does** (he, she, it).

Do you **like** turkey?	Magst du Truthahn?
Does Jacob **like** chocolate?	Mag Jacob Schokolade?

– Fragen im **simple past** beginnst du mit **did** für alle Personen.

Did you **travel** by car last year?	Bist du letztes Jahr mit dem Auto verreist?
Did it **rain** last December?	Hat es im letzten Dezember geregnet?

– Fragen im **will-future** beginnst du mit **will** für alle Personen.

Will you **call** us again tomorrow?	Wirst du uns morgen nochmal anrufen?

Fragen mit Fragewörtern

What do you **like**?	Was magst du gerne?
Where did you **spend** your summer?	Wo hast du deinen Sommer verbracht?
When will you **go** to Boston?	Wann wirst du nach Boston fahren?

Fragen mit who
– Das Fragewort who? kann **verschiedene Bedeutungen** haben:
– Heißt es **Wer?** wird **keine Form von do** verwendet.
– Heißt es **Wen?** oder **Wem?** muss **eine Form von do** verwendet werden.

Who lives in Boston?	**Wer** lebt in Boston?
Who do you **like**?	**Wen** magst du?
Who did you **help** last week?	**Wem** hast du letzte Woche geholfen?

Präpositonen bleiben in Fragen meistens beim Verb stehen. Im Deutschen dagegen steht die Präposition meistens beim Fragewort. Vergleiche:

Who did you **talk to?**	**Mit wem** hast du dich unterhalten?
Where do you **come from?**	**Woher** kommst du?

(TEST YOURSELF) Put in do, does, did, will – if necessary.

1. —— you often have a turkey dinner?
2. Where —— your uncle live?
3. Who —— you invite next Friday?
4. —— you see the snow storm on TV last Sunday?
5. Who —— got stuck in his car last night?
6. Who —— Mark talk to yesterday?

G8 R: Bedingungssätze Typ II

Revision: If-clauses type II

Bei den Bedingungssätzen Typ II ist eine Bedingung unwahrscheinlich oder nicht erfüllbar. Du verwendest im **if**-Satz **simple past**. Im Hauptsatz steht **would / wouldn't + Grundform des Verbs**.

Bedingung (condition)	Folge (consequence)	
If it **rained**	I **would stay** at home.	Wenn es regnen würde, würde ich zu Hause bleiben.
If you **didn't call**,	I **would be** very sad.	Wenn du nicht anrufen würdest, wäre ich sehr traurig.

Bedingungssätze können auch mit dem Hauptsatz beginnen. Dann entfällt das Komma.

Folge (consequence)	Bedingung (condition)	
I **would buy** new clothes	if I **had** more money.	Ich würde mir neue Kleidung kaufen, wenn ich genug Geld hätte.
I **wouldn't have** problems with my clothes,	if I **lived** in the Amish community.	Ich hätte keine Kleidungsprobleme, wenn ich in der Gemeinschaft der Amish leben würde.

Statt **If I was** … wird oft **If I were** … gebraucht.

If I **were** a film star,	I **would live** in Beverly Hills.	Wenn ich ein Filmstar wäre, würde ich in Beverly Hills wohnen.

Im **if**-Satz steht nie **would / wouldn't**!

Im Deutschen verwendet man in beiden Satzteilen **würde**, **wäre** oder **hätte (Konjunktiv)**.

(TEST YOURSELF) Complete the sentences.

1. If you — (visit) your grandma on Sundays, she — (be) very glad.
2. If she — (have) less time, she — (not meet) her friends every week.
3. If I — (be) in Pennsylvania, I — (like) to see the Amish community.
4. I — really — (miss) you if you — (not come) back.
5. Jennifer — (not worry) about clothes if she — (live) with the Amish community.
6. Maybe it — (be) better if you — (not phone) me every day.

Unit 4

G9 R: Gegenüberstellung: Simple present – present progressive

Revision: Simple present – present progressive

Du kennst schon die Zeiten **simple present** und **present progressive**. Hier findest du noch einmal die Situationen, in denen du sie benutzen kannst und siehst, wie sie gebildet werden.

Simple present

Das **simple present** verwendest du, wenn du sagen willst, dass jemand etwas häufig oder regelmäßig tut.

Signalwörter: always, never, sometimes, often, usually, every …

Aussagen bildest du mit der Grundform des Verbs.

I **work** every day. You never **listen**.

Achtung: **He**, **she**, **it** – das **s** muss mit:
He work**s**. She talk**s**. It rain**s**. Aber: He go**es**.

Sätze mit Vollverben verneinst du mit **don't** und **doesn't**:

I **don't play** football.

Bei Fragen mit Vollverben musst du mit **do** oder **does** beginnen:

Do you **eat** fish? **Does** he **like** games?

Present progressive

Mit dem **present progressive** kannst du sagen, was jemand gerade tut oder was im Augenblick passiert.

Signalwörter: now, at the moment

Aussagen bildest du so:
am / are / is + Verb + -ing

I'**m working** at the moment. It **is raining** now.

Achtung Schreibweise: make → mak**ing**; write → writ**ing**; run → run**ning**; sit → sit**ting**

So verneinst du Sätze:
am / are / is not + Verb + -ing:

He **isn't eating** at the moment.

Bei Fragen stellst du **am / are / is** an den Satzanfang:

Are you **listening**? **Is** she **dancing**?

Simple present und present progressive kannst du auch einsetzen, um ein **Bild** zu beschreiben. Zunächst sagst du, wen oder was du siehst. Dann beschreibst du, was jemand tut.

Simple present

Du benutzt es, um zu sagen, wer oder was auf dem Bild zu sehen ist, oder in welchem Zustand etwas ist.

There is a boy in the picture.
There are a man and a woman.
She **looks** happy.
She **has** two dogs.
The weather **is** nice. It **is** warm.

Present progressive

Du benutzt es für alle Handlungen, die im Bild zu sehen sind und für alles, was jemand tut.

The boy **is riding** a mountain bike.
They**'re sitting** in camping chairs.
She**'s wearing** boots.
They **are playing** with a ball.
The sun **is shining**. It **isn't raining**.

(TEST YOURSELF) Use present progressive or simple present.

1. Sandy often —— (go) surfing.
2. But at the moment she —— (not surf).
3. "—— you really —— (listen), Sandy?"
4. Students —— (not like) tests.
5. What —— you usually —— (do) after school?
6. We sometimes —— (meet) some friends.

G10 R: Adjektive und Adverbien

Revision: Adjectives and adverbs

Ein **Adjektiv** (Eigenschaftswort) beschreibt eine Person oder eine Sache.

Sandra is a **good** surfer.	Sandra ist eine gute Surferin.
A helicopter tour is **fantastic**.	Ein Hubschrauberflug ist fantastisch.

Ein **Adverb** beschreibt, wie jemand etwas tut oder wie etwas geschieht.
Man erkennt Adverbien durch ein angehängtes **-ly**.

Look, she is running **slowly**.	Schau, sie läuft langsam.
It happened **quickly**.	Es geschah schnell.

Achtung Schreibweise: happy – happ**ily**; careful – careful**ly**; comfortable – comfortab**ly**; fantastic – fantstic**ally**

Es gibt Adverbien, die sich nicht verändern:

Basketball is a **fast** game.	(Adjektiv)	Basketball ist ein schnelles Spiel.
Look, the players are running **fast**.	(Adverb)	Schau, die Spieler rennen schnell.
That was a **hard** exercise.	(Adjektiv)	Das war eine schwierige Übung.
Tom has to work **hard** every day.	(Adverb)	Tom muss jeden Tag schwer arbeiten.

Es gibt auch unregelmäßige Adverbien:

This is a **good** surfboard.	(Adjektiv)	Das ist ein gutes Surfbrett.
I can surf very **well** with it.	(Adverb)	Ich kann sehr gut damit surfen.

Achtung Ausnahme! Manche Verben drücken **keine** Tätigkeit aus, z. B. **look**, **feel**, **seem**, **sound**.
Nach diesen Verben verwendest du ein **Adjektiv**:

I **feel** so **sad**.	Ich fühle mich so traurig.
You **look** **happy** today.	Du siehst heute glücklich aus.
This exercise **seems** **easy**.	Diese Aufgabe scheint leicht zu sein.
That **sounds** **good**.	Das klingt gut.

(TEST YOURSELF) Use adjectives or adverbs.

1. Don't speak so ___ (fast). Speak more ___ (slow), please.
2. She surfed so ___ (good) that she ___ (easy) won the race.
3. Sandy looks ___ (pretty) in her new dress.
4. I don't feel ___ (good) today. I think I've worked too ___ (hard).
5. Yesterday it rained ___ (heavy).
6. You seem ___ (unhappy) with the results of the last test.

G11 R: Das Perfekt

Revision: The present perfect

Wenn eine Handlung in der Vergangenheit beginnt und in der Gegenwart zu einem Ergebnis führt, verwendest du das **present perfect**:
have/has + 3. Form des Verbs (past participle).
Bei den meisten Verben hängst du ein **-ed** an das Verb: help → help**ed**

Signalwörter	
already	schon
just	gerade
not … yet	noch … nicht
never	noch nie
ever (in Fragen)	jemals (in Fragen)
since	seit (Zeitpunkt)
for	seit (Zeitspanne)

Eine Liste der unregelmäßigen Verben findest du ab Seite 224.

Einige Verben haben unregelmäßige 3. Formen: z. B. be → **been**; write → **written**

I **have** just **posted** a photo.	Ich habe gerade ein Foto verschickt.
She **has** already **written** ten text messages.	Sie hat schon zehn SMS geschrieben.

Um Sätze zu verneinen, benutzt du **haven't** oder **hasn't** (bei he, she, it):

I **haven't been** to California yet.	Ich bin noch nicht in Kalifornien gewesen.
She **hasn't seen** Los Angeles yet.	Sie hat Los Angeles noch nicht gesehen.

Fragen und Kurzantworten bildest du so:

Have you ever **been** to San Francisco?	Yes, I **have**.	No, I **haven't**.
Has your sister ever **met** a famous star?	Yes, she **has**.	No, she **hasn't**.

Present perfect mit **for** und **since**
since (**seit**) verwendest du vor einem **Zeitpunkt**, z. B. **since** 5 o'clock, **since** July, **since** 2013.
for (**seit**) verwendest du vor einer **Zeitspanne**, z. B. **for** five hours, **for** three years, **for** a long time.

I haven't seen Lara **since** Monday.	Ich habe Lara **seit** Montag nicht gesehen.
I haven't seen Lara **for** a week.	Ich habe Lara **seit** einer Woche nicht gesehen.

Im Deutschen verwendet man oft die **Gegenwart**, wenn man sagen will, seit wann oder wie lange etwas schon andauert. Wie im Präsens gibt es im Perfekt eine Verlaufsform (**present perfect progressive**). Damit betonst du die Dauer der Handlung. Vergleiche:

I **have been living** in Los Angeles for two years.	Ich **lebe seit** zwei Jahren in Los Angeles.

(TEST YOURSELF) Put the verbs in the present perfect.

1. Linda — never — (meet) a Hollywood star.
2. I — (not see) you for two months.
3. Why — your sister — (not call) yet?
4. — you — (forget) your homework again?
5. We — (not be) on holiday since 2010.
6. — you ever — (watch) video clips?

G12 Das Passiv

Passive voice (simple present and simple past)

English is important.
It is spoken all over the world.

Mit dem Passiv kannst du über eine Handlung Auskunft geben, ohne zu sagen, wer die Handlung ausführt. Im Vordergrund steht die Handlung.

So bildest du das **Passiv** im **simple present: am / are / is + 3. Form des Verbs** (past participle)

English **is spoken** in a lot of countries.	Englisch **wird** in vielen Ländern **gesprochen**.
Racism **isn't accepted**.	Rassismus **wird nicht akzeptiert**.
Spices and flour **are mixed**.	Gewürze und Mehl **werden gemischt**.

So bildest du das Passiv im **simple past: was / were + 3. Form des Verbs** (past participle)

Raleigh **was founded** in the 18th century.	Raleigh **wurde** im 18. Jahrhundert **gegründet**.
The airport **wasn't finished** until 1929.	Der Flughafen **wurde nicht** vor 1929 **fertiggestellt**.
The streets **were built** in a special way.	Die Straßen **wurden** auf besondere Weise **gebaut**.

Willst du in einem Passivsatz sagen, **wer** die Handlung ausführt, ergänzt du ihn oder sie mit **by**.

The city of Raleigh **was founded by** the French.	Die Stadt Raleigh **wurde von** den Franzosen **gegründet**.
New dishes **were brought** here **by** the slaves.	Neue Gerichte **wurden von** den Sklaven hierher **gebracht**.

(TEST YOURSELF) Use the passive voice, simple present or simple past.

1. The fried chicken — (introduce) by people from Scotland hundreds of years ago.
2. Today this dish — (make) with flour and spices.
3. The chicken and the rice — (not cook) for a long time.
4. Many cities in the South — (found) by the French in the 18th century.
5. Every year the famous Mardi Gras carnival — (celebrate) in New Orleans.
6. The city — (not build) by Sir Walter Raleigh.

G13 Indirekte Rede (ohne Zeitverschiebung)

Reported speech (without backshift)

Oh no!
Dad says we have to take a shower now!

Mit der indirekten Rede kannst du über das berichten, was jemand anderes **gerade gesagt hat**. Du beginnst mit **He says that … / She says that …** usw. Das Wort **that** kann man auch weglassen.

Positive Aussagen und verneinte Sätze in der indirekten Rede bildest du so:

Direkte Rede	Indirekte Rede
Anna says, "**I like** Florida."	Anna says (that) **she likes** Florida.
Anna says, "**We want** to see the alligators."	Anna says (that) **they want** to see the alligators.
Anna says, "**I don't need** a hotel."	Anna says (that) **she doesn't need** a hotel.

Beachte die Änderungen:

I	→ **he/she**	**my**	→ **his/her**
we	→ **they**	**our**	→ **their**
(I) **like**	→ (he/she) **likes**		
(I) **don't** …	→ (he/she) **doesn't** …		

Fragen in der indirekten Rede werden so wiedergegeben:
Du beginnst z. B. mit **She asks if …** – Sie fragt, **ob** …
Bei Fragen mit Fragewörtern beginnst du z. B. mit **He asks where …** – Er fragt, **wo/wohin** …

Direkte Rede	Indirekte Rede
Anna asks Ethan, "**Do you like** alligators?"	She asks Ethan **if he likes** alligators.
Nick asks, "**Where do you go** camping?"	He asks **where they go** camping.

Erkenne die Zeitform in der **Frage** der direkten Rede (hier: **simple present**) und bilde in der indirekten Rede einen **Satz** im **simple present** nach der Regel **S**ubjekt – **V**erb – **O**bjekt!

(TEST YOURSELF) Report what Anna says.

1. "We prefer the Everglades."
2. "I want to go on a boat tour."
3. "I don't like all those crowds."
4. "I don't want to feed the alligators."
5. "Ethan, do you know Florida?"
6. "Ethan, what do you think?"

G14 Indirekte Rede (mit Zeitverschiebung)

Reported speech (with backshift)

Look, I've got a new boyfriend.
But he's a bat!
And he told me he was a pilot.

Mit der indirekten Rede kannst du über etwas berichten, was jemand **vor einiger Zeit gesagt hat**. Du beginnst mit **He said that . . . / She told me that . . .** usw. Das Wort **that** kann man auch weglassen. Das Verb des Satzes wird vom **simple present** in das **simple past** zurückgesetzt. Das nennt man **backshift**.
Backshift gilt auch für die Verneinung: aus **don't / doesn't** wird **didn't**.

Positive Aussagen und verneinte Sätze in der indirekten Rede bildest du so:

Direkte Rede	Indirekte Rede
Al Lane said, "I **get up** at 6 a.m."	Al Lane told me (that) he **got up** at 6 a.m.
He said, "There **are** 20 alligators."	He said (that) there **were** 20 alligators.
He said, "We **don't get** a lot of visitors."	He said (that) they **didn't get** a lot of visitors.

(TEST YOURSELF) **Report what Al Lane said.**

1. "I often work with the alligators."
2. "Some tourists don't like alligators."
3. "We feed the animals at 10 o'clock."
4. "It's too late to feed the alligators."
5. "I don't speak German."
6. "The visitors love the warm weather."

(FÜR PROFIS)

Fragen werden in der indirekten Rede so wiedergegeben:

Du beginnst z.B. mit	**She asked if . . .**	Sie fragte, **ob** . . .
Bei Fragewörtern beginnst du z. B. mit	**He asked when . . .**	Er fragte, **wann** . . .

Direkte Rede	Indirekte Rede
Al Lane asked, "Anna, **do** you **want** to feed the alligators?"	Al Lane asked Anna **if** she **wanted** to feed the alligators.
Anna asked, "**When does** the alligator show **start**?"	Anna wanted to know **when** the alligator show **started**.

Erkenne die Zeitform in der **Frage** der direkten Rede (hier: **simple present**) und bilde in der indirekten Rede einen **Satz** im **simple past** nach der Regel **S**ubjekt – **V**erb – **O**bjekt!

Methods

1-minute-presentation

Step 1

Nimm ein Blatt DIN A4-Papier quer und falte es so, dass das untere Drittel nach hinten wegknickt.

Step 2

Schreibe den Vortragstext auf die oberen zwei Drittel.

Step 3

Streiche nun die wichtigsten Stichpunkte im Text an. Notiere sie noch einmal auf dem unteren Drittel. Das ist dein Spickzettel.

Step 4

In deiner Präsentation verwendest du nur den Spickzettel. Wenn du steckenbleibst, darfst du ihn umknicken und kurz auf den Text oben schauen.

Bus stop

(Lerntempoduett)

Step 1

Bearbeite die Aufgabe zunächst allein. Schreibe deine Lösungen auf.

Step 2

Wenn du fertig bist, gehe zum „bus stop“. Warte dort auf die nächste Person bzw. triff die Person, die dort schon wartet. Vergleicht und korrigiert eure Ergebnisse.

Step 3

Gehe danach wieder zu deinem Platz zurück. Bearbeite die nächste Aufgabe.

Dramatic reading

(Szenisches Lesen)

Step 1

Verteilt die Rollen innerhalb eurer Gruppe.

Step 2

Lies dir deinen Text lautlos oder ganz leise immer wieder vor, bis du ihn gut kennst.

Step 3

Übt euren Text in der Gruppe mit der Methode „Read and look up" (Seite 178).

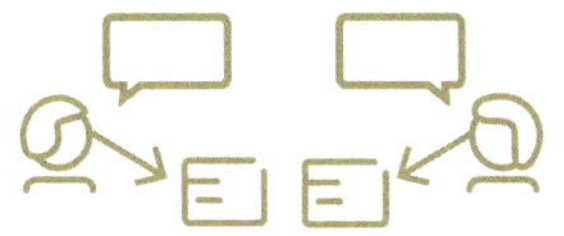

Step 4

Überlegt euch, wie ihr euch in der Rolle fühlt und wie ihr euch bewegen würdet. Tragt euren Text so frei wie möglich vor.

Gallery walk

Step 1

Hängt nach eurer Gruppenarbeit euer Produkt gut sichtbar im Klassenzimmer auf.

Step 2

Einer von euch, der „Experte", bleibt bei eurem Produkt stehen und erklärt es den anderen. Die anderen gehen herum. Nach jedem Durchgang wechselt der Experte.

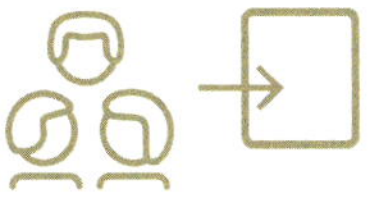

Step 3

Seht euch die Produkte der anderen an und bewertet sie.

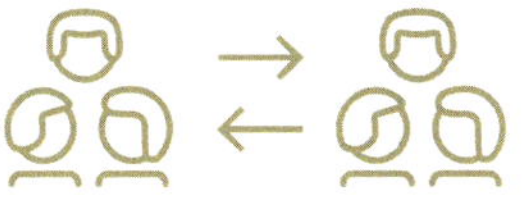

Step 4

Wertet im Anschluss eure Ergebnisse in der Klasse aus.

Jigsaw

(Gruppenpuzzle)

Step 1

Bildet Stammgruppen („home groups“).
Jedes Gruppenmitglied wählt einen Text aus, liest ihn und bearbeitet ihn. Macht euch Notizen dazu.

Step 2

Trefft euch in Expertengruppen („expert groups“) mit den Mitgliedern der anderen Stammgruppen, die denselben Text wie ihr bearbeitet haben. Vergleicht eure Notizen, besprecht sie gemeinsam und ergänzt sie.

Step 3

Geht zurück in eure Stammgruppe. Präsentiert dort die Informationen aus eurem Text. Macht euch Notizen zu den Texten der anderen, so dass am Ende jeder die Informationen aus allen Texten hat.

Milling around

(Marktplatz)

Step 1

Bearbeite die Aufgabe zunächst allein.
Auf ein Zeichen vom Lehrer oder der Lehrerin steht ihr auf und geht durch den Raum.
Nimm die Aufgabe und einen Stift mit.

Step 2

Wenn ein Signal ertönt, bleibt ihr stehen.
Besprecht mit der Person die Aufgabe, die euch am nächsten steht.

Step 3

Beim nächsten Signal trennt ihr euch und geht weiter durch den Raum. Wiederholt den Vorgang.

Peer correction

(Partnerkontrolle)

Step 1

Bearbeite die Aufgabe zunächst selbstständig.

Step 2

Tausche deine Lösungen mit einem Partner/einer Partnerin. Kontrolliere seine oder ihre Lösungen.

Step 3

Tauscht euch danach zu der Aufgabe aus und korrigiert den Text.

Placemat

(Platzdeckchen)

Step 1

Bildet Vierergruppen.

Step 2

Teilt ein großes Blatt Papier in fünf Bereiche ein.

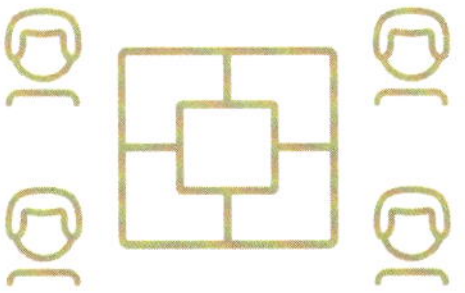

Step 3

Setzt euch so hin, dass alle in eine Ecke des Blattes schreiben können.

Step 4

Jedes Gruppenmitglied denkt allein über das Thema nach und schreibt Ideen auf seinen Teil des Blattes.

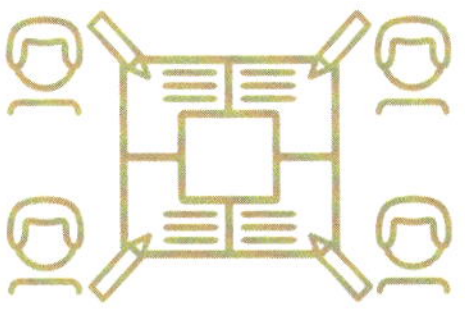

Step 5

Tauscht euch über die Ideen aus. Einigt euch auf die besten Ideen und schreibt diese in die Mitte des Blattes.

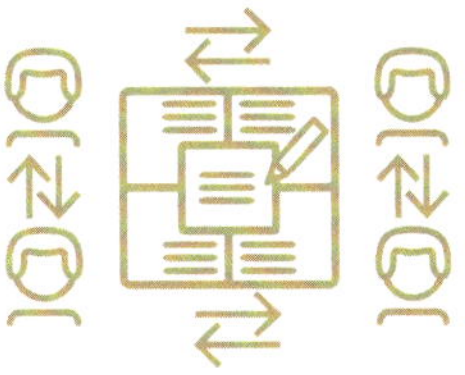

Read and look up

(Lesen und Aufschauen)

Step 1

Schaue auf deinen Text und präge dir die erste Zeile oder den ersten Satz ein. Schaue hoch und sprich deine Zeile/deinen Satz lautlos oder leise vor dich hin. Nimm dir die nächste Zeile/den nächsten Satz vor.

Step 2

Übe nun mit einer Partnerin/einem Partner. Erzähle deinen Text, Zeile für Zeile oder Satz für Satz. Dazwischen schaust du immer wieder nach unten auf deinen Text.

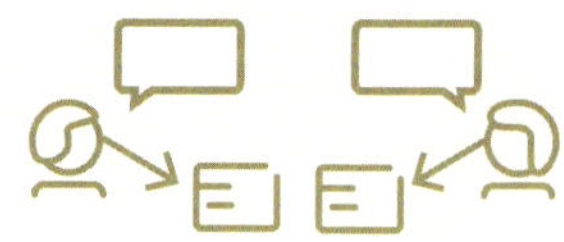

Step 3

Wiederhole alles, bis es gut klappt. Überlege dir, wo du stehen und wie du dich bewegen willst.

Round robin

(Blitzlicht)

Step 1

Bildet Gruppen und setzt euch in einen Kreis.

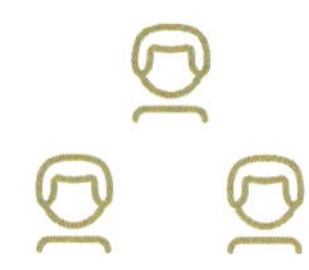

Step 2

Jedes Gruppenmitglied überlegt sich kurz einen Satz, der seine persönliche Meinung zum Thema ausdrückt.

Step 3

Wenn alle bereit sind, sagen die Gruppenmitglieder der Reihe nach ihre Meinung.

Step 4

Die anderen Gruppenmitglieder dürfen die Sätze nicht kommentieren.

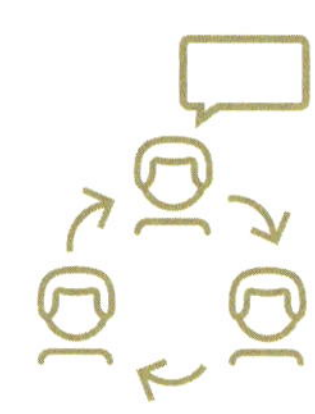

Think – pair – share

Step 1
Schreibe deine Ideen, Gedanken oder Lösungen zur Aufgabe auf.

Step 2
Tauscht eure Notizen zu zweit aus und besprecht sie.

Step 3
Präsentiert euer Ergebnis anderen Paaren oder der gesamten Klasse.

Tip top

Step 1
Sage zunächst, was dir gut gefallen hat – was „top“ war.

Step 2
Sage nun, was noch nicht so gut war, und gib einen Tipp, was man noch verbessern könnte.

Writers’ conference
(Schreibwerkstatt)

Step 1
Bildet Vierergruppen.

Step 2
Lest euch eure Sätze/Texte gegenseitig vor.

Step 3
Die anderen sagen, was ihnen gefallen hat.

Step 4
Die Zuhörer machen Verbesserungsvorschläge.

Step 5
Jede Gruppe wählt den besten Text aus und liest ihn der Klasse vor.

Du kennst schon einige Tipps und Tricks zum Vokabellernen. Erinnerst du dich? Hier gibt es weitere Tipps.

Vocabulary

Vocabulary tips

Lerntipp: Englisch im Alltag

Achte während des Tages auf alle englischen Wörter, die dir begegnen. Ob im Supermarkt, im Fernsehen, in Büchern, auf Werbeplakaten oder Schildern am Bahnhof, Flughafen etc.: Du wirst erstaunt sein, wie oft man im Alltag auf die englische Sprache stößt. Das ist ein gutes Training, um auf noch unbekannte Vokabeln aufmerksam zu werden. Deinen Sprachschatz erweiterst du ganz leicht, indem du dir ein schönes Heft oder Notizbuch kaufst, das speziell für solche Vokabeln da ist. Nimm es so oft wie möglich mit, vor allem, wenn du verreist! Die noch unbekannten Wörter kannst du dann zu Hause in einem Wörterbuch nachschlagen. Da du mit jedem Wort eine kleine Geschichte oder bestimmte besondere Umstände verbindest (zum Beispiel: „Ach ja! Dieses Wort habe ich am Bahnhof gesehen, im Kino gehört" etc.), wirst du es dir sehr leicht merken können!

Wortbildung

Es gibt verschiedene Möglichkeiten, um aus einem Verb ein Nomen abzuleiten.

1. Du kannst die Endung *-ing* anhängen:
   to build → a building
   to meet → a meeting
2. Manche Nomen werden mit der Endung *-er* oder *-or* gebildet.
   Solche Nomen bezeichnen meistens eine Person:
   to ride → a rider
   to visit → a visitor
3. Es gibt auch die Endung *-ion*:
   to define → a definition
   to invent → an invention
4. Sehr oft haben auch Verb und Nomen dieselbe Form:
   to call → a call
   to dream → a dream

Diese Checkliste kann dir helfen, Fehler zu vermeiden und deine Rechtschreibung zu verbessern. Prüfe alle deine Texte damit.

- **Schreibung:**
  - ☐ *gh* wird meist nicht gesprochen. Vergiss es beim Schreiben nicht.
  - ☐ *k* kommt vor *t* so gut wie nie vor, z. B. action – Aktion, October – Oktober

- **Gleiche Aussprache, unterschiedliche Schreibung:**
  - ☐ [iː] z. B. teacher, meeting, media, magazine, people, field
  - ☐ [uː] z. B. food, route, to do, swimsuit, supermarket, true, crew

- **Gleiche Aussprache, unterschiedliche Schreibung und Bedeutung:**
  - ☐ [iː] z. B. see – sehen, sea – Meer; meet – treffen, meat – Fleisch
  - ☐ [uː] z. B. two – zwei, too – auch

- **Verdoppelung der Endkonsonanten:**
  - ☐ to stop – stopping, stopped
  - ☐ to plan – planning, planned

- ***y* wird zu *ie*:**
  - ☐ in der 3. Person Singular: z. B. to carry – he carries; aber: to buy – she buys
  - ☐ im Plural: z. B. city – cities, party – parties; aber: boy – boys
  - ☐ bei der Steigerung von Adjektiven: z. B. happy – happier – (the) happiest; easy – easier – (the) easiest

- **Ähnlich und doch anders:**
  - ☐ Wortendung *le*: z. B. engl. title – dt. Titel; engl. middle – dt. Mittel
  - ☐ *ph* statt *f*: z. B. engl. phone – dt. Telefon; engl. photo – dt. Foto

- **Großschreibung:**
  - ☐ Monatsnamen: z. B. January, July, December
  - ☐ Wochentage: z. B. Monday, Wednesday, Saturday
  - ☐ Eigennamen: z. B. Tom, Lisa, the Brooks, the London Eye, the Thames
  - ☐ geografische Namen: Bristol, Greenwich, Germany, Italy

- **Plural:**
  - ☐ Der Plural bekommt normalerweise ein *-s*: z. B. friend – friends, chair – chairs, film – films
  - ☐ Endet ein Wort auf *s* oder *x*, wird *-es* angehängt: z. B. bus – buses, box – boxes
  - ☐ Manche Wörter haben einen unregelmäßigen Plural: z. B. man – men, child – children, shelf – shelves, mouse – mice

- **Apostroph:**
  - ☐ bei Kurzformen: z. B. she is → she's; they are → they're
  - ☐ beim Genitiv-s: z. B. Sam's bike, Emma's family, the Jacksons' house, the children's games

- **Wörterbuch:**
  - ☐ Prüfe die Schreibung aller Wörter, bei denen du dir nicht ganz sicher bist, indem du sie im Wörterbuch nachschlägst.

Vocabulary

Das Vocabulary enthält alle neuen Wörter und Wendungen. Sie stehen in der Reihenfolge, wie sie im Buch vorkommen.

Die Wortliste ist in drei Spalten aufgeteilt:

Links findest du das englische Wort mit der Lautschrift in Klammern. (Die Lautschrift wird ganz unten auf jeder Seite im *Dictionary* erklärt.)

In der mittleren Spalte steht die deutsche Übersetzung.

Rechts findest du Beispielsätze, Hinweise und Tipps, die dir beim Lernen helfen.

Die **fett** gedruckten Wörter musst du lernen.
Die blau gedruckten Wörter kannst du lernen, musst du aber nicht.
Die Wörter aus den Checkpoints musst du nicht lernen.

Symbole und Abkürzungen:

Achte auf die Aussprache!
Achte auf die Schreibung!
↔ ist das Gegenteil von
→ ist verwandt mit
sth something
sb somebody

= entspricht
(sg) Einzahl (Singular)
(pl) Mehrzahl (Plural)
R ähnlich wie im Russischen
T ähnlich wie im Türkischen

Die *Word bank*-Seiten helfen dir, die *Your turn*-Aufgaben in den *Units* zu bearbeiten.
Du findest dort nützlichen individuellen Wortschatz zum Thema der *Unit*, der dir hilft, über deine eigene Situation zu sprechen oder zu schreiben. Diese Wörter findest du auch im *Dictionary*.

Wenn du ein Wort nicht weißt und im Wörterbuch nachschlagen willst, schau auf den *Dictionary*-Seiten ab S. 229 nach. Oder bei den *Instructions* auf S. 224.

Zoom in – The USA

p. 8	**fall** *(AE)* [fɔ:l]	Herbst	AE: **fall** BE: autumn
	state [steɪt]	Staat; Bundesstaat; Land	There are 50 **states** in the USA.
	to shine [ʃaɪn], **shone** [ʃɒn], **shone** [ʃɒn]	scheinen; glänzen	The sun is **shining** today.
	bright [braɪt]	hell; leuchtend; strahlend	**bright** ↔ dark
	color *(AE)* ['kʌlə]	Farbe	AE: **color** BE: colour
p. 9	**huge** [hju:dʒ]	riesig; riesengroß	**huge** = very big
	area ['eəriə]	Fläche	The USA has an **area** of over 9,000,000 km².
	corn [kɔ:n]	Korn; Mais; Getreide	
	soy bean ['sɔɪ ˌbi:n]	Sojabohne	You can see **soy beans** in the Midwest.

	field [fiːld]	Feld; Wiese; Weide	There are corn **fields** in the Midwest.
	surfer ['sɜːfə]	Wellenreiter; Wellenreiterin; Surfer; Surferin	T sörfçü 
	paradise ['pærədaɪs]	Paradies	Hawaii is a surfer's **paradise**.
	perfect ['pɜːfɪkt]	perfekt; vollkommen	Today is the **perfect** weather for a picnic.
	wave [weɪv]	Welle	
p. 8	**North America** [ˌnɔːθ‿ə'merɪkə]	Nordamerika	Denali is the highest mountain in **North America**.
p. 9	**landscape** ['lændskeɪp]	Landschaft	Tourists enjoy the beautiful **landscape**.
	American [ə'merɪkən]	amerikanisch; Amerikanisch; aus Amerika; Amerikaner; Amerikanerin	**American** → America
	swamp [swɒmp]	Sumpf	There are **swamps** in the American south.
	alligator ['ælɪgeɪtə]	Alligator	R аллигатор T alligator 
p. 8	**rose** [rəʊz]	Rose	R роза 
	bald eagle [ˌbɔːld 'iːgl]	Weißkopfseeadler	The **bald eagle** is an American symbol.
	total ['təʊtl]	Gesamt-; gesamt	The **total** area is all of the area.
	square mile (= sq. mi.) [ˌskweə 'maɪl]	Quadratmeile	The United States' total area is about 3,600,000 **square miles**.
	currency ['kʌrnsi]	Währung	The **currency** in Germany is the euro.
	dollar ['dɒlə]	Dollar *(amer. Währungseinheit)*	R доллар T dolar
	time zone ['taɪm ˌzəʊn]	Zeitzone	There are nine **time zones** in the USA.
	major ['meɪdʒə]	Haupt-; wichtig; bedeutend	There are three **major** rivers in the USA.
p. 9	**to name** [neɪm]	benennen	**to name** → name
	north of ['nɔːθ‿əv]	nördlich von	Denmark is **north of** Germany.
	south of ['saʊθ‿əv]	südlich von	Italy is **south of** Germany.
	ocean ['əʊʃn]	Ozean; Meer	R океан T okyanus
	east of ['iːst‿əv]	östlich von	Poland is **east of** Germany.
	west of ['west‿əv]	westlich von	France is **west of** Germany.
	distance ['dɪstns]	Entfernung; Distanz	Find out the **distance** from A to B.

Unit 1 Gateway NYC

p. 12	**gateway** ['geɪtweɪ]	Tor; Eingangstor	NYC is the **gateway** to America.

Way in

borough ['bʌrə]	Stadtteil; Bezirk	NYC has five **boroughs**.
nickname ['nɪkneɪm]	Spitzname	Most US cities have a **nickname**.
to stand out ['stænd‚aʊt]	auffallen; herausragen; herausstechen	One building **stands out**. 
skyline ['skaɪlaɪn]	Skyline	
foot [fʊt]	Fuß *(Längenmaß: 30,48 cm)*	The building is 400 **feet** high.
to replace [rɪ'pleɪs]	ersetzen	They **replaced** the old World Trade Center.
attack [ə'tæk]	Angriff; Attacke	There were **attacks** on September 11, 2001.
p. 13 **baseball** ['beɪsbɔ:l]	Baseball	R бейсбол T beyzbol 
New Yorker [ˌnju: 'jɔ:kə]	New Yorker; New Yorkerin	**New Yorkers** live in New York City.
especially [ɪ'speʃli]	besonders; vor allem	We like sport, **especially** baseball.
best-paid ['bestˌpeɪd]	bestbezahlt	He is the **best-paid** star.
center *(AE)* ['sentə]	Zentrum; Mitte; Center	AE: **center** BE: centre
theater *(AE)* ['θɪətə]	Theater	AE: **theater** BE: theatre
collection [kə'lekʃn]	Sammlung; Kollektion	**collection** → to collect
cultural movement [ˌkʌltʃrl 'mu:vmənt]	Kulturbewegung	There are many **cultural movements**.
independence [ˌɪndɪ'pendəns]	Unabhängigkeit	They celebrated 100 years of **independence**.
immigrant ['ɪmɪgrənt]	Immigrant; Immigrantin; Einwanderer; Einwandererin	A lot of **immigrants** went to America.
symbol ['sɪmbl]	Symbol	R символ T sembol
hope [həʊp]	Hoffnung	**hope** → to hope
event [ɪ'vent]	Ereignis; Veranstaltung	My birthday was a big **event**.
on TV [ɒn ˌti:'vi:]	im Fernsehen	You could see everything **on TV**.
top [tɒp]	Spitze	It took 30 seconds to travel to the **top**.
elevator *(AE)* ['elɪveɪtə]	Aufzug; Lift	AE: **elevator** BE: lift 
light [laɪt]	Licht	
to be located [bi: ləʊ'keɪtɪd]	gelegen sein; sich befinden	The museum **is located** in the city centre.
grounds *(pl)* [graʊndz]	Gelände; Gebiet	The house is in the **grounds** of the school.
billion ['bɪliən]	Milliarde	R биллион

Station 1

City words

traffic jam ['træfɪk ˌdʒæm]	Stau	**avenue** ['ævənju:]	Allee; Boulevard
rush hour ['rʌʃ ˌaʊə]	Hauptverkehrszeit	**lights** [laɪts]	Ampel
roadwork *(AE)* ['rəʊdwɜ:k]	Straßenbauarbeiten	**intersection** *(AE)* [ˌɪntə'sekʃn]	Kreuzung
downtown *(AE)* [ˌdaʊn'taʊn]	im Stadtzentrum	**sightseeing** ['saɪtsi:ɪŋ]	Besichtigungstour
landmark ['lænmɑ:k]	Wahrzeichen	**sidewalk** *(AE)* ['saɪdwɔ:k]	Gehweg; Bürgersteig
skyscraper ['skaɪskreɪpə]	Wolkenkratzer	**parking lot** *(AE)* ['pɑ:kɪŋ ˌlɒt]	Parkplatz
story *(AE)* ['stɔ:ri]	Stock; Stockwerk; Etage	**commuter** [kə'mju:tə]	Pendler; Pendlerin
block [blɒk]	Block; Häuserblock	**construction site** [kən'strʌkʃn ˌsaɪt]	Baustelle
subway *(AE)* ['sʌbweɪ]	U-Bahn	**suburb** ['sʌbɜ:b]	Vorort

p. 14	**ride** [raɪd]	Fahrt; Ritt	A taxi **ride** in NYC is very interesting.
	even ['i:vn]	lieber	Don't **even** ask me what I think.
	snow [snəʊ]	Schnee	
	to get into [ˌget‿'ɪntə]	hineinkommen; hineingelangen	I usually **get into** town by bus.
	to get tired of sth [ˌget 'taɪəd‿əv]	etw. sattbekommen; etw. satthaben	I never **get tired of** it.
	financial [faɪ'nænʃl]	finanziell; Finanz-	Where is the **financial** centre of the world?
	in the distance [ˌɪn ðə 'dɪstns]	in der Ferne	I can see the bridge **in the distance**.
	back then ['bæk ˌðen]	damals	It was the tallest building **back then**.
	view [vju:]	Aussicht; Sicht; Ausblick; Blick	The **view** from the top is amazing.
	anyway ['eniweɪ]	eigentlich	How long are you here for, **anyway**?
	bagel ['beɪgl]	Bagel *(weiches, ringförmiges Brötchen)*	
	coffee ['kɒfi]	Kaffee	R кофе T kahve 
	to check out [ˌtʃek‿'aʊt]	anschauen; ausprobieren	I want to **check out** the zoo before we go.
	star sign ['stɑ: ˌsaɪn]	Sternzeichen	Look at the **star signs** at the station.
	ceiling ['si:lɪŋ]	Zimmerdecke	There are pictures on the **ceiling**.
	correct [kə'rekt]	richtig; korrekt	**correct** = right

	to **have no idea** [hæv ˌnəʊ aɪˈdɪə]	keine Ahnung haben	**I have no idea.** = I don't know.
	around [əˈraʊnd]	um … herum	The café is **around** the corner.
	hot dog [ˈhɒt ˌdɒg]	Hot Dog *(Würstchen im Brötchen)*	R хот-дог T hot dog 
	cart [kɑːt]	*hier:* Stand	We can get a hot dog from that **cart**.
	to **belong (to)** [bɪˈlɒŋ (tə)]	gehören (zu)	it **belongs** to me = it's mine
	to **get to** [ˈget tə]	hinkommen zu; gelangen	Can you tell us how to **get to** the park?
	Let's get moving! [ˌlets get ˈmuːvɪŋ]	Lasst uns weiterfahren!; Auf geht's!	**Let's get moving** or we'll be late.
p. 15	**shopping mall** [ˈʃɒpɪŋ ˌmɔːl]	Einkaufszentrum	We went shopping in the **shopping mall**.
	right ahead [ˌraɪt‿əˈhed]	geradeaus	Look, the museum is **right ahead**.
	to **point out** [ˌpɔɪnt‿ˈaʊt]	zeigen; darauf hinweisen	The driver **pointed out** the sights.
	down there [ˌdaʊn ˈðeə]	dahin; da unten	I went on a trip **down there**.
p. 16	**Native American** [ˌneɪtɪv‿əˈmerɪkən]	Ureinwohner Amerikas; Ureinwohnerin Amerikas; Indianer; Indianerin; indianisch	**Native Americans** live in the USA.

Station 2

Going to a new country

to **immigrate** [ˈɪmɪgreɪt]	einwandern; immigrieren
decision [dɪˈsɪʒn]	Entscheidung
unemployed [ˌʌnɪmˈplɔɪd]	arbeitslos
chance [tʃɑːns]	Möglichkeit
community [kəˈmjuːnəti]	Gemeinde; Gemeinschaft
career [kəˈrɪə]	Beruf; Laufbahn; Karriere
culture [ˈkʌltʃə]	Kultur
motivated [ˈməʊtɪveɪtɪd]	motiviert
ambitious [æmˈbɪʃəs]	ehrgeizig
opportunity [ˌɒpəˈtjuːnəti]	Gelegenheit; Chance
citizen [ˈsɪtɪzn]	Staatsbürger; Staatsbürgerin; Staatsangehöriger; Staatsangehörige
contact [ˈkɒntækt]	Kontakt
foreign [ˈfɒrɪn]	fremd; ausländisch
to **get used to (sth)** [ˌget ˈjuːzd tə]	sich an (etw.) gewöhnen
to **emigrate** [ˈemɪgreɪt]	auswandern; emigrieren
to **succeed (in)** [səkˈsiːd (ɪn)]	Erfolg haben (mit/bei); nachfolgen
to **fail (at)** [feɪl (ət)]	versagen (in/bei); ausfallen; fehlschlagen
support [səˈpɔːt]	Unterstützung; Hilfe
to **adapt to** [əˈdæpt (tə)]	sich anpassen
to **cross the border** [ˌkrɒs ðə ˈbɔːdə]	über die Grenze gehen; die Grenze überschreiten

p. 18	**interviewer** [ˈɪntəvjuːə]	Interviewer; Interviewerin; Befrager; Befragerin	**interviewer** → interview → to interview
	to **go ahead** [ˌɡəʊ əˈhed]	fortfahren; loslegen; vorangehen	**Go ahead** with your questions.
	season [ˈsiːzn]	Saison; Jahreszeit	It is a good baseball **season** this year.
	so far [ˌsəʊ ˈfɑː]	bis jetzt	The season has been good **so far**.
	Latin America [ˌlætɪn əˈmerɪkə]	Lateinamerika	In **Latin America** the first language isn't English.
	league [liːɡ]	Liga	There are **leagues** for many sports.
	Cuba [ˈkjuːbə]	Kuba	R Куба T Küba
	mom *(AE)* [mɒm]	Mama	AE: **mom** BE: mum
	strange [streɪndʒ]	fremd	It's hard to move to a **strange** place.
	poor [pɔː]	arm	**poor** ↔ rich
	above all [əbʌv‿ˈɔːl]	vor allen Dingen; in erster Linie	**Above all** they wanted to give us the best.
	Cuban [ˈkjuːbən]	kubanisch; aus Kuba; Kubaner; Kubanerin	**Cuban** → Cuba
	goods *(no pl)* [ɡʊdz]	Güter; Waren	My parents sell **goods** in a small shop.
	to **count** [kaʊnt]	zählen	I can **count** in English, German and French.
	to **begin** [bɪˈɡɪn], **began** [bɪˈɡæn], **begun** [bɪˈɡʌn]	beginnen; anfangen	**to begin** ↔ to finish
	to **take sth seriously** [ˌteɪk ˈsɪəriəsli]	etw. ernst nehmen	I don't **take** sport **seriously**, I do it for fun.
	high school [ˈhaɪ ˌskuːl]	Highschool *(weiterführende Schule, Oberstufe)*	I worked hard at **high school**.
	to **take off** [ˌteɪk‿ˈɒf]	durchstarten; abheben	My career **took off** afer school.
	certainly [ˈsɜːtnli]	allerdings	You have **certainly** been successful.
	example [ɪɡˈzɑːmpl]	Beispiel	Give me an **example** of a good book.
	to **come true** [ˌkʌm ˈtruː]	wahr werden; in Erfüllung gehen	It is a dream **come true**.
	US [juːˈes]	US-amerikanisch	It is a **US** school, not a British one.
	to **develop** [dɪˈveləp]	(sich) entwickeln	We have **developed** two new games.
	tourism [ˈtʊərɪzm]	Tourismus	R туризм T turizm
p. 19	**home country** [ˌhəʊm ˈkʌntri]	Heimat; Heimatland	My **home country** is Germany.
p. 21	**The Philippines** [ˌðə ˈfɪlɪpiːnz]	die Philippinen	Angela is from **the Philippines**.
	reader [ˈriːdə]	Leser; Leserin	**reader** → to read

Reading corner

p. 22	**immigration** [ˌɪmɪˈgreɪʃn]	Immigration; Zuwanderung	**immigration** → to immigrate → immigrant
	to bring to life [ˌbrɪŋ tə‿ˈlaɪf]	zum Leben erwecken; veranschaulichen	The pictures **brought** the story **to life**.
	statement [ˈsteɪtmənt]	Aussage; Behauptung; Erklärung	I gave a **statement** to the police.
	descendant [dɪˈsendənt]	Abkömmling; Nachfahre; Nachfahrin	They're the **descendants** of immigrants.
	to search [sɜːtʃ]	durchsuchen; suchen	We **searched** the passenger lists.
	to save [seɪv]	sparen	I'm **saving** my money to buy a bike.
	statistics *(no pl)* [stəˈtɪstɪks]	Statistik	R статистика T istatistik
	to work off [ˌwɜːk‿ˈɒf]	abarbeiten	It took years to **work off** our tickets.
	steamship [ˈstiːmʃɪp]	Dampfschiff; Dampfer	
	condition [kənˈdɪʃn]	Bedingung; Zustand	The **conditions** were very hard.
	crowded [ˈkraʊdɪd]	überfüllt	**crowded** → crowd
	space [speɪs]	Ort; Stelle; Platz; Raum; Fläche	It was a small, dirty **space** in the ship.
	little [ˈlɪtl]	wenig; kaum	We had very **little** space on the ship.
	deck [dek]	Schiffsdeck	The **deck** of the ship was dirty.
	area [ˈeəriə]	Bereich	The **area** for passengers was small.
	air [eə]	Luft	You have to put **air** in the tyres.
	crossing [ˈkrɒsɪŋ]	Überfahrt; Überquerung	The **crossing** took 21 days.
	majority [məˈdʒɒrəti]	Mehrheit; Mehrzahl	The **majority** of people were sick.
	physical [ˈfɪzɪkl]	physisch; körperlich	**Physical** is about the body.
	mental [ˈmentl]	geistig	**Mental** is about inside the head.
	state [steɪt]	Zustand	We weren't in a very good **state**.
	over [ˈəʊvə]	vorbei	After 21 days the journey was **over**.
	disease [dɪˈziːz]	Krankheit	Doctors checked for **diseases**.
	inspection [ɪnˈspekʃn]	Inspektion; Kontrolle; Überprüfung	Doctors also did an **inspection** of the ship.
	harbor *(AE)* [ˈhɑːbə]	Hafen	AE: **harbor** BE: harbour
	arrival [əˈraɪvl]	Ankömmling	**arrival** → to arrive
	word [wɜːd]	Wort	I know so many English **words** now.
	Polish [ˈpəʊlɪʃ]	polnisch; Polnisch; aus Polen	**Polish** → Poland
	goddess [ˈgɒdes]	Göttin	The Statue of Liberty is like a **goddess**.

V

	powerful ['paʊəfl]	stark; mächtig; bedeutend; beeindruckend	America is a **powerful** country.
	to dock [dɒk]	andocken	The ship **docked** at the harbour.
	medical ['medɪkl]	medizinisch; ärztlich	Doctors checked our **medical** condition.
	unpleasant [ʌn'pleznt]	unangenehm; unerfreulich	The inspections were very **unpleasant**.
	certain ['sɜ:tn]	bestimmte	They looked for **certain** diseases.
	percent (%) [pə'sent]	Prozent	50 **percent** of ten is five.
	to return [rɪ'tɜ:n]	zurückkehren; zurückgeben	My friends had to **return** home.
	minority [maɪ'nɒrəti]	Minderheit	**minority** ↔ majority
	check [tʃek]	Kontrolle	**check** → to check
	the rest [ðə 'rest]	der Rest	**The rest** of us left for our new life.
	free [fri:]	frei	The slaves were **free** after the Civil War.
	ahead of [ə'hed‿əv]	vor	There were many problems **ahead of** us.
p. 23	**Scandinavia** [ˌskændɪ'neɪviə]	Skandinavien	Denmark is in **Scandinavia**.
	Greece [gri:s]	Griechenland	**Greece** is in the south of Europe.
	Eastern Europe ['i:stn ˌjʊərəp]	Osteuropa	Poland is in **Eastern Europe**.
	Russia ['rʌʃə]	Russland	**Russia** is to the east of Germany.
	religious [rɪ'lɪdʒəs]	religiös; gläubig	Are you **religious**?
	political [pə'lɪtɪkl]	politisch	People have different **political** opinions.
	freedom *(no pl)* ['fri:dəm]	Freiheit; Unabhängigkeit	**Freedom** hat keine Mehrzahl.
	to escape [ɪ'skeɪp]	entkommen; fliehen; entfliehen; flüchten	They wanted to **escape** their problems.
	poverty ['pɒvəti]	Armut	**Poverty** is when you have no money.
	Mexico ['meksɪkəʊ]	Mexiko	R Мексика T Meksika
	China ['tʃaɪnə]	China	Achtung Aussprache!
	The Dominican Republic [ðə dəˌmɪnɪkn rɪ'pʌblɪk]	Dominikanische Republik	**The Dominican Republic** is to the east of Cuba.
	Vietnam [ˌvjet'næm]	Vietnam	**Vietnam** is south of China.
	source [sɔ:s]	Quelle	What was the **source** for your text?

Film corner

p. 25	**once** [wʌns]	einst; einmal	at a time in the past
	honor *(AE)* ['ɒnə]	Ehre	There's a Wall of **Honor** on Ellis Island.

great-grandparents [ˌgreɪtˈgrænˌpeərənts]	Urgroßeltern	My **great-grandparents** are my grandparents' parents.
inside [ˌɪnˈsaɪd]	innen; drinnen	In summer it can get hot **inside**.

Checkpoint

angel [ˈeɪndʒl]	Engel	ethnic [ˈeθnɪk]	ethnisch; Volks-

V

Word bank: City guide

skyscraper

cathedral

tower

museum

gallery

station

bridge

building

monument

Over there you can see …
Don't miss …
Around this corner we'll come to …
Right/Straight ahead are …
You must visit …
In the distance you can see …
Have a look at/Look at …

Make sure you visit …
I'd like to point out …
Down there/Over there is …
From here …
… built it in …
It opened in …
It is special because …

Word bank: Presenting personal information

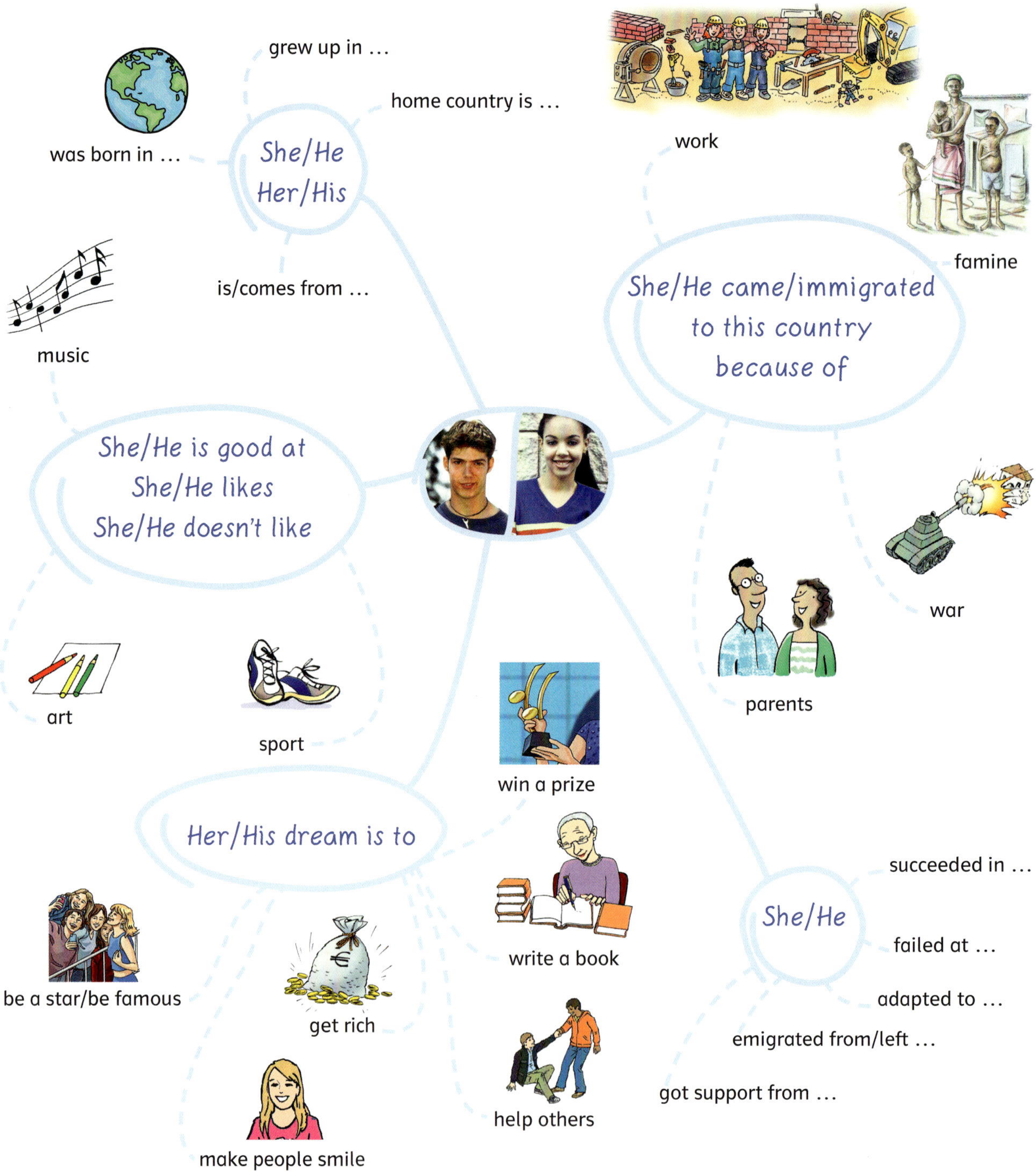

Unit 2 Teens in the Midwest

Way in

p. 32	**best known** [ˌbest ˈnəʊn]	weltberühmt	NYC is **best known** for its skyline.
	flat [flæt]	flach; platt	When the land is **flat** you can see lots.
	farmland [ˈfɑːmlænd]	Ackerland; Ackerboden; Landwirtschaftsflächen	You can see corn on **farmland** in the Midwest.
	tornado [tɔːˈneɪdəʊ]	Tornado; Wirbelsturm	R торнадо
	alley [ˈæli]	Gasse; Weg	An **alley** is a small street.
	terrifying [ˈterəfaɪɪŋ]	furchterregend; erschreckend	The movie we watched was **terrifying**.
	storm [stɔːm]	Sturm	The **storm** was awful and I was sick.
	European [ˌjʊərəˈpiːən]	europäisch; Europäisch; aus Europa; Europäer; Europäerin	T Avrupalı
	settler [ˈsetlə]	Siedler; Siedlerin	Thousands of **settlers** came to the West.
	government [ˈɡʌvnmənt]	Regierung	Achtung Schreibweise! gover<u>n</u>ment
	to force [fɔːs]	zwingen	We were **forced** to sell our land.
	reservation [ˌrezəˈveɪʃn]	Reservat	We had to live on **reservations**.
p. 33	**part-time** [ˌpɑːtˈtaɪm]	Teilzeit-; Halbtags-	Students often have **part-time** jobs.
	store *(AE)* [stɔː]	Laden; Geschäft	AE: **store** BE: shop
	to clear [klɪə]	abräumen; ausräumen	I **clear** the tables in a café on Fridays.
	to serve [sɜːv]	servieren	Sarah **serves** ice cream in the new café.
	grade *(AE)* [ɡreɪd]	Note; Klasse	AE: **grade** BE: mark; class
	schedule *(AE)* [ˈskedʒuːl]	Stundenplan; Fahrplan	AE: **schedule** BE: timetable
	former [ˈfɔːmə]	ehemalige; frühere	He is a **former** student from my school.
	Homecoming *(AE)* [ˈhəʊmˌkʌmɪŋ]	Ehemaligentreffen	The **Homecoming** Dance is always fun.
	dance [dɑːns]	Tanz; Tanzveranstaltung; Ball	**dance** → to dance
	to vote for [ˈvəʊt fə]	abstimmen über; wählen	
p. 32	**to earn** [ɜːn]	verdienen	I have a job and **earn** money.
p. 33	**to present** [prɪˈzent]	präsentieren	He **presented** the information well.
	to report (on) [rɪˈpɔːt (ɒn)]	berichten (über)	They **reported** the storms on the radio.
	to drive [draɪv], **drove** [drəʊv], **driven** [ˈdrɪvn]	fahren; treiben	
	per [pɜː]	pro	I earn $40 **per** week.

chaser ['tʃeɪsə]	Jäger; Jägerin; Verfolger; Verfolgerin	Warren is a storm **chaser**.
direction [dɪ'rekʃn]	Richtung	The wind comes from all **directions**.
cloud [klaʊd]	Wolke	
to tear (up) [teər (ʌp)], **tore (up)** [tɔ:r (ʌp)], **torn (up)** [tɔ:n (ʌp)]	kaputt machen; zerreißen; reißen	The storm **tore up** many houses.

Station 1

At American schools

locker ['lɒkə]	Schließfach; Spind
morning message ['mɔ:nɪŋ ˌmesɪdʒ]	morgendliche Ansprache
principal *(AE)* ['prɪnsɪpl]	Schulleiter; Schulleiterin
pledge of allegiance [ˌpledʒ‿əv‿ə'li:dʒns]	Treueeid
pledge [pledʒ]	Versprechen
class [klɑ:s]	Unterrichtsstunde; Kurs
freshman *(AE)* ['freʃmən]	Neuntklässler; Neuntklässlerin
Math *(AE)* [mæθ]	Mathematik; Mathe
elective [ɪ'lektɪv]	Wahlfach
study hall period ['stʌdi hɔ:l ˌpɪəriəd]	Freistunde
hall [hɔ:l]	Flur; Korridor; Diele
pass [pɑ:s]	Ausweis; Pass
extracurricular [ˌekstrəkə'rɪkjələ]	außerhalb des Lehrplans; außerunterrichtlich *(Zusatzunterricht)*
cheerleader ['tʃɪəˌli:də]	Cheerleader *(Mädchen, das in einer Gruppe eine Sportmannschaft anfeuert)*
cheerleading ['tʃɪəˌli:dɪŋ]	Cheerleading *(Aktivitäten der Cheerleader)*
detention [dɪ'tenʃn]	Nachsitzen
campus ['kæmpəs]	Campus; Schulgelände
core subject [ˌkɔ: 'sʌbdʒɪkt]	Pflichtfach
vacation *(AE)* [və'keɪʃn]	Ferien; Urlaub
recess *(AE)* ['ri:ses]	Pause
dress code ['dres ˌkəʊd]	Kleiderordnung; Bekleidungsvorschriften

p. 34	**exchange** [ɪks'tʃeɪndʒ]	Austausch	Luise did a student **exchange** in the USA.
	to be stuck [bi: 'stʌk]	festsitzen; feststecken; nicht weg können; hängen bleiben	The sheep **is stuck** in the mud.
	nowhere ['nəʊweə]	nirgendwo; nirgendwohin	We live in the middle of **nowhere**.
	(a) couple of [ə 'kʌpl‿əv]	(ein) paar	I missed home in the first **couple of** days.
	familiar [fə'mɪliə]	vertraut; bekannt	Everything was so **familiar**.

to **be allowed to (do sth)** [bi: ə'laʊd tə]	(etw.) dürfen	We **were allowed to** talk in class.
to **keep** [ki:p], **kept** [kept], **kept** [kept]	aufbewahren; behalten	You can't **keep** things in the classroom.
stuff [stʌf]	Zeug	No **stuff** was allowed in the classroom.
instead [ɪn'sted]	stattdessen	I don't like ham, let's have cheese **instead**.
a while [ə 'waɪl]	eine Weile	It took **a while** to get used to things.
to **be able to (do sth)** [bi: 'eɪbl tə]	(zu etw.) fähig sein; (etw.) können; (etw.) dürfen	I **was able to** find my own way.
to **promise** ['prɒmɪs]	versprechen	I **promise** to work hard at school.
true [tru:]	*hier:* treu	The students are **true** to the US.
pretty ['prɪti]	ziemlich; ganz schön	AE: **pretty** BE: really
astronomy [ə'strɒnəmi]	Astronomie	R астрономия T astronomi
journalism ['dʒɜ:nlɪzm]	Journalistik; Journalismus	R журналистика
option ['ɒpʃn]	Möglichkeit; Option; Wahl	There are many **options** to choose from.
to **study** ['stʌdi]	studieren; lernen	You can **study** or do your homework here.
strict [strɪkt]	streng; strikt	The school rules are very **strict**.
bathroom *(AE)* ['bɑ:θrʊm]	Toilette; Bad(ezimmer)	AE: **bathroom** BE: toilet
for example [fər ɪg'zɑ:mpl]	zum Beispiel	I like fruit, **for example** apples.
to **end** [end]	enden; beenden; aufhören	Classes **ended** at 3:30 p.m.
competition [ˌkɒmpə'tɪʃn]	Konkurrenz	There was lots of **competition** for places.
squad [skwɒd]	Gruppe; Team; Mannschaft	**squad** = team
awesome ['ɔ:səm]	super; spitze	**awesome** = amazing, great
host family ['həʊst ˌfæmli]	Gastfamilie	I really liked my **host family**.
so that [səʊ 'ðæt]	damit; so dass	I went to the coast, **so that** I could see the sea.
blast [blɑ:st]	*hier:* Wahnsinnsspaß	My exchange year was a **blast**.
p. 36 to **stay up** [steɪ 'ʌp]	aufbleiben	I **stayed up** late last night.

Station 2

Describing people

helpful ['helpfl]	hilfsbereit	**disorganized** [ˌdɪs'ɔ:gənaɪzd]	unorganisiert; ungeordnet
cooperative [kəʊ'ɒprətɪv]	kooperativ; hilfsbereit	**generous** ['dʒenrəs]	großzügig
responsible [rɪs'pɒnsəbl]	verantwortlich; verantwortungsvoll	**rude** [ru:d]	unhöflich; unverschämt
bossy ['bɒsi]	rechthaberisch	**stubborn** ['stʌbən]	eigensinnig; störrisch
unmotivated [ˌʌn'məʊtɪveɪtɪd]	unmotiviert	**selfish** ['selfɪʃ]	selbstsüchtig
lazy ['leɪzi]	faul	**willing** ['wɪlɪŋ]	bereitwillig
hard-working [ˌhɑ:d'wɜ:kɪŋ]	fleißig	**shy** [ʃaɪ]	schüchtern

p. 38	**lesson** ['lesn]	Lektion; Lehre	A **lesson** outside school is different.
	outside [ˌaʊt'saɪd]	außerhalb	Extracurricular activites are **outside** school.
	year-old [ˌjɪər‿'əʊld]	jährig; Jahre alt	My sister is 16. I've got a 16-**year-old** sister.
	badly ['bædli]	dringend	Michael **badly** needed money.
	allowance *(AE)* [ə'laʊəns]	Taschengeld; Unterhaltsgeld	AE: **allowance** BE: pocket money
	just [dʒʌst]	einfach	My allowance **just** wasn't enough.
	driver's license *(AE)* ['draɪvəz ˌlaɪsns]	Führerschein	AE: **driver's license** BE: driving licence
	girlfriend ['gɜ:lfrend]	Freundin *(in einer Paarbeziehung)*	Sarah is Michael's **girlfriend**.
	ad(vert) (= advertisement) ['æd(vɜ:t) (əd'vɜ:tɪsmənt)]	Annonce	I saw an **advert** for a student job.
	job title ['dʒɒb ˌtaɪtl]	Stellenbezeichnung; Berufsbezeichnung	What is the **job title** of your new job?
	sales associate *(AE)* [ˌseɪlz ə'səʊʃiət]	Verkäufer; Verkäuferin	AE: **sales associate** BE: sales assistant
	education [ˌedʒʊ'keɪʃn]	Ausbildung; Erziehung; Bildung	My **education** was at the local school.
	to waste [weɪst]	verschwenden	Michael didn't **waste** any time.
	to apply (for) [ə'plaɪ (fə)]	sich bewerben (für/um)	He **applied for** the student job.
	interview ['ɪntəvju:]	Vorstellungsgespräch	He had an **interview** on Thursday.
	manager ['mænɪdʒə]	Manager; Managerin; Geschäftsführer; Geschäftsführerin	R менеджер
	tricky ['trɪki]	schwierig; knifflig	**tricky** = hard
	to react [ri'ækt]	reagieren	Sometimes I don't know how to **react**.

	to steal [sti:l], **stole** [stəʊl], **stolen** ['stəʊlən]	stehlen	I saw the boy **steal** a T-shirt.
	luckily ['lʌkɪli]	glücklicherweise	**Luckily** I wasn't late.
	to offer ['ɒfə]	anbieten; bieten	The manager **offered** Michael the job.
	minimum ['mɪnɪməm]	Minimum; minimal; Mindest-	T minimum
	wage [weɪdʒ]	Lohn	He earned the minimum **wage**.
	staff *(no pl)* [stɑ:f]	Personal; Belegschaft; Kollegium	All the **staff** were really nice.
	co-worker ['kəʊˌwɜ:kə]	Arbeitskollege; Arbeitskollegin	My **co-workers** are friendly.
	to fold [fəʊld]	falten; klappen	Michael **folded** trousers all day.
	pants *(pl) (AE)* [pænts]	Hose	AE: **pants** BE: trousers
	twice [twaɪs]	zweimal; doppelt	**twice** = two times
	to dust [dʌst]	abstauben; Staub wischen	He cleaned and **dusted** the shelves.
	to sort [sɔ:t]	sortieren	He **sorted** the colourful T-shirts.
	to tease [ti:z]	hänseln; sticheln; reizen	People came in and **teased** Michael.
	lame [leɪm]	lahm; schwach	People said, "Your job is **lame**."
	such [sʌtʃ]	solch	It was **such** a nice day.
	pinhead ['pɪnhed]	Trottel	Michael thought they were **pinheads**.
	to throw [θrəʊ], **threw** [θru:], **thrown** [θrəʊn]	werfen	He **threw** them out of the store.
	reaction [ri'ækʃn]	Reaktion	**reaction** → to react
	behavior *(AE)* [bɪ'heɪvjə]	Verhalten	AE: **behavior** BE: behaviour
	to behave [bɪ'heɪv]	sich benehmen; sich verhalten	**to behave** → behaviour
	working hours *(pl)* ['wɜ:kɪŋ ˌaʊəz]	Arbeitszeit	9:00 to 5:00 are my **working hours**.
	pay [peɪ]	Bezahlung; Lohn; Gehalt	**pay** = wage
p. 39	**bonus** ['bəʊnəs]	Bonus; Prämie	I worked hard and got a **bonus**.
	strength [streŋθ]	Stärke; Kraft	I made a list of my **strengths**.
	weakness ['wi:knəs]	Schwäche	**weakness** ↔ strength
p. 40	**to leave** [li:v]	gehen	I had to **leave** early on Monday.
p. 41	**restroom** *(AE)* ['restrʊm]	Toilette	AE: **restroom** BE: toilet
	broken ['brəʊkn]	gebrochen; kaputt	My sunglasses are **broken**.
	pair [peə]	Paar	Do you like my new **pair** of trainers?
	dog walker ['dɒg ˌwɔ:kə]	Hundeausführer; Hundeausführerin	a person who takes dogs for a walk
	paperboy ['peɪpəˌbɔɪ]	Zeitungsausträger	I'm Dave, I'm a **paperboy**.

	papergirl ['peɪpəˌgɜ:l]	Zeitungsausträgerin	A paperboy or **papergirl** works every day.
	babysitter ['beɪbɪˌsɪtə]	Babysitter; Babysitterin	a person who looks after children
	to take care of sb [ˌteɪk 'keər‿əv]	sich um jmdn. kümmern; für jmdn. sorgen	I **take care** of my neighbour's kids.
	mostly ['məʊstli]	meistens; hauptsächlich	I work **mostly** in the evenings.

Reading corner

p. 42	**date** [deɪt]	Verabredung; Date	They went on their first **date**.
	to ask sb out [ˌɑ:sk … 'aʊt]	sich mit jmdm. verabreden	Dylan **asked Abby out** on a date.
	boyfriend ['bɔɪfrend]	Freund *(in einer Paarbeziehung)*	**boyfriend** ↔ girlfriend
	to fall out of [ˌfɔ:l 'aʊt‿əv]	herausfallen aus	All my books **fell out of** my locker.
	right [raɪt]	gerade; genau; in dem Moment als	It happened **right** when he walked past.
	to show up [ˌʃəʊ‿'ʌp]	auftauchen; erscheinen	He **showed up** late for school.
	in tow [ɪn 'təʊ]	im Schlepptau	Abby had Scott **in tow**, of course.
	embarrassing [ɪm'bærəsɪŋ]	peinlich	It was so **embarrassing**, I went red.
	guy [gaɪ]	Typ; Kerl	Who is the **guy** in the hall?
	gym(nasium) [dʒɪm (dʒɪm'neɪziəm)]	Turnhalle	the room in a school where PE lessons are
	to attack [ə'tæk]	angreifen	The boys **attacked** him in the gym.
p. 43	**to pick up** [ˌpɪk‿'ʌp]	abholen	Dylan **picked** Abby **up** at seven o'clock.
	everybody ['evriˌbɒdi]	jeder; alle	**everybody** = everyone
	dancing ['dɑ:nsɪŋ]	Tanzen; Tanz-	T dans

Film corner

p. 45	**buddy** *(infml)* ['bʌdi]	Kumpel	David is my best **buddy**.
	homeroom ['həʊmru:m]	erste Stunde *(in der Schule)*	We are in the same **homeroom**.

Checkpoint

atmosphere ['ætməsfɪə]	Atmosphäre; Stimmung	**to interest** ['ɪntrəst]	interessieren
relationship [rɪ'leɪʃnʃɪp]	Beziehung	**field trip** ['fi:ld ˌtrɪp]	Schulausflug

Presentation skills

p. 51	**presentation** [ˌprezn'teɪʃn]	Präsentation; Vortrag	My **presentation** is about cats.
	topic ['tɒpɪk]	Thema	My next **topic** is the rules of the game.
	second ['seknd]	zweitens	**Second**, the cats are loud.

V

Word bank: Comparing schools

dress code

cheerleading

marching band

pledge of allegiance

school bus

locker

Homecoming Dance

schedule

grade

hall pass

class

I would like to compare …
In/At American high schools …
In/At German schools …
Both countries have detention/principals/…

In America there is … but not in Germany.
… is the same.
… is different.

Word bank: Jobs

waitress

waiter

serve ice cream

work on a market stall

shop assistant

wash up in a café/ restaurant

babysitter

dog walker

paperboy/girl

help in the garden/ mow the lawn

do the shopping for people

I earn …
I work inside/outside.
I work every day/at the weekends/in the holidays/on …
I work in the mornings/afternoons/evenings.
I start work at …

I like it/don't like it because …
I'm a … person.
It's hard/easy work.
It's fun/boring.
I work with nice/interesting/fun/strange/ quiet/… people.

Unit 3 In the Northeast

Way in

p. 52	**to stretch** [stretʃ]	sich strecken; erstrecken; dehnen	The land **stretches** into the distance.
	whale watching ['weɪl ˌwɒtʃɪŋ]	Walbeobachtung	Let's go **whale watching** in the Northeast.
	lobster ['lɒbstə]	Hummer	
	leaf *(sg)* [li:f], **leaves** *(pl)* [li:vz]	Blatt	one **leaf** → two leaves 
	member ['membə]	Mitglied	The **members** of my family live together.
	apart [ə'pɑ:t]	auseinander; entfernt	They don't work miles **apart**.
	to get together [ˌge‿tə'gəðə]	zusammenkommen; zusammenfinden	We like to **get together** for birthdays.
	celebration [ˌselə'breɪʃn]	Feier	**celebration** → to celebrate
p. 53	**Thanksgiving** [ˌθæŋks'gɪvɪŋ]	Erntedankfest	**Thanksgiving** is the 4th Thursday in November.
	turkey ['tɜ:ki]	Truthahn; Pute	
	dinner ['dɪnə]	Essen	meals: breakfast, lunch, **dinner**
	president ['prezɪdnt]	Präsident; Präsidentin	[R] президент
	to pardon ['pɑ:dn]	begnadigen; entschuldigen; verzeihen	The President **pardons** a turkey.
	creepy ['kri:pi]	gruselig	**Creepy** films are often made in Maine.
	novel ['nɒvl]	Roman	I have to read this **novel** for school.
	forest ['fɒrɪst]	Wald	
	few [fju:]	wenige	**few** people = not many people
	mystery story ['mɪstri ˌstɔ:ri]	Krimi (= Kriminalgeschichte); Detektivgeschichte	Maine is very popular for **mystery stories**.
	land of the free [ˌlænd‿əv ðə 'fri:]	Land der Freien	The USA is called the **land of the free**.
	control [kən'trəʊl]	Kontrolle; Steuerung	[R] контроль
	the Amish [ði 'ɑ:mɪʃ]	die Amischen	**The Amish** don't have mobile phones.
	Christian ['krɪstʃn]	christlich	[T] Hıristiyan
	barrel ['bærl]	Fass; Tonne	
	stuntman ['stʌntmæn]	Stuntman	**Stuntmen** work in films.
	daredevil ['deəˌdevl]	Draufgänger; Draufgängerin	The **daredevil** did dangerous tricks.

amazed [ə'meɪzd]	erstaunt; verblüfft	**amazed** → amazing
to **sign autographs** [ˌsaɪn 'ɔ:təgra:fs]	Autogramme geben	The actor **signed autographs** for us.

Station 1

Small talk

What's up? [ˌwɒts‿'ʌp]	Wie geht's?	**What have you been up to?** [ˌwɒt‿əv ju: bi:n 'ʌp tə]	Was hast du (in letzter Zeit) gemacht?; Wie läuft's bei dir?
How's it going? [ˌhaʊz‿ɪt 'gəʊɪŋ]	Wie geht's?; Wie läuft's?		
How are you doing? [ˌhaʊ‿ə jə 'du:ɪŋ]	Wie geht's dir?		

p. 54	to **get ready** [ˌget 'redi]	sich vorbereiten; sich fertig machen	We have to **get ready** for the party.
	husband ['hʌzbənd]	Ehemann	**husband** ↔ wife
	teenage ['ti:neɪdʒ]	jugendlich	**teenage** → teenager
	to **get stuck** [ˌget 'stʌk]	stecken bleiben	I **got stuck** in my car for two hours.
	doorbell ['dɔ:bel]	Türklingel	
	elderly ['eldəli]	älter	I have **elderly** grandparents.
	neighbor *(AE)* ['neɪbə]	Nachbar; Nachbarin	AE: **neighbor** BE: neighbour
	freezing ['fri:zɪŋ]	eiskalt; gefrierend	Come in, it's **freezing** outside.
	glad [glæd]	froh	We were **glad** you liked the flowers.
	to **make it** ['meɪk‿ɪt]	es schaffen	I'm glad you could **make it**.
	to **enter** ['entə]	hineingehen; hereinkommen; betreten; eintreten	**to enter** ↔ to leave
	Have a seat. [ˌhæv‿ə 'si:t]	Setzen Sie sich.; Setz dich.	Come in. **Have a seat.**
	original [ə'rɪdʒnl]	original; ursprünglich	R оригинал T orijinal
	across [ə'krɒs]	hinüber; herüber; quer durch	We went **across** the river in a boat.
	a little something [ə ˌlɪtl 'sʌmθɪŋ]	eine Kleinigkeit	I have brought you **a little something**.
	chocolate ['tʃɒklət]	Praline	T çikolata 
	video ['vɪdiəʊ]	Video	I'm making a **video** of Thanksgiving.
	thankful ['θæŋkfl]	dankbar	**thankful** → Thank you.
	engine ['endʒɪn]	Motor	Cars don't work without an **engine**.

	to land [lænd]	landen	Our plane **lands** at seven o'clock.
	to save [seɪv]	aufheben	We will **save** you some turkey.
p. 57	**bored** [bɔ:d]	gelangweilt	I was so **bored** in Math today.
	stress [stres]	Stress	Phew, I had so much **stress** today.

Station 2

Agreeing and disagreeing

Exactly. [ɪg'zæktli]	Genau.	I'm convinced that … [ˌaɪm kən'vɪnst ðət]	Ich bin überzeugt, dass …
Absolutely not. [ˌæbsə'lu:tli nɒt]	Ganz und gar nicht.; Auf keinen Fall!	It's clear to me that … [ɪts 'klɪə tə ˌmi: ðæt]	Mir ist klar, dass …
As far as I know, … [ˌəz 'fɑ:r‿əz‿aɪ nəʊ]	Soweit ich weiß, …	I doubt that … [aɪ 'daʊt ˌðæt]	Ich bezweifle, dass …
I guess … [aɪ 'ges]	Ich nehme an, dass …		

Devices

device [dɪ'vaɪs]	Gerät; Vorrichtung	**hair straightener** ['heə ˌstreɪtnə]	Haarglätter
tablet ['tæblət]	Tablet	fan [fæn]	Ventilator
dryer ['draɪə]	Wäschetrockner	dishwasher ['dɪʃˌwɒʃə]	Spülmaschine
microwave ['maɪkrəweɪv]	Mikrowelle	vacuum cleaner ['vækju:m ˌkli:nə]	Staubsauger
headphones *(pl)* ['hedfəʊnz]	Kopfhörer	razor ['reɪzə]	Rasierer; Rasierapparat
cell phone *(AE)* ['sel fəʊn]	Mobiltelefon; Handy	radiator ['reɪdieɪtə]	Heizkörper

p. 58	**Amish** ['ɑ:mɪʃ]	amisch	We live in an **Amish** community.
	to lead [li:d], **led** [led], **led** [led]	führen; anführen	We **lead** a simple life.
	to concentrate ['kɒnsntreɪt]	(sich) konzentrieren	This is hard. I have to **concentrate**.
	to cover ['kʌvə]	bedecken; abdecken	Amish girls often **cover** their hair.
	make-up ['meɪkʌp]	Make-up; Schminke	T makyaj
	to grow [grəʊ], **grew** [gru:], **grown** [grəʊn]	anbauen; züchten; ziehen; wachsen	We **grow** our own vegetables.
	to care about [ˌkeər‿ə'baʊt]	wichtig nehmen; sich kümmern um; sich interessieren für	If you **care about** sth, it's important to you.

	outside world [ˌaʊtsaɪd ˈwɜːld]	Außenwelt	I don't work in the **outside world**.
	forbidden [fəˈbɪdn]	verboten	I never do **forbidden** things. 
	alcohol *(no pl)* [ˈælkəhɒl]	Alkohol	R алкоголь T alkol
	to **regret** [rɪˈgret]	bedauern	I'm sure I won't **regret** my decision.
	to **guess** [ges]	vermuten; schätzen	I **guess** my parents are proud of me.
	average [ˈævrɪdʒ]	durchschnittlich	I'm an **average** American teenager.
	fashion *(no pl)* [ˈfæʃn]	Mode	I love clothes and the newest **fashion**.
	gossip [ˈgɒsɪp]	Klatsch; Tratsch; Gerede	I read the **gossip** about the stars too.
	to **iron** [aɪən]	bügeln	I don't wear clothes that I haven't **ironed**.
	alright [ɔːlˈraɪt]	okay	**alright** = OK
	to **hang out (with)** [ˌhæŋ‿ˈaʊt (wɪð)]	rumhängen (mit); sich treffen (mit); sich herumtreiben (mit)	I **hang out with** my friends after school. 
	bowling [ˈbəʊlɪŋ]	Bowlen	R боулинг T bowling
	the movies *(AE)* [ðə ˈmuːviz]	Kino	AE: **the movies** BE: cinema
p. 59	**electric** [ɪˈlektrɪk]	elektrisch	T elektrik
p. 61	**superhero** [ˈsuːpəˌhɪərəʊ] *(sg)*, **superheroes** [ˈsuːpəˌhɪərəʊz] *(pl)*	Superheld	Spiderman is a **superhero**.
	before [bɪˈfɔː]	vor	**before** ↔ after
	all in all [ˌɔːl‿ɪn ˈɔːl]	alles in allem; insgesamt	**All in all** I'm happy with my life.

Reading corner

p. 62	**body** [ˈbɒdi]	Leiche	There was a man's **body** on the beach.
	to **learn** [lɜːn]	erfahren; herausfinden	They **learned** that a boy had died.
	to **disappear** [ˌdɪsəˈpɪə]	verschwinden	The man **disappeared** two weeks ago.
	gun [gʌn]	Schusswaffe	He had a **gun** in his hand.
	thought [θɔːt]	Gedanke	The **thought** of dinner made me happy.
	to **roll up** [ˌrəʊl‿ˈʌp]	zusammenrollen; aufrollen; aufkrempeln	We **rolled up** our clothes.
	blanket [ˈblæŋkɪt]	Decke; Bettdecke; Wolldecke	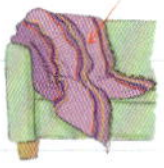
	to **tie** [taɪ]	binden; zubinden; fesseln	Be careful! **Tie** your shoes right.
	belt [belt]	Gürtel	
	back [bæk]	Hinter-	We went in the **back** door.

V

to avoid [ə'vɔɪd]	vermeiden; meiden; aus dem Weg gehen; ausweichen	We have to **avoid** the teachers.
towards [tə'wɔ:dz]	in Richtung; auf … zu	We were walking **towards** the station.
clubhouse ['klʌbhaʊs]	Klubhaus; Vereinsheim	We meet at the **clubhouse** on Tuesdays.
to catch up with [kætʃ‿'ʌp wɪð]	einholen	I was slow so they **caught up with** me.
at the bottom [æt ðə 'bɒtəm]	ganz am Ende	He stopped **at the bottom** of the alley.
trash *(AE)* [træʃ]	Abfall; Müll	AE: **trash** BE: rubbish
to puke [pju:k]	erbrechen; sich übergeben	**to puke** = to be sick
into ['ɪntu]	in; hinein	He put his hand **into** the bag.
backpack ['bækpæk]	Rucksack	
desk [desk]	Schreibtisch	
wine [waɪn]	Wein	
… to keep them drunk [tə ˌki:p ðəm 'drʌŋk]	… dass sie betrunken bleiben	They have enough **to keep them drunk.**
beer [bɪə]	Bier	
p. 63 bullet ['bʊlɪt]	Kugel; Geschoss	There are no **bullets** in the gun.
to shoot (at) [ʃu:t (ət)], **shot (at)** [ʃɒt (ət)], **shot (at)** [ʃɒt (ət)]	schießen (auf)	He **shot at** the bottles on the wall.
sat [sæt]	simple past, past participle von *to sit* (sitzen)	I **sat** = ich saß/ich habe gesessen
tin [tɪn]	Dose; Büchse; *hier:* Mülleimer	
smelly [smeli]	stinkend; übelriechend	There was **smelly** trash in it.
to spill [spɪl], spilt [spɪlt], spilt [spɪlt]	auslaufen; verschütten	I **spilt** the milk, sorry.
to squeeze [skwi:z]	drücken; pressen; quetschen	She took my hand and **squeezed** it.
to jump [dʒʌmp]	springen	
wrist [rɪst]	Handgelenk	It is between your hand and your arm.
evil ['i:vl]	böse; schlecht	**evil** ↔ nice
magician [mə'dʒɪʃn]	Zauberer; Zauberin; Magier; Magierin	
amused [ə'mju:zd]	amüsiert; vergnügt	Was Chris **amused** or scared?
to shut up [ʃʌt‿'ʌp]	die Klappe halten	**Shut up** and listen to me!
by [baɪ]	an	He grabbed me **by** the shirt.
to reach [ri:tʃ]	erreichen	We **reached** the station at two o'clock.

to slow to a walk [ˌsləʊ tʊ‿ə 'wɔ:k]	in Schritttempo verfallen	We were early and **slowed to a walk**.
it's a pity [ˌɪts‿ə 'pɪti]	(es ist) schade	**It's a pity** it rained.
face [feɪs]	Gesicht	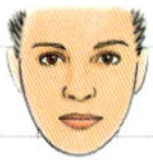
mean [mi:n]	gemein	Chris did a **mean** trick.
honestly ['ɒnɪstli]	ehrlich	**Honestly**, I didn't know it was broken.
innocent ['ɪnəsnt]	unschuldig	He didn't do it, he is **innocent**.
laugh [lɑ:f]	Lachen	**laugh** → to laugh
might [maɪt]	könnten	We **might** see a wild animal.
frightening ['fraɪtnɪŋ]	furchterregend	The forest is **frightening** at night.
p. 64 to **put up** [ˌpʊt‿'ʌp]	aufstellen; errichten	We **put** the pictures **up** next to each other.
to **turn on** [ˌtɜ:n‿'ɒn]	einschalten	It was dark and I **turned on** the lamp.
to slap [slæp]	einen Klaps geben; schlagen	He **slapped** me hard and it hurt.
back [bæk]	Rücken; Rückseite	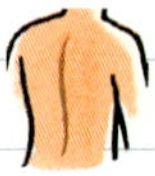
to **grin** [grɪn]	grinsen	He **grinned** from ear to ear.
nearly ['nɪəli]	fast; beinahe; annähernd	**nearly** = almost
to **stand up** [stænd‿'ʌp]	aufstehen	He **stood up** and left the room.
to gather ['gæðə]	(sich) sammeln	We **gathered** round him and listened.
railway track ['reɪlweɪ ˌtræk]	Gleis	We went across the bridge on the **railway tracks**.

Film corner

p. 67 **pecan** ['pi:kæn]	Pekannuss	**Pecan** pie is my favourite pie.
pardon ['pɑ:dn]	Begnadigung; Entschuldigung; Verzeihung	The President's **pardon** is for a turkey.

Checkpoint

to **control** [kən'trəʊl]	kontrollieren	**annoying** [ə'nɔɪɪŋ]	ärgerlich; lästig
out [aʊt]	aus; draußen; außerhalb		

Writing skills

p. 73 to **deal (with)** [di:l (wɪð)], **dealt (with)** [delt (wɪð)], **dealt (with)** [delt (wɪð)]	sich befassen (mit); umgehen (mit)	The text **deals with** the culture.
to **sum up** [ˌsʌm‿'ʌp]	zusammenfassen	To **sum up** you can say this food is better.
in general [ɪn 'dʒenrl]	allgemein; generell	**In general** the news is good.

Word bank: **Giving opinions**

I agree with the statement …

I agree with you.

I think you're right (there).

That's true.

I think so because …

In my opinion …

I think …

I also think that … because …

So my answer is …

I tried it when I was …

One reason is …

Another reason is …

To conclude I would like to say …

It had an impact on my life because …

I don't agree/disagree with the statement …

I don't agree/disagree with you.

That's false.

I don't think so because …

In my opinion …

I think …

You can't be serious!

I think you're wrong (there).

I tried it when I was …

Another reason is …

One reason is …

To conclude I would like to say …

It had an impact/influence on my life because …

Unit 4 California dreams

Way in

p. 74	**dense** [dens]	dicht	The forest was **dense** with trees.
	populated ['pɒpjəleɪtɪd]	bevölkert; besiedelt	**populated** → population
	redwood (tree) ['redwʊd (triː)]	Mammutbaum	
	relaxed [rɪ'lækst]	entspannt; locker; gelassen	People are very **relaxed** in California.
	lifestyle ['laɪfstaɪl]	Lebensart; Lifestyle	the way you live your life
	volleyball ['vɒlibɔːl]	Volleyball	[R] волейбол [T] voleybol
	to take a ride [ˌteɪk‿ə 'raɪd]	fahren	We **took a ride** on a bus.
	old-fashioned [ˌəʊld'fæʃnd]	altmodisch	The houses here are **old-fashioned**.
	cable car ['keɪbl ˌkɑː]	Seilbahn	
	hill [hɪl]	Berg; Hügel	
	Asia ['eɪʒə]	Asien	[R] азия [T] Asya
p. 75	**golden** ['gəʊldn]	golden; Gold-	California is called 'The **Golden** State'.
	number ['nʌmbə]	Anzahl	There are a **number** of big museums.
	high-tech [ˌhaɪ'tek]	Hightech-	I work for a **high-tech** company.
	to settle ['setl]	besiedeln; sich niederlassen	We moved from NYC and **settled** here.
	glamor *(AE) (no pl)* ['glæmə]	Glanz; Zauber	Hollywood means **glamor** to me.
	excitement [ɪk'saɪtmənt]	Aufregung	The **excitement** at the show was huge.
	show-business ['ʃəʊˌbɪznɪs]	Showbusiness; Showgeschäft; Unterhaltungsindustrie	[R] шоу-бизнес
	studio ['stjuːdiəʊ]	Studio	They make movies in **studios**.
	length *(no pl)* [leŋθ]	Länge; Dauer	**length** → long
	to paint [peɪnt]	streichen; anmalen; malen	
	bay [beɪ]	Bucht	
	architect ['ɑːkɪtekt]	Architekt; Architektin	[R] архитектор
	safety net ['seɪfti ˌnet]	Sicherheitsnetz	There's a **safety net** to catch you.
	fog [fɒg]	Nebel	
	to rust [rʌst]	rosten	The bridge **rusted** very quickly.
	lane [leɪn]	Fahrspur; Weg; Gasse	There are four **lanes** of cars on the bridge.

Station 1

Adjectives for ads

catchy ['kætʃi]	eingängig; einprägsam	**unappealing** [ˌʌnə'pi:lɪŋ]	uninteressant
informative [ɪn'fɔ:mətɪv]	informativ	**fascinating** ['fæsɪneɪtɪŋ]	faszinierend
clear [klɪə]	klar; eindeutig; deutlich	**pointless** ['pɔɪntləs]	sinnlos
appealing [ə'pi:lɪŋ]	ansprechend	**unusual** [ʌn'ju:ʒl]	ungewöhnlich; außergewöhnlich
		dull [dʌl]	langweilig

p. 76	to **chill out** [ˌtʃɪlˌ'aʊt]	chillen; sich entspannen	**Chill out** in sunny California.
	reservation [ˌrezə'veɪʃn]	Reservierung	T rezervasyon
	to **book** [bʊk]	buchen; reservieren	We booked our **flights** yesterday.
	lifetime ['laɪftaɪm]	Leben; Lebenszeit	It will be the holiday of a **lifetime**.
	tour [tʊə]	Tour; Fahrt; Reise	We went on the Grand Canyon **tour**.
	to **stroll** [strəʊl]	schlendern; bummeln	We **strolled** along the beach in the sun.
	ancient ['eɪnʃnt]	alt; altertümlich	**ancient** = very old
	earth [ɜ:θ]	die Erde; Boden; Erde; Erdboden	
p. 77	**layout** ['leɪaʊt]	Layout; Anordnung	Look at the **layout** of this ad.
	design [dɪ'zaɪn]	Design; Gestaltung	I like the **design** of this one.
	headline ['hedlaɪn]	Überschrift; Schlagzeile	We need a good **headline** for our ad.
	slogan ['sləʊgən]	Slogan; Werbespruch	We thought of a catchy **slogan** too.
	expert ['ekspɜ:t]	Experte; Expertin	R эксперт
p. 78	**climbing** ['klaɪmɪŋ]	Kletter-	Always wear a good **climbing** helmet.
	swimmer ['swɪmə]	Schwimmer; Schwimmerin	**swimmer** → to swim
p. 79	**helicopter** ['helɪkɒptə]	Helikopter; Hubschrauber	T helikopter 
	experience [ɪk'spɪəriəns]	Erfahrung; Erlebnis	It was a fantastic **experience**. 
	pilot ['paɪlət]	Pilot; Pilotin	
	to **last** [lɑ:st]	dauern; andauern; anhalten	The tour **lasted** three hours.

Station 2

Social media

social media [ˌsəʊʃl ˈmiːdiə]	soziale Medien	**post** [pəʊst]	Post *(online gestellte Nachricht)*
site [saɪt]	*hier:* Seite *(im Internet)*	**blogger** [ˈblɒgə]	Blogger; Bloggerin
		to **dislike** [dɪˈslaɪk]	nicht mögen
account [əˈkaʊnt]	Konto	**request** [rɪˈkwest]	Anfrage
to **post** [pəʊst]	online stellen; posten	to **friend** [frend]	befreunden *(jmdn. zu seiner Freundesliste hinzufügen)*
pic (picture) [pɪk]	Foto		
clip [klɪp]	Clip; Ausschnitt; Kurzfilm		
tutorial [tjuːˈtɔːriəl]	Anleitung; Tutorial	to **unfriend** [ʌnˈfrend]	entfreunden *(jmdn. von seiner Freundesliste streichen)*
to **stream** [striːm]	*hier:* streamen *(im Internet)*		
mobile [ˈməʊbaɪl]	mobil; tragbar; beweglich	**follower** [ˈfɒləʊə]	Follower; Followerin; Anhänger; Anhängerin
smartphone [ˈsmɑːtˌfəʊn]	Smartphone	to **subscribe** [səbˈskraɪb]	abonnieren
		trending [ˈtrendɪŋ]	trendsetzend
cyberbullying [ˈsaɪbəˌbʊliɪŋ]	Cyber-Mobbing	to **update** [ˈʌpdeɪt]	updaten; auf den neuesten Stand bringen
comment [ˈkɒment]	Kommentar	**status** [ˈsteɪtəs]	Status
link [lɪŋk]	Link	**selfie** [ˈselfi]	Selfie *(Schnappschuss von sich selbst)*

p. 80	to **welcome** [ˈwelkəm]	begrüßen; willkommen heißen	California **welcomes** new ideas.
	innovation [ˌɪnəˈveɪʃn]	Innovation; Neuheit	Achtung Aussprache!
	gaming [ˈgeɪmɪŋ]	Computerspiele-	The **gaming** industry is huge.
	to **be around** [biː əˈraʊnd]	geben; existieren	The WWW has **been around** for 30 years.
	for [fɔː]	seit	I have lived here **for** two months.
	trend [trend]	Trend; Entwicklung; Richtung	There are always new **trends** to follow.
	since [sɪns]	seit; seitdem	I have lived here **since** March.
	to **deserve** [dɪˈzɜːv]	verdienen	He did well, he **deserves** a prize.
	extremely [ɪkˈstriːmli]	äußerst; sehr	Climbing is **extremely** popular.
	impact [ˈɪmpækt]	Einfluss; Auswirkung	Social media had a big **impact** on us.
	basically [ˈbeɪsɪkli]	eigentlich; grundsätzlich; im Grunde genommen	**Basically**, I think it's a good idea.
	ton [tʌn]	Tonne *(Gewicht)*	There is **tons** of information to look at.

	favorite *(AE)* ['feɪvrɪt]	Lieblings-	AE: **favorite** BE: favourite
	to **influence** ['ɪnfluəns]	beeinflussen	Social media **influences** our lives.
	to **communicate** [kə'mju:nɪkeɪt]	kommunizieren; sich verständigen	Today we **communicate** differently.
	map [mæp]	Karte; Plan	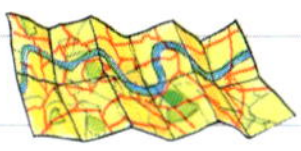
	daily ['deɪli]	täglich	**daily** = every day
	half *(sg)* [hɑ:f], **halves** *(pl)* [hɑ:vz]	(die) Hälfte	**half** a lemon 
	several ['sevrl]	einige; mehrere; verschiedene	**several** = three or more, but not many
	right away [ˌraɪt‿ə'weɪ]	sofort; gleich	I answer my messages **right away**.
p. 81	**outdated** [ˌaʊt'deɪtɪd]	veraltet	Listening to CDs is very **outdated**.
	out of fashion [ˌaʊt‿əv 'fæʃn]	altmodisch; nicht mehr aktuell	**out of fashion** ↔ in fashion
	trendy ['trendi]	trendy; modisch	**trendy** ↔ outdated
	jumping fitness ['dʒʌmpɪŋ ˌfɪtnəs]	Jumping Fitness *(Trendsportart)*	**Jumping fitness** is a new sport.
p. 83	**torn** [tɔ:n]	zerrissen; aufgerissen	The jeans are **torn**. 
	veganism *(no pl)* ['vi:gənɪzm]	Veganismus	T veganizm

Reading corner

p. 84	**gold rush** ['gəʊld ˌrʌʃ]	Goldrausch	Everyone wanted gold in the **gold rush**.
	report [rɪ'pɔ:t]	Bericht	T rapor
	official [ə'fɪʃl]	offiziell	We won the game, it's **official**.
	to **confirm** [kən'fɜ:m]	bestätigen; bekräftigen	Can you **confirm** when you arrive?
	discovery [dɪ'skʌvri]	Entdeckung	I made an awesome **discovery** – gold!
	Swiss [swɪs]	schweizerisch; aus der Schweiz; Schweizer; Schweizerin	He was a **Swiss** immigrant.
	businessman ['bɪznɪsmæn]	Geschäftsmann	R бизнесмен
	farming ['fɑ:mɪŋ]	Landwirtschaft; Ackerbau	He didn't give up his **farming** plans.
	landowner ['lændˌəʊnə]	Grundbesitzer; Grundbesitzerin	He owns the land, he's the **landowner**.
	to **allow** [ə'laʊ]	erlauben; gestatten	He didn't **allow** us to say anything.
	to **prove** [pru:v]	beweisen	He has to **prove** he owns the land.
	at first [ət 'fɜ:st]	zuerst; zunächst	I wasn't happy **at first**, then it was OK.
	simply ['sɪmpli]	*hier:* einfach nur	It was **simply** the best thing to do.

to set off [ˌset‿ˈɒf]	aufbrechen; sich aufmachen; auslösen	We **set off** to the West to find gold.
fever [ˈfiːvə]	Fieber	The gold rush is also called gold **fever**.
to increase [ɪnˈkriːs]	zunehmen; vergrößern	The population has **increased**.
to keep sb informed [ˌkiːp‿ɪnˈfɔːmd]	jmdn. auf dem Laufenden halten	They **kept us informed** about the trip.
edition [ɪˈdɪʃn]	Ausgabe; Auflage; Edition	Find out more in our next **edition**.
p. 85 **hunter** [ˈhʌntə]	Jäger; Jägerin	Lots of gold **hunters** went to California.
beloved [bɪˈlʌvɪd]	geliebt	It's weeks since I left my **beloved** family.
finally [ˈfaɪnli]	endlich; letztlich; zuletzt	**Finally**, I have time to write to you.
to rest [rest]	rasten; ausruhen; liegen	I work so hard and have no time to **rest**.
desperately [ˈdesprətli]	dringend; verzweifelt	I'm **desperately** waiting to go home.
jungle [ˈdʒʌŋgl]	Dschungel	 
to sail [seɪl]	segeln	
spirit [ˈspɪrɪt]	Stimmung; Geist	Our **spirits** were high and we had fun.
to hire [haɪə]	mieten; anheuern; einstellen	We **hired** a car on holiday.
wagon [ˈwægən]	Waggon; Planwagen	The horses pulled the **wagons** for us.
to pass [pɑːs]	vorbeigehen; durchgehen	We **passed** the museum on the tour.
to hang [hæŋ]	*hier:* erhängen	They **hung** the men for stealing.
wilderness [ˈwɪldənəs]	Wildnis	Our camp was in the **wilderness**.
fortune [ˈfɔːtʃuːn]	Vermögen; Reichtum	I dream of making a **fortune**.
to dig [dɪg], dug [dʌg], dug [dʌg]	graben; schürfen	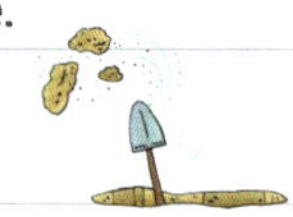
to imagine (sth) [ɪˈmædʒɪn]	sich etw. vorstellen	Can you **imagine** acting in a movie?
shiny [ˈʃaɪni]	glänzend	The gold I found was very **shiny**.
love [lʌv]	Liebe	**love** → to love
to keep going [kiːp ˈgəʊɪŋ]	weitergehen; weitermachen	I will **keep going** until I find more gold.
ice-cold [aɪsˈkəʊld]	eiskalt	The water we worked in was **ice-cold**.
prayer [preə]	Gebet	Say a **prayer** for me on Sunday.
loving [ˈlʌvɪŋ]	liebend; liebevoll	Edward is a **loving** husband.
p. 86 **encyclopedia** [ɪnˌsaɪkləˈpiːdiə]	Enzyklopädie; Lexikon	✎ Achtung Schreibweise! en<u>cy</u>clop<u>e</u>di<u>a</u>
entry [ˈentri]	Eintrag	What does the **entry** for Gold Rush say?
to cause [kɔːz]	verursachen	The driver **caused** the accident.

V

abroad [ə'brɔ:d]	im Ausland; ins Ausland	The problems caused trouble **abroad**.
surface ['sɜ:fɪs]	Oberfläche	The **surface** of the table is white.
to **continue** [kən'tɪnju:]	andauern; weitermachen; fortsetzen	The problems **continued** for years.
non- [nɒn]	nicht-	**non**-native ↔ native
native ['neɪtɪv]	eingeboren; einheimisch	The **native** population was only 20%.
boomtown ['bu:mtaʊn]	Boomtown *(eine Stadt, die sehr schnell wächst)*	It went from a village to a **boomtown**.
to spring up [ˌsprɪŋ‿'ʌp], sprang up [ˌspræŋ‿'ʌp], sprung up [ˌsprʌŋ‿'ʌp]	entstehen; entspringen	During the gold rush many new towns **sprang up**.
transport ['trænspɔ:t]	Verkehrs-	The money helped to build **transport** links.
transcontinental [ˌtrænsˌkɒntɪ'nentl]	transkontinental *(über den Kontinent hinweg)*	**Transcontinental** trains make long journeys.
railway ['reɪlweɪ]	Eisenbahn	
slave [sleɪv]	Sklave; Sklavin	There were **slaves** before the Civil War.
boom years ['bu:m ˌjɪəz]	Blütezeit; fette Jahre *(ugs.)*	The **boom years** didn't last long.
empty ['emti]	leer	**empty** ↔ full
ghost town ['gəʊst ˌtaʊn]	Geisterstadt	The **ghost towns** are empty of people.
to **step** [step]	treten; steigen	We went there and **stepped** back in time.
region ['ri:dʒn]	Region; Gegend	There were ghost towns in the **region**.

Film corner

p. 89	**helper** ['helpə]	Helfer; Helferin	**helper** → to help → help
	as soon as [əz 'su:n‿əz]	sobald	**as soon as** → soon
	regular ['regjələ]	regelmäßig; normal; üblich; gleichmäßig	I work **regular** hours in my job.
	to **respect** [rɪ'spekt]	respektieren	I love and **respect** animals.
	to **care (for)** ['keə (fɔ:)]	sich kümmern (um)	He **cares for** old people.
	energetic [ˌenə'dʒetɪk]	tatkräftig	I am **energetic** and fit for the job.
	practical ['præktɪkl]	praktisch	I like making things, I'm **practical**.
	attitude ['ætɪtju:d]	Einstellung; Haltung	I have a practical **attitude** to work.
	waitress ['weɪtrəs]	Kellnerin; Bedienung	She is a **waitress** in the new café.
	groceries *(pl)* ['grəʊsriz]	Lebensmittel	We buy our **groceries** at the supermarket.

Checkpoint

technology [tek'nɒlədʒi]	Technologie
entertainment *(no pl)* [ˌentə'teɪnmənt]	Unterhaltung
creative [kri'eɪtɪv]	kreativ
fun-filled ['fʌnfɪld]	lustig; witzig
Japan [dʒə'pæn]	Japan
home-packed [ˌhəʊm'pækt]	zu Hause gemacht
Japanese [ˌdʒæpən'i:z]	japanisch; Japanisch; aus Japan; Japaner; Japanerin
bamboo [bæm'bu:]	Bambus

Communication skills

p. 94	**podcast** ['pɒdkɑ:st]	Podcast	I got the new **podcast** last night.
	Thanks so much. [ˌθæŋk‿səʊ 'mʌtʃ]	Vielen Dank.; Herzlichen Dank.	**Thanks so much** for your help!
	to **interrupt** [ˌɪntə'rʌpt]	unterbrechen	I have to **interrupt** here.

V

Word bank: Talking about a region

Which region?

north

west  east

south

How many people live in the region/visit the region?

thousands millions billions

What does it look like?

mountains

beach

countryside

town

city

coastline

What can you do there?

museum

amusement park

zoo

church

skiing

shopping

hiking

sightseeing

It's in the … of …
It's near the …
There are …
There is …

… people live in the region/visit the region.
I like it because …
It's nice/quiet/busy/beautiful/…

Unit 5 Southern Life

p. 96	**southern** ['sʌðən]	südlich	**northern** ↔ southern

Way in

	way of life [ˌweɪ əv 'laɪf]	Lebensart; Lebensweise	I like the southern **way of life**.
	the outdoors [ˌði 'aʊtdɔːz]	die freie Natur	They are fans of **the outdoors**.
	protest ['prəʊtest]	Protest; Demonstration	R протест
	wide [waɪd]	breit	wide
	destination [ˌdestɪ'neɪʃn]	Ziel; Reiseziel	Our holiday **destination** is England.
	African American [ˌæfrɪkən ə'merɪkən]	Afroamerikaner; Afroamerikanerin	There were lots of **African Americans** in the South.
	right [raɪt]	Recht	African Americans wanted the same **rights**.
	discrimination [dɪˌskrɪmɪ'neɪʃn]	Diskriminierung	There was a lot of **discrimination**.
	civil rights *(pl)* [ˌsɪvl 'raɪts]	Bürgerrechte	King fought for **civil rights** in the 1950s.
	peaceful ['piːsfl]	friedlich	Protests aren't always **peaceful**.
p. 97	**African** ['æfrɪkən]	afrikanisch; aus Afrika; Afrikaner; Afrikanerin	T Afrikalı
	plantation [plæn'teɪʃn]	Plantage	People had to work on the **plantations**.
	custom ['kʌstəm]	Brauch; Sitte	The South has its own culture and **customs**.
	both … and … ['bəʊθ … ənd]	sowohl … als auch …	I eat **both** fruit **and** vegetables.
	Southerner ['sʌðənə]	Südstaatler; Südstaatlerin	**Southern** → south → southern
	root [ruːt]	Wurzel	Some music has its **roots** in the South.
	to originate [ə'rɪdʒneɪt]	entstehen	Rock'n'roll **originated** in the south.
	to be alive with … [biː ə'laɪv wɪð]	erfüllt sein von …; vor … wimmeln	New Orleans **is alive with** jazz music.
	hit [hɪt]	Hit; Treffer	Taylor Swift had lots of **hits**.
	charts *(pl only)* [tʃɑːts]	*hier:* Hitparade	There are **charts** for different types of music.
	business ['bɪznɪs]	Geschäft; Branche	R бизнес
	to release [rɪ'liːs]	veröffentlichen; herausgeben; freigeben; freisetzen; loslassen	In 2006 Taylor Swift **released** her first CD.
	copy ['kɒpi]	Exemplar	The CD sold two million **copies**.
	celebrity [sə'lebrəti]	Prominenter; Prominente; berühmte Person	**celebrity** = famous person

Station 1

Nationalities

Spanish ['spænɪʃ]	spanisch; Spanisch; aus Spanien	**Greek** [gri:k]	griechisch; Griechisch; aus Griechenland
Vietnamese [ˌvjetnə'mi:z]	vietnamesisch; Vietnamesisch; aus Vietnam; Vietnamese; Vietnamesin	**Russian** ['rʌʃn]	russisch; Russisch; aus Russland; Russe; Russin
		Turkish ['tɜ:kɪʃ]	türkisch; Türkisch; aus der Türkei
Chinese [tʃaɪ'ni:z]	chinesisch; Chinesisch; aus China; Chinese; Chinesin	**Japanese** [ˌdʒæpən'i:z]	japanisch; Japanisch; aus Japan; Japaner; Japanerin

Conflicts and solutions

to **compromise** ['kɒmprəmaɪz]	sich einigen; Kompromisse schließen	to **stand** [stænd]	ertragen; ausstehen
debate [dɪ'beɪt]	Diskussion; Debatte	to **accept** [ək'sept]	akzeptieren; annehmen; hinnehmen
to **tolerate** ['tɒlreɪt]	tolerieren; dulden	to **appreciate** [ə'pri:ʃieɪt]	schätzen; anerkennen; würdigen
to **confront** [kən'frʌnt]	konfrontieren; entgegentreten; sich stellen	to **reject** [rɪ'dʒekt]	zurückweisen; ablehnen
solution [sə'lu:ʃn]	Lösung	to **resent** [rɪ'zent]	übelnehmen; verübeln
to **ban** [bæn]	verbannen; verbieten; sperren	**negative** ['negətɪv]	negativ

p. 98	to **follow** ['fɒləʊ]	folgen; befolgen	You have to **follow** the recipe.
	down there ['daʊn ˌðeə]	dahin; da unten	I went on a trip **down there**.
	West Africa [ˌwest 'æfrɪkə]	Westafrika	The slaves were from **West Africa**.
	influence ['ɪnfluəns]	Einfluss	He is a bad **influence** on her.
	chicken ['tʃɪkɪn]	Hähnchen	
	to **introduce** [ˌɪntrə'dju:s]	einführen; einleiten	They **introduced** new food ideas.
	to **mix** [mɪks]	mischen; vermischen; mixen	If you **mix** blue and yellow, you get green.
	to **dry** [draɪ]	trocknen	**to dry** → dry
	to **cover in flour** [ˌkʌvər‿ɪn 'flaʊə]	in Mehl wenden	First **cover** the chicken **in flour**.
	to **fry** [fraɪ]	braten; frittieren	

	oil [ɔɪl]	Öl	
	to found [faʊnd]	gründen	The city was **founded** in 1718.
	the French [ðə 'frenʃ]	die Franzosen	The city was founded by **the French**.
	rule [ru:l]	Herrschaft	The city was under Spanish **rule**. 
	port [pɔ:t]	Hafen	
	identity [aɪ'dentəti]	Identität	Everyone has their own **identity**.
	multicultural [ˌmʌlti'kʌltʃrl]	multikulturell	The south is a **multicultural** area.
	to **experience** [ɪk'spɪəriəns]	erleben; erfahren	I **experienced** it best at Mardi Gras.
	carnival ['kɑ:nɪvl]	Karneval; Fasching	R карнавал T karnaval
	to need to ['ni:d ˌtə]	müssen	We **need to** buy some more eggs.
	case [keɪs]	Fall; Verhandlung	It was the **case** of the lost bag.
	a number of [ə 'nʌmbər‿əv]	einige; mehrere	I spoke to **a number of** people.
	historic [hɪ'stɒrɪk]	historisch	**historic** → history
	pride [praɪd]	Stolz	This flag is a symbol of **pride**.
	racism ['reɪsɪzm]	Rassismus	Some say the flag is a symbol of **racism**.
	State House *(AE)* ['steɪt ˌhaʊs]	Regierungsgebäude	The US flag flies over the **State House**.
	to **remove** [rɪ'mu:v]	entfernen	I **removed** the plaster from my knee.
	media ['mi:diə]	Medien	The **media** reported the protest.
	killing ['kɪlɪŋ]	Tötung; Ermordung	There have been a number of **killings**.
	protester [prə'testə]	Gegner; Gegnerin	**protester** → protest
	state government ['steɪt ˌgʌvnmənt]	Landesregierung	Protesters confronted the **state government**.
	to **attract** [ə'trækt]	anziehen	The South **attracts** lots of visitors.
p. 99	**paella** [paɪ'elə]	Paella	T paella
	sushi ['su:ʃi]	Sushi	R суши T sushi
	nothing ['nʌθɪŋ]	nichts	**nothing** ↔ something
p. 100	**society** [sə'saɪəti]	Gesellschaft	We live in a multicultural **society**.
	to **support** [sə'pɔ:t]	unterstützen	My parents **supported** my idea.
p. 101	**adventurer** [əd'ventʃrə]	Abenteurer; Abenteuerin	Sir Walter Raleigh was an **adventurer**.
	grid [grɪd]	Gitter; Raster	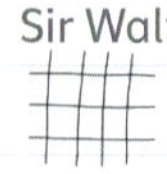
	to **complete** [kəm'pli:t]	fertigstellen; vervollständigen	The building was **completed** in 2015.

owner ['əʊnə]	Besitzer; Besitzerin	**owner** → to own
African-American [ˌæfrɪkənə'merɪkən]	afroamerikanisch	Obama was the first **African-American** president of the USA.
college *(AE)* ['kɒlɪdʒ]	Universität; Institut; College	There are different **colleges** in Raleigh.
to **add** [æd]	hinzufügen; addieren	Let's **add** some tomatoes to this salad.

Station 2

Understanding things

I didn't get that. [aɪ ˌdɪdnt 'get ðæt]	Ich habe es nicht verstanden.	**I know what you mean.** [aɪ ˌnəʊ wɒt jə 'mi:n]	Ich verstehe, was du meinst.
I didn't catch that. [aɪ ˌdɪdnt 'kætʃ ðæt]	Das habe ich nicht verstanden.; Das habe ich nicht gehört.	**I see.** [aɪ 'si:]	Ich verstehe.
		Absolutely! [ˌæbsə'lu:tli]	Auf jeden Fall!

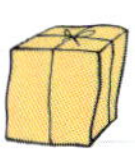

p. 102	**calendar** ['kæləndə]	Kalender	R календарь
	package ['pækɪdʒ]	Paket	T paket
	to **include** [ɪn'klu:d]	enthalten; beinhalten	It **includes** lots of surprises.
	excellent ['ekslnt]	exzellent; hervorragend	The ticket prices are **excellent**.
	choice [tʃɔɪs]	Auswahl; Wahl	**choice** → to choose
	transfer [træns'fɜ:]	Transport; Transfer	There is a free **transfer** by bus.
	track [træk]	Strecke	The race **track** isn't far away.
	deluxe [dɪ'lʌks]	Luxus-	The **deluxe** bus will pick us up.
	booklet ['bʊklət]	Broschüre; Heft	
	detail ['di:teɪl]	Detail; Einzelheit	T detay
	deep [di:p]	tief	I want to go **deep** into the forest.
	airboat ['eəbəʊt]	Propellerboot	We can go on an **airboat** there.
	wildlife ['waɪldlaɪf]	Tierwelt *(in freier Wildbahn)*	There is lots of **wildlife** in Florida.
	show [ʃəʊ]	Show; Schau; Aufführung	There is a **show** every 30 minutes.
	pick-up ['pɪkʌp]	Abholung; Pick-up	Look, there is a free hotel **pick-up** too.
	degree [dɪ'gri:]	Grad	It was really hot, 35 **degrees**.
	turn [tɜ:n]	Drehung	**turn** → to turn
	trail [treɪl]	Wanderweg; Spur	There is a **trail** through the swamps.
	seat [si:t]	Sitzplatz; Platz	If we book early, we'll get good **seats**.
	the wild [ðə 'waɪld]	Wildnis; freie Wildbahn	I've never seen a cat in **the wild**.

	heat [hiːt]	Hitze	This **heat** is too much for me.
	speech impaired ['spiːtʃ ɪmˌpeərd]	sprachbehindert	He can't speak, he's **speech impaired**.
	to translate [trænz'leɪt]	übersetzen	I can **translate** the text for you.
	outnumbered [ˌaʊt'nʌmbərd]	in der Unterzahl	I think I'm **outnumbered**, aren't I?
p. 103	**trainer** ['treɪnə]	Trainer; Trainerin	The **trainer** fed the alligators.
	to feel sick [ˌfiːl 'sɪk]	Übelkeit verspüren; sich schlecht fühlen	I **felt sick** after the airboat ride.
p. 104	**vacation** *(AE)* [və'keɪʃn]	Ferien; Urlaub	AE: **vacation** BE: holiday 
	fishing ['fɪʃɪŋ]	Angeln; Fischen	
p. 105	**opening times** ['əʊpnɪŋ ˌtaɪmz]	Öffnungszeiten	We have to look at the **opening times**.

Reading corner

p. 106	**segregation** [ˌsegrɪ'geɪʃn]	Rassentrennung; Trennung	Not everyone believed in **segregation**.
	complete [kəm'pliːt]	vollständig	**complete** → to complete
	segregated ['segrɪgeɪtɪd]	getrennt	**segregated** → segregation
	separate ['seprət]	getrennt; separat; verschieden	**separated** = segregated
	movie theater *(AE)* ['muːvi ˌθiːətə]	Kino	AE: **movie theater** BE: cinema
	at the back [ət ðə 'bæk]	hinten; am Ende; im hinteren Teil	**at the back** ↔ at the front
	unjust [ʌn'dʒʌst]	ungerecht	**unjust** = unfair
p. 107	**to refuse** [rɪ'fjuːz]	sich weigern; ablehnen	Claudette **refused** to move.
	to drag [dræg]	schleppen; schleifen; ziehen	They **dragged** him away from the dog.
	off [ɒf]	von … weg	They pulled the dog **off** the man.
	to arrest [ə'rest]	festnehmen; verhaften	She was **arrested** by the police. 
	jail [dʒeɪl]	Gefängnis	
	shotgun ['ʃɒtgʌn]	Schrotflinte; Jagdgewehr	**shotgun** → to shoot
	courage ['kʌrɪdʒ]	Mut; Tapferkeit; Courage	She showed a lot of **courage** on the bus.
	on the other (hand) [ɒn ði 'ʌðə (hænd)]	andererseits	I liked the music, but **on the other hand** it was loud.
	action ['ækʃn]	Handlung; Action	Did her **actions** make things worse?
	although [ɔːl'ðəʊ]	obwohl	**Although** she was slow, she wasn't late.
	witness ['wɪtnəs]	Zeuge; Zeugin	She saw it, she was a **witness**.

court case ['kɔ:t ˌkeɪs]	Gerichtsverhandlung; Rechtsfall	The **court case** ended segregation.
reputation [ˌrepjə'teɪʃn]	Ruf; Ansehen	He had a bad **reputation** at school.
to link [lɪŋk]	verbinden	**to link** → link
to **bother** ['bɒðə]	stören; belästigen; nerven	It didn't **bother** me that he forgot me.
role [rəʊl]	Rolle	I played an important **role** in the fight.
to **abolish** [ə'bɒlɪʃ]	abschaffen	It took a long time to **abolish** segregation.
system ['sɪstəm]	System	It was a long fight to abolish the **system**.

Film corner

p. 109	**reliable** [rɪ'laɪəbl]	verlässlich; zuverlässig; vertrauenswürdig	She's very **reliable**. She's always on time.
	to **trust** [trʌst]	vertrauen	She's reliable and you can **trust** her.

Checkpoint

feature story ['fi:tʃə ˌstɔ:ri]	Leitartikel; Sonderbericht	to wait one's turn [ˌweɪt wʌnz 'tɜ:n]	warten, bis man an der Reihe ist
stall [stɔ:l]	Stand; Bude	saleswoman ['seɪlz ˌwʊmən]	Verkäuferin
line [laɪn]	Schlange		

Writing skills

p. 115	**nowadays** ['naʊədeɪz]	heutzutage	**Nowadays** people help others less.
	point [pɔɪnt]	Punkt	The next **point** is very important.
	on the one hand [ɒn ðə 'wʌn hænd]	einerseits	**On one hand** I agree with you.
	after all [ˌɑ:ftər‿'ɔ:l]	schließlich; immerhin	**After all** you have to decide.

Word bank: Talking about culture

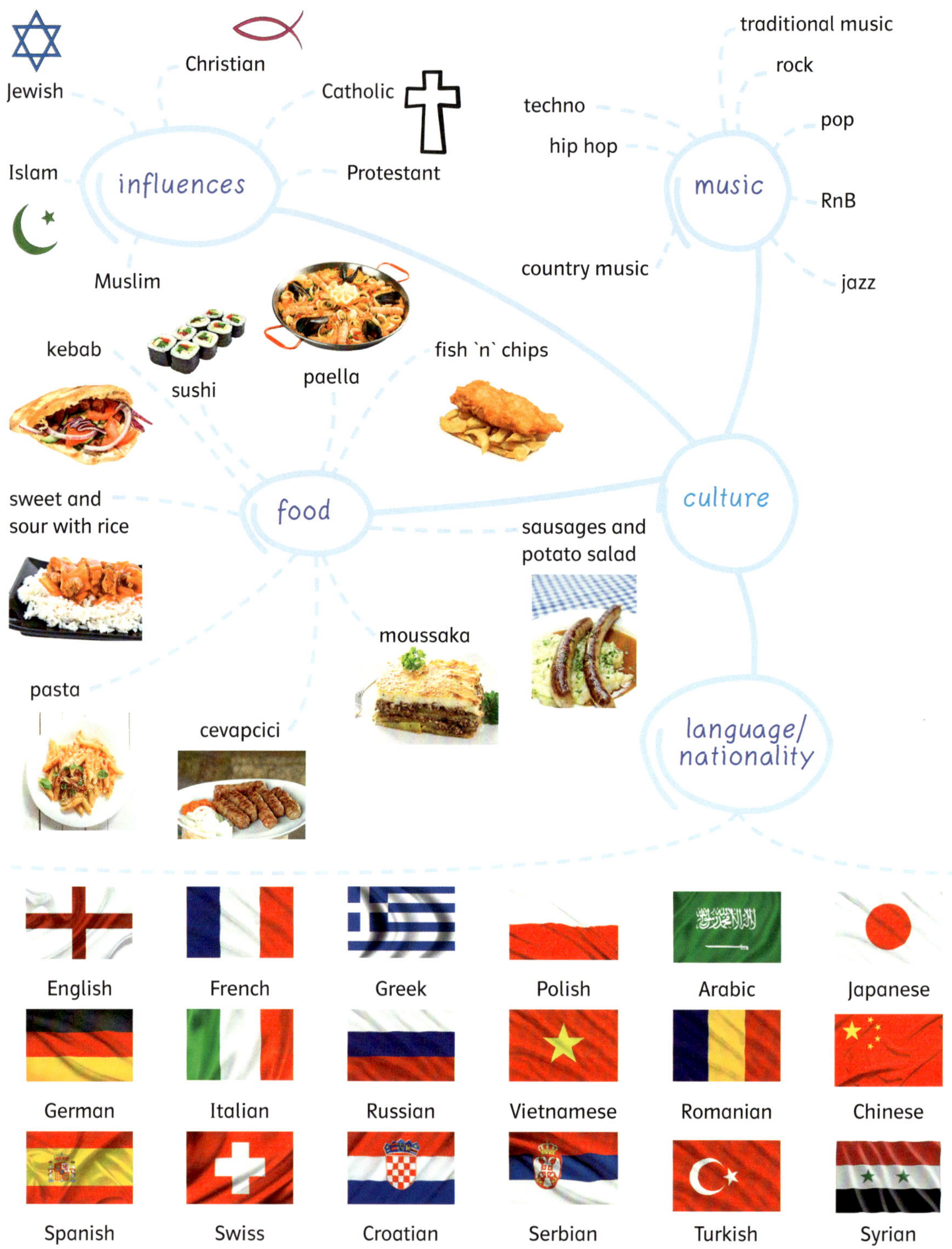

V

Word bank: A day trip

opening times

all day half day
from 9:00 a.m. until 5:00 p.m.
weekends only
last entry one hour before closing time
afternoons/morning only
closed on Mondays

tickets

adults	£ 10.00
children (under 14)	£ 5.00
senior citizens/OAPs	£ 5.00
students	£ 5.00
family (2 adults + 2 children)	£ 17.50

places

museum

zoo

amusement/
theme park

city

beach

transport

coach

train

tram

car

bike

boat

activities

hiking

sightseeing

fishing

a guided tour

cycling

Instructions

Arbeitsanweisungen mit Operatoren

Act the dialogue • the role play.	**Spielt** den Dialog • das Rollenspiel.
Add more words.	**Ergänze** mehr Wörter.
Answer the questions.	**Beantworte** die Fragen.
Ask a partner.	**Frage** eine Partnerin / einen Partner.
Check the sentences.	**Überprüfe** die Sätze.
Choose one of the tasks • the right answer.	**Wähle** eine der Aufgaben • die richtige Antwort **aus**.
Collect ideas.	**Sammle** Ideen.
Compare with your partner.	**Vergleicht** zu zweit.
Complete the sentences • the dialogue.	**Vervollständige** die Sätze • den Dialog.
Copy the list.	**Schreibe** die Liste **ab**.
Correct the wrong sentences.	**Verbessere** die falschen Sätze.
Decide on the best order.	**Entscheide dich für** die beste Reihenfolge.
Describe the picture.	**Beschreibe** das Bild.
Discuss in groups.	**Besprecht euch** in Gruppen.
Draw a picture.	**Zeichne** ein Bild.
Exchange your lists.	**Tauscht** eure Listen aus.
Explain the rules.	**Erkläre** die Regeln.
Finish the sentences.	**Vervollständige** die Sätze.
Give feedback.	**Gib** Rückmeldung.
Give reasons.	**Gib Gründe an.**
Guess.	**Überlege.**
Interview your partner.	**Interviewe** deine Partnerin / deinen Partner.
Label the picture.	**Beschrifte** das Bild.
Listen to the dialogue.	**Höre** dir den Dialog **an**.
Look at the photos • pictures (again).	**Schau** dir die Fotos • Bilder (noch einmal) **an**.
Make a list • a chart • a mind map.	**Erstelle** eine Liste • eine Tabelle • ein Wörternetz.
Make notes.	**Mache dir Stichpunkte.**
Make up more verses.	**Denke dir** weitere Strophen **aus**.
Match the sentences with the pictures.	**Ordne** den Bildern die richtigen Sätze **zu**.
Name the place.	**Nenne** den Ort.
Plan your role play.	**Plant** euer Rollenspiel.
Practise with a partner.	**Übe** mit einer Partnerin / einem Partner.
Present your profile to the class.	**Stelle** dein Profil deiner Klasse **vor**.
Put in the right verbs.	**Setze** die richtigen Verben **ein**.
Put the words **in the right order**.	**Bringe** die Wörter **in die richtige Reihenfolge**.
Read the story **again**.	**Lies** die Geschichte **noch einmal**.
Record your dialogue.	**Nehmt** euren Dialog **auf**.

Rewrite the sentences.	**Schreibe** die Sätze **um**.
Say how you feel.	**Sage**, wie du dich fühlst.
Show your text to a partner.	**Zeige** deinen Text einer Partnerin / einem Partner.
Sort the words **into groups**.	**Sortiere** die Wörter **in Gruppen**.
Take notes.	**Mache dir Notizen.**
Talk about the photos.	**Rede** über die Fotos.
Tell the class.	**Erzähle** es der Klasse.
Think about the story.	**Denke über** die Geschichte **nach**.
Think of a number.	**Denke** dir eine Nummer **aus.**
Use your own ideas.	**Benutze** deine eigenen Ideen.
Watch the film.	**Schau** den Film **an**.
Write a poem • a heading • a draft.	**Schreibe** ein Gedicht • einen Titel • einen Entwurf.

Classroom phrases

You and your teacher

I'm sorry I'm late.	Tut mir leid, dass ich mich verspätet habe.
I'm sorry I don't have my exercise book.	Tut mir leid, ich habe mein Heft nicht dabei.
What's the homework?	Was haben wir als Hausaufgabe auf?
Can you help me, please?	Können Sie / Kannst du mir bitte helfen?
Can you say that again, please?	Können Sie / Kannst du das bitte wiederholen?
Can I go to the toilet, please?	Kann ich bitte auf Toilette gehen?
Mr / Mrs / Miss ..., I don't feel well.	Herr / Frau ..., mir geht es nicht gut.
What page is it, please?	Auf welcher Seite ist das?
What's the German / English word for ...?	Was ist das deutsche / englische Wort für ...?
How do you spell ...?	Wie schreibt man ...?
What does that mean?	Was heißt / bedeutet das?
Sorry, I don't understand/ I don't know.	Tut mir leid, ich verstehe das nicht / ich weiß es nicht.

Working together

Can we work in pairs / groups?	Können wir zu zweit / in Gruppen arbeiten?
Do you want to work with me / us?	Willst du / Wollt ihr mit mir / uns arbeiten?
Let's make a / draw a ...	Lass(t) uns ein ... machen / zeichnen.
Whose turn is it? – It's my / your turn.	Wer ist dran? – Ich bin dran. / Du bist dran.

Your teacher can say ...

Turn to page ...	Schlagt Seite ... auf.
Look at the board.	Schaut an die Tafel.
Put your hands up, please!	Meldet euch, bitte!
Try again!	Versuche es noch einmal.

List of irregular verbs

Hier findest du alle unregelmäßigen Verben, die im Buch vorkommen.
Die Liste enthält jeweils alle drei Formen, auch wenn sie noch nicht alle in den Units vorgekommen sind.

infinitive	simple past	past participle	German
be [bi:]	was, were [wɒz, wɜ:]	been [bi:n]	sein
beat [bi:t]	beat [bi:t]	beaten ['bi:tn]	schlagen; besiegen
become [bɪ'kʌm]	became [bɪ'keɪm]	become [bɪ'kʌm]	werden
begin [bɪ'gɪn]	began [bɪ'gæn]	begun [bɪ'gʌn]	beginnen; anfangen
bleed [bli:d]	bled [bled]	bled [bled]	bluten
break [breɪk]	broke [brəʊk]	broken ['brəʊkn]	brechen
bring [brɪŋ]	brought [brɔ:t]	brought [brɔ:t]	bringen; mitbringen
build [bɪld]	built [bɪlt]	built [bɪlt]	bauen
burn [bɜ:n]	burned/burnt [bɜ:nt]	burned/burnt [bɜ:nt]	brennen
buy [baɪ]	bought [bɔ:t]	bought [bɔ:t]	kaufen
choose [tʃu:z]	chose [tʃəʊz]	chosen ['tʃəʊzn]	auswählen; wählen
come [kʌm]	came [keɪm]	come [kʌm]	kommen
cost [kɒst]	cost [kɒst]	cost [kɒst]	kosten
cut [kʌt]	cut [kʌt]	cut [kʌt]	(sich) schneiden
deal (with) [di:l]	dealt [delt]	dealt [delt]	sich befassen mit; umgehen mit
dig [dɪg]	dug [dʌg]	dug [dʌg]	graben
do [du:]	did [dɪd]	done [dʌn]	machen; tun
draw [drɔ:]	drew [dru:]	drawn [drɔ:n]	zeichnen
dream [dri:m]	dreamed/dreamt [dremt]	dreamed/dreamt [dremt]	träumen
drink [drɪŋk]	drank [dræŋk]	drunk [drʌŋk]	trinken
drive [draɪv]	drove [drəʊv]	driven ['drɪvn]	fahren; treiben
eat [i:t]	ate [eɪt]	eaten ['i:tn]	essen
fall [fɔ:l]	fell [fel]	fallen ['fɔ:ln]	fallen; hinfallen
feed [fi:d]	fed [fed]	fed [fed]	füttern; ernähren
feel [fi:l]	felt [felt]	felt [felt]	(sich) fühlen
fight [faɪt]	fought [fɔ:t]	fought [fɔ:t]	kämpfen; streiten
find [faɪnd]	found [faʊnd]	found [faʊnd]	finden
fly [flaɪ]	flew [flu:]	flown [fləʊn]	fliegen
forget [fə'get]	forgot [fə'gɒt]	forgotten [fə'gɒtn]	vergessen
freeze [fri:z]	froze [frəʊz]	frozen ['frəʊzn]	frieren; gefrieren
get [get]	got [gɒt]	got [gɒt]	bekommen; werden
give [gɪv]	gave [geɪv]	given ['gɪvn]	geben
go [gəʊ]	went [went]	gone [gɒn]	gehen; fahren
grow [grəʊ]	grew [gru:]	grown [grəʊn]	anbauen; züchten; ziehen; wachsen
grow up [ˌgrəʊ_'ʌp]	grew up [ˌgru:_'ʌp]	grown up [ˌgrəʊn_'ʌp]	aufwachsen
hang [hæŋ]	hung [hʌŋ]	hung [hʌŋ]	hängen

infinitive	simple past	past participle	German
have [hæv]	had [hæd]	had [hæd]	haben; besitzen
hear [hɪə]	heard [hɜ:d]	heard [hɜ:d]	hören
hide [haɪd]	hid [hɪd]	hidden ['hɪdn]	verstecken
hit [hɪt]	hit [hɪt]	hit [hɪt]	schlagen; treffen
hold [həʊld]	held [held]	held [held]	halten; festhalten
hurt [hɜ:t]	hurt [hɜ:t]	hurt [hɜ:t]	verletzen; weh tun
keep [ki:p]	kept [kept]	kept [kept]	halten
know [nəʊ]	knew [nju:]	known [nəʊn]	wissen; kennen
lay [leɪ]	laid [leɪd]	laid [leɪd]	legen; (den Tisch) decken
lead [li:d]	led [led]	led [led]	führen; anführen
leave [li:v]	left [left]	left [left]	verlassen; lassen; abfahren
lend [lend]	lent [lent]	lent [lent]	leihen; verleihen
lose [lu:z]	lost [lɒst]	lost [lɒst]	verlieren
make [meɪk]	made [meɪd]	made [meɪd]	machen; tun; bilden
mean [mi:n]	meant [ment]	meant [ment]	bedeuten; meinen
meet [mi:t]	met [met]	met [met]	kennen lernen; (sich) treffen
pay [peɪ]	paid [peɪd]	paid [peɪd]	bezahlen
put [pʊt]	put [pʊt]	put [pʊt]	setzen; legen; stellen
read [ri:d]	read [red]	read [red]	lesen
ride [raɪd]	rode [rəʊd]	ridden ['rɪdn]	fahren; reiten
ring [rɪŋ]	rang [ræŋ]	rung [rʌŋ]	klingeln; läuten
run [rʌn]	ran [ræn]	run [rʌn]	laufen; rennen
say [seɪ]	said [sed]	said [sed]	sagen; sprechen
see [si:]	saw [sɔ:]	seen [si:n]	sehen
sell [sel]	sold [səʊld]	sold [səʊld]	verkaufen
send [send]	sent [sent]	sent [sent]	schicken; senden
shine [ʃaɪn]	shone [ʃɒn]	shone [ʃɒn]	glänzen; scheinen
shoot [ʃu:t]	shot [ʃɒt]	shot [ʃɒt]	schießen
show [ʃəʊ]	showed [ʃəʊd]	shown [ʃəʊn]	zeigen
sing [sɪŋ]	sang [sæŋ]	sung [sʌŋ]	singen
sink [sɪŋk]	sank [sæŋk]	sunk [sʌŋk]	untergehen; sinken
sit [sɪt]	sat [sæt]	sat [sæt]	sitzen
sleep [sli:p]	slept [slept]	slept [slept]	schlafen
smell [smel]	smelled/smelt [smelt]	smelled/smelt [smelt]	riechen
speak [spi:k]	spoke [spəʊk]	spoken ['spəʊkn]	sprechen
spell [spel]	spelled/spelt [spelt]	spelled/spelt [spelt]	buchstabieren
spill [spɪl]	spilt [spɪlt]	spilt [spɪlt]	auslaufen; verschütten
spend [spend]	spent [spent]	spent [spent]	ausgeben; verbringen

infinitive	simple past	past participle	German
stand [stænd]	stood [stʊd]	stood [stʊd]	stehen
steal [sti:l]	stole [stəʊl]	stolen ['stəʊlən]	stehlen
sweep [swi:p]	swept [swept]	swept [swept]	fegen
swim [swɪm]	swam [swæm]	swum [swʌm]	schwimmen
take [teɪk]	took [tʊk]	taken ['teɪkn]	nehmen; mitnehmen
tear (up) [teə]	tore [tɔ:]	torn [tɔ:n]	kaputt machen; (zer) reißen
tell [tel]	told [təʊld]	told [təʊld]	erzählen; sagen
think [θɪŋk]	thought [θɔ:t]	thought [θɔ:t]	denken; glauben
throw [θrəʊ]	threw [θru:]	thrown [θrəʊn]	werfen
understand [ˌʌndə'stænd]	understood [ˌʌndə'stʊd]	understood [ˌʌndə'stʊd]	verstehen
wake up [weɪk‿'ʌp]	woke up [wəʊk‿'ʌp]	woken up [ˌwəʊkn‿'ʌp]	aufwachen
wear [weə]	wore [wɔ:]	worn [wɔ:n]	tragen
win [wɪn]	won [wʌn]	won [wʌn]	gewinnen; siegen
write [raɪt]	wrote [rəʊt]	written ['rɪtn]	schreiben

Dictionary

Im *Dictionary* sind alle wichtigen Wörter aus deinem Buch enthalten. Die Wörter stehen in alphabetischer Reihenfolge. Englische Wörter schlägst du ab S. 229 nach, deutsche Wörter ab S. 283.

Die Abkürzungen geben an, wo das Wort zum ersten Mal im Buch erscheint.

account	[ə'kaʊnt]	Konto	IV	U4	80
englisches Wort	Aussprache	deutsche Übersetzung	Band 4	Unit 4	Seite 80

Die mit einem Sternchen (*) gekennzeichneten Verben sind unregelmäßige Verben (→ *List of irregular verbs*, S. 226 – 228).

Manche Wörter haben verschiedene Bedeutungen. Am besten liest du alle, bevor du dich für eine entscheidest.

practice ['præktɪs] Training; Übung I[1]
angel ['eɪndʒl] Engel <IV U1, 26>[3]

*to **spend** [spend] ausgeben *(Geld)*; verbringen *(Zeit)* II[1]
accident ['æksɪdnt] Unfall III[1]

to **adapt** (to) [ə'dæpt (tə)] sich anpassen IV U1, 19[2]
address [ə'dres] Adresse II[2]

1 Lernwortschatz für alle: schwarz; 2 Differenzierungswortschatz: blau; 3 kein Lernwortschatz: < >

A

a [ə] ein, eine I
a **bit** [ə 'bɪt] ein bisschen; ein wenig II
a **few** [ə 'fju:] ein paar; wenige; einige III
a **five minute walk** [ə 'faɪv mɪnɪt ˌwɔ:k] fünf Minuten zu Fuß III
a **little** [ə 'lɪtl] ein bisschen II
a **lot** [ə 'lɒt] viel I; sehr II
a **lot of** [ə 'lɒt‿əv] viel(e); eine Menge I
a **number of** [ə 'nʌmbər‿əv] einige; mehrere IV U5, 98
a **pair of** [ə 'peər‿əv] ein Paar II
a/one **hundred** ['hʌndrəd] einhundert; hundert I
a/one **thousand** [ə/wʌn 'θaʊznd] eintausend; tausend II
a.m. [ˌeɪ'em] vormittags *(Uhrzeit)* II

*to **be able** to (do sth) [bi: 'eɪbl tə] (zu etw.) fähig sein; (etw.) können; (etw.) dürfen IV U2, 34
to **abolish** [ə'bɒlɪʃ] abschaffen IV U5, 107
about [ə'baʊt] über I; ungefähr; circa; etwa II
to be **about** [bi: ə'baʊt] gehen um; handeln von III
to care **about** [ˌkeər‿ə'baʊt] wichtig nehmen; sich kümmern um; sich interessieren für IV U3, 58
out and **about** [ˌaʊt‿ən‿ə'baʊt] unterwegs I
above all [əbʌv‿'ɔ:l] vor allen Dingen; in erster Linie IV U1, 18
abroad [ə'brɔ:d] im Ausland; ins Ausland IV U4, 86
to **abseil** ['æbseɪl] sich abseilen II
absolutely [ˌæbsə'lu:tli] absolut; völlig IV U3, 59
accent ['æksnt] Akzent <III>

to **accept** [ək'sept] akzeptieren; annehmen; hinnehmen IV U5, 99
accident ['æksɪdnt] Unfall III
according to [ə'kɔ:dɪŋ tə] laut; gemäß III
account [ə'kaʊnt] Konto IV U4, 80
stomach **ache** ['stʌmək ˌeɪk] Bauchweh; Bauchschmerzen II
across [ə'krɒs] über III; hinüber; herüber; quer durch IV U3, 54
to **act** [ækt] spielen II
acting ['æktɪŋ] Schauspielen; Schauspielerei III
acting workshop ['æktɪŋ ˌwɜ:kʃɒp] Schauspielworkshop II
action ['ækʃn] Handlung; Action IV U5, 107; Actionfilm <IV U4, 142>
Action! ['ækʃn] Achtung, Aufnahme! <III>
to take **action** [teɪk‿'ækʃn] eingreifen <IV U5, 114>
active ['æktɪv] aktiv <IV U3, 72>

activist ['æktɪvɪst] Aktivist; Aktivistin *(jmd. der sich für etw. engagiert)* <IV U3, 140>
activity [æk'tɪvəti] Aktivität I
  activity centre [æk'tɪvəti ˌsentə] Jugendzentrum III
actor ['æktə] Schauspieler; Schauspielerin II
actually ['æktʃuəli] eigentlich; tatsächlich; wirklich III
AD (= Anno Domini) [ˌeɪ'di:] nach Christus III
to **adapt** (to) [ə'dæpt (tə)] sich anpassen IV U1, 19
adaptor [ə'dæptə] Adapter III
to **add** [æd] hinzufügen; addieren IV U5, 101
addicted [ə'dɪktɪd] süchtig <IV U3, 72>
chemical **additive** [ˌkemɪkl 'ædətɪv] chemischer Zusatzstoff <IV U3, 72>
address [ə'dres] Adresse II
to **address** [ə'dres] ansprechen; adressieren <IV U2, 46>
adjective ['ædʒɪktɪv] Adjektiv; Eigenschaftswort III
adult ['ædʌlt] Erwachsene; Erwachsener III
adventure [əd'ventʃə] Abenteuer I
adventurer [əd'ventʃrə] **Abenteurer; Abenteurerin** IV U5, 101
adverb ['ædvɜ:b] Adverb <III>
ad(vert) (= advertisement) ['æd(vɜ:t) (əd'vɜ:tɪsmənt)] Anzeige; Werbespot II; Annonce IV U2, 38
advertising text ['ædvətaɪzɪŋ ˌtekst] Werbetext <IV U4, 78>
advice [əd'vaɪs] Rat; Ratschlag III
afraid [ə'freɪd] ängstlich II
  to be afraid [bi: ə'freɪd] sich fürchten; Angst haben II
African ['æfrɪkən] afrikanisch; aus Afrika; Afrikaner; Afrikanerin IV U5, 97
  African American [ˌæfrɪkən ə'merɪkən] Afroamerikaner; Afroamerikanerin IV U5, 96
African-American [ˌæfrɪkənə'merɪkən] afroamerikanisch IV U5, 101

after ['ɑ:ftə] nach I; danach; später III
  after all [ˌɑ:ftər‿'ɔ:l] schließlich; immerhin IV U5, 115
  after that ['ɑ:ftə ðæt] danach I
afternoon [ˌɑ:ftə'nu:n] Nachmittag I
  in the afternoon [ˌɪn ði ˌɑ:ftə'nu:n] nachmittags I
afterwards ['ɑ:ftəwədz] danach; hinterher <IV U5, 114>
again [ə'gen] wieder; noch einmal II
  then again [ˌðen ə'gen] andererseits III
against [ə'genst] gegen II
age [eɪdʒ] Alter I; Zeitalter <IV U4, 142>
ago [ə'gəʊ] vor II
to **agree** [ə'gri:] zustimmen II
  to agree (on) [ə'gri:] sich einigen (auf) <III>
  to agree (with) [ə'gri:] einer Meinung sein (mit) III
right **ahead** [ˌraɪt‿ə'hed] geradeaus IV U1, 15
ahead of [ə'hed‿əv] vor IV U1, 22
aim [eɪm] Ziel <IV U2, 50>
ain't (= isn't/aren't) [eɪnt] ist nicht; sind nicht <IV U1, 19>
air [eə] Luft IV U1, 22
airboat ['eəbəʊt] Propellerboot IV U5, 102
airport ['eəpɔ:t] Flughafen II
alarm [ə'lɑ:m] Alarmanlage <IV U4, 142>
  alarm clock [ə'lɑ:m ˌklɒk] Wecker I
Alaskan [ə'læskən] Alaska-; alaskisch <IV U1, 29>
alcohol *(no pl)* ['ælkəhɒl] Alkohol IV U3, 58
alcoholic [ˌælkə'hɒlɪk] alkoholisch; Alkohol- <IV U3, 72>
alert [ə'lɜ:t] Alarm <IV U1, 30>
algebra ['ældʒɪbrə] Algebra <IV U2, 48>
alien ['eɪliən] Außerirdischer; Außerirdische I
alive [ə'laɪv] am Leben III
  to be alive with … [bi: ə'laɪv wɪð] erfüllt sein von …; vor … wimmeln IV U5, 97

all [ɔ:l] alle I; ganz II
  above all [əbʌv‿'ɔ:l] vor allen Dingen; in erster Linie IV U1, 18
  after all [ˌɑ:ftər‿'ɔ:l] schließlich; immerhin IV U5, 115
  all alone [ˌɔ:l‿ə'ləʊn] ganz allein I
  all around the world [ɔ:l‿əˌraʊnd ðə 'wɜ:ld] in aller Welt III
  all day [ˌɔ:l 'deɪ] den ganzen Tag III
  all in all [ˌɔ:l‿ɪn 'ɔ:l] alles in allem; insgesamt IV U3, 61
  all over [ˌɔ:l‿'əʊvə] überall I
  all right [ˌɔ:l 'raɪt] in Ordnung; alles klar II
  all the time [ˌɔ:l ðə 'taɪm] die ganze Zeit III
allegiance [ə'li:dʒns] Treue IV U2, 34
  pledge of allegiance [ˌpledʒ‿əv‿ə'li:dʒns] Treueeid IV U2, 34
allergic to [ə'lɜ:dʒɪk tə] allergisch gegen II
allergy ['ælədʒi] Allergie II
alley ['æli] Gasse; Weg IV U2, 32
alligator ['ælɪgeɪtə] Alligator IV ZI, 9
to **allow** [ə'laʊ] erlauben; gestatten IV U4, 84
  to be allowed to (do sth) [bi: ə'laʊd tə] (etw.) dürfen IV U2, 34
allowance *(AE)* [ə'laʊəns] Taschengeld; Unterhaltsgeld IV U2, 38
almost ['ɔ:lməʊst] fast; beinahe III
alone [ə'ləʊn] allein I
  all alone [ˌɔ:l‿ə'ləʊn] ganz allein I
along [ə'lɒŋ] entlang I
alphabet ['ælfəbet] Alphabet I
already [ɔ:l'redi] schon; bereits II
alright [ɔ:l'raɪt] okay IV U3, 58
also ['ɔ:lsəʊ] auch I
alternative [ɔ:l'tɜ:nətɪv] alternativ; abwechselnd <IV U3, 58>
although [ɔ:l'ðəʊ] obwohl IV U5, 107
aluminium [ˌæljə'mɪniəm] Aluminium III
always ['ɔ:lweɪz] immer I
amazed [ə'meɪzd] erstaunt; verblüfft IV U3, 53
amazing [ə'meɪzɪŋ] unglaublich; toll; erstaunlich II

ambition [æm'bɪʃn] Ziel III; Ehrgeiz; Streben; Ambitionen <IV U3, 141>
ambitious [æm'bɪʃəs] ehrgeizig IV U1, 18
ambulance ['æmbjələns] Krankenwagen III
American [ə'merɪkən] amerikanisch; Amerikanisch; aus Amerika; Amerikaner; Amerikanerin IV ZI, 9
American football [əˌmerɪkən 'fʊtbɔ:l] American Football <IV U2, 50>
Native American [ˌneɪtɪv‿ə'merɪkən] Ureinwohner Amerikas; Ureinwohnerin Amerikas; Indianer; Indianerin; indianisch IV U1, 16
Amish ['ɑ:mɪʃ] amisch IV U3, 58
the **Amish** [ði 'ɑ:mɪʃ] die Amischen IV U3, 53
among [ə'mʌŋ] unter; inmitten III
amount (of) [ə'maʊnt (əv)] Menge; Summe <IV U1, 24>
amused [ə'mju:zd] amüsiert; vergnügt IV U3, 63
amusement park [ə'mju:zmənt ˌpɑ:k] Freizeitpark <IV U4, 215>
an [ən] ein, eine I
ancient ['eɪnʃnt] alt; altertümlich IV U4, 76
and [ænd] und I
angel ['eɪndʒl] Engel <IV U1, 26>
angle ['æŋgl] Winkel <III>
Anglo-American [ˌæŋgləʊə'merɪkən] anglo-amerikanisch <IV U5, 144>
angry ['æŋgri] wütend; zornig; verärgert; böse II
animal ['ænɪml] Tier I
animal rescue shelter [ˌænɪml 'reskju: ˌʃeltə] Tierheim I
ankle ['æŋkl] Fußgelenk; Fußknöchel II
announcement [ə'naʊnsmənt] Durchsage; Ankündigung II
annoyed [ə'nɔɪd] verärgert III
annoying [ə'nɔɪɪŋ] ärgerlich; lästig <IV U3, 68>
annual ['ænjuəl] jährlich III

another [ə'nʌðə] ein anderer; noch ein; ein andere II
answer ['ɑ:nsə] Antwort II
to **answer** ['ɑ:nsə] antworten; beantworten I
to answer the phone [ˌɑ:nsə ðə 'fəʊn] ans Telefon gehen III
antenna [æn'tenə] Antenne III
any ['eni] irgendein; irgendwelche II; jede III
not … any [ˌnɒt … eni] kein II
anything ['eniθɪŋ] irgendetwas II
Anything else? ['eniθɪŋ ˌels] Darf es sonst noch etwas sein? I
anything to drink ['eniθɪŋ tə 'drɪŋk] etwas zu trinken II
anyway ['eniweɪ] trotzdem; jedenfalls III; eigentlich IV U1, 14
anywhere ['eniweə] überall; irgendwo <IV U1, 19>
apart [ə'pɑ:t] auseinander; entfernt IV U3, 52
apostrophe [ə'pɒstrəfi] Apostroph <III>
appealing [ə'pi:lɪŋ] ansprechend IV U4, 77
to **appear** [ə'pɪə] auftauchen; erscheinen III
apple crumble [ˌæpl 'krʌmbl] Apfelauflauf *(mit Streuseln bedeckt)* II
to **apply** (for) [ə'plaɪ (fə)] sich bewerben (für/um) IV U2, 38
to **appreciate** [ə'pri:ʃieɪt] schätzen; anerkennen; würdigen IV U5, 99
approval form [ə'pru:vl ˌfɔ:m] Einverständnisformular <IV U2, 44>
April ['eɪprl] April I
Arabic ['ærəbɪk] arabisch; Arabisch <IV U5, 222>
architect ['ɑ:kɪtekt] Architekt; Architektin IV U4, 75
archive ['ɑ:kaɪv] Archiv II
are [ɑ:] bist; sind I
are required [rɪ'kwaɪəd] werden gebeten <IV U2, 48>
Are you serious? [ˌɑ: ju 'sɪəriəs] Im Ernst? III
… are 99p. [ɑ: 'naɪntinaɪn ˌpens] … kosten 99 Pence. I
area ['eəriə] Gegend; Gebiet; Areal III; Fläche IV ZI, 9; Bereich IV U1, 22
to **argue** ['ɑ:gju:] argumentieren; streiten <IV U4, 89>
argument ['ɑ:gjəmənt] Auseinandersetzung; Streit II; Argument <IV U3, 61>
arm [ɑ:m] Arm I
armour ['ɑ:mə] Rüstung III
army ['ɑ:mi] Armee; Heer III
around [ə'raʊnd] herum; umher I; gegen; ungefähr um III; um … herum IV U1, 14
around the house [ə'raʊnd ðə haʊs] im Haus I
to be around [bi: ə'raʊnd] geben; existieren IV U4, 80
to get around [ˌget ə'raʊnd] herumkommen III
to turn around [ˌtɜ:n‿ə'raʊnd] (sich) umdrehen III
to **arrange** [ə'reɪndʒ] arrangieren <IV U1, 27>
to **arrest** [ə'rest] festnehmen; verhaften IV U5, 107
arrival [ə'raɪvl] Ankömmling IV U1, 22
to **arrive** [ə'raɪv] ankommen II
Art [ɑ:t] Kunst I
article ['ɑ:tɪkl] Artikel; Bericht *(in einer Zeitung)* <IV U1, 12>
artist ['ɑ:tɪst] Künstler; Künstlerin <IV U1, 136>
make-up artist ['meɪkʌp ˌɑ:tɪst] Maskenbildner; Maskenbildnerin; Visagist; Visagistin <III>
as [æz] wie II; als III
as … as [əz … əz] so … wie II
as far as [ˌəz 'fɑ:r‿əz] soweit IV U3, 59
as soon as [əz 'su:n‿əz] sobald IV U4, 89
to **ask** [ɑ:sk] fragen I
to ask about ['ɑ:sk‿əˌbaʊt] sich erkundigen nach; fragen nach II
to ask for ['ɑ:sk fɔ:] bitten um II

to ask sb out [ˌɑ:sk … 'aʊt] sich mit jmdm. verabreden IV U2, 42
asking the way ['ɑ:skɪŋ ðə ˌweɪ] nach dem Weg fragen I
*to be **asleep** [bi: ə'sli:p] schlafen III
to fall asleep [ˌfɔ:lˌə'sli:p] einschlafen III
aspect ['æspekt] Aspekt; Gesichtspunkt; Blickwinkel <IV U2, 37>
to **assassinate** [ə'sæsɪneɪt] ermorden <IV U3, 140>
assistant [ə'sɪstnt] Verkäufer; Verkäuferin III
shop assistant ['ʃɒpˌəˌsɪstnt] Verkäufer; Verkäuferin II
sales **associate** *(AE)* [ˌseɪlz ə'səʊʃiət] Verkäufer; Verkäuferin IV U2, 38
astronomy [ə'strɒnəmi] Astronomie IV U2, 34
at [æt] an; in; um; bei; auf I
at break [ət 'breɪk] in der Pause I
at first [ət 'fɜ:st] zuerst; zunächst IV U4, 84
at home [ət 'həʊm] zu Hause I
at last [ət 'lɑ:st] endlich; zu guter Letzt II
at least [ət 'li:st] wenigstens; mindestens III
at school [ət 'sku:l] in der Schule I
at the back [ət ðə 'bæk] hinten; am Ende; im hinteren Teil IV U5, 106
at the bottom [æt ðə 'bɒtəm] unten III; ganz am Ende IV U3, 62
at the front [ət ðə 'frʌnt] vorn; im vorderen Bereich <IV U1, 17>
at the front of [ət ðə 'frʌntˌəv] an der Spitze (von); im vorderen Bereich II
at the seaside [ət ðə 'si:saɪd] am Meer I
at the top [æt ðə 'tɒp] oben III
at the weekend [ˌət ðə 'wi:kend] am Wochenende I
at this stage [æt ðɪs 'steɪdʒ] zu diesem Zeitpunkt <IV U5, 108>
ate [eɪt] simple past von *to eat* II
atmosphere ['ætməsfɪə] Atmosphäre; Stimmung <IV U2, 46>

to **attach** [ə'tætʃ] verbinden III
attack [ə'tæk] Angriff; Attacke IV U1, 12
to **attack** [ə'tæk] angreifen IV U2, 42
attempt [ə'tempt] Versuch <IV U4, 88>
to **attend** [ə'tend] teilnehmen; anwesend sein; besuchen <IV U2, 48>
attention [ə'tenʃn] Aufmerksamkeit <IV U2, 51>
to catch sb's attention [ˌkætʃˌ ə'tenʃn] jmdn. auf sich aufmerksam machen <IV U3, 68>
to pay attention to [ˌpeɪˌə'tenʃn tʊ] beachten <III>
attic ['ætɪk] Dachboden I
attitude ['ætɪtju:d] Einstellung; Haltung IV U4, 89
to **attract** [ə'trækt] anziehen IV U5, 98
audience ['ɔ:diəns] Publikum <IV U2, 51>
audition [ɔ:'dɪʃn] Vorspielen; Vorsprechen; Vorsingen; Vortanzen II
August ['ɔ:gəst] August I
in August [in 'ɔ:gəst] im August I
aunt [ɑ:nt] Tante II
author ['ɔ:θə] Autor; Autorin <IV U3, 71>
autograph ['ɔ:təgrɑ:f] Autogramm IV U3, 53
to sign autographs [ˌsaɪn 'ɔ:təgrɑ:fs] Autogramme geben IV U3, 53
available [ə'veɪləbl] erhältlich; verfügbar <IV U2, 44>
avenue ['ævənju:] Allee; Boulevard IV U1, 14
average ['ævrɪdʒ] durchschnittlich IV U3, 58
to **avoid** [ə'vɔɪd] vermeiden; meiden; aus dem Weg gehen; ausweichen IV U3, 62
awake [ə'weɪk] bei Bewusstsein; wach III
away [ə'weɪ] weg; entfernt II
right away [ˌraɪtˌə'weɪ] sofort; gleich IV U4, 80
awesome ['ɔ:səm] super; spitze IV U2, 34

awful ['ɔ:fl] schrecklich; furchtbar I

B

baby ['beɪbi] Baby II
babysitter ['beɪbɪˌsɪtə] Babysitter; Babysitterin IV U2, 41
back [bæk] Rückseite; Rücken IV U3, 64
at the back [ət ðə 'bæk] hinten; am Ende; im hinteren Teil IV U5, 106
back [bæk] Hinter- IV U3, 62
back [bæk] zurück I
back home [bæk 'həʊm] zu Hause II
back then ['bæk ˌðen] damals IV U1, 14
background ['bækgraʊnd] Hintergrund III
in the background [ɪn ðə 'bækgraʊnd] im Hintergrund III
backpack ['bækpæk] Rucksack IV U3, 62
bad [bæd] schlecht I
badly ['bædli] sehr; schwer III; dringend IV U2, 38
bag [bæg] Tasche; Tüte; Sack I
tea bag ['ti: ˌbæg] Teebeutel <IV U5, 113>
bagel ['beɪgl] Bagel *(weiches, ringförmiges Brötchen)* IV U1, 14
baggies *(pl) (coll)* ['bægiz] kurze Hosen *(ugs.)* <IV U4, 77>
bagpipes *(pl)* ['bægpaɪps] Dudelsack III
baguette [bæg'et] **Baguette** *(Stangenweißbrot)* <IV U5, 112>
pasta **bake** [ˌpæstə 'beɪk] Nudelauflauf II
baker ['beɪkə] Bäcker; Bäckerin III
baker's ['beɪkəz] Bäckerei III
bald eagle [ˌbɔ:ld 'i:gl] Weißkopfseeadler IV ZI, 8
ball [bɔ:l] Ball II
cannon ball ['kænən ˌbɔ:l] Kanonenkugel II
balloon [bə'lu:n] Luftballon I

bamboo [bæm'bu:] Bambus <IV U4, 90>
to **ban** [bæn] verbannen; verbieten; sperren IV U5, 99
banana [bə'nɑ:nə] Banane I
band [bænd] Band; Musikgruppe II
brass band [ˌbrɑ:s 'bænd] Blaskapelle; Blasensemble <IV U5, 108>
marching band ['mɑ:tʃɪŋ ˌbænd] Marschkapelle <IV U2, 199>
to start a band [ˌstɑ:t‿ə 'bænd] eine Band gründen II
bandage ['bændɪdʒ] Verband III
bar chart ['bɑ: ˌtʃɑ:t] Balkendiagramm; Säulendiagramm <IV U1, 27>
bar of chocolate [bɑ:r‿əv 'tʃɒklət] Tafel Schokolade I
barbecue ['bɑ:bɪkju:] Grill; Grillparty I
bargain ['bɑ:gɪn] Schnäppchen II
to **bark** [bɑ:k] bellen III
barrel ['bærl] Fass; Tonne IV U3, 53
baseball ['beɪsbɔ:l] Baseball IV U1, 13
basic ['beɪsɪk] grundlegend; einfach <IV U1, 24>
basically ['beɪsɪkli] eigentlich; grundsätzlich; im Grunde genommen IV U4, 80
basketball ['bɑ:skɪtbɔ:l] Basketball II
bat [bæt] Fledermaus I
Turkish **bath** [ˌtɜ:kɪʃ 'bɑ:θ] Dampfbad III
bathroom ['bɑ:θrʊm] Badezimmer; Bad I
bathroom *(AE)* ['bɑ:θrʊm] Toilette; Bad(ezimmer) IV U2, 34
battle ['bætl] Schlacht; Kampf III
bay [beɪ] Bucht IV U4, 75
BC (= before Christ) [ˌbi:'si:] vor Christus <IV U2, 138>
*to **be** [bi:] sein I
to be able to (do sth) [bi: 'eɪbl tə] (zu etw.) fähig sein; (etw.) können; (etw.) dürfen IV U2, 34
to be about [bi: ə'baʊt] gehen um; handeln von III
to be afraid [bi: ə'freɪd] sich fürchten; Angst haben II
to be alive with ... [bi: ə'laɪv wɪð] erfüllt sein von ...; vor ... wimmeln IV U5, 97
to be allowed to (do sth) [bi: ə'laʊd tə] dürfen IV U2, 34
to be around [bi: ə'raʊnd] geben; existieren IV U4, 80
to be asleep [bi: ə'sli:p] schlafen III
to be born [bi: 'bɔ:n] geboren werden III
to be called [bi: 'kɔ:ld] heißen; genannt werden II
to be fed up (with) [bi: fed‿'ʌp (wɪð)] die Nase voll haben (von); sauer sein III
to be good at [bi: 'gʊd‿ət] gut sein in/bei I
to be homesick [bi: 'həʊmsɪk] Heimweh haben III
to be included [bi: ɪn'klu:dɪd] enthalten sein III
to be interested in [bi: 'ɪntrəstɪd‿ɪn] sich interessieren für; interessiert sein an III
to be known as [bi: 'nəʊn‿əz] bekannt sein als <IV U3, 70>
to be located [bi: ləʊ'keɪtɪd] liegen III; gelegen sein; sich befinden IV U1, 13
to be lucky [bi: 'lʌki] Glück haben III
to be made of [bi: 'meɪd‿əv] hergestellt sein aus III
to be on fire [bi: ɒn 'faɪə] brennen II
to be right [bi: 'raɪt] recht haben II
to be scared [bi: 'skeəd] Angst haben; erschrocken sein II
to be sick [bi: 'sɪk] sich übergeben I
to be sorry [bi: 'sɒri] leidtun III
to be stuck [bi: 'stʌk] feststecken; nicht weg können; festsitzen; hängen bleiben IV U2, 34
to be unlucky [bi: ʌn'lʌki] Pech haben <IV U5, 114>
to be up to [bi: 'ʌp tə] vorhaben III
to be worth [bi: 'wɜ:θ] wert sein III
to be wrong [bi: 'rɒŋ] unrecht haben; sich irren III
Be careful! [bi: 'keəfl] Sei vorsichtig! I
beach [bi:tʃ] Strand I
to go beach combing [gəʊ 'bi:tʃ ˌkəʊmɪŋ] den Strand nach Strandgut absuchen II
kidney **bean** ['kɪdni ˌbi:n] Kidneybohne II
soy **bean** ['sɔɪ ˌbi:n] Sojabohne IV ZI, 9
bear [beə] Bär I
grizzly bear ['grɪzli ˌbeə] Grizzlybär <IV U1, 30>
*to **beat** [bi:t] besiegen; schlagen III
beat [bi:t] simple past von *to beat* III
beaten ['bi:tn] past participle von *to beat* III
beautiful ['bju:tɪfl] schön; hübsch I
became [bɪ'keɪm] simple past von *to become* II
because [bɪ'kɒz] weil; da I
because of [bɪ'kɒz‿əv] wegen III
That's because ... [ˌðæts bɪ'kɒz] Das liegt daran, dass ... III
*to **become** [bɪ'kʌm] werden II
become [bɪ'kʌm] past participle von *to become* II
bed [bed] Bett I
bed and breakfast (B & B) [ˌbed‿ən 'brekfəst] Frühstückspension III
to go to bed [ˌgəʊ tə 'bed] ins Bett gehen I
bedroom ['bedrʊm] Schlafzimmer; Kinderzimmer I
beef [bi:f] Rindfleisch II
roast beef [ˌrəʊst 'bi:f] Roastbeef; Rinderbraten <IV U5, 112>
been [bi:n] past particple von *to be* II
beer [bɪə] Bier IV U3, 62
before [bɪ'fɔ:] vorher; zuvor II; schon einmal III; bevor; bis zu II; vor IV U3, 61
before that [bɪ'fɔ: ðæt] davor III
began [bɪ'gæn] simple past von *to begin* IV U1, 18
*to **begin** [bɪ'gɪn] beginnen; anfangen IV U1, 18

beginner [bɪ'gɪnə] Anfänger; Anfängerin <IV U5, 145>
beginning [bɪ'gɪnɪŋ] Anfang; Beginn III
begun [bɪ'gʌn] past participle von *to begin* IV U1, 18
to **behave** [bɪ'heɪv] sich benehmen; sich verhalten IV U2, 38
behavior *(AE)* [bɪ'heɪvjə] Verhalten IV U2, 38
behaviour [bɪ'heɪvjə] Verhalten <IV U3, 65>
behind [bɪ'haɪnd] hinter II
from behind [ˌfrəm bɪ'haɪnd] von hinten I
to **believe** [bɪ'li:v] glauben II
bell [bel] Glocke II
to **belong (to)** [bɪ'lɒŋ (tə)] gehören (zu) IV U1, 14
beloved [bɪ'lʌvɪd] geliebt IV U4, 85
belt [belt] Gürtel IV U3, 62
bench [benʃ] Bank; Sitzbank III
best [best] beste II
best known [ˌbest 'nəʊn] weltberühmt IV U2, 32
to like … best [ˌlaɪk 'best] am meisten mögen; am liebsten mögen I
Best wishes, [ˌbest 'wɪʃɪz] Viele Grüße, I
the best [ðə 'best] die besten II
best-paid ['bestˌpeɪd] bestbezahlt IV U1, 13
best-paying [ˌbest'peɪɪŋ] bestbezahlt IV U2, 39
*to **bet** [bet] wetten (auf) III
bet [bet] simple past, past participle von *to bet* III
better ['betə] besser I
better quality food [ˌbetə 'kwɒləti ˌfu:d] qualitativ besseres Essen <IV U3, 72>
between [bɪ'twi:n] zwischen II
in between [ˌɪn bɪ'twi:n] dazwischen <IV U4, 92>
big [bɪg] groß I
big wheel [ˌbɪg 'wi:l] Riesenrad II
bike [baɪk] Fahrrad I
bill [bɪl] Rechnung III
to pay the bill [ˌpeɪ ðə 'bɪl] die Rechnung bezahlen III
billion ['bɪliən] Milliarde IV U1, 13
biography [baɪ'ɒgrəfi] Biografie <III>
Biology [baɪ'ɒlədʒi] Biologie I
bird [bɜ:d] Vogel I
bird watching ['bɜ:d ˌwɒtʃɪŋ] Vogelbeobachtung III
birthday ['bɜ:θdeɪ] Geburtstag I
Happy birthday! [ˌhæpi 'bɜ:θdeɪ] Alles Gute zum Geburtstag! I
biscuit ['bɪskɪt] Keks II
dog biscuit ['dɒg ˌbɪskɪt] Hundekeks II
a **bit** [ə 'bɪt] ein bisschen; ein wenig II
bits and pieces *(pl only)* [ˌbɪts‿ən 'pi:sɪz] Stückchen <IV U1, 136>
black [blæk] schwarz I
blanket ['blæŋkɪt] Decke; Bettdecke; Wolldecke IV U3, 62
blast [blɑ:st] Wahnsinnsspaß IV U2, 34
bled [bled] simple past, past participle von *to bleed* III
*to **bleed** [bli:d] bluten III
blew [blu:] simple past von *to blow* <IV U2, 138>
block [blɒk] Block; Häuserblock IV U1, 14
blockbuster ['blɒkˌbʌstə] Kassenschlager; Bestseller <IV U4, 142>
blog [blɒg] Blog; Internettagebuch II
blogger ['blɒgə] Blogger; Bloggerin IV U4, 81
blond [blɒnd] blond <IV U4, 77>
bloody ['blʌdi] blutig <IV U2, 138>
blouse [blaʊz] Bluse I
*to **blow** [bləʊ] wehen; blasen; pusten <IV U2, 138>
blue [blu:] blau I
blue cheese [ˌblu: 'tʃi:s] Schimmelkäse II
blues [blu:z] Blues *(Musikrichtung)* IV U5, 97
board [bɔ:d] Tafel I; Brett <IV U3, 72>
on board ['ɒn bɔ:d] an Bord III
boarding school ['bɔ:dɪŋ ˌsku:l] Internat <IV U2, 139>
boat [bəʊt] Boot II
boat trip ['bəʊt ˌtrɪp] Bootsfahrt; Schiffsfahrt II
bodhran ['baʊrɑ:n] *schottisch-irische Trommel* <III>
body ['bɒdi] Körper III; Leiche IV U3, 62
body language ['bɒdi ˌlæŋgwɪdʒ] Körpersprache <III>
body lotion ['bɒdi ˌləʊʃn] Körperlotion III
to **boil** [bɔɪl] kochen <IV U5, 113>
boiling [bɔɪlɪŋ] kochend <IV U5, 113>
bold [bəʊld] fett gedruckt <IV U2, 49>
bonus ['bəʊnəs] Bonus; Prämie IV U2, 39
book [bʊk] Buch; Heft I
exercise book ['eksəsaɪz ˌbʊk] Übungsheft I
to **book** [bʊk] buchen; reservieren IV U4, 76
booklet ['bʊklət] Broschüre; Heft IV U5, 102
to **bookmark** ['bʊkmɑ:k] zu … hinzufügen II
boom years ['bu:m ˌjɪəz] Blütezeit; fette Jahre *(ugs.)* IV U4, 86
boomtown ['bu:mtaʊn] Boomtown *(eine Stadt, die sehr schnell wächst)* IV U4, 86
boot [bu:t] Stiefel II; Schuh <IV U2, 50>
border ['bɔ:də] Grenze III
to cross the border [ˌkrɒs ðə 'bɔ:də] über die Grenze gehen; die Grenze überschreiten IV U1, 19
bored [bɔ:d] gelangweilt IV U3, 57
boring ['bɔ:rɪŋ] langweilig I
*to **be born** [bi: 'bɔ:n] geboren werden III
borough ['bʌrə] Stadtteil; Bezirk IV U1, 12
to **borrow** ['bɒrəʊ] ausleihen II
boss [bɒs] Boss; Chef; Chefin II
bossy ['bɒsi] rechthaberisch IV U2, 39
both [bəʊθ] beide III

both … and … ['bəʊθ … ənd] sowohl … als auch … IV U5, 97

to **bother** ['bɒðə] stören; belästigen; nerven IV U5, 107

bottle ['bɒtl] Flasche I

bottle bank ['bɒtl bæŋk] Altglascontainer II

bottom ['bɒtəm] unterer Teil; Boden; Grund III

at the bottom [æt ðə 'bɒtəm] unten III; ganz am Ende IV U3, 62

bought [bɔːt] simple past von *to buy* I; past participle von *to buy* II

boulevard ['buːləvɑːd] Boulevard <IV U4, 143>

bow [bəʊ] Bogen <IV U2, 138>

bowl [bəʊl] Schale; Schälchen; Schüssel II

bowling ['bəʊlɪŋ] Bowlen IV U3, 58

box [bɒks] Box; Kiste; Schachtel I

telephone box ['telɪfəʊn ˌbɒks] Telefonzelle II

boy [bɔɪ] Junge I

boyfriend ['bɔɪfrend] Freund *(in einer Paarbeziehung)* IV U2, 42

to **brainstorm** ['breɪnstɔːm] brainstormen; sammeln <IV U3, 68>

brand [brænd] Marke III

brass band [ˌbrɑːs 'bænd] Blaskapelle; Blasensemble <IV U5, 108>

brave [breɪv] tapfer; mutig III

bread [bred] Brot II

sliced bread [ˌslaɪst 'bred] in Scheiben geschnittenes Brot III

break [breɪk] Pause I

at break [ət 'breɪk] in der Pause I

to take a break [ˌteɪk‿ə 'breɪk] Pause machen II

*to **break** [breɪk] brechen; zerbrechen II

breakdancing ['breɪkdɑːnsɪŋ] Breakdance <IV U1, 136>

breakfast ['brekfəst] Frühstück I

bed and breakfast (B & B) [ˌbed‿ən 'brekfəst] Frühstückspension III

to have breakfast [ˌhæv 'brekfəst] frühstücken I

breast [brest] Brust <IV U3, 72>

to **breathe** [briːð] atmen III

breathing ['briːðɪŋ] Atmung <IV U4, 88>

brewing time ['bruːɪŋ ˌtaɪm] Brühzeit <IV U5, 113>

brick [brɪk] Stein; Ziegelstein II

bridge [brɪdʒ] Brücke II

briefcase ['briːfkeɪs] Aktenkoffer; Aktentasche III

fire **brigade** ['faɪə brɪˌgeɪd] Feuerwehr <III>

bright [braɪt] hell; leuchtend; strahlend IV ZI, 8

brilliant ['brɪliənt] toll I

*to **bring** [brɪŋ] bringen; mitbringen II

to bring down [ˌbrɪŋ 'daʊn] herunterbringen <IV U2, 35>

to bring to life [ˌbrɪŋ tə ˈlaɪf] zum Leben erwecken; veranschaulichen IV U1, 22

British ['brɪtɪʃ] britisch II

broadcast ['brɔːdkɑːst] Sendung; Ausstrahlung; Übertragung <IV U5, 97>

brochure ['brəʊʃə] Broschüre; Prospekt III

broke [brəʊk] simple past von *to break* II

broken ['brəʊkn] past participle von *to break* II

broken ['brəʊkn] gebrochen; kaputt IV U2, 41

brother ['brʌðə] Bruder I

brought [brɔːt] simple past von *to bring* II

brown [braʊn] braun I

bubble wrap ['bʌbl ˌræp] Luftpolsterfolie <IV U3, 71>

speech **bubble** ['spiːtʃ ˌbʌbl] Sprechblase <III>

thought **bubble** ['θɔːt ˌbʌbl] Denkblase; Gedankenblase <IV U1, 19>

bucket of water ['bʌkɪt‿əv ˌwɔːtə] Eimer Wasser I

buddy *(infml)* ['bʌdi] Kumpel IV U2, 45

buffalo ['bʌfləʊ] Büffel <IV U2, 138>

buffet ['bʊfeɪ] Büfett III

*to **build** [bɪld] bauen II

builder ['bɪldə] Bauarbeiter; Bauarbeiterin II

ship builder ['ʃɪp ˌbɪldə] Schiffsbauer; Schiffsbauerin III

building ['bɪldɪŋ] Gebäude II

built [bɪlt] simple past, past participle von *to build* II

light **bulb** ['laɪt ˌbʌlb] Glühbirne III

bullet ['bʊlɪt] Kugel; Geschoss IV U3, 63

burger ['bɜːgə] Hamburger II

burglar ['bɜːglə] Einbrecher; Einbrecherin I

*to **burn** [bɜːn] verbrennen; brennen III

to burn down [bɜːn 'daʊn] niederbrennen; verbrennen II

burnt [bɜːnt] simple past, past participle von *to burn* III

bus [bʌs] Bus I

bus stop ['bʌs ˌstɒp] Bushaltestelle II

on the bus [ˌɒn ðə 'bʌs] im Bus II

bushy ['bʊʃi] buschig <IV U4, 77>

business ['bɪznɪs] Geschäft; Branche IV U5, 97

businessman ['bɪznɪsmæn] Geschäftsmann IV U4, 84

busy ['bɪzi] beschäftigt; arbeitsreich I; belebt; voller Menschen <III>

a busy day [ə ˌbɪzi 'deɪ] ein ausgefüllter Tag I

but [bʌt] aber I

butcher's ['bʊtʃəz] Metzgerei III

butter ['bʌtə] Butter I

peanut butter [ˌpiːnʌt 'bʌtə] Erdnussbutter III

*to **buy** [baɪ] kaufen I

my head is **buzzing** [maɪ ˌhed‿ɪz 'bʌzɪŋ] mir schwirrt der Kopf <IV U5, 114>

by [baɪ] von II; bis (spätestens); vorbei <III>; an IV U3, 63

by *(train)* [baɪ] mit *(dem Zug)* I

by the end [ˌbaɪ ði 'end] am Schluss II

by yourself [baɪ 'jɔːself] allein II

Bye. [baɪ] Tschüss. I

C

cabbage ['kæbɪdʒ] Kohl; Kraut II

cable car ['keɪbl ˌkɑ:] Seilbahn IV U4, 74

café ['kæfeɪ] Café I

cafeteria [kæfə'tɪəriə] Cafeteria; Mensa I

cage [keɪdʒ] Käfig I

cake [keɪk] Kuchen I
- to make a cake [ˌmeɪk‿ə 'keɪk] einen Kuchen backen I
- piece of cake ['pi:s‿əv keɪk] einfach <IV U3, 68>

calculator ['kælkjəleɪtə] Rechner; Taschenrechner I

calendar ['kæləndə] Kalender IV U5, 102

call [kɔ:l] Anruf; Ruf III
- call-and-response [ˌkɔ:lənrɪ'spɒns] Ruf-Antwort <IV U5, 108>
- phone call ['fəʊn ˌkɔ:l] Telefonanruf I

to **call** [kɔ:l] rufen; anrufen I; nennen III
- to be called [bi: 'kɔ:ld] heißen; genannt werden II

caller ['kɔ:lə] Anrufer; Anruferin II

*to keep **calm** [ˌki:p 'kɑ:m] Ruhe bewahren; ruhig bleiben <IV U3, 55>

calorie ['kælri] Kalorie <IV U3, 72>

came [keɪm] simple past von *to come* I

camel ['kæml] Kamel I

camera ['kæmrə] Fotoapparat; Kamera <III>
- camera operator ['kæmrə ˌɒpreɪtə] Kameramann; Kamerafrau <III>

camp [kæmp] Camp; Lager II

camper ['kæmpə] Camper; Camperin <IV U1, 30>

camping ['kæmpɪŋ] Camping; Zelten III
- to go camping [ˌgəʊ 'kæmpɪŋ] campen gehen; zelten II

campsite ['kæmpsaɪt] Campingplatz; Zeltplatz III

campus ['kæmpəs] Campus; Schulgelände IV U2, 35

can [kæn] Dose I

can [kæn; kən] können I
- can't [kɑ:nt] nicht können I

Canadian [kə'neɪdiən] kanadisch; aus Kanada; Kanadier; Kanadierin <IV U5, 144>

canary [kə'neəri] Kanarienvogel III

candidate ['kændɪdət] Kandidat; Kandidatin <IV U5, 109>

candle ['kændl] Kerze I

cannon ['kænən] Kanone II
- cannon ball ['kænən ˌbɔ:l] Kanonenkugel II

cannot ['kænɒt] nicht können III

canoe [kə'nu:] Kanu <IV U2, 138>

canoeing [kə'nu:ɪŋ] Kanufahren I

canvas ['kænvəs] Leinwand <IV U1, 136>

cap [kæp] Kappe; Mütze I

capital (city) ['kæpɪtl (sɪti)] Hauptstadt III

capital letter [ˌkæpɪtl 'letə] Großbuchstabe <III>

captain ['kæptɪn] Kapitän; Kapitänin I

caption ['kæpʃn] Untertitel; Bildunterschrift <II>

car [kɑ:] Auto I

caravan ['kærəvæn] Wohnwagen III

card [kɑ:d] Karte; Spielkarte I
- ID card [ˌaɪ'di: ˌkɑ:d] Ausweis; Personalausweis <IV U2, 44>
- playing card ['pleɪɪŋ ˌkɑ:d] Spielkarte <IV U4, 92>
- prompt card ['prɒmt ˌkɑ:d] Stichwortkarte <IV U2, 51>

cardboard ['kɑ:dbɔ:d] Pappe; Karton III

to **care** (for) ['keə (fɔ:)] sich kümmern (um) III
- to care about [ˌkeər‿ə'baʊt] wichtig nehmen; sich kümmern um; sich interessieren für IV U3, 58
- to take **care** of sb [ˌteɪk 'keər‿əv] sich um jmdn. kümmern; für jmdn. sorgen IV U2, 41

career [kə'rɪə] Beruf; Laufbahn; Karriere IV U1, 18

careful ['keəfl] vorsichtig; sorgfältig II
- Be careful! [bi: 'keəfl] Sei vorsichtig! I

caretaker ['keəˌteɪkə] Hausmeister; Hausmeisterin I

carnival ['kɑ:nɪvl] Karneval; Fasching IV U5, 98

carpenter ['kɑ:pəntə] Zimmermann; Zimmerin; Tischler; Tischlerin II

carpet ['kɑ:pɪt] Teppich I

carrot ['kærət] Karotte II

to **carry** ['kæri] tragen; befördern II

cart [kɑ:t] Stand IV U1, 14

cartoon [kɑ:'tu:n] Cartoon; Zeichentrickfilm <IV U4, 81>

case [keɪs] Fall; Verhandlung IV U5, 98
- court case ['kɔ:t ˌkeɪs] Gerichtsverhandlung; Rechtsfall IV U5, 107
- pencil case ['pensl ˌkeɪs] Federmäppchen I

cash [kæʃ] (mit) Bargeld II

casino [kə'si:nəʊ] Kasino; Spielkasino <IV U2, 139>

cast [kɑ:st] Gips III

castle ['kɑ:sl] Schloss; Burg II

cat [kæt] Katze I

*to **catch** [kætʃ] fangen II; finden <IV U4, 77>
- to catch sb's attention [ˌkætʃ‿ə'tenʃn] jmdn. auf sich aufmerksam machen <IV U3, 68>
- to catch up with [kætʃ‿'ʌp wɪð] einholen IV U3, 62
- I didn't catch that. [aɪ ˌdɪdnt 'kætʃ ðæt] Das habe ich nicht verstanden.; Das habe ich nicht gehört. IV U5, 102

catchy ['kætʃi] eingängig; einprägsam IV U4, 77

category ['kætəgri] Kategorie <IV U4, 142>

catering college ['keɪtərɪŋ ˌkɒlɪdʒ] Hotelfachschule II

cathedral [kə'θi:drl] Dom; Kathedrale <IV U1, 191>

Catholic ['kæθlɪk] katholisch; Katholik; Katholikin III
caught [kɔ:t] simple past, past participle von *to catch* II
to **cause** [kɔ:z] verursachen IV U4, 86
'cause (= because) [kɒz] weil <IV U2, 35>
cautious ['kɔ:ʃəs] vorsichtig; behutsam III
cave [keɪv] Höhle II
ceiling ['si:lɪŋ] Zimmerdecke IV U1, 14
to **celebrate** ['seləbreɪt] feiern I
celebration [ˌselə'breɪʃn] Feier IV U3, 52
celebrity [sə'lebrəti] Prominenter; Prominente; berühmte Person IV U5, 97
cell phone *(AE)* ['sel fəʊn] Mobiltelefon; Handy IV U3, 59
cemetery ['semətri] Friedhof <IV U3, 140>
cent [sent] Cent *(Währung)* III
center *(AE)* ['sentə] Zentrum; Mitte; Center IV U1, 13
centimetre (cm) ['sentɪˌmi:tə] Zentimeter (cm) I
centre ['sentə] Zentrum; Mitte; Center III
activity centre [æk'tɪvəti ˌsentə] Jugendzentrum III
city centre [ˌsɪti 'sentə] Stadtzentrum; Stadtmitte III
shopping centre ['ʃɒpɪŋ ˌsentə] Einkaufszentrum I
in the centre of [ˌɪn ðə 'sentər‿əv] in der Mitte von III
century ['senʃri] Jahrhundert III
cereal ['sɪəriəl] Müsli; Cornflakes III
ceremony ['serɪməni] Zeremonie <IV U4, 142>
certain ['sɜ:tn] bestimmte IV U1, 22
certainly ['sɜ:tnli] allerdings IV U1, 18
cevapcici [səvæp'tʃətʃi] Cevapcici <IV U5, 222>
chain [tʃeɪn] Kette <III>
chair [tʃeə] Stuhl I
chalk [tʃɔ:k] Kreide <IV U1, 28>
chance [tʃɑ:ns] Chance; Gelegenheit II; Möglichkeit IV U1, 18
change [tʃeɪndʒ] Münzgeld; Wechselgeld II
to **change** [tʃeɪndʒ] wechseln II; (sich) ändern; verändern; umsteigen III
to change one's mind [ˌtʃeɪndʒ wʌnz 'maɪnd] seine Meinung ändern III
chant [tʃɑ:nt] Sprechgesang <I>
chapter ['tʃæptə] Kapitel <IV U3, 64>
character ['kærəktə] Charakter; Figur <III>
charades [ʃə'rɑ:dz] Scharaden <II>
charger ['tʃɑ:dʒə] Ladegerät III
chart [tʃɑ:t] Diagramm; Tabelle <I>
bar chart ['bɑ: ˌtʃɑ:t] Balkendiagramm; Säulendiagramm <IV U1, 27>
pie chart ['paɪ ˌtʃɑ:t] Kuchendiagramm; Tortendiagramm <IV U1, 23>
charts *(pl only)* [tʃɑ:ts] Hitparade IV U5, 97
chaser ['tʃeɪsə] Jäger; Jägerin; Verfolger; Verfolgerin IV U2, 33
video **chat** ['vɪdiəʊ ˌtʃæt] Video-Chat III
to **chat** [tʃæt] chatten; plaudern II
cheap [tʃi:p] billig II
check [tʃek] Kontrolle IV U1, 22
spell check ['spel ˌtʃek] Rechtschreibprüfprogramm <III>
to **check** [tʃek] überprüfen; kontrollieren III
to check in [ˌtʃek‿'ɪn] einchecken III
to check out [ˌtʃek‿'aʊt] auschecken III; anschauen; ausprobieren IV U1, 14
checklist ['tʃeklɪst] Checkliste <I>
cheeky ['tʃi:ki] frech III
to **cheer** sb up [ˌtʃɪər‿'ʌp] jmdn. aufheitern; jmdn. aufmuntern III
cheerleader ['tʃɪəˌli:də] Cheerleader *(Mädchen, das in einer Gruppe eine Sportmannschaft anfeuert)* IV U2, 34
cheerleading ['tʃɪəˌli:dɪŋ] Cheerleading *(Aktivitäten der Cheerleader)* IV U2, 34
cheese [tʃi:z] Käse I
blue cheese [ˌblu: 'tʃi:s] Schimmelkäse II
cheesecake ['tʃi:skeɪk] Käsekuchen II
chef [ʃef] Koch; Köchin II
head chef ['hed ʃef] Chefkoch II
chemical additive [ˌkemɪkl 'ædətɪv] chemischer Zusatzstoff <IV U3, 72>
chewing gum ['tʃu:ɪŋ ˌgʌm] Kaugummi I
chic [ʃɪk] schick; elegant I
chicken ['tʃɪkɪn] Huhn I; Hähnchen IV U5, 98
child [tʃaɪld] Kind II
child labour [ˌtʃaɪld 'leɪbə] Kinderarbeit <IV U4, 74>
children *(pl)* ['tʃɪldrn] Kinder II
to **chill** out [ˌtʃɪl‿'aʊt] chillen; sich entspannen IV U4, 76
chilli ['tʃɪli] Chili II
china ['tʃaɪnə] Porzellan III
Chinese [tʃaɪ'ni:z] chinesisch; Chinesisch; aus China; Chinese; Chinesin IV U5, 99
chips *(pl)* [tʃɪps] Pommes frites I
chocolate ['tʃɒklət] Schokolade I; Praline IV U3, 54
choice [tʃɔɪs] Auswahl; Wahl IV U5, 102
*to **choose** [tʃu:z] auswählen; wählen II
chorus ['kɔ:rəs] Refrain <I>
chose [tʃəʊz] simple past von *to choose* II
chosen ['tʃəʊzn] past participle von *to choose* II
Christian ['krɪstʃn] christlich IV U3, 53
Christmas ['krɪsməs] Weihnachten I
chronological [ˌkrɒnə'lɒdʒɪkl] chronologisch <III>
church [tʃɜ:tʃ] Kirche II
cinema ['sɪnəmə] Kino I
circle ['sɜ:kl] Kreis; Ring III
to **cite** [saɪt] zitieren; anführen <IV U1, 15>

citizen ['sɪtɪzn] Staatsbürger; Staatsbürgerin; Staatsangehöriger; Staatsangehörige IV U1, 18
citizenship ['sɪtɪznʃɪp] Staatsangehörigkeit; Staatsbürgerschaft <IV U1, 24>
city ['sɪti] Stadt; Großstadt II
city centre [ˌsɪti 'sentə] Stadtzentrum; Stadtmitte III
city hall [ˌsɪti 'hɔːl] Rathaus <IV U5, 114>
civil rights *(pl)* [ˌsɪvl 'raɪts] Bürgerrechte IV U5, 96
Civil War [ˌsɪvl 'wɔː] Bürgerkrieg IV U3, 140
to **clap** [klæp] klatschen <I>
class [klɑːs] Unterricht I; Klasse III; Unterrichtsstunde; Kurs IV U2, 34
classic ['klæsɪk] Klassiker <IV U4, 142>
classical ['klæsɪkl] klassisch *(Musik)* III
classmate ['klɑːsmeɪt] Klassenkamerad; Klassenkameradin; Mitschüler; Mitschülerin <II>
classroom ['klɑːsrʊm] Klassenzimmer I
to **clean** [kliːn] sauber machen; putzen I
clean [kliːn] sauber I
vacuum **cleaner** ['vækjuːm ˌkliːnə] Staubsauger IV U3, 59
to **clear** [klɪə] abräumen; ausräumen IV U2, 33
to clear the table [ˌklɪə ðə 'teɪbl] den Tisch abräumen II
clear [klɪə] klar; deutlich; eindeutig IV U4, 77
clever ['klevə] schlau; klug; intelligent I
to **click** [klɪk] klicken I
to **climb** [klaɪm] besteigen; steigen; klettern III
rock **climbing** ['rɒk ˌklaɪmɪŋ] Klettern I
climbing ['klaɪmɪŋ] Kletter- IV U4, 78
clip [klɪp] Clip; Ausschnitt; Kurzfilm IV U4, 80
clock [klɒk] Uhr II
alarm clock [ə'lɑːm ˌklɒk] Wecker I
clock tower ['klɒk ˌtaʊə] Uhrenturm II
o'clock [ə'klɒk] Uhr *(Zeitangabe bei vollen Stunden)* I
to **close** [kləʊz] schließen; zumachen I
close [kləʊs] genau <III>
clothes *(pl)* [kləʊðz] Kleider *(Pl.)*; Kleidung I
cloud [klaʊd] Wolke IV U2, 33
cloudy ['klaʊdi] wolkig I
club [klʌb] Klub; Verein II
clubhouse ['klʌbhaʊs] Klubhaus; Vereinsheim IV U3, 62
clue [kluː] Hinweis; Spur I
coach [kəʊtʃ] Trainer; Trainerin <III>; Reisebus <IV U5, 223>
coal [kəʊl] Kohle III
coast [kəʊst] Küste III
on the coast [ˌɒn ðə 'kəʊst] an der Küste III
roller **coaster** ['rəʊlə ˌkəʊstə] Achterbahn II
coastguard ['kəʊstgɑːd] Küstenwache <III>
coastline ['kəʊstlaɪn] Küste <IV U4, 215>
coat [kəʊt] Jacke I
cocktail sauce ['kɒkteɪl ˌsɔːs] Cocktailsoße <IV U5, 112>
coconut ['kəʊkənʌt] Kokosnuss II
dress **code** ['dres ˌkəʊd] Kleiderordnung; Bekleidungsvorschriften IV U2, 36
coffee ['kɒfi] Kaffee IV U1, 14
coin [kɔɪn] Münze III
coke [kəʊk] Cola I
cold [kəʊld] kalt I
to get cold [ˌget 'kəʊld] frieren III
coleslaw ['kəʊlslɔː] Krautsalat <IV U5, 112>
collar ['kɒlə] Halsband I
to **collect** [kə'lekt] sammeln I
collection [kə'lekʃn] Sammlung; Kollektion IV U1, 13
college *(AE)* ['kɒlɪdʒ] Universität; Institut; College IV U5, 101
catering college ['keɪtərɪŋ ˌkɒlɪdʒ] Hotelfachschule II
colonist ['kɒlənɪst] Kolonist; Kolonistin; Siedler; Siedlerin <IV U1, 24>
colony ['kɒləni] Kolonie <IV U3, 70>
color *(AE)* ['kʌlə] Farbe IV ZI, 8
colour ['kʌlə] Farbe I
coloured ['kʌləd] buntes <IV U3, 71>
colourful ['kʌləfl] bunt II
comb ['kəʊm] Kamm III
combination [ˌkɒmbɪ'neɪʃn] Kombination II
*to **come** [kʌm] kommen I
to come to mind [ˌkʌm tə 'maɪnd] einem einfallen; zufällig einfallen <IV U4, 95>
to come true [ˌkʌm 'truː] wahr werden; in Erfüllung gehen IV U1, 18
to come up [ˌkʌm‿'ʌp] bevorstehen III
Come on! [ˌkʌm‿'ɒn] Komm jetzt! I; Komm schon! III
comedy ['kɒmədi] Komödie III
comfortable ['kʌmftəbl] bequem; angenehm III
comic ['kɒmɪk] Comic(heft) II
comic strip ['kɒmɪk strɪp] Comic <III>
comment ['kɒment] Kommentar IV U4, 80
to put a comment [ˌpʊt‿ə 'kɒment] einen Kommentar schreiben <I>
to **comment** (on) ['kɒment (ɒn)] kommentieren <IV U3, 61>
to **communicate** [kə'mjuːnɪkeɪt] kommunizieren; sich verständigen IV U4, 80
community [kə'mjuːnəti] Gemeinde; Gemeinschaft IV U1, 18
commuter [kə'mjuːtə] Pendler; Pendlerin IV U1, 15
company ['kʌmpəni] Gesellschaft; Firma II
to **compare** [kəm'peə] vergleichen I
comparison [kəm'pærɪsn] Vergleich <IV U2, 37>
competition [ˌkɒmpə'tɪʃn] Wettbewerb II; Konkurrenz IV U2, 34

competitive [kəm'petɪtɪv] wettkampforientiert; leistungsorientiert III
to **complain** [kəm'pleɪn] sich beschweren; sich beklagen III
complaint [kəm'pleɪnt] Beschwerde III
to **complete** [kəm'pli:t] vervollständigen I; absolvieren; abschließen <IV U2, 44>; fertigstellen IV U5, 101
complete [kəm'pli:t] vollständig IV U5, 106
completely [kəm'pli:tli] völlig III
to **compromise** ['kɒmprəmaɪz] sich einigen; Kompromisse schließen IV U5, 98
computer [ˌkəm'pju:tə] Computer I
computer science [kəmˌpju:tə 'saɪəns] Informatik <III>
to **concentrate** ['kɒnsntreɪt] (sich) konzentrieren IV U3, 58
concert ['kɒnsət] Konzert II
to **conclude** [kən'klu:d] schließen; zusammenfassen <IV U3, 207>
conclusion [kən'klu:ʒn] Schlussfolgerung; Schluss III
concrete ['kɒŋkri:t] Beton III
condition [kən'dɪʃn] Bedingung; Zustand IV U1, 22
working **conditions** *(pl only)* ['wɜ:kɪŋ kənˌdɪʃnz] Arbeitsbedingungen <IV U4, 88>
confident ['kɒnfɪdnt] selbstsicher; selbstbewusst III
to **confirm** [kən'fɜ:m] bestätigen; bekräftigen IV U4, 84
conflict ['kɒnflɪkt] Auseinandersetzung; Konflikt <III>
to **confront** [kən'frʌnt] konfrontieren; entgegentreten; sich stellen IV U5, 98
confused [kən'fju:zd] verwirrt; wirr III
Congratulations! [ˌkɒŋgrætjʊ'leɪʃnz] Glückwunsch! II
to **connect** [kə'nekt] verbinden III
connecting [kə'nektɪŋ] verbindend <II>
connective [kə'nektɪv] Bindewort <III>
consent [kən'sent] Zustimmung; Einwilligung <IV U4, 88>
consequence ['kɒnsɪkwəns] Konsequenz; Folge; Auswirkung <IV U2, 40>
constant ['kɒnstənt] ständig; konstant; stetig; permanent <IV U4, 88>
construction site [kən'strʌkʃn ˌsaɪt] Baustelle IV U1, 15
contact ['kɒntækt] Kontakt IV U1, 18
to **contact** ['kɒntækt] sich in Verbindung setzen; kontaktieren <IV U1, 30>
container [kən'teɪnə] Container; Behälter; Behältnis <IV U1, 30>
content ['kɒntent] Inhalt III
to **continue** [kən'tɪnju:] fortfahren; weitergehen <IV U2, 43>; andauern; weitermachen; fortsetzen IV U4, 86
pro and **contra** [ˌprəʊ ən 'kɒntrə] für und wider <IV U5, 115>
to **contribute** [kən'trɪbju:t] beitragen; mitwirken <IV U2, 49>
control [kən'trəʊl] Kontrolle; Steuerung IV U3, 53
to **control** [kən'trəʊl] kontrollieren <IV U3, 68>
controversial [ˌkɒntrə'vɜ:ʃl] umstritten; strittig <IV U5, 98>
convenience food [kən'vi:niəns ˌfu:d] Fertignahrung <IV U3, 72>
conversation [ˌkɒnvə'seɪʃn] Konversation; Gespräch; Unterhaltung III
to **convince** [kən'vɪns] überzeugen <IV U2, 47>
convinced [kən'vɪnst] überzeugt IV U3, 59
convincing [kən'vɪnsɪŋ] überzeugend III
to **cook** [kʊk] kochen II
cooking ['kʊkɪŋ] Kochen II
to **cool** [ku:l] kühlen III; abkühlen lassen <IV U5, 113>
cool [ku:l] cool; super; kühl I
to keep **cool** [ˌki:p 'ku:l] Ruhe bewahren <III>
cooperative [kəʊ'ɒprətɪv] kooperativ; hilfsbereit IV U2, 38
copy ['kɒpi] Kopie II; Abschrift <III>; Exemplar IV U5, 97
to **copy** ['kɒpi] kopieren II; abschreiben <III>
core subject [ˌkɔ: 'sʌbdʒɪkt] Pflichtfach IV U2, 35
corn [kɔ:n] Korn; Mais; Getreide IV ZI, 9
corner ['kɔ:nə] Ecke III
corner shop ['kɔ:nə ˌʃɒp] Tante-Emma-Laden I
Cornish ['kɔ:nɪʃ] Cornish; aus Cornwall II
to **correct** [kə'rekt] verbessern I
correct [kə'rekt] richtig; korrekt IV U1, 14
corridor ['kɒrɪdɔ:] Gang; Flur II
*to **cost** [kɒst] kosten III
cost [kɒst] simple past, past participle von *to cost* III
costume ['kɒstju:m] Kostüm I
cosy ['kəʊzi] gemütlich III
cottage ['kɒtɪdʒ] Häuschen III
cotton ['kɒtn] Baumwolle III
to **cough** [kɒf] husten III
could [kʊd] konnte; könnte III
to **count** [kaʊnt] zählen IV U1, 18
countdown ['kaʊntdaʊn] Countdown <I>
counter ['kaʊntə] Zähler <IV U2, 49>
country ['kʌntri] ländliche Gegend; Land I; Countrymusik IV U5, 97
country and western music [ˌkʌntri ənd 'westən ˌmju:zɪk] Countrymusik <IV U5, 145>
home **country** [ˌhəʊm 'kʌntri] Heimat; Heimatland IV U1, 19
in the **country** [ɪn ðə 'kʌntri] auf dem Land I
countryside ['kʌntrɪsaɪd] Land; Landschaft III
(a) **couple** of [ə 'kʌplˌəv] (ein) paar IV U2, 34
courage ['kʌrɪdʒ] Mut; Tapferkeit; Courage IV U5, 107
course [kɔ:s] Kurs III

main course [ˌmeɪn ˈkɔːs] Hauptgericht II

of course [əv ˈkɔːs] natürlich; selbstverständlich I

court [kɔːt] Spielfeld III; Gericht IV U5, 107

court case [ˈkɔːt ˌkeɪs] Gerichtsverhandlung; Rechtsfall IV U5, 107

cousin [ˈkʌzn] Cousin; Cousine II

to **cover** [ˈkʌvə] bedecken; abdecken IV U3, 58

to cover in flour [ˌkʌvər‿ɪn ˈflaʊə] in Mehl wenden IV U5, 98

cow [kaʊ] Kuh III

co-worker [ˈkəʊˌwɜːkə] Arbeitskollege; Arbeitskollegin IV U2, 38

cranberry [ˈkrænbri] Cranberry; Preiselbeer- <IV U3, 72>

crazy [ˈkreɪzi] verrückt I

to drive sb crazy [ˌdraɪv … ˈkreɪzi] jmdn. verrückt machen III

ice cream [ˌaɪs ˈkriːm] Eiscreme; Eis I

to **create** [kriˈeɪt] schaffen; erschaffen <III>; machen <IV U2, 48>

creative [kriˈeɪtɪv] kreativ <IV U4, 90>

credit [ˈkredɪt] Schein <IV U2, 48>

credit card [ˈkredɪt ˌkɑːd] Kreditkarte <IV U2, 39>

creepy [ˈkriːpi] gruselig IV U3, 53

crew [kruː] Crew; Besatzung; Mannschaft III

cricket [ˈkrɪkɪt] Kricket II

crime [kraɪm] Verbrechen <IV U5, 114>

crisp [krɪsp] Kartoffelchip I

critic [ˈkrɪtɪk] Kritiker; Kritikerin <IV U1, 28>

Croatian [krəʊˈeɪʃn] kroatisch; Kroatisch; aus Kroatien; Kroate; Kroatin <IV U5, 222>

crocodile [ˈkrɒkədaɪl] Krokodil I

to **cross** [krɒs] überqueren III

to cross the border [ˌkrɒs ðə ˈbɔːdə] über die Grenze gehen; die Grenze überschreiten IV U1, 19

crossed [krɒst] verschränkt <IV U4, 95>

crossing [ˈkrɒsɪŋ] Überfahrt; Überquerung IV U1, 22

crossroads *(pl only)* [ˈkrɒsrəʊdz] Kreuzung <IV U1, 15>

crowd [kraʊd] Menschenmenge II

crowded [ˈkraʊdɪd] überfüllt IV U1, 22

crushed ice [ˈkrʌʃt ˌaɪs] zerstoßenes Eis <IV U5, 113>

to **cry** [kraɪ] weinen; schreien <IV U5, 114>

Cuban [ˈkjuːbən] kubanisch; aus Kuba; Kubaner; Kubanerin IV U1, 18

cuddly [ˈkʌdli] knuddelig III

cuddly toy [ˈkʌdli ˌtɔɪ] Kuscheltier III

cultural [ˈkʌltʃrl] kulturell IV U1, 13

cultural movement [ˌkʌltʃrl ˈmuːvmənt] Kulturbewegung IV U1, 13

culture [ˈkʌltʃə] Kultur IV U1, 18

cup [kʌp] Tasse II

cupboard [ˈkʌbəd] Schrank III

curious [ˈkjʊəriəs] neugierig <IV U5, 115>

currency [ˈkʌrnsi] Währung IV ZI, 8

curry [ˈkʌri] Curry II

custard [ˈkʌstəd] Vanillesauce II

custom [ˈkʌstəm] Brauch; Sitte IV U5, 97

customer [ˈkʌstəmə] Kunde; Kundin III

*to **cut** [kʌt] (sich) schneiden II

cut [kʌt] simple past, past participle von *to cut* II

cute [kjuːt] niedlich; süß I

CV (= Curriculum Vitae) [ˌsiːˈviː] Lebenslauf <IV U2, 48>

cyberbullying [ˈsaɪbəˌbʊliɪŋ] Cyber-Mobbing IV U4, 80

cycling [ˈsaɪklɪŋ] Radfahren III

D

dad [dæd] Papa I

daily [ˈdeɪli] täglich IV U4, 80

dairy product [ˈdeəri ˌprɒdʌkt] Milchprodukt; Milcherzeugnis <IV U3, 72>

dance [dɑːns] Tanz III; Tanzveranstaltung; Ball IV U2, 33

folk dance [ˈfəʊk ˌdɑːns] Volkstanz <IV U5, 145>

line dance [ˈlaɪn ˌdɑːns] Line Dance *(alle tanzen zusammen in einer Reihe)* <IV U5, 145>

to **dance** [dɑːns] tanzen I

dancer [ˈdɑːnsə] Tänzer; Tänzerin III

dancing [ˈdɑːnsɪŋ] Tanzen; Tanz- IV U2, 43

danger [ˈdeɪndʒə] Gefahr <IV U5, 114>

dangerous [ˈdeɪndʒrəs] gefährlich III

daredevil [ˈdeəˌdevl] Draufgänger; Draufgängerin IV U3, 53

the **dark** [ðə ˈdɑːk] Dunkelheit III

dark [dɑːk] dunkel I

data [ˈdeɪtə] Daten; Angaben <IV U1, 26>

date [deɪt] Datum I; Verabredung; Date IV U2, 42

daughter [ˈdɔːtə] Tochter I

day [deɪ] Tag I

a day off [ə ˌdeɪ‿ˈɒf] ein freier Tag III

all day [ɔːl ˈdeɪ] den ganzen Tag III

in the old days [ɪn ði ˈəʊld ˌdeɪz] früher III

lucky day [ˌlʌki ˈdeɪ] Glückstag II

one day [wʌn ˈdeɪ] eines Tages III

a busy day [ə ˌbɪzi ˈdeɪ] ein ausgefüllter Tag I

four hours a day [ˌaʊəz‿ə ˈdeɪ] vier Stunden täglich I

dead [ded] tot III

deadline [ˈdedlaɪn] Termin; Abgabetermin <IV U2, 49>

deadly [ˈdedli] tod-; tödlich III

deaf [def] gehörlos; schwerhörig; taub III

*to **deal** (with) [diːl (wɪð)] sich befassen (mit); umgehen (mit) IV U3, 73

dealt (with) [delt (wɪð)] simple past, past participle von *to deal with* IV U3, 73

Dear …, [dɪə] Liebe/Lieber …, *(Anrede in Briefen)* I

death [deθ] Tod <IV U5, 108>

debate [dɪˈbeɪt] Diskussion; Debatte IV U5, 98

December [dɪ'sembə] Dezember I
to **decide** [dɪ'saɪd] (sich) entscheiden III
decision [dɪ'sɪʒn] Entscheidung IV U1, 18
to make a decision [ˌmeɪk‿ə dɪ'sɪʒn] eine Entscheidung treffen <III>
deck [dek] Schiffsdeck IV U1, 22
to **decorate** ['dekreɪt] dekorieren; verzieren; schmücken <IV U3, 71>
deep [di:p] tief IV U5, 102
to **defeat** [dɪ'fi:t] besiegen <IV U3, 140>
definition [ˌdefɪ'nɪʃn] Definition <III>
degree [dɪ'gri:] Grad IV U5, 102
delicious [dɪ'lɪʃəs] köstlich II
deluxe [dɪ'lʌks] Luxus- IV U5, 102
democracy [dɪ'mɒkrəsi] Demokratie <IV U3, 141>
dense [dens] dicht IV U4, 74
department [dɪ'pɑ:tmənt] Abteilung II
department store [dɪ'pɑ:tmənt ˌstɔ:] Kaufhaus II
to **depend** (on) [dɪ'pend (ɒn)] abhängen (von) <IV U2, 48>
descendant [dɪ'sendənt] Abkömmling; Nachfahre; Nachfahrin IV U1, 22
to **describe** [dɪ'skraɪb] beschreiben IV U3, 73
description [dɪ'skrɪpʃn] Beschreibung <IV U2, 43>
to **deserve** [dɪ'zɜ:v] verdienen IV U4, 80
design [dɪ'zaɪn] Design; Gestaltung IV U4, 77
Design Technology (DT) [dɪˌzaɪn tek'nɒlədʒi, ˌdi:'ti:] Technik I
graphic design [ˌgræfɪk dɪ'zaɪn] Grafikdesign; grafische Gestaltung <IV U2, 49>
to **design** [dɪ'zaɪn] entwerfen; gestalten <III>
desk [desk] Schreibtisch IV U3, 62
information desk [ɪnfə'meɪʃn ˌdesk] Information II
desperately ['desprətli] dringend; verzweifelt IV U4, 85

dessert [dɪ'zɜ:t] Nachspeise II
destination [ˌdestɪ'neɪʃn] Ziel; Reiseziel IV U5, 96
detail ['di:teɪl] Detail; Einzelheit IV U5, 102
language detectives ['læŋgwɪdʒ ˌdɪtektɪvz] Sprachdetektive <I>
detector [dɪ'tektə] Detektor III
detention [dɪ'tenʃn] Nachsitzen IV U2, 35
to **develop** [dɪ'veləp] (sich) entwickeln IV U1, 18
development [dɪ'veləpmənt] Entwicklung <IV U5, 144>
device [dɪ'vaɪs] Gerät; Vorrichtung IV U3, 58
dialect ['daɪəlekt] Dialekt <IV U3, 58>
dialogue ['daɪəlɒg] Dialog; Gespräch <III>
diamond ['daɪəmənd] Diamant <II>
diary ['daɪəri] Tagebuch I
dictionary ['dɪkʃnri] Wörterbuch <III>
did [dɪd] simple past von *to do* I
to **die** [daɪ] sterben III
difference ['dɪfrns] Unterschied <III>
different ['dɪfrnt] anders; unterschiedlich I
difficult ['dɪfɪklt] schwierig III
difficulty ['dɪfɪklti] Schwierigkeit <IV U4, 88>
*to **dig** [dɪg] graben; schürfen IV U4, 85
dining room ['daɪnɪŋ ˌrʊm] Esszimmer I
dinner ['dɪnə] Abendessen II; Essen IV U3, 53
direct [dɪ'rekt] direkt <III>
direct speech [dɪˌrekt 'spi:tʃ] direkte Rede <IV U3, 73>
direction [dɪ'rekʃn] Richtung IV U2, 33
directions *(pl)* [dɪ'rekʃnz] Anweisungen; Wegbeschreibung <III>
director [dɪ'rektə] Regisseur; Regisseurin II
dirty ['dɜ:ti] dreckig; schmutzig I
to **disagree** [ˌdɪsə'gri:] anderer Meinung sein; nicht einverstanden sein II

to **disappear** [ˌdɪsə'pɪə] verschwinden IV U3, 62
disaster [dɪ'zɑ:stə] Desaster; Katastrophe; Unglück III
to **discover** [dɪ'skʌvə] entdecken <IV U2, 138>
discovery [dɪ'skʌvri] Entdeckung IV U4, 84
discrimination [dɪˌskrɪmɪ'neɪʃn] Diskriminierung IV U5, 96
to **discuss** [dɪ'skʌs] diskutieren <III>
disease [dɪ'zi:z] Krankheit IV U1, 22
dish [dɪʃ] Gericht; Speise II
dishwasher ['dɪʃˌwɒʃə] Spülmaschine IV U3, 59
to **dislike** [dɪ'slaɪk] nicht mögen IV U4, 81
disorganized [ˌdɪs'ɔ:gənaɪzd] unorganisiert; ungeordnet IV U2, 39
distance ['dɪstns] Entfernung; Distanz IV ZI, 9
in the distance [ˌɪn ðə 'dɪstns] in der Ferne IV U1, 14
to **distract** sb (from sth) [dɪ'strækt (frəm)] jmdn. (von etw.) ablenken <IV U2, 47>
to **dive** [daɪv] springen <IV U5, 114>
to **divide** (up) [dɪ'vaɪd (ʌp)] teilen; aufteilen; unterteilen <IV U4, 79>
division [dɪ'vɪʒn] Abteilung <IV U5, 114>
DJing [ˌdi:'dʒeɪɪŋ] Musikauflegen <IV U1, 136>
*to **do** [du:] machen; tun I
to do homework [ˌdu: 'həʊmwɜ:k] Hausaufgabe(n) machen I
to do the right thing [ˌdu: ðə 'raɪt θɪŋ] das Richtige tun III
to do the shopping [ˌdu: ðə 'ʃɒpɪŋ] Einkäufe machen; Besorgungen machen II
to do the washing up [ˌdu: ðə 'wɒʃɪŋ‿ʌp] abspülen II
to **dock** [dɒk] andocken IV U1, 22
doctor ['dɒktə] Arzt; Ärztin II
document ['dɒkjəmənt] Dokument <IV U3, 141>

documentary [ˌdɒkjəˈmentri] Dokumentarfilm <IV U4, 142>

dog [dɒg] Hund I

dog biscuit [ˈdɒg ˌbɪskɪt] Hundekeks II

dog walker [ˈdɒg ˌwɔːkə] Hundeausführer; Hundeausführerin IV U2, 41

dollar [ˈdɒlə] Dollar *(amer. Währungseinheit)* IV ZI, 8

dolphin [ˈdɒlfɪn] Delfin <III>

dome [dəʊm] Kuppel II

done [dʌn] past participle von *to do* II

door [dɔː] Tür I

doorbell [ˈdɔːbel] Türklingel IV U3, 54

to **double-check** [ˌdʌblˈtʃek] genau nachprüfen <III>

to **doubt** [daʊt] bezweifeln IV U3, 59

down [daʊn] entlang; herunter; hinunter III; deprimiert III

down there [ˌdaʊn ˈðeə] dahin; da unten IV U5, 98

to **download** [ˌdaʊnˈləʊd] herunterladen II

downtown *(AE)* [ˌdaʊnˈtaʊn] im Stadtzentrum IV U1, 14

Dr [ˈdɒktə] Dr. *(Anrede)* III

draft [drɑːft] Entwurf <II>

drafting [ˈdrɑːftɪŋ] Formulieren <III>

to **drag** [dræg] schleppen; schleifen; ziehen IV U5, 107

drama [ˈdrɑːmə] Theater II; Drama III

drank [dræŋk] simple past von *to drink* II

*to **draw** [drɔː] zeichnen II

drawing [ˈdrɔːɪŋ] Zeichnung; Bild <IV U4, 79>

drawn [drɔːn] past participle von *to draw* II

dreadful [ˈdredfl] furchtbar III

dream [driːm] Traum I

*to **dream** [driːm] träumen III

dreamt [dremt] simple past, past participle von *to dream* III

dress [dres] Kleid I

dress code [ˈdres ˌkəʊd] Kleiderordnung; Bekleidungsvorschriften IV U2, 36

fancy dress [ˌfænsi ˈdres] Verkleidung; Kostüm I

dressed [drest] angezogen; verkleidet III

to get dressed [ˌget ˈdrest] sich anziehen II

drew [druː] simple past von *to draw* II

drink [drɪŋk] Getränk II

*to **drink** [drɪŋk] trinken II

anything to drink [ˈeniθɪŋ tə ˈdrɪŋk] etwas zu trinken II

drinking straw [ˈdrɪŋkɪŋ ˌstrɔː] Trinkhalm <IV U3, 71>

*to **drive** [draɪv] fahren; treiben IV U2, 33

to drive sb crazy [ˌdraɪv … ˈkreɪzi] jmdn. verrückt machen III

driven [ˈdrɪvn] past participle von *to drive* IV U2, 33

driver [ˈdraɪvə] Fahrer; Fahrerin III

driver's license *(AE)* [ˈdraɪvəz ˌlaɪsns] Führerschein IV U2, 38

lorry driver [ˈlɒri ˌdraɪvə] LKW-Fahrer; LKW-Fahrerin II

driving [ˈdraɪvɪŋ] Fahren; Fahr- <IV U2, 44>

driving school [ˈdraɪvɪŋ ˌskuːl] Fahrschule <IV U2, 44>

drove [drəʊv] simple past von *to drive* IV U2, 33

to **drown** [draʊn] ertrinken <IV U5, 114>

drug [drʌg] Droge <IV U3, 72>

drum [drʌm] Trommel <III>

drumming [ˈdrʌmɪŋ] Trommel- III

drunk [drʌŋk] past participle von *to drink* II; betrunken IV U3, 62

… to keep them drunk [tə ˌkiːp ðəm ˈdrʌŋk] … dass sie betrunken bleiben IV U3, 62

to **dry** [draɪ] trocknen IV U5, 98

dry [draɪ] trocken III

dryer [ˈdraɪə] Wäschetrockner IV U3, 58

dug [dʌg] simple past, past participle von *to dig* IV U4, 85

dull [dʌl] langweilig; matt IV U4, 77

dumpling [ˈdʌmplɪŋ] Kloß II

during [ˈdjʊərɪŋ] während III

to **dust** [dʌst] abstauben; Staub wischen IV U2, 38

E

each [iːtʃ] jeder <I>

each other [ˌiːtʃ‿ˈʌðə] einander; sich; sich gegenseitig III

each [iːtʃ] pro Stück II

bald **eagle** [ˌbɔːld ˈiːgl] Weißkopfseeadler IV ZI, 8

ear [ɪə] Ohr II

early [ˈɜːli] früh I

earlier [ˈɜːliə] früher I

to **earn** [ɜːn] verdienen IV U2, 32

to earn a living [ˌɜːn‿ə ˈlɪvɪŋ] seinen Lebensunterhalt verdienen <IV U4, 88>

earth [ɜːθ] die Erde; Boden; Erde; Erdboden IV U4, 76

east [iːst] Osten III

east of [ˈiːst‿əv] östlich von IV ZI, 9

easy [ˈiːzi] einfach; leicht I

*to **eat** [iːt] essen I

eaten [ˈiːtn] past participle von *to eat* II

editing [ˈedɪtɪŋ] Kontrolle <III>; Bearbeitung; Redaktion <IV U2, 49>

edition [ɪˈdɪʃn] Ausgabe; Auflage; Edition IV U4, 84

education [ˌedʒʊˈkeɪʃn] Ausbildung; Erziehung; Bildung IV U2, 38

effect [ɪˈfekt] Effekt; Wirkung <IV U3, 72>

special effect [ˌspeʃl ɪˈfekt] Spezialeffekt <IV U4, 142>

egg [eg] Ei I

scrambled egg [ˌskræmbld‿ˈeg] Rührei II

eight [eɪt] acht I

eighteen [ˌeɪˈtiːn] achtzehn I

eighty [ˈeɪti] achtzig I

not … either [nɒt … 'aɪðə] auch nicht III
either way ['aɪðə ˌweɪ] ganz egal; so oder so <IV U1, 137>
elderly ['eldəli] älter IV U3, 54
to **elect** [ɪ'lekt] wählen <IV U2, 46>
election [ɪ'lekʃn] Wahl <IV U2, 46>
elective [ɪ'lektɪv] Wahlfach IV U2, 34
electric [ɪ'lektrɪk] elektrisch IV U3, 59
electricity [ˌelɪk'trɪsəti] Strom; Elektrizität III
element ['elɪmənt] Element <IV U3, 67>
elephant ['elɪfənt] Elefant I
elevator *(AE)* ['elɪveɪtə] Aufzug; Lift IV U1, 13
eleven [ɪ'levn] elf I
e-mail ['i:meɪl] E-Mail I
embarrassed [ɪm'bærəst] verlegen II
embarrassing [ɪm'bærəsɪŋ] peinlich IV U2, 42
emergency [ɪ'mɜ:dʒnsi] Notfall III
emergency call [ɪ'mɜ:dʒnsi ˌkɔ:l] Notruf III
emergency service [ɪ'mɜ:dʒnsi ˌsɜ:vɪs] Notdienst; Rettungsdienst III
to **emigrate** ['emɪgreɪt] auswandern; emigrieren IV U1, 19
emotion [ɪ'məʊʃn] Gefühl; Emotion <IV U3, 57>
to **emphasize** ['emfəsaɪz] betonen <IV U2, 51>
empire ['empaɪə] Reich; Kaiserreich III
to **employ** [ɪm'plɔɪ] einstellen; anstellen; beschäftigen <IV U4, 88>
empty ['emti] leer IV U4, 86
encyclopedia [ɪnˌsaɪklə'pi:diə] Enzyklopädie; Lexikon IV U4, 86
end [end] Ende; Schluss II
by the end [ˌbaɪ ði 'end] am Schluss II
in the end [ɪn ði 'end] schließlich; zum Schluss II
to **end** [end] enden; beenden; aufhören IV U2, 34
to end up [ˌend‿'ʌp] enden; landen <IV U5, 114>
ending ['endɪŋ] Schluss; Ende III
happy ending [ˌhæpi 'endɪŋ] Happy End <III>
enemy ['enəmi] Feind; Feindin III
energetic [ˌenə'dʒetɪk] tatkräftig IV U4, 89
engine ['endʒɪn] Motor IV U3, 54
fire engine ['faɪər‿ˌendʒɪn] Feuerwehrauto II
search engine ['sɜ:tʃ‿ˌendʒɪn] Suchmaschine <IV U1, 31>
steam engine ['sti:m‿ˌendʒɪn] Dampfmaschine III
engineer [ˌendʒɪ'nɪə] Ingenieur; Ingenieurin; Techniker; Technikerin II
English ['ɪŋglɪʃ] englisch; Englisch; aus England I
the **English** [ði 'ɪŋglɪʃ] die Engländer III
to **enjoy** [ɪn'dʒɔɪ] genießen II; mögen III
to enjoy oneself [ɪn'dʒɔɪ] Spaß haben; sich amüsieren III
enough [ɪ'nʌf] genug; genügend III
to **enter** ['entə] hineingehen; hereinkommen; betreten; eintreten IV U3, 54
entertainment *(no pl)* [ˌentə'teɪnmənt] Unterhaltung <IV U4, 90>
entry ['entri] Eintrag IV U4, 86; Einlass <IV U5, 223>
entry form ['entri ˌfɔ:m] Anmeldeformular II
envelope ['envələʊp] Umschlag; Briefumschlag <IV U4, 142>
environment [ɪn'vaɪrnmənt] Umgebung; Umwelt <IV U2, 138>
equal ['i:kwəl] gleich <IV U5, 108>
equipment [ɪ'kwɪpmənt] Ausrüstung III
Victorian **era** [vɪkˌtɔ:riən 'ɪərə] viktorianisches Zeitalter III
eraser [ɪ'reɪzə] Radiergummi I
escalator ['eskəleɪtə] Rolltreppe II
to **escape** [ɪ'skeɪp] entkommen; fliehen; entfliehen; flüchten IV U1, 23
especially [ɪ'speʃli] besonders; vor allem IV U1, 13
establishing shot [ɪ'stæblɪʃɪŋ ˌʃɒt] Anfangsszene; Eingangsszene <IV U2, 45>
estimate ['estɪmeɪt] Schätzung <IV U4, 88>
ethnic ['eθnɪk] ethnisch; Volks- <IV U1, 26>
euro ['jʊərəʊ] Euro *(Währung)* III
European [ˌjʊərə'pi:ən] europäisch; Europäisch; aus Europa; Europäer; Europäerin IV U2, 32
even ['i:vn] noch; sogar II; lieber IV U1, 14
evening ['i:vnɪŋ] Abend I
in the evenings [ɪn ði 'i:vnɪŋz] abends III
event [ɪ'vent] Ereignis; Veranstaltung IV U1, 13
sporting event ['spɔ:tɪŋ ɪˌvent] Sportereignis; Sportveranstaltung <IV U2, 50>
ever ['evə] jemals II
every ['evri] jeder I
everybody ['evriˌbɒdi] jeder; alle IV U2, 43
everyday ['evrideɪ] alltäglich <IV U1, 15>
everyone ['evriwʌn] jeder I; zusammen; alle II
everything ['evriθɪŋ] alles II
evil ['i:vl] böse; schlecht IV U3, 63
exact [ɪg'zækt] exakt; genau III
exactly [ɪg'zæktli] genau IV U3, 59
exam [ɪg'zæm] Prüfung; Examen <IV U1, 24>
example [ɪg'zɑ:mpl] Beispiel IV U1, 18
for example [fər‿ɪg'zɑ:mpl] zum Beispiel IV U2, 34
excellent ['ekslnt] exzellent; hervorragend IV U5, 102
except [ɪk'sept] außer III
exception [ɪk'sepʃn] Ausnahme <IV U1, 24>
exceptionally [ɪk'sepʃnli] außergewöhnlich; besonders <IV U5, 114>

exchange [ɪks'tʃeɪndʒ] Austausch IV U2, 34
to **exchange** [ɪks'tʃeɪndʒ] tauschen; austauschen <III>
excited [ɪk'saɪtɪd] aufgeregt; begeistert II
excitement [ɪk'saɪtmənt] Aufregung IV U4, 75
exciting [ɪk'saɪtɪŋ] spannend; aufregend I
excuse [ɪk'skju:s] Entschuldigung; Ausrede <III>
Excuse me! [ɪk'skju:z mi] Entschuldigung! I
exercise ['eksəsaɪz] Übung I
exercise book ['eksəsaɪz ˌbʊk] Übungsheft I
exhausted [ɪg'zɔ:stɪd] erschöpft III
exhibition [ˌeksɪ'bɪʃn] Ausstellung III
to **exist** [ɪg'zɪst] existieren; bestehen <IV U1, 28>
to **expect** [ɪk'spekt] erwarten III
expensive [ɪk'spensɪv] teuer II
experience [ɪk'spɪəriəns] Erfahrung; Erlebnis IV U4, 79
to **experience** [ɪk'spɪəriəns] erleben; erfahren IV U5, 98
experiment [ɪk'sperɪmənt] Versuch II
expert ['ekspɜ:t] Experte; Expertin IV U4, 77
to **explain** [ɪk'spleɪn] erklären III
explanation [ˌeksplə'neɪʃn] Erklärung; Erläuterung <IV U2, 51>
to **explode** [ɪk'spləʊd] explodieren III
to **explore** [ɪk'splɔ:] erkunden; erforschen II
explosion [ɪk'spləʊʒn] Explosion III
to **express** [ɪk'spres] ausdrücken <III>
expression [ɪk'spreʃn] Ausdruck; Wendung; Äußerung <IV U4, 81>
facial expression ['feɪʃl ɪkˌspreʃn] Gesichtsausdruck; Mimik <IV U4, 95>
extra ['ekstrə] Extra; Zusatz <IV U5, 112>
extra ['ekstrə] zusätzlich; Zusatz- II
extra activities ['ekstrə ˌæktɪvətiz] Zusatzaktivitäten <I>
extracurricular [ˌekstrəkə'rɪkjələ] außerhalb des Lehrplans; außerunterrichtlich *(Zusatzunterricht)* IV U2, 34
extreme [ɪk'stri:m] Extreme <IV U1, 29>
extremely [ɪk'stri:mli] äußerst; sehr IV U4, 80
eye [aɪ] Auge II
eye-catching ['aɪˌkætʃɪŋ] auffallend; plakativ <IV U1, 27>

F

fable ['feɪbl] Fabel; Märchen III
face [feɪs] Gesicht IV U3, 63
to **face** [feɪs] schauen <IV U5, 145>
facial expression ['feɪʃl ɪkˌspreʃn] Gesichtsausdruck; Mimik <IV U4, 95>
fact [fækt] Fakt; Tatsache II
in fact [ɪn 'fækt] eigentlich; tatsächlich; genau genommen III
factory ['fæktri] Fabrik; Werk III
to **fail** (at) [feɪl (ət)] versagen (in/bei); ausfallen; fehlschlagen IV U1, 19
failed [feɪld] fehlgeschlagen; gescheitert; erfolglos <IV U4, 88>
Fair enough. [ˌfeər‿ɪ'nʌf] Na schön. III
fall *(AE)* [fɔ:l] Herbst IV ZI, 8
*to **fall** [fɔ:l] fallen I
to fall (over) [ˌfɔ:l‿'əʊvə] fallen; hinfallen; umfallen III
to fall asleep [ˌfɔ:l‿ə'sli:p] einschlafen III
to fall behind [ˌfɔ:l bɪ'haɪnd] zurückfallen <IV U2, 35>
to fall in love (with) [ˌfɔ:l‿ɪn 'lʌv] sich verlieben (in) III
to fall off [ˌfɔ:l‿'ɒf] fallen; herunterfallen III
to fall out of [ˌfɔ:l‿'aʊt‿əv] herausfallen aus IV U2, 42
false [fɔ:ls] falsch <II>
familiar [fə'mɪliə] vertraut; bekannt IV U2, 34
family ['fæmli] Familie I
host family ['həʊst ˌfæmli] Gastfamilie IV U2, 34
famine ['fæmɪn] Hungersnot <IV U1, 192>
famous ['feɪməs] berühmt I
fan [fæn] Fan I; Ventilator IV U3, 59
fancy dress [ˌfænsi 'dres] Verkleidung; Kostüm I
fantastic [fæn'tæstɪk] fantastisch; großartig II
fantasy ['fæntəsi] Fantasie; Fantasy II
FAQ (= frequently asked questions) [ˌefeɪ'kju: (ˌfri:kwəntli ˌɑ:skt 'kwestʃənz)] häufig gestellte Fragen <IV U1, 30>
far [fɑ:] weit III
as far as [ˌəz 'fɑ:r‿əz] soweit IV U3, 59
so far [ˌsəʊ 'fɑ:] bis jetzt IV U1, 18
fare [feə] Fahrpreis III
farewell speech [feə'wel spi:tʃ] Abschiedsrede II
farm [fɑ:m] Bauernhof I
wind farm ['wɪnd fɑ:m] Windpark III
farmer ['fɑ:mə] Landwirt; Landwirtin; Bauer; Bäuerin I
farmers' market [ˌfɑ:məz 'mɑ:kɪt] Bauernmarkt <IV U3, 72>
farming ['fɑ:mɪŋ] Landwirtschaft; Ackerbau IV U4, 84
farmland ['fɑ:mlænd] Ackerland; Ackerboden; Landwirtschaftsflächen IV U2, 32
fascinating ['fæsɪneɪtɪŋ] faszinierend IV U4, 77
fashion *(no pl)* ['fæʃn] Mode IV U3, 58
out of fashion [ˌaʊt‿əv 'fæʃn] altmodisch; nicht mehr aktuell IV U4, 81
fashionable ['fæʃnəbl] modisch II
fast [fɑ:st] schnell II
fast food [ˌfɑ:st 'fu:d] Fastfood I
fast food restaurant [ˌfɑ:st fu:d 'restrɒnt] Fastfood-Restaurant I
the fastest [ðə 'fɑ:stɪst] der/die/das schnellste I
father ['fɑ:ðə] Vater I
founding father [ˌfaʊndɪŋ 'fɑ:ðə] Gründungsvater <IV U3, 140>

favorite *(AE)* ['feɪvrɪt] Lieblings- IV U4, 80
favourite ['feɪvrɪt] Lieblings- I
fear [fɪə] Angst; Furcht <IV U5, 114>
feature ['fi:tʃə] Merkmal <III>; Feature; Artikel <IV U2, 49>
feature story ['fi:tʃə ˌstɔ:ri] Leitartikel; Sonderbericht <IV U5, 110>
February ['februri] Februar I
fed [fed] simple past von *to feed* I; past participle von *to feed* II
*to be **fed** up (with) [bi: fed‿'ʌp (wɪð)] die Nase voll haben (von); sauer sein III
federal ['fedrl] Bundes-; föderalistisch <IV U4, 88>
fee [fi:] Gebühr <IV U3, 66>
*to **feed** [fi:d] füttern I
feedback ['fi:dbæk] Feedback; Rückmeldung <II>
*to **feel** [fi:l] (sich) fühlen II
to feel sick [ˌfi:l 'sɪk] Übelkeit verspüren; sich schlecht fühlen IV U5, 103
to feel sorry for [ˌfi:l 'sɒri fə] Mitleid haben mit; bedauern III
to make sb feel like sth [ˌmeɪk … 'fi:l laɪk] jmdm. das Gefühl geben etw. zu sein III
feeling ['fi:lɪŋ] Gefühl <III>
fell [fel] simple past von *to fall* I
felt [felt] simple past von *to feel* II
felt-tip [ˌfelt'tɪp] Filzstift I
festival ['festɪvl] Festival; Fest III
fever ['fi:və] Fieber IV U4, 84
few [fju:] wenige IV U3, 53
a few [ə 'fju:] ein paar; wenige; einige III
science **fiction** [ˌsaɪəns 'fɪkʃn] Science-Fiction I
fictional ['fɪkʃnl] fiktiv <IV U1, 137>
field [fi:ld] Feld; Wiese; Weide IV ZI, 9
field goal ['fi:ld ˌgəʊl] Feldtor <IV U2, 50>
field trip ['fi:ld ˌtrɪp] Schulausflug <IV U2, 46>
fifteen [ˌfɪf'ti:n] fünfzehn I
fifty ['fɪfti] fünfzig I
fight [faɪt] Kampf; Streit III
*to **fight** [faɪt] kämpfen; (sich) streiten III
file [faɪl] Datei II
to **fill** [fɪl] (sich) füllen III; befüllen <IV U3, 71>
filled with ['fɪld ˌwɪð] gefüllt mit <IV U3, 72>
filling ['fɪlɪŋ] Füllung <IV U5, 112>
film [fɪlm] Film I
film maker ['fɪlm ˌmeɪkə] Filmemacher; Filmemacherin <III>
to **film** [fɪlm] filmen; drehen <III>
filming ['fɪlmɪŋ] Filmen; Drehen <IV U3, 54>
final match [ˌfaɪnl 'mætʃ] Endspiel <IV U2, 50>
finally ['faɪnli] schließlich; zum Schluss II; endlich; letztlich; zuletzt IV U4, 85
financial [faɪ'nænʃl] finanziell; Finanz- IV U1, 14
*to **find** [faɪnd] finden; herausfinden I
to find out [ˌfaɪnd‿'aʊt] herausfinden I
fine [faɪn] schön; gut; in Ordnung II
finger ['fɪŋgə] Finger III
fingerprint ['fɪŋgəprɪnt] Fingerabdruck II
to **finish** ['fɪnɪʃ] beenden; enden; aufhören; fertigstellen; vervollständigen II
fire [faɪə] Feuer I
to be on fire [bi: ɒn 'faɪə] brennen II
fire brigade ['faɪə brɪˌgeɪd] Feuerwehr <III>
fire engine ['faɪər‿ˌendʒɪn] Feuerwehrauto II
fired ['faɪəd] gefeuert; hinausgeworfen III
firework ['faɪəwɜ:k] Feuerwerk <IV U3, 141>
first [fɜ:st] zuerst; als Erstes; erste I
at first [ət 'fɜ:st] zuerst; zunächst IV U4, 84
first name [ˌfɜ:st 'neɪm] Vorname <III>
very first ['veri fɜ:st] allererste III
fish *(sg)* [fɪʃ], **fish** *(pl)* [fɪʃ] Fisch I
fisherman ['fɪʃəmən] Fischer <IV U2, 138>
fishing ['fɪʃɪŋ] Angeln; Fischen IV U5, 104
to **fit** [fɪt] passen II
to fit (in) [fɪt (ɪn)] hineinpassen (in) <IV U2, 35>
fit [fɪt] fit; in Form III
fitness ['fɪtnəs] Fitness <IV U3, 72>
fitness instructor ['fɪtnəs ɪnˌstrʌktə] Fitnesstrainer; Fitnesstrainerin <IV U3, 72>
jumping fitness ['dʒʌmpɪŋ ˌfɪtnəs] Jumping Fitness *(Trendsportart)* IV U4, 81
five [faɪv] fünf I
to **fix** [fɪks] fixieren; befestigen <IV U3, 71>
flag [flæg] Flagge; Fahne II
flame [fleɪm] Flamme III
flamingo [flə'mɪŋgəʊ] Flamingo I
flat [flæt] Wohnung I
flat [flæt] flach; platt IV U2, 32
flew [flu:] simple past von *to fly* II
flexible ['fleksɪbl] flexibel <IV U3, 68>
flight [flaɪt] Flug II
to **float** [fləʊt] treiben <IV U3, 71>
flood [flʌd] Flut; Hochwasser; Überschwemmung <IV U5, 114>
to **flood** [flʌd] fluten; überfluten; überschwemmen <IV U5, 114>
floor [flɔ:] Fußboden I; Stockwerk II
flour [flaʊə] Mehl II
to cover in flour [ˌkʌvər‿ɪn 'flaʊə] in Mehl wenden IV U5, 98
to **flow** [fləʊ] fließen; strömen <IV U5, 144>
flower ['flaʊə] Blume III
flown [fləʊn] past participle von *to fly* II
fluent ['flu:ənt] fließend; flüssig III
*to **fly** [flaɪ] fliegen II
flyer ['flaɪə] Flyer; Faltblatt II

to **focus** (on) ['fəʊkəs] sich konzentrieren (auf) <IV U1, 17>
fog [fɒg] Nebel IV U4, 75
foggy ['fɒgi] neblig I
to **fold** [fəʊld] falten; klappen IV U2, 38
to fold in half [ˌfəʊld‿ɪn 'hɑ:f] in der Mitte falten <IV U4, 92>
folder ['fəʊldə] Ordner; Mappe <III>
folk dance ['fəʊk ˌdɑ:ns] Volkstanz <IV U5, 145>
to **follow** ['fɒləʊ] folgen; befolgen IV U5, 98
follower ['fɒləʊə] Follower; Followerin; Anhänger; Anhängerin IV U4, 81
font [fɒnt] Schriftart <IV U2, 49>
food [fu:d] Essen; Nahrung; Lebensmittel I
convenience food [kən'vi:niəns ˌfu:d] Fertignahrung <IV U3, 72>
food stall ['fu:d ˌstɔ:l] Essensstand II
frozen food ['frəʊzn ˌfu:d] Tiefkühlkost; Tiefkühlprodukte <IV U3, 72>
better quality food [ˌbetə 'kwɒləti ˌfu:d] qualitativ besseres Essen <IV U3, 72>
foot [fʊt] Fuß *(Längenmaß: 30,48 cm)* IV U1, 12
on foot [ɒn 'fʊt] zu Fuß I
foot *(sg)* [fʊt], **feet** *(pl)* [fi:t] Fuß I
football ['fʊtbɔ:l] Fußball I
American football [əˌmerɪkən 'fʊtbɔ:l] American Football <IV U2, 50>
for [fɔ:] für I; seit IV U4, 80
for a start [ˌfɔ:r‿ə 'stɑ:t] zunächst III
for five months [fə 'faɪv ˌmʌnθs] fünf Monate lang I
for fun [fə 'fʌn] zum Spaß III
forbidden [fə'bɪdn] verboten IV U3, 58
to **force** [fɔ:s] zwingen IV U2, 32
foreground ['fɔ:graʊnd] Vordergrund III
in the foreground [ɪn ðə 'fɔ:graʊnd] im Vordergrund III
foreign ['fɒrɪn] fremd; ausländisch IV U1, 19
forest ['fɒrɪst] Wald IV U3, 53
*to **foretell** [fɔ:'tel] vorhersagen III
forever [fə'revə] für immer; ewig II
*to **forget** [fə'get] vergessen I
forgot [fə'gɒt] simple past von *to forget* I
forgotten [fə'gɒtn] past participle von *to forget* II
fork [fɔ:k] Gabel II
form [fɔ:m] Form <III>; Art <IV U2, 48>
approval form [ə'pru:vl ˌfɔ:m] Einverständnisformular <IV U2, 44>
entry form ['entri ˌfɔ:m] Anmeldeformular II
to **form** [fɔ:m] bilden <III>
to **format** ['fɔ:mæt] formatieren <IV U2, 49>
former ['fɔ:mə] ehemalige; frühere IV U2, 33
fortune ['fɔ:tʃu:n] Vermögen; Reichtum IV U4, 85
forty ['fɔ:ti] vierzig I
forward ['fɔ:wəd] vorwärts <IV U2, 139>
fought [fɔ:t] simple past, past participle von *to fight* III
to **found** [faʊnd] gründen IV U5, 98
found [faʊnd] simple past von *to find* I
founding father [ˌfaʊndɪŋ 'fɑ:ðə] Gründungsvater <IV U3, 140>
four [fɔ:] vier I
fourteen [ˌfɔ:'ti:n] vierzehn I
fourth [fɔ:θ] vierte I
land of the **free** [ˌlænd‿əv ðə 'fri:] Land der Freien IV U3, 53
free [fri:] kostenlos III; frei IV U1, 22
free range [ˌfri: 'reɪndʒ] Freiland- II
free time [ˌfri: 'taɪm] Freizeit I
freedom *(no pl)* ['fri:dəm] Freiheit; Unabhängigkeit IV U1, 23
religious freedom [ˌrɪlɪdʒəs 'fri:dəm] Religionsfreiheit <IV U3, 70>
free-time [ˌfri:'taɪm] Freizeit- <III>
*to **freeze** [fri:z] frieren; gefrieren III
freeze frame ['fri:z ˌfreɪm] Standbild <I>
freezing ['fri:zɪŋ] eiskalt; gefrierend IV U3, 54
French [frentʃ] Französisch I
the **French** [ðə 'frenʃ] die Franzosen IV U5, 98
fresh [freʃ] frisch II
freshman *(AE)* ['freʃmən] Neuntklässler; Neuntklässlerin IV U2, 34
Friday ['fraɪdeɪ] Freitag I
fridge [frɪdʒ] Kühlschrank III
fried [fraɪd] (in der Pfanne) gebraten II
friend [frend] Freund; Freundin I
to make friends [ˌmeɪk 'frendz] Freundschaften schließen I
to see friends [si: 'frendz] Freunde treffen I
to **friend** [frend] befreunden *(jmdn. zu seiner Freundesliste hinzufügen)* IV U4, 81
friendly ['frendli] freundlich; nett III
frightening ['fraɪtnɪŋ] furchterregend IV U3, 63
frisbee ['frɪzbi] Frisbee; Frisbeescheibe I
from [frɒm] aus; von I
from behind [ˌfrəm bɪ'haɪnd] von hinten I
at the **front** [ət ðə 'frʌnt] vorn <IV U1, 17>
at the **front** of [ət ðə 'frʌnt‿əv] an der Spitze (von); im vorderen Bereich II
in **front** of [ɪn 'frʌnt‿əv] vor; davor II
froze [frəʊz] simple past von *to freeze* III
frozen ['frəʊzn] past participle von *to freeze* III
frozen food ['frəʊzn ˌfu:d] Tiefkühlkost; Tiefkühlprodukte <IV U3, 72>
fruit [fru:t] Frucht; Obst I
to **fry** [fraɪ] braten; frittieren IV U5, 98
to **fulfill** [fʊl'fɪl] erfüllen <IV U1, 24>
full [fʊl] voll III; vollwertig <IV U2, 138>
full stop [ˌfʊl 'stɒp] Punkt <III>
full length [ˌfʊl 'leŋθ] volle Länge; ganze Länge <IV U1, 19>

fun [fʌn] Freude; Spaß I
for fun [fə 'fʌn] zum Spaß III
fundamental [ˌfʌndə'mentl] Grundlage <IV U2, 49>
funeral ['fju:nrəl] Beerdigung; Begräbnis <IV U5, 108>
fun-filled ['fʌnfɪld] lustig; witzig <IV U4, 90>
funny ['fʌni] lustig; witzig I; merkwürdig; seltsam II
furious ['fjʊəriəs] wütend III
further ['fɜ:ðə] weiter <IV U2, 138>
future ['fju:tʃə] Zukunft III

G

galaxy ['gæləksi] Galaxie; Galaxis <IV U2, 48>
gallery ['gæləri] Galerie <IV U1, 28>
game [geɪm] Spiel I
gamer ['geɪmə] Spieler *(Computer)*; Spielerin *(Computer)* II
gaming ['geɪmɪŋ] Computerspiele IV U4, 80
street **gang** ['stri:t ˌgæŋ] Straßengang <IV U1, 136>
garbage *(AE)* ['gɑ:bɪdʒ] Müll; Abfall <IV U1, 30>
garden ['gɑ:dn] Garten I
garlic ['gɑ:lɪk] Knoblauch II
gas [gæs] Gas III
gas *(AE)* [gæs] Benzin <IV U3, 66>
gate [geɪt] Tor III
gateway ['geɪtweɪ] Tor; Eingangstor IV U1, 12
to **gather** ['gæðə] (sich) sammeln IV U3, 64
gave [geɪv] simple past von *to give* II
gel [dʒel] Gel III
hair gel ['heə ˌdʒel] Haargel III
shower gel ['ʃaʊə ˌdʒel] Duschgel III
general ['dʒenrl] allgemein <III>
in general [ɪn 'dʒenrl] allgemein; generell IV U3, 73
generation [ˌdʒenə'reɪʃn] Generation <IV U2, 139>
generous ['dʒenrəs] großzügig IV U2, 39

geocaching ['dʒiəʊkæʃɪŋ] Geocaching I
Geography [dʒi'ɒgrəfi] Geografie; Erdkunde I
German ['dʒɜ:mən] Deutsch I; deutsch; aus Deutschland III
gesture ['dʒestʃə] Geste; Gebärde <IV U5, 103>
*to **get** [get] bekommen; werden I; holen II; verstehen III
to get around [ˌget ə'raʊnd] herumkommen III
to get cold [ˌget 'kəʊld] frieren III
to get dressed [ˌget 'drest] sich anziehen II
to get in ['get‿ɪn] hereinkommen I
to get into [ˌget‿'ɪntə] hineinkommen; hineingelangen IV U1, 14
to get lost [get lɒst] sich verirren I
to get married [ˌget 'mærɪd] heiraten II
to get off [ˌget‿'ɒf] aussteigen II
to get on [ˌget‿'ɒn] einsteigen III
to get on one's nerves [ˌget‿ɒn wʌnz 'nɜ:vz] auf die Nerven gehen III
to get out [ˌget 'aʊt] herauskommen III
to get ready [ˌget 'redi] sich vorbereiten; sich fertig machen IV U3, 54
to get sth [get] etw. verstehen IV U5, 102
to get stuck [ˌget 'stʌk] stecken bleiben IV U3, 54
to get there ['get‿ðeə] hinkommen III
to get tired of sth [ˌget 'taɪəd‿əv] etw. sattbekommen; etw. satthaben IV U1, 14
to get to ['get tə] hinkommen zu; gelangen IV U1, 14
to get to know [ˌget tə 'nəʊ] kennen lernen II
to get together [ˌge‿tə'geðə] zusammenkommen; zusammenfinden IV U3, 52
to get up [ˌget‿'ʌp] aufstehen I

to get used to (sth) [ˌget 'ju:zd tə] sich an (etw.) gewöhnen IV U1, 19
gherkin ['gɜ:kɪn] Essiggurke <IV U5, 112>
ghost [gəʊst] Geist II
ghost town ['gəʊst ˌtaʊn] Geisterstadt IV U4, 86
giant [dʒaɪənt] Riese III
giant [dʒaɪənt] Riesen-; riesig III
giraffe [dʒɪ'rɑ:f] Giraffe I
girl [gɜ:l] Mädchen I
girlfriend ['gɜ:lfrend] Freundin *(in einer Paarbeziehung)* IV U2, 38
gist [dʒɪst] das Wesentliche <III>
*to **give** [gɪv] geben I
to give a talk [ˌgɪv‿ə 'tɔ:k] einen Vortrag halten <III>
to give reasons [ˌgɪv 'ri:znz] Gründe nennen; Gründe angeben III
to give sth a miss [ˌgɪv sʌmθɪŋ‿ə 'mɪs] auf etw. verzichten; etw. bleiben lassen III
to give up [ˌgɪv‿'ʌp] aufgeben III
glad [glæd] froh IV U3, 54
glamor *(AE)* ['glæmə] Glanz; Zauber IV U4, 75
glass [glɑ:s] Glas II
global ['gləʊbl] weltweit; global <IV U1, 136>
glove [glʌv] Handschuh <IV U2, 50>
glue [glu:] Klebstoff I
glue stick ['glu: ˌstɪk] Klebestift <IV U3, 71>
*to **go** [gəʊ] gehen; fahren I
to go ahead [ˌgəʊ ə'hed] fortfahren; loslegen; vorangehen IV U1, 18
to go beach combing [gəʊ 'bi:tʃ ˌkəʊmɪŋ] den Strand nach Strandgut absuchen II
to go camping [ˌgəʊ 'kæmpɪŋ] campen gehen; zelten II
to go on [ˌgəʊ‿'ɒn] hineingehen II; weitergehen <III>
to go out [ˌgəʊ‿'aʊt] ausgehen III
to go quiet [ˌgəʊ 'kwaɪət] still werden III

to go shopping [ˌgəʊ ˈʃɒpɪŋ] einkaufen gehen II
to go sightseeing [gəʊ ˈsaɪtsiːɪŋ] eine Besichtigungstour machen II
to go swimming [ˌgəʊ ˈswɪmɪŋ] schwimmen gehen I
to go to bed [ˌgəʊ tə ˈbed] ins Bett gehen I
field **goal** [ˈfiːld ˌgəʊl] Feldtor <IV U2, 50>
goat [gəʊt] Ziege III
God [gɒd] Gott <IV U2, 45>
thank God [ˌθæŋk‿ˈgɒd] Gott sei Dank <IV U3, 70>
goddess [ˈgɒdes] Göttin IV U1, 22
gold [gəʊld] Gold III
gold [gəʊld] golden; Gold- III
gold rush [ˈgəʊld ˌrʌʃ] Goldrausch IV U4, 84
golden [ˈgəʊldn] golden; Gold- IV U4, 75
gone [gɒn] past participle von *to go* II
good [gʊd] gut I
to be good at [biː ˈgʊd‿ət] gut sein in/bei I
Good morning. [ˌgʊd ˈmɔːnɪŋ] Guten Morgen. II
good luck [ˌgʊd ˈlʌk] viel Glück II
Goodbye. [gʊdˈbaɪ] Auf Wiedersehen. I
goods *(no pl)* [gʊdz] Güter; Waren IV U1, 18
gospel [ˈgɒspl] Gospel *(Musikrichtung)* IV U5, 97
gossip [ˈgɒsɪp] Klatsch; Tratsch; Gerede IV U3, 58
got [gɒt] simple past von *to get* I
*to have **got** [hæv ˈgɒt] besitzen; haben II
government [ˈgʌvnmənt] Regierung IV U2, 32
state government [ˈsteɪt ˌgʌvnmənt] Landesregierung IV U5, 98
GPS *(Global Positioning System)* [ˌdʒiːpiːˈes] GPS I

to **grab** [græb] schnappen; greifen; ergreifen III
grade *(AE)* [greɪd] Note; Klasse IV U2, 33
graduation [ˌgrædʒuˈeɪʃn] Schulabschluss <IV U2, 48>
graffiti [grəˈfiːti] Graffiti <IV U1, 136>
grammar [ˈgræmə] Grammatik <I>
grammatical [grəˈmætɪkl] grammatikalisch <IV U5, 111>
grand [grænd] großartig III
grandad [ˈgrændæd] Opa III
great-great-grandad [ˌgreɪtgreɪt ˈgrændæd] Ururopa I
grandfather [ˈgrænˌfɑːðə] Großvater II
grandma [ˈgrænmɑː] Oma II
grandmother [ˈgrænˌmʌðə] Großmutter III
grandparent [ˈgrænˌpeərənt] Großelternteil <III>
grandparents *(pl)* [ˈgrænˌpeərənts] Großeltern II
graphic design [ˌgræfɪk dɪˈzaɪn] Grafikdesign; grafische Gestaltung <IV U2, 49>
grass [grɑːs] Gras I
grated [ˈgreɪtɪd] gerieben <IV U5, 112>
grave [greɪv] Grab III
great [greɪt] großartig; toll I
great-grandparents [ˌgreɪtˈgrænˌpeərənts] Urgroßeltern IV U1, 25
Greek [griːk] griechisch; Griechisch; aus Griechenland IV U5, 99
green [griːn] grün I
greengrocer's [ˈgriːnˌgrəʊsəz] Obst- und Gemüseladen III
grew [gruː] simple past von *to grow* IV U3, 58
grey [greɪ] grau I
grid [grɪd] Gitter; Raster IV U5, 101
to **grin** [grɪn] grinsen IV U3, 64
grizzly bear [ˈgrɪzli ˌbeə] Grizzlybär <IV U1, 30>
groceries *(pl)* [ˈgrəʊsriz] Lebensmittel IV U4, 89
ground [graʊnd] Boden; Erdboden III

grounds *(pl)* [graʊndz] Gelände; Gebiet IV U1, 13
group [gruːp] Gruppe I
tutor group [ˈtjuːtə ˌgruːp] Klasse *(in einer englischen Schule)* I
*to **grow** [grəʊ] anbauen; züchten; ziehen; wachsen IV U3, 58
to grow up [ˌgrəʊ‿ˈʌp] aufwachsen III
grown [grəʊn] past participle von *to grow* IV U3, 58
guarded [ˈgɑːdɪd] vorsichtig; zurückhaltend III
to **guess** [ges] erraten; raten; überlegen II; vermuten; schätzen IV U3, 58; annehmen IV U3, 59
guest [gest] Gast III
guestbook [ˈgestbʊk] Gästebuch <I>
guide [gaɪd] Führer; Führerin II
guided tour [ˈgaɪdɪd ˌtɔː] Führung <IV U1, 13>
guinea pig [ˈgɪni ˌpɪg] Meerschweinchen I
guitar [gɪˈtɑː] Gitarre III
gun [gʌn] Schusswaffe IV U3, 62
guy [gaɪ] Typ; Kerl IV U2, 42
guys *(pl)* [gaɪz] Leute II
gym(nasium) [dʒɪm (dʒɪmˈneɪziəm)] Turnhalle IV U2, 42
gymnasium [dʒɪmˈneɪziəm] Fitnessraum III

H

had [hæd] simple past von *to have* I; past participle von *to have* II
hair [heə] Haar; Haare III
hair gel [ˈheə ˌdʒel] Haargel III
hair straightener [ˈheə ˌstreɪtnə] Haarglätter IV U3, 59
hairbrush [ˈheəbrʌʃ] Haarbürste III
haircut [ˈheəkʌt] Haarschnitt II
to have a haircut [ˈheəkʌt] sich die Haare schneiden lassen II
hairdo [ˈheəduː] Frisur <IV U4, 77>
hairdresser [ˈheəˌdresə] Friseur; Friseurin II
hairdryer [ˈheəˌdraɪə] Fön III

half *(sg)* [hɑːf], **halves** *(pl)* [hɑːvz] (die) Hälfte IV U4, 80
to fold in half [ˌfəʊld‿ɪn ˈhɑːf] in der Mitte falten <IV U4, 92>

half [hɑːf] halb III
half a million [ˌhɑːf‿ə ˈmɪljən] eine halbe Million III
half past (two) [ˌhɑːf ˈpɑːst] halb (drei) I

half-mast [ˌhɑːfˈmɑːst] halbmast <IV U3, 140>

hall [hɔːl] Flur; Diele; Korridor IV U2, 34
city hall [ˌsɪti ˈhɔːl] Rathaus <IV U5, 114>
town hall [ˌtaʊn ˈhɔːl] Rathaus II

ham [hæm] Schinken II

hand [hænd] Hand I

*to **hang** [hæŋ] hängen II; erhängen IV U4, 85
to hang out (with) [ˌhæŋ‿ˈaʊt (wɪð)] rumhängen (mit); sich treffen (mit); sich herumtreiben (mit) IV U3, 58

to **happen** [ˈhæpn] geschehen; passieren II

happy [ˈhæpi] glücklich I
happy ending [ˌhæpi ˈendɪŋ] Happy End <III>
Happy birthday! [ˌhæpi ˈbɜːθdeɪ] Alles Gute zum Geburtstag! I

harbor *(AE)* [ˈhɑːbə] Hafen IV U1, 22

harbour [ˈhɑːbə] Hafen II

hard [hɑːd] hart; schwer; schwierig II

hardly [ˈhɑːdli] kaum <IV U4, 88>

hard-working [ˌhɑːdˈwɜːkɪŋ] fleißig IV U2, 39

harp [hɑːp] Harfe <III>

harvest [ˈhɑːvɪst] Ernte <IV U3, 67>

hat [hæt] Hut II

to **hate** [heɪt] hassen; nicht mögen I

*to **have** [hæv] haben I; essen II
to have a haircut [ˈheəkʌt] sich die Haare schneiden lassen II
to have a look [ˌhæv‿ə ˈlʊk] anschauen II
to have breakfast [ˌhæv ˈbrekfəst] frühstücken I
to have to [ˈhæv tə] müssen II
to have no idea [hæv ˌnəʊ aɪˈdɪə] keine Ahnung haben IV U1, 14
Have a seat. [ˌhæv‿ə ˈsiːt] Setzen Sie sich.; Setz dich. IV U3, 54

*to **have got** [hæv ˈgɒt] besitzen; haben II

he [hiː] er I

head [hed] Kopf II
head chef [ˈhed ʃef] Chefkoch II
head first [ˈhed fɜːst] kopfüber III
my head is buzzing [maɪ ˌhed‿ɪz ˈbʌzɪŋ] mir schwirrt der Kopf <IV U5, 114>

headache [ˈhedeɪk] Kopfschmerzen; Kopfweh II

heading [ˈhedɪŋ] Überschrift; Titel <III>

headline [ˈhedlaɪn] Schlagzeile; Überschrift IV U4, 77

headphones *(pl)* [ˈhedfəʊnz] Kopfhörer IV U3, 59

headspin [ˈhedspɪn] Kopfdrehung <IV U1, 136>

health [helθ] Gesundheits-; gesundheitlich <IV U3, 72>

healthy [ˈhelθi] gesund III

*to **hear** [hɪə] hören I

heard [hɜːd] simple past von *to hear* I; past participle von *to hear* II

heart [hɑːt] Herz III

heartbeat [ˈhɑːtbiːt] Herzschlag <IV U2, 35>

heat [hiːt] Hitze IV U5, 102

heaven [ˈhevn] Himmel <IV U5, 108>

heavy [ˈhevi] schwer; stark II

hectic [ˈhektɪk] hektisch <IV U2, 47>

height [haɪt] Höhe II

held [held] simple past, past participle von *to hold* III

helicopter [ˈhelɪkɒptə] Helikopter; Hubschrauber IV U4, 79

Hello. [həˈləʊ] Hallo. I
Hello there. [həˈləʊ ˌðeə] Hallo.; Grüß dich. I

helmet [ˈhelmət] Helm III

help [help] Hilfe II

to **help** [help] helfen I
to help oneself [ˌhelp wʌnˈself] sich bedienen III
I couldn't help but … [ˌaɪ kʊdnt ˈhelp bʌt] Ich konnte nicht anders als … III

helper [ˈhelpə] Helfer; Helferin IV U4, 89

helpful [ˈhelpfl] hilfreich; nützlich III; hilfsbereit IV U2, 38

her [hɜː] ihr, ihre; sie I

here [hɪə] hier I
Here you are. [ˌhɪə ju‿ˈɑː] Bitte schön. I

hero *(sg)* [ˈhɪərəʊ], **heroes** *(pl)* [ˈhɪərəʊz] Held III

heroism [ˈherəʊɪzm] Heldentum <IV U5, 114>

hers [hɜːz] ihre II

herself [hɜːˈself] sie selbst; sich selbst III

Hi. [haɪ] Hi.; Hallo. I
to say hi to [ˌseɪ ˈhaɪ tə] grüßen; Grüße ausrichten I

hid [hɪd] simple past von *to hide* III

hidden [ˈhɪdn] past participle von *to hide* III

*to **hide** [haɪd] (sich) verstecken III

high [haɪ] hoch; groß I
high school [ˈhaɪ ˌskuːl] Highschool *(weiterführende Schule, Oberstufe)* IV U1, 18

high-action [ˌhaɪˈækʃn] mit Action vollgepackt <IV U4, 142>

highlighted [ˈhaɪlaɪtɪd] hervorgehoben <III>

high-tech [ˌhaɪˈtek] Hightech- IV U4, 75

to **hike** [haɪk] wandern II

hiking [ˈhaɪkɪŋ] Wandern III

hill [hɪl] Berg; Hügel IV U4, 74

him [hɪm] ihm; ihn I

himself [hɪmˈself] sich (selbst); er selbst III

hip hop [ˈhɪp hɒp] Hip-Hop *(Musik)* III

to **hire** [haɪə] mieten; anheuern; einstellen IV U4, 85

his [hɪz] sein I; seins; seiner II

historic [hɪˈstɒrɪk] historisch IV U5, 98

historical [hɪˈstɒrɪkl] historisch; geschichtlich <III>
History [ˈhɪstri] Geschichte I
history [ˈhɪstri] Geschichte III
hit [hɪt] Hit; Treffer IV U5, 97
*to **hit** [hɪt] treffen; schlagen II; (sich) stoßen; anstoßen; gegen etw. fahren III
hit [hɪt] simple past, past participle von *to hit* II
hobby [ˈhɒbi] Hobby III
*to **hold** [həʊld] halten; festhalten III
hole [həʊl] Loch I
holiday [ˈhɒlədeɪ] Ferien; Urlaub I; Feiertag III
  national holiday [ˌnæʃnl ˈhɒlədeɪ] Nationalfeiertag <IV U1, 24>
home [həʊm] Zuhause; Heim; nach Hause I
  at home [ət ˈhəʊm] zu Hause I
  back home [bæk ˈhəʊm] zu Hause II
  home country [ˌhəʊm ˈkʌntri] Heimat; Heimatland IV U1, 19
  to make oneself at home [ˌmeɪk wʌnself ət ˈhəʊm] sich wie zu Hause fühlen III
Homecoming *(AE)* [ˈhəʊmˌkʌmɪŋ] Ehemaligentreffen IV U2, 33
home-packed [ˌhəʊmˈpækt] zu Hause gemacht <IV U4, 90>
homepage [ˈhəʊmpeɪdʒ] Homepage III
homeroom [ˈhəʊmruːm] erste Stunde *(in der Schule)* IV U2, 45
homeschooled [ˈhəʊmˌskuːld] zu Hause unterrichtet <IV U2, 34>
homeschooling [ˈhəʊmˌskuːlɪŋ] Hausunterricht <IV U2, 34>
*to be **homesick** [biː ˈhəʊmsɪk] Heimweh haben III
homework [ˈhəʊmwɜːk] Hausaufgabe(n) I
  to do homework [ˌduː ˈhəʊmwɜːk] Hausaufgabe(n) machen I
honest [ˈɒnɪst] ehrlich III
honestly [ˈɒnɪstli] ehrlich IV U3, 63
honor *(AE)* [ˈɒnə] Ehre IV U1, 25
to **hoover** [ˈhuːvə] staubsaugen II
hope [həʊp] Hoffnung IV U1, 13
to **hope** [həʊp] hoffen I
hopeful [ˈhəʊpfl] hoffnungsvoll III
horrible [ˈhɒrəbl] schrecklich; furchtbar III
horror [ˈhɒrə] Horrorfilm <IV U4, 142>
horse [hɔːs] Pferd I
  horse riding [ˈhɔːs ˌraɪdɪŋ] Reiten I
hospital [ˈhɒspɪtl] Hospital; Krankenhaus I
host [həʊst] Talkmaster; Gastgeber; Gastgeberin <IV U3, 69>
  host family [ˈhəʊst ˌfæmli] Gastfamilie IV U2, 34
youth **hostel** [ˈjuːθ ˌhɒstl] Jugendherberge III
hot [hɒt] heiß I
  hot BBQ sauce [hɒt ˈbɑːbɪkjuː ˌsɔːs] scharfe Grillsoße <IV U5, 112>
  hot dog [ˈhɒt ˌdɒg] Hot Dog *(Würstchen im Brötchen)* IV U1, 14
hotel [həʊˈtel] Hotel II
hour [aʊə] Stunde I
  rush hour [ˈrʌʃ ˌaʊə] Hauptverkehrszeit IV U1, 14
  working hours *(pl)* [ˈwɜːkɪŋ ˌaʊəz] Arbeitszeit IV U2, 38
  40 kilometres an hour [kɪˈlɒmɪtəz‿ən‿ˈaʊə] 40 Kilometer pro Stunde I
house [haʊs] Haus I
  around the house [əˈraʊnd ðə haʊs] im Haus I
  State House *(AE)* [ˈsteɪt ˌhaʊs] Regierungsgebäude IV U5, 98
how [haʊ] wie I
  How about …? [ˌhaʊ‿əˈbaʊt] Wie wäre es mit …? II
  How are you? [ˌhaʊ‿ˈɑː jə] Wie geht es dir? I
  How are you doing? [ˌhaʊ‿ə jə ˈduːɪŋ] Wie geht's dir? IV U3, 55
  How do I get there? [ˌhaʊ du aɪ ˈget ðeə] Wie komme ich dahin? III
  how many [ˌhaʊ ˈmeni] wie viele II
  how much [ˌhaʊ ˈmʌtʃ] wie sehr III
  How much (is/are) …? [ˌhaʊ ˈmʌtʃ‿ɪz/ɑː] Wie viel (kostet/kosten) …? I
  How old are you? [haʊ‿ˈəʊld‿ə ˌjuː] Wie alt bist du? I
  How to … [ˈhaʊ tə] Wie man … II
  How's it going? [ˌhaʊz‿ɪt ˈgəʊɪŋ] Wie geht's?; Wie läuft's? IV U3, 54
however [haʊˈevə] jedoch III
huge [hjuːdʒ] riesig; riesengroß IV ZI, 9
human [ˈhjuːmən] menschlich III
a/one **hundred** [ˈhʌndrəd] einhundert; hundert I
hung [hʌŋ] simple past, past participle von *to hang* II
hunger [ˈhʌŋgə] Hunger <IV U2, 138>
hungry [ˈhʌŋgri] hungrig I
to **hunt** [hʌnt] jagen <IV U2, 138>
hunter [ˈhʌntə] Jäger; Jägerin IV U4, 85
to **hurry** [ˈhʌri] sich beeilen II
*to **hurt** [hɜːt] weh tun; verletzen II
hurt [hɜːt] simple past, past participle von *to hurt* II
hurt [hɜːt] verletzt II
husband [ˈhʌzbənd] Ehemann IV U3, 54
husky [ˈhʌski] Husky *(Schlittenhunderasse)* <IV U1, 29>

I

I [aɪ] ich I
  I didn't catch that. [aɪ ˌdɪdnt ˈkætʃ ðæt] Das habe ich nicht verstanden.; Das habe ich nicht gehört. IV U5, 102
  I don't know! [ˌaɪ ˌdəʊnt ˈnəʊ] Ich weiß (es) nicht! I
  I see. [aɪ ˈsiː] Ich verstehe. IV U5, 103
  I wouldn't like (to) … [aɪ ˈwʊdnt laɪk (tə)] Ich möchte nicht …; Ich würde nicht gerne … I
  I'd like (to) … (= I would like to) [aɪd ˈlaɪk (tə)] Ich möchte …; Ich würde gerne … I
  I'd love to … (= I would love to) [aɪd ˈlʌv tə] Ich würde sehr gern … III
  I'd rather [aɪd ˈrɑːðə] ich würde lieber III

I'm from … ['aɪm ˌfrɒm] Ich komme aus … I

I'm sorry. [aɪm 'sɒrɪ] Es tut mir leid.; Entschuldigung. I

ice [aɪs] Eis IV U4, 85

crushed **ice** ['krʌʃt ˌaɪs] zerstoßenes Eis <IV U5, 113>

ice cream [ˌaɪs 'kri:m] Eiscreme; Eis I

ice rink ['aɪs ˌrɪŋk] Eislaufbahn <IV U1, 25>

iceberg ['aɪsbɜ:g] Eisberg III

ice-cold [aɪs'kəʊld] eiskalt IV U4, 85

ID [ˌaɪ'di:] Ausweis; Personalausweis III

ID card [ˌaɪ'di: ˌkɑ:d] Ausweis; Personalausweis <IV U2, 44>

idea [aɪ'dɪə] Idee; Ahnung I

to have no **idea** [hæv ˌnəʊ aɪ'dɪə] keine Ahnung haben IV U1, 14

ideal [aɪ'dɪəl] ideal; optimal <IV U3, 72>

identity [aɪ'dentəti] Identität IV U5, 98

if [ɪf] wenn; falls II

ill [ɪl] krank; schlecht II

illegally [ɪ'li:gli] illegal; unrechtmäßig; rechtswidrig <IV U4, 88>

illness ['ɪlnəs] Krankheit <IV U2, 138>

to **imagine** (sth) [ɪ'mædʒɪn] sich (etw.) vorstellen IV U4, 85

immigrant ['ɪmɪgrənt] Immigrant; Immigrantin; Einwanderer; Einwanderin IV U1, 13

to **immigrate** ['ɪmɪgreɪt] einwandern; immigrieren IV U1, 18

immigration [ˌɪmɪ'greɪʃn] Immigration; Einwanderung <IV U1, 12>; Zuwanderung IV U1, 22

impact ['ɪmpækt] Einfluss; Auswirkung IV U4, 80

speech **impaired** ['spi:tʃ ɪmˌpeəd] sprachbehindert IV U5, 102

impairment [ɪm'peəmənt] Beeinträchtigung; Einschränkung <IV U1, 24>

imperative [ɪm'perətɪv] Imperativ <III>

imperial unit [ɪm'pɪəriəl ˌju:nɪt] englische Maßeinheit <IV U5, 112>

important [ɪm'pɔ:tnt] wichtig; einflussreich II

impossible [ɪm'pɒsəbl] unmöglich III

to **impress** [ɪm'pres] beeindrucken III

impression [ɪm'preʃn] Eindruck <IV U4, 76>

in [ɪn] in I; drinnen II

in August [ɪn 'ɔ:gəst] im August I

in between [ˌɪn bɪ'twi:n] dazwischen <IV U4, 92>

in fact [ɪn 'fækt] eigentlich; tatsächlich; genau genommen III

in front of [ɪn 'frʌnt‿əv] vor; davor II

in my opinion [ɪn 'maɪ‿əˌpɪnjən] meiner Meinung nach III

in the afternoon [ˌɪn ði ˌɑ:ftə'nu:n] nachmittags I

in the background [ɪn ðə 'bækgraʊnd] im Hintergrund III

in the centre of [ˌɪn ðə 'sentər‿əv] in der Mitte von III

in the country [ɪn ðə 'kʌntri] auf dem Land I

in the distance [ˌɪn ðə 'dɪstns] in der Ferne IV U1, 14

in the end [ɪn ði 'end] schließlich; zum Schluss II

in the evenings [ɪn ði 'i:vnɪŋz] abends III

in the south of [ˌɪn ðə 'saʊθ‿əv] im Süden von III

in the world [ɪn ðə 'wɜ:ld] auf der Welt II

in time [ɪn 'taɪm] rechtzeitig I

in tow [ɪn 'təʊ] im Schlepptau IV U2, 42

inch [ɪnʃ] Zoll (Längenmaß: 2,54 cm) <IV U5, 112>

to **include** [ɪn'klu:d] beinhalten; einschließen <IV U2, 48>; enthalten IV U5, 102

*to be **included** [bi: ɪn'klu:dɪd] enthalten sein III

income ['ɪnkʌm] Einkommen <IV U4, 88>

to **increase** [ɪn'kri:s] zunehmen; vergrößern IV U4, 84

independence [ˌɪndɪ'pendəns] Unabhängigkeit IV U1, 13

Indian ['ɪndiən] Indianer; Indianerin <IV U3, 70>

Indian ['ɪndiən] indisch II

individual [ˌɪndɪ'vɪdʒuəl] Einzelperson; Individuum <IV U1, 24>

individual [ˌɪndɪ'vɪdʒuəl] individuell; einzeln <IV U2, 48>

indoor [ˌɪn'dɔ:] Hallen-; Innen- III

Industrial Revolution [ɪnˌdʌstriəl revl'u:ʃn] industrielle Revolution III

industry ['ɪndəstri] Industrie III

influence ['ɪnfluəns] Einfluss IV U5, 98

to **influence** ['ɪnfluəns] beeinflussen IV U4, 80

information *(no pl)* [ˌɪnfə'meɪʃn] Information; Informationen I

information desk [ɪnfə'meɪʃn ˌdesk] Information II

informative [ɪn'fɔ:mətɪv] informativ IV U4, 77

*to keep sb **informed** [ˌki:p‿ɪn'fɔ:md] jmdn. auf dem Laufenden halten IV U4, 84

ingredient [ɪn'gri:diənt] Zutat II

inhabitant [ɪn'hæbɪtnt] Einwohner; Einwohnerin; Bewohner; Bewohnerin III

injection [ɪn'dʒekʃn] Spritze III

injured ['ɪndʒəd] verletzt <IV U4, 88>

injury ['ɪndʒri] Verletzung III

innocent ['ɪnəsnt] unschuldig IV U3, 63

innovation [ˌɪnə'veɪʃn] Innovation; Neuheit IV U4, 80

insect ['ɪnsekt] Insekt III

to **insert** ['ɪnsɜ:t] einfügen <IV U2, 49>

inside [ˌɪn'saɪd] in; innen in; im Innern III; in … hinein II; innen; drinnen IV U1, 25

inspection [ɪn'spekʃn] Inspektion; Kontrolle; Überprüfung IV U1, 22

to **inspire** [ɪn'spaɪə] inspirieren; anregen <IV U5, 114>

instead [ɪn'sted] stattdessen IV U2, 34

instruction [ɪn'strʌkʃn] Unterricht; Anweisung <IV U2, 44>
instructor [ɪn'strʌktə] Lehrer; Lehrerin III
fitness instructor ['fɪtnəs ɪn,strʌktə] Fitnesstrainer; Fitnesstrainerin <IV U3, 72>
instrument ['ɪnstrəmənt] Instrument <III>
intelligent [ɪn'telɪdʒnt] intelligent; klug; vernünftig III
interact [,ɪntər'ækt] interagieren; zusammenspielen <IV U5, 109>
interest ['ɪntrəst] Interesse <IV U1, 25>
interest (in) ['ɪntrəst (ɪn)] Interesse (an) <III>
to **interest** ['ɪntrəst] interessieren <IV U4, 89>
*to be **interested** in [bi: 'ɪntrəstɪd‿ɪn] sich interessieren für; interessiert sein an III
interesting ['ɪntrəstɪŋ] interessant I
internet ['ɪntənet] Internet II
to surf the internet [,sɜ:f ði 'ɪntənet] im Internet surfen II
to **interrupt** [,ɪntə'rʌpt] unterbrechen IV U4, 94
intersection *(AE)* [,ɪntə'sekʃn] Kreuzung IV U1, 15
interview ['ɪntəvju:] Interview; Befragung II; Vorstellungsgespräch IV U2, 38
to **interview** ['ɪntəvju:] interviewen; befragen I
interviewer ['ɪntəvju:ə] Interviewer; Interviewerin; Befrager; Befragerin IV U1, 18
into ['ɪntu] in; hinein IV U3, 62
to **introduce** [,ɪntrə'dju:s] vorstellen III; einführen; einleiten IV U5, 98; zeigen <IV U2, 48>
introduction [,ɪntrə'dʌkʃn] Einleitung; Einführung III; Vorstellung <IV U3, 68>
to **invade** [ɪn'veɪd] einmarschieren (in); eindringen (in) III
to **invent** [ɪn'vent] erfinden III
invention [ɪn'venʃn] Erfindung III
inventor [ɪn'ventə] Erfinder; Erfinderin III
invincible [ɪn'vɪnsəbl] unschlagbar; unbesiegbar <IV U2, 35>
invitation [,ɪnvɪ'teɪʃn] Einladung I
to **invite** [ɪn'vaɪt] einladen I
Irish ['aɪrɪʃ] irisch; Irisch III
the **Irish** [ði 'aɪrɪʃ] die Iren III
to **iron** [aɪən] bügeln IV U3, 58
is [ɪz] ist I
... is **£1.25.** [ɪz 'wʌn paʊnd twenti,faɪv] ... kostet ein Pfund fünfundzwanzig. I
Islam ['ɪzlɑ:m] Islam <IV U5, 222>
island ['aɪlənd] Insel II
isn't it? ['ɪznt‿ɪt] nicht wahr?; stimmt's? II
it [ɪt] es I
It says ... [ɪt 'sez] Hier steht ...; Es heißt ... <III>
IT (Information Technology) [,aɪ'ti:, ɪnfə,meɪʃn tek'nɒlədʒi] Informatik; Informationstechnik I
Italian [ɪ'tæliən] italienisch; Italienisch; Italiener; Italienerin II
its [ɪts] sein; ihr III
itself [ɪt'self] (sich) selbst III

J

jacket ['dʒækɪt] Jacke II
jacket potato [,dʒækɪt pə'teɪtəʊ] Ofenkartoffel II
jail [dʒeɪl] Gefängnis IV U5, 107
jam [dʒæm] Marmelade; Konfitüre III
traffic jam ['træfɪk ,dʒæm] Stau IV U1, 14
Jamaican [dʒə'meɪkən] jamaikanisch II
January ['dʒænjuri] Januar I
Japanese [,dʒæpən'i:z] japanisch; Japanisch; aus Japan; Japaner; Japanerin IV U5, 99
jar [dʒɑ:] Glas III
jazz [dʒæz] Jazz *(Musikrichtung)* IV U5, 97
jealous ['dʒeləs] eifersüchtig; neidisch II
jeans *(pl)* [dʒi:nz] Jeans I
jersey ['dʒɜ:zi] Trikot <IV U2, 50>
jeweller's ['dʒu:ələz] Juwelierladen III
jewellery ['dʒu:əlri] Schmuck II
Jewish ['dʒu:ɪʃ] jüdisch <IV U5, 222>
job [dʒɒb] Job I; Aufgabe; Tätigkeit; Arbeit; Beruf II
job title ['dʒɒb ,taɪtl] Stellenbezeichnung; Berufsbezeichnung IV U2, 38
to **join** [dʒɔɪn] sich anschließen III; verbinden <IV U2, 48>
joke [dʒəʊk] Witz I
to **joke** [dʒəʊk] Witze machen; scherzen III
journalism ['dʒɜ:nlɪzm] Journalistik; Journalismus IV U2, 34
journalistic ['dʒɜ:nlɪstɪk] journalistisch <IV U2, 49>
journey ['dʒɜ:ni] Fahrt; Reise III
to **joust** [dʒaʊst] einen Turnierzweikampf austragen; turnieren III
jousting ['dʒaʊstɪŋ] Turnierzweikampf III
joyful ['dʒɔɪfl] freudig <IV U5, 108>
judge [dʒʌdʒ] Juror; Jurorin II
juice [dʒu:s] Saft II
July [dʒʊ'laɪ] Juli I
jumble sale ['dʒʌmbl ,seɪl] Flohmarkt II
to **jump** [dʒʌmp] zusammenzucken; erschrecken III; springen IV U3, 63
jumping fitness ['dʒʌmpɪŋ ,fɪtnəs] Jumping Fitness *(Trendsportart)* IV U4, 81
June [dʒu:n] Juni I
jungle ['dʒʌŋgl] Dschungel IV U4, 85
junior ['dʒu:niə] Nachwuchs- <IV U2, 139>
just [dʒʌst] gerade (eben); soeben; nur II; einfach IV U2, 38

K

kebab [kɪ'bæb] Döner <IV U5, 222>
*to **keep** [ki:p] halten II; aufbewahren; behalten IV U2, 34

to keep calm [ˌki:p ˈkɑ:m] Ruhe bewahren; ruhig bleiben <IV U3, 55>
to keep cool [ˌki:p ˈku:l] Ruhe bewahren <III>
to keep going [ki:p ˈgəʊɪŋ] weitergehen; weitermachen IV U4, 85
to keep in touch [ˌki:p ɪn ˈtʌtʃ] in Verbindung bleiben II
to keep out [ˌki:p ˈaʊt] draußen halten III
to keep quiet [ˌki:p ˈkwaɪət] ruhig sein <III>
to keep safe [ˌki:p ˈseɪf] schützen III
to keep sb informed [ˌki:p‿ɪnˈfɔ:md] jmdn. auf dem Laufenden halten IV U4, 84
… to keep them drunk [tə ˌki:p ðəm ˈdrʌŋk] … dass sie betrunken bleiben IV U3, 62

kennel [ˈkenl] Hundezwinger <IV U1, 30>
kept [kept] simple past, past participle von *to keep* II
ketchup [ˈketʃʌp] Ketchup II
key [ki:] Legende <IV U1, 23>
keyword [ˈki:ˌwɜ:d] Stichwort; Schlüsselbegriff <III>
to **kick** [kɪk] schießen; treten III
kid [kɪd] Kind II
kidney bean [ˈkɪdni ˌbi:n] Kidneybohne II
to **kill** [kɪl] töten III
killing [ˈkɪlɪŋ] Tötung; Ermordung IV U5, 98
kilogram (kg) [ˈkɪləgræm] Kilogramm (kg) I
7 kilograms a day [ˌkɪləgræmz‿ə ˈdeɪ] sieben Kilogramm täglich I
kilometre (km) [kɪˈlɒmɪtə] Kilometer (km) I
40 kilometres an hour [kɪˈlɒmɪtəz‿ən‿ˈaʊə] 40 Kilometer pro Stunde I
kilt [kɪlt] Schottenrock; Kilt III
kind [kaɪnd] Art; Sorte III
kind [kaɪnd] freundlich; nett II
king [kɪŋ] König III
kiss [kɪs] Kuss II
to **kiss** [kɪs] küssen III
kitchen [ˈkɪtʃɪn] Küche I
knee [ni:] Knie III
knew [nju:] simple past von *to know* IV U4, 84
knife *(sg)* [naɪf], **knives** *(pl)* [naɪvz] Messer II
knight [naɪt] Ritter III
*to **know** [nəʊ] wissen; kennen I; verstehen IV U5, 103
to get to know [ˌget tə ˈnəʊ] kennen lernen II
I don't know! [ˌaɪ ˌdəʊnt ˈnəʊ] Ich weiß (es) nicht! I
knowledge *(no pl)* [ˈnɒlɪdʒ] Wissen; Kenntnisse <IV U1, 24>
known [nəʊn] past participle von *to know* IV U4, 84
to be known as [bi: ˈnəʊn‿əz] bekannt sein als <IV U3, 70>
best known [ˌbest ˈnəʊn] weltberühmt IV U2, 32

L

lab fee [ˈlæb ˌfi:] Laborgebühr <IV U2, 48>
label [ˈleɪbl] Etikett; Beschriftung <IV U1, 23>
to **label** [ˈleɪbl] beschriften <III>
laborer *(AE)* [ˈleɪbərə] Arbeiter; Arbeiterin; Arbeitskraft <IV U4, 88>
child **labour** [ˌtʃaɪld ˈleɪbə] Kinderarbeit <IV U4, 74>
ladder [ˈlædə] Leiter I
lady [ˈleɪdi] Dame; Frau II
laid [leɪd] simple past, past participle von *to lay* II
lake [leɪk] See III
lamb [læm] Lamm II
lame [leɪm] lahm; schwach IV U2, 38
lamp [læmp] Lampe I
land [lænd] Land II
land of the free [ˌlænd‿əv ðə ˈfri:] Land der Freien IV U3, 53
to **land** [lænd] landen IV U3, 54
landlord [ˈlændlɔ:d] Eigentümer II
landmark [ˈlænmɑ:k] Wahrzeichen IV U1, 14
landowner [ˈlændˌəʊnə] Grundbesitzer; Grundbesitzerin IV U4, 84
landscape [ˈlændskeɪp] Landschaft IV ZI, 9
lane [leɪn] Fahrspur; Weg; Gasse IV U4, 75
language [ˈlæŋgwɪdʒ] Sprache II
language detectives [ˈlæŋgwɪdʒ dɪˌtektɪvz] Sprachdetektive <I>
language tip [ˌlæŋgwɪdʒ ˈtɪp] Grammatikhinweis <I>
body language [ˈbɒdi ˌlæŋgwɪdʒ] Körpersprache <III>
sign language [ˈsaɪn ˌlæŋgwɪdʒ] Gebärdensprache; Zeichensprache III
laptop [ˈlæptɒp] Laptop I
large [lɑ:dʒ] groß II
lasagne [ləˈzænjə] Lasagne II
to **last** [lɑ:st] dauern; andauern; anhalten IV U4, 79
last [lɑ:st] letzte I
at last [ət ˈlɑ:st] endlich; zu guter Letzt II
late [leɪt] (zu) spät I
later [ˈleɪtə] später I
laugh [lɑ:f] Lachen IV U3, 63
to **laugh** [lɑ:f] lachen II
law [lɔ:] Gesetz III
to mow the **lawn** [ˌməʊ ðə ˈlɔ:n] den Rasen mähen <IV U2, 200>
*to **lay** [leɪ] legen; decken II
to lay the table [ˌleɪ ðə ˈteɪbl] den Tisch decken II
layout [ˈleɪaʊt] Layout; Anordnung IV U4, 77
lazy [ˈleɪzi] faul IV U2, 39
lead [li:d] Leine I
*to **lead** [li:d] führen; anführen IV U3, 58
leader [ˈli:də] Anführer; Anführerin; Führer; Führerin III
leaf *(sg)* [li:f], **leaves** *(pl)* [li:vz] Blatt IV U3, 52
league [li:g] Liga IV U1, 18
to **learn** [lɜ:n] lernen II; erfahren; herausfinden IV U3, 62

to learn about sth [ˌlɜːn əˈbaʊt] etwas erfahren über III

least [liːst] geringste; am wenigsten <IV U3, 59>

at least [ət ˈliːst] wenigstens; mindestens III

leather [ˈleðə] Leder III

*to **leave** [liːv] lassen; verlassen; abfahren II; gehen IV U2, 40

to leave out [ˌliːv‿ˈaʊt] weglassen <III>

leaving [ˈliːvɪŋ] Abschieds- II

led [led] simple past, past participle von *to lead* IV U3, 58

left [left] simple past, past participle von *to leave* II

left [left] links; übrig III

to turn left [ˌtɜːn ˈleft] (nach) links abbiegen I

on the left [ɒn ðə ˈleft] auf der linken Seite; links I

leg [leg] Bein II

legal [ˈliːgl] legal; rechtlich; Rechts- <IV U4, 88>

legendary [ˈledʒəndri] legendär <IV U1, 137>

lemon [ˈlemən] Zitrone II

lemonade [ˌleməˈneɪd] Limonade II

*to **lend** [lend] leihen; verleihen II

length *(no pl)* [leŋθ] Länge; Dauer IV U4, 75

full length [ˌfʊl ˈleŋθ] volle Länge; ganze Länge <IV U1, 19>

lent [lent] simple past von *to lend* II

less [les] weniger III

lesson [ˈlesn] Schulstunde; Unterricht I; Lektion; Lehre IV U2, 38

*to **let** [let] lassen III

let's [lets] lass uns I

Let's get moving! [ˌlets get ˈmuːvɪŋ] Lasst uns weiterfahren!; Auf geht's! IV U1, 14

Let's see … [ˌlets ˈsiː] Lass mal sehen …; Also … I

let [let] simple past, past participle von *to let* III

letter [ˈletə] Buchstabe; Brief III

capital letter [ˌkæpɪtl ˈletə] Großbuchstabe <III>

lettuce [ˈletɪs] Kopfsalat II

water **level** [ˈwɔːtə ˌlevl] Wasserpegel; Wasserstand <IV U5, 144>

library [ˈlaɪbri] Bibliothek; Bücherei III

licence [ˈlaɪsns] Lizenz; Erlaubnis <IV U1, 15>

license *(AE)* [ˈlaɪsns] Lizenz; Erlaubnis <IV U1, 15>

driver's license *(AE)* [ˈdraɪvəz ˌlaɪsns] Führerschein IV U2, 38

lid [lɪd] Deckel <IV U3, 71>

*to **lie** [laɪ] liegen <IV U1, 25>

life *(sg)* [laɪf], **lives** *(pl)* [laɪvz] Leben I

to bring to life [ˌbrɪŋ tə‿ˈlaɪf] zum Leben erwecken; veranschaulichen IV U1, 22

way of life [ˌweɪ əv ˈlaɪf] Lebensart; Lebensweise IV U5, 96

lifeboat [ˈlaɪfbəʊt] Rettungsboot III

lifestyle [ˈlaɪfstaɪl] Lebensart; Lifestyle IV U4, 74

lifetime [ˈlaɪftaɪm] Leben; Lebenszeit IV U4, 76

light [laɪt] Licht IV U1, 13

light bulb [ˈlaɪt ˌbʌlb] Glühbirne III

tea light [ˈtiː ˌlaɪt] Teelicht <IV U3, 71>

lighting [ˈlaɪtɪŋ] Beleuchtung <III>

lights [laɪts] Ampel IV U1, 14

to **like** [laɪk] mögen I

to like … best [ˌlaɪk ˈbest] am meisten mögen; am liebsten mögen I

would like [wʊd ˈlaɪk] würde(n) gern; hätte(n) gern II

I wouldn't like (to) … [aɪ ˈwʊdnt laɪk (tə)] Ich möchte nicht …; Ich würde nicht gerne … I

I'd like (to) … (= I would like to) [aɪd ˈlaɪk (tə)] Ich möchte …; Ich würde gerne … I

Would you like (to) …? [ˌwʊd jə ˈlaɪk (tə)] Möchtest du? I

like [laɪk] wie I

like this [laɪk ˈðɪs] so; auf diese Weise I; ähnlich <III>

line [laɪn] Zeile; Linie II; Schlange <IV U5, 110>

line dance [ˈlaɪn ˌdɑːns] Line Dance *(alle tanzen zusammen in einer Reihe)* <IV U5, 145>

lines *(pl)* [laɪnz] Text II

link [lɪŋk] Link; Verbindung IV U4, 80

to **link** [lɪŋk] verbinden IV U5, 107

linking word [ˌlɪŋkɪŋ ˈwɜːd] Verbindungswort <IV U3, 73>

lion [ˈlaɪən] Löwe I

list [lɪst] Liste II

ranking list [ˈræŋkɪŋ lɪst] Rangliste; Rangfolge <IV U3, 59>

shopping list [ˈʃɒpɪŋ ˌlɪst] Einkaufszettel I

to **listen** (to) [ˈlɪsn] zuhören; anhören; hören I

listener [ˈlɪsənə] Zuhörer; Zuhörerin II

listening [ˈlɪsnɪŋ] Hörverstehen <I>

little [ˈlɪtl] klein II; wenig; kaum IV U1, 22

a little [ə ˈlɪtl] ein bisschen II

a little something [ə ˌlɪtl ˈsʌmθɪŋ] eine Kleinigkeit IV U3, 54

to **live** [lɪv] wohnen; leben I

to live off [ˈlɪv‿ɒf] von leben <IV U3, 72>

lively [ˈlaɪvli] lebhaft; lebendig <IV U5, 111>

to earn a **living** [ˌɜːn‿ə ˈlɪvɪŋ] seinen Lebensunterhalt verdienen <IV U4, 88>

living room [ˈlɪvɪŋ ˌrʊm] Wohnzimmer I

loaf *(sg)* [ləʊf], **loaves** *(pl)* [ləʊvz] Brotlaib III

lobster [ˈlɒbstə] Hummer IV U3, 52

local [ˈləʊkl] hiesig; lokal; örtlich III

to **locate** [ləʊˈkeɪt] finden <IV U2, 48>

to be located [biː ləʊˈkeɪtɪd] liegen III; gelegen sein; sich befinden IV U1, 13

location [ləʊˈkeɪʃn] Drehort; Lage III; Aufenthaltsort <IV U5, 111>

loch [lɒk] See *(in Schottland)* III

to **lock** [lɒk] abschließen I
locker ['lɒkə] Schließfach; Spind IV U2, 34
lonely ['ləʊnli] einsam III
long [lɒŋ] lang I
*to have a **look** [ˌhæv‿ə 'lʊk] anschauen II
to **look** [lʊk] schauen; nachschauen I; aussehen; sehen II
to look after [ˌlʊk‿'ɑ:ftə] aufpassen; hüten II
to look at ['lʊk‿ət] anschauen I
to look for ['lʊk fə] suchen nach II
to look up [ˌlʊk‿'ʌp] aufschauen; nachschauen II
Look … [lʊk] Schau mal …; Schau … nach. I
lookout point ['lʊkaʊt ˌpɔɪnt] Aussichtspunkt II
loose [lu:s] locker; lose II
lorry driver ['lɒri ˌdraɪvə] LKW-Fahrer; LKW-Fahrerin II
*to **lose** [lu:z] verlieren II
lost [lɒst] simple past von *to lose* II; past participle von *to lose* III
to get lost [get lɒst] sich verirren I
a **lot** [ə 'lɒt] viel I; sehr II
a lot of [ə 'lɒt‿əv] viel(e); eine Menge I
parking **lot** *(AE)* ['pɑ:kɪŋ ˌlɒt] Parkplatz IV U1, 15
body **lotion** ['bɒdi ˌləʊʃn] Körperlotion III
lots [lɒts] viel; jede Menge III
lots of ['lɒts‿əv] viel; jede Menge I
loud [laʊd] laut III
love [lʌv] Liebe IV U4, 85
to fall in love (with) [ˌfɔ:l‿ɪn 'lʌv] sich verlieben (in) III
to **love** [lʌv] lieben; gern mögen I
I'd love to … (= I would love to) [aɪd 'lʌv tə] Ich würde sehr gern … III
loved ones ['lʌvd ˌwʌnz] Angehörige; Nahestehende <IV U5, 108>
lovely ['lʌvli] schön; herrlich; hübsch II
loving ['lʌvɪŋ] liebend; liebevoll IV U4, 85
low [ləʊ] niedrig II
lower ['ləʊə] untere III
good **luck** [ˌgʊd 'lʌk] viel Glück II
luckily ['lʌkɪli] glücklicherweise IV U2, 38
*to be **lucky** [bi: 'lʌki] Glück haben III
lucky day [ˌlʌki 'deɪ] Glückstag II
lucky number [ˌlʌki 'nʌmbə] Glückszahl I
lunch [lʌnʃ] Mittagessen I
packed lunch [ˌpækt 'lʌnʃ] Lunchpaket; Vesper II
lunchtime ['lʌnʃtaɪm] Mittagszeit; Mittagspause I
lyrics *(pl)* ['lɪrɪks] Liedtext <II>

M

machine [mə'ʃi:n] Automat; Maschine II
payment machine ['peɪmənt ˌməʃi:n] Bezahlautomat II
made [meɪd] simple past von *to make* I; past participle von *to make* II
magazine [ˌmægə'zi:n] Zeitschrift I
magic ['mædʒɪk] Magie; Zauberei II
magic ['mædʒɪk] magisch; Zauber- II
magician [mə'dʒɪʃn] Zauberer; Zauberin; Magier; Magierin IV U3, 63
main [meɪn] Haupt- <III>
main course [ˌmeɪn 'kɔ:s] Hauptgericht II
mainly ['meɪnli] hauptsächlich; in erster Linie; vorwiegend <IV U5, 108>
major ['meɪdʒə] Haupt-; wichtig; bedeutend IV ZI, 8
majority [mə'dʒɒrəti] Mehrheit; Mehrzahl IV U1, 22
*to **make** [meɪk] erstellen; machen; tun; bilden I
to be made of [bi: 'meɪd‿əv] hergestellt sein aus III
to make a cake [ˌmeɪk‿ə 'keɪk] einen Kuchen backen I
to make a decision [ˌmeɪk‿ə dɪ'sɪʒn] eine Entscheidung treffen <III>
to make a reservation [ˌmeɪk‿ə 'rezəveɪʃn] reservieren III
to make friends [ˌmeɪk 'frendz] Freundschaften schließen I
to make it ['meɪk‿ɪt] es schaffen IV U3, 54
to make oneself at home [ˌmeɪk wʌnself ət 'həʊm] sich wie zu Hause fühlen III
to make sb feel like sth [ˌmeɪk … 'fi:l laɪk] jmdm. das Gefühl geben etw. zu sein III
to make sense [ˌmeɪk 'sens] Sinn ergeben; einleuchten <III>
to make sure [ˌmeɪk 'ʃɔ:] dafür sorgen; sich versichern III
to make up [ˌmeɪk‿'ʌp] erfinden; sich ausdenken <III>
maker ['meɪkə] Macher; Macherin <IV U4, 79>
film maker ['fɪlm ˌmeɪkə] Filmemacher; Filmemacherin <III>
make-up ['meɪkʌp] Make-up; Schminke IV U3, 58
make-up artist ['meɪkʌp ˌɑ:tɪst] Maskenbildner; Maskenbildnerin; Visagist; Visagistin <III>
shopping **mall** ['ʃɒpɪŋ ˌmɔ:l] Einkaufszentrum IV U1, 15
mama ['mæmə] Mama II
man *(sg)* [mæn], **men** *(pl)* [men] Mann I
to **manage** ['mænɪdʒ] schaffen <IV U5, 114>
management ['mænɪdʒmənt] Management; Verwaltung; Geschäftsführung <IV U5, 114>
manager ['mænɪdʒə] Manager; Managerin; Geschäftsführer; Geschäftsführerin IV U2, 38
many ['meni] viele II
how many [ˌhaʊ 'meni] wie viele II
map [mæp] Stadtplan; Landkarte III; Karte; Plan IV U4, 80
mind map ['maɪnd ˌmæp] Wörternetz <I>

marathon ['mærəθn] Marathon <IV U1, 25>
March [mɑ:tʃ] März I
to **march** [mɑ:tʃ] marschieren <IV U5, 108>
marching band ['mɑ:tʃɪŋ ˌbænd] Marschkapelle <IV U2, 199>
to **mark** [mɑ:k] markieren; kennzeichnen III
market ['mɑ:kɪt] Markt II
farmers' market [ˌfɑ:məz 'mɑ:kɪt] Bauernmarkt <IV U3, 72>
market stall ['mɑ:kɪt ˌstɔ:l] Marktstand; Marktbude <IV U2, 200>
marquee [mɑ:'ki:] Partyzelt; Festzelt <IV U1, 19>
*to get **married** [ˌget 'mærɪd] heiraten II
mascot ['mæskət] Maskottchen <III>
mashed potatoes [ˌmæʃt pə'teɪtəʊz] Kartoffelbrei II
mast [mɑ:st] Mast <IV U3, 71>
master ['mɑ:stə] Herr; Meister <IV U3, 71>
match [mætʃ] Spiel I
final match [ˌfaɪnl 'mætʃ] Endspiel <IV U2, 50>
to **match** [mætʃ] zuordnen I; zusammenpassen <IV U4, 95>
material [mə'tɪəriəl] Material; Stoff III
Math *(AE)* [mæθ] Mathematik; Mathe IV U2, 34
Maths [mæθs] Mathematik; Mathe I
It doesn't **matter**. [ɪt ˌdʌznt 'mætə] Es ist egal. II
May [meɪ] Mai I
may [meɪ] vielleicht; können; dürfen II
maybe ['meɪbi] vielleicht I
mayonnaise [ˌmeɪə'neɪz] Mayonnaise II
me [mi:] mich; ich; mir I
meal [mi:l] Essen; Mahlzeit II
*to **mean** [mi:n] bedeuten; meinen III
mean [mi:n] gemein IV U3, 63
meaning ['mi:nɪŋ] Bedeutung <III>
meant [ment] simple past, past participle von *to mean* III
to **measure** ['meʒə] messen <IV U5, 112>
meat [mi:t] Fleisch I
media ['mi:diə] Medien IV U5, 98
social media [ˌsəʊʃl 'mi:diə] soziale Medien IV U4, 80
mediation [ˌmi:'di'eɪʃn] Sprachmittlung <I>
medical ['medɪkl] medizinisch; ärztlich IV U1, 22
medicine ['medsn] Medikamente; Medizin III
*to **meet** [mi:t] kennen lernen; treffen I
member ['membə] Mitglied IV U3, 52
in **memory** of [ɪn 'memri əv] in Erinnerung an <IV U3, 141>
mental ['mentl] geistig IV U1, 22
to **mention** ['menʃn] erwähnen <IV U3, 61>
menu ['menju:] Speisekarte II
mess [mes] Unordnung; Durcheinander I
message ['mesɪdʒ] Botschaft; Nachricht; SMS II
morning message ['mɔ:nɪŋ ˌmesɪdʒ] morgendliche Ansprache IV U2, 34
text message ['tekst ˌmesɪdʒ] SMS II
met [met] simple past von *to meet* I
metal ['metl] Metall III
method ['meθəd] Methode II
metre ['mi:tə] Meter I
microwave ['maɪkrəweɪv] Mikrowelle IV U3, 59
mid [mɪd] mittel <IV U5, 108>
middle ['mɪdl] Mitte III; Mittel- <IV U2, 44>
in the middle [ɪn ðə 'mɪdl] in der Mitte III
middle-aged [ˌmɪdl'eɪdʒd] mittleren Alters <IV U5, 114>
midnight ['mɪdnaɪt] Mitternacht III
might [maɪt] könnten IV U3, 63
migrant ['maɪgrnt] Migrant; Migrantin <IV U4, 88>
to **migrate** [maɪ'greɪt] wandern; umherziehen <IV U2, 138>
mild [maɪld] mild I
mile [maɪl] Meile II
square mile (= sq. mi.) [ˌskweə 'maɪl] Quadratmeile IV ZI, 8
milk [mɪlk] Milch I
to **milk** [mɪlk] melken III
milkshake ['mɪlkˌʃeɪk] Milchmischgetränk; Milchshake III
million ['mɪljən] Million III
half a million [ˌhɑ:f‿ə 'mɪljən] eine halbe Million III
*to come to **mind** [ˌkʌm tə 'maɪnd] einem einfallen; zufällig einfallen <IV U4, 95>
mind map ['maɪnd ˌmæp] Wörternetz <I>
Never **mind**. [ˌnevə 'maɪnd] Macht nichts.; Schon gut.; Mach dir nichts draus. II
mine [maɪn] Bergwerk III
mine [maɪn] meins; meine II
of mine [əv 'maɪn] von mir II
miner ['maɪnə] Bergarbeiter; Bergarbeiterin III
mineral water ['mɪnrl ˌwɔ:tə] Mineralwasser III
minimum ['mɪnɪməm] Minimum; minimal; Mindest- IV U2, 38
minority [maɪ'nɒrəti] Minderheit IV U1, 22
minute ['mɪnɪt] Minute II
mirror ['mɪrə] Spiegel III
miserable ['mɪzrəbl] elend; armselig; jämmerlich III
*to give sth a **miss** [ˌgɪv sʌmθɪŋ‿ə 'mɪs] auf etw. verzichten; etw. bleiben lassen III
to **miss** [mɪs] verpassen; vermissen II
mistake [mɪ'steɪk] Fehler <III>
to **mix** [mɪks] mischen; vermischen; mixen IV U5, 98
mixed pickles [ˌmɪkst 'pɪklz] gemischtes Essiggemüse <IV U5, 112>

mobile ['məʊbaɪl] mobil; tragbar; beweglich IV U4, 80
mobile (phone) ['məʊbaɪl (ˌfəʊn)] Handy; Mobiltelefon I
modern ['mɒdn] modern I
mom *(AE)* [mɒm] Mama IV U1, 18
moment ['məʊmənt] Moment; Augenblick II
Monday ['mʌndeɪ] Montag I
money ['mʌni] Geld I
monkey ['mʌŋki] Affe I
monster ['mɒnstə] Ungeheuer; Monster III
month [mʌnθ] Monat I
monthly ['mʌnθli] monatlich III
monument ['mɒnjəmənt] Denkmal II
mood [mu:d] Stimmung; Laune <III>
moral ['mɒrl] moralisch <IV U1, 24>
more [mɔ:] mehr I
morning ['mɔ:nɪŋ] Morgen; Vormittag I
Good morning. [ˌgʊd 'mɔ:nɪŋ] Guten Morgen. II
morning message ['mɔ:nɪŋ ˌmesɪdʒ] morgendliche Ansprache IV U2, 34
mosque [mɒsk] Moschee II
most [məʊst] die meisten; die Mehrheit I; am meisten II
mostly ['məʊstli] meistens; hauptsächlich IV U2, 41
mother ['mʌðə] Mutter I
to motivate ['məʊtɪveɪt] motivieren <IV U2, 50>
motivated ['məʊtɪveɪtɪd] motiviert IV U1, 18
motorbike ['məʊtəbaɪk] Motorrad I
motorboat ['məʊtəbəʊt] Motorboot <IV U5, 114>
mountain ['maʊntɪn] Berg III
in the mountains [ˌɪn ðə 'maʊntɪnz] in den Bergen III
mouse *(sg)* [maʊs], **mice** *(pl)* [maɪs] Maus I
moussaka [mu'sa:kə] Moussaka II
mouth [maʊθ] Mund II
move [mu:v] Bewegung III
to move [mu:v] (sich) bewegen III
to move (house) [mu:v] umziehen II
movement ['mu:vmənt] Bewegung IV U1, 13
cultural movement [ˌkʌltʃrl 'mu:vmənt] Kulturbewegung IV U1, 13
movie ['mu:vi] Film I
movie theater *(AE)* ['mu:vi ˌθi:ətə] Kino IV U5, 106
the movies *(AE)* [ðə 'mu:viz] Kino IV U3, 58
to mow the lawn [ˌməʊ ðə 'lɔ:n] den Rasen mähen <IV U2, 200>
Mr ['mɪstə] Herr *(Anrede)* I
Mrs ['mɪsɪz] Frau *(Anrede)* I
Ms [mɪz] Frau *(Anrede)* I
much [mʌtʃ] viel I
so much ['səʊ ˌmʌtʃ] so sehr III
too much [ˌtu: 'mʌtʃ] zu sehr II
how much [ˌhaʊ 'mʌtʃ] wie sehr III
mud [mʌd] Schlamm; Matsch III
muddy ['mʌdi] schlammig I
multicultural [ˌmʌlti'kʌltʃrl] multikulturell IV U5, 98
mum [mʌm] Mama I
mural ['mjʊərəl] Wandgemälde III
murderer ['mɜ:drə] Mörder; Mörderin III
museum [mju:'zi:əm] Museum II
music ['mju:zɪk] Musik I
country and western music [ˌkʌntri ənd 'westən ˌmju:zɪk] Countrymusik <IV U5, 145>
musical ['mju:zɪkl] Musical <IV U1, 136>
musical ['mju:zɪkl] Musik-; musikalisch III
Muslim ['mʊzlɪm] Muslim; Muslimin I; muslimisch <IV U5, 222>
must [mʌst] müssen I
must not/never [ˌmʌst 'nɒt/'nevə] nicht/nie dürfen III
mustn't ['mʌsnt] nicht dürfen III
mustard ['mʌstəd] Senf II
my [maɪ] mein, meine I
My name is ... [maɪ 'neɪm‿ɪz] Ich heiße ... I
myself [maɪ'self] selbst; selber III
mystery ['mɪstri] Rätsel; Geheimnis I
mystery story ['mɪstri ˌstɔ:ri] Krimi (= Kriminalgeschichte); Detektivgeschichte IV U3, 53

N

nacho ['nɑ:tʃəʊ] Nacho <IV U5, 112>
to nag [næg] nörgeln; meckern III
nail [neɪl] Nagel III
nail scissors *(pl)* ['neɪl ˌsɪzəz] Nagelschere III
name [neɪm] Name I
first name [ˌfɜ:st 'neɪm] Vorname <III>
to name [neɪm] benennen IV ZI, 9
named after ['neɪmd ˌɑ:ftə] benannt nach <IV U3, 70>
napkin ['næpkɪn] Serviette II
narrator [nə'reɪtə] Erzähler; Erzählerin I
nation ['neɪʃn] Nation; Land; Staat <IV U2, 45>
national ['næʃnl] National-; national III
national holiday [ˌnæʃnl 'hɒlədeɪ] Nationalfeiertag <IV U1, 24>
national park [ˌnæʃnl 'pɑ:k] Nationalpark; Naturpark <IV U4, 89>
nationality [ˌnæʃn'æləti] Nationalität; Staatsangehörigkeit <IV U5, 99>
native ['neɪtɪv] eingeboren; einheimisch IV U4, 86
Native American [ˌneɪtɪv‿ə'merɪkən] Ureinwohner Amerikas; Ureinwohnerin Amerikas; Indianer; Indianerin; indianisch IV U1, 16
natural ['nætʃrl] Natur-; natürlich <IV U5, 108>
naturally ['nætʃrli] natürlich <IV U2, 47>
nature ['neɪtʃə] Natur III
naughty ['nɔ:ti] frech; böse III
near [nɪə] in der Nähe von I; nah III
nearly ['nɪəli] fast; beinahe; annähernd IV U3, 64
neat [ni:t] ordentlich; hübsch; gepflegt <IV U1, 27>

necessary ['nesəsri] nötig; notwendig; erforderlich <IV U3, 73>
with special **needs** [wɪð ˌspeʃl 'ni:dz] mit Behinderung III
to **need** [ni:d] brauchen I
needn't ['ni:dnt] nicht brauchen; nicht müssen I
to **need to** ['ni:d ˌtə] müssen IV U5, 98
negative ['negətɪv] negativ IV U5, 99
neighbor *(AE)* ['neɪbə] Nachbar; Nachbarin IV U3, 54
neighbour ['neɪbə] Nachbar; Nachbarin III
*to get on one's **nerves** [ˌget ˌɒn wʌnz 'nɜ:vz] auf die Nerven gehen III
nervous ['nɜ:vəs] nervös; aufgeregt II
net [net] Netz IV U4, 75
safety net ['seɪfti ˌnet] Sicherheitsnetz IV U4, 75
netball ['netbɔ:l] Korbball I
never ['nevə] nie; niemals I
Never mind. [ˌnevə 'maɪnd] Macht nichts.; Schon gut.; Mach dir nichts draus. II
new [nju:] neu I
New Yorker [ˌnju: 'jɔ:kə] New Yorker; New Yorkerin IV U1, 13
news [nju:z] Neuigkeit(en); Nachricht(en) II
newsagent's ['nju:zˌeɪdʒnts] Zeitschriftenladen III
newspaper ['nju:sˌpeɪpə] Zeitung II
next [nekst] nächste I; als Nächstes II
next to ['nekst tə] neben I
nice [naɪs] schön; nett I; lecker; gut III
nickname ['nɪkneɪm] Spitzname IV U1, 12
niece [ni:s] Nichte III
night [naɪt] Nacht I
night walk [ˌnaɪt 'wɔ:k] Nachtwanderung I
that night [ˌðæt 'naɪt] an jenem Abend; in jener Nacht II
nightmare ['naɪtmeə] Alptraum <IV U3, 68>
nine [naɪn] neun I
nineteen [ˌnaɪn'ti:n] neunzehn I
ninety ['naɪnti] neunzig I
no [nəʊ] kein; keine; nein I
no one ['nəʊ wʌn] niemand I
No way! [ˌnəʊ 'weɪ] Auf keinen Fall!; Was?!; Echt?! III
nobody ['nəʊbədi] niemand III
noise [nɔɪz] Geräusch I
noisy ['nɔɪzi] laut III
non- [nɒn] nicht- IV U4, 86
the **Normans** [ðə 'nɔ:mənz] die Normannen III
north [nɔ:θ] Norden III
north of ['nɔ:θ‿əv] nördlich von IV ZI, 9
to the north of [ˌtə ðə 'nɔ:θ‿əv] nördlich von III
northeast [ˌnɔ:θ'i:st] Nordosten III
northern ['nɔ:ðən] nördlich III
northwest [ˌnɔ:θ'west] Nordwesten III
northwest of [ˌnɔ:θ'west‿əv] nordwestlich III
nose [nəʊz] Nase I
not [nɒt] nicht I
not … any [ˌnɒt … eni] kein II
not at all [ˌnɒt‿ət‿'ɔ:l] überhaupt nicht; gar nicht II
not … any more [ˌnɒt … eni 'mɔ:] nicht mehr III
not … either [nɒt … 'aɪðə] auch nicht III
not … yet [nɒt … 'jet] noch nicht II
not possibly [nɒt 'pɒsəbli] unmöglich III
note [nəʊt] Geldschein II; Notiz <III>
nothing ['nʌθɪŋ] nichts IV U5, 99
to **notice** ['nəʊtɪs] bemerken; wahrnehmen III
noun [naʊn] Nomen; Hauptwort <I>
novel ['nɒvl] Roman IV U3, 53
November [nə'vembə] November I
now [naʊ] jetzt; nun I; heutzutage II
right now [ˌraɪt 'naʊ] jetzt gerade III
nowadays ['naʊədeɪz] heutzutage IV U5, 115
nowhere ['nəʊweə] nirgendwo; nirgendwohin IV U2, 34
nugget ['nʌgɪt] Klumpen; Nugget <IV U4, 92>
number ['nʌmbə] Nummer; Zahl I; Anzahl IV U4, 75
a number of [ə 'nʌmbər‿əv] einige; mehrere IV U5, 98
lucky number [ˌlʌki 'nʌmbə] Glückszahl I
ordinal number [ˌɔ:dɪnəl 'nʌmbə] Ordinalzahl <I>
phone number ['fəʊn ˌnʌmbə] Telefonnummer III
nurse [nɜ:s] Krankenschwester; Krankenpfleger II
nut [nʌt] Nuss I

O

o'clock [ə'klɒk] Uhr *(Zeitangabe bei vollen Stunden)* I
oak [əʊk] Eiche <IV U5, 144>
OAP [ˌəʊeɪ'pi:] Rentner; Rentnerin <IV U5, 223>
oat [əʊt] Hafer III
object ['ɒbdʒɪkt] Objekt; Gegenstand <III>
observation [ˌɒbzə'veɪʃn] Beobachtung <IV U2, 48>
obviously ['ɒbviəsli] offensichtlich <IV U1, 136>
ocean ['əʊʃn] Ozean; Meer IV ZI, 9
October [ɒk'təʊbə] Oktober I
the **odd** one out [ˌɒd wʌn‿'aʊt] das Wort, das nicht in die Gruppe passt <III>
of [ɒv] von I
of course [əv 'kɔ:s] natürlich; selbstverständlich I
of mine [əv 'maɪn] von mir II
off [ɒf] abseits von <IV U1, 136>; von … weg IV U5, 107
a day off [ə ˌdeɪ‿'ɒf] ein freier Tag III
to set off [ˌset‿'ɒf] aufbrechen; sich aufmachen; auslösen IV U4, 84
to turn off [ˌtɜ:n‿'ɒf] abschalten; ausschalten <IV U1, 25>
Off we went. ['ɒf wi went] Nichts wie weg. III

special offer [ˌspeʃl‿ˈɒfə] Sonderangebot III
to offer [ˈɒfə] anbieten; bieten IV U2, 38
office [ˈɒfɪs] Büro II
post office [ˈpəʊst‿ˌɒfɪs] Postamt I
officer [ˈɒfɪsə] Beamter; Beamtin <IV U1, 24>
police officer [pəˈliːs‿ˌɒfɪsə] Polizeibeamter; Polizeibeamtin I
official [əˈfɪʃl] offiziell IV U4, 84
officially [əˈfɪʃli] offiziell <III>
often [ˈɒfn] oft; häufig I
oh [əʊ] null *(bei Uhrzeiten und Telefonnummern)* I
oil [ɔɪl] Öl IV U5, 98
OK [əʊˈkeɪ] okay I
old [əʊld] alt I
in the old days [ɪn ði ˈəʊld ˌdeɪz] früher III
old-fashioned [ˌəʊldˈfæʃnd] altmodisch IV U4, 74
on [ɒn] auf; an I
on board [ˈɒn bɔːd] an Bord III
on foot [ɒn ˈfʊt] zu Fuß I
on purpose [ɒn ˈpɜːpəs] absichtlich II
on 7th July [ɒn ðə ˈsevnθ əv ˌdʒʊlaɪ] am 7. Juli I
on the bus [ˌɒn ðə ˈbʌs] im Bus II
on the left [ɒn ðə ˈleft] auf der linken Seite; links I
on the one hand [ɒn ðə‿ˈwʌn ˌhænd] einerseits IV U5, 115
on the other (hand) [ɒn ði ˈʌðə (hænd)] andererseits <IV U2, 138>
on the right [ɒn ðə ˈraɪt] auf der rechten Seite; rechts I
on the way [ˌɒn ðə ˈweɪ] auf dem Weg; unterwegs I
on Tuesday [ˌɒn ˈtjuːzdeɪ] am Dienstag I
on TV [ɒn ˌtiːˈviː] im Fernsehen IV U1, 13
on Wednesdays [ɒn ˈwenzdeɪz] mittwochs I
on weekdays [ɒn ˈwiːkdeɪz] unter der Woche; an Werktagen III
to try on [ˌtraɪ‿ˈɒn] anprobieren II
once [wʌns] einst; einmal IV U1, 25
once more [ˈwʌns ˌmɔː] noch einmal II
one [wʌn] eins I
a/one hundred [ˈhʌndrəd] einhundert; hundert I
one day [wʌn ˈdeɪ] eines Tages III
one stop [ˌwʌn ˈstɒp] einmal Umsteigen <IV U3, 66>
one(s) [wʌn(z)] *Platzhalter für ein Nomen* III
loved ones [ˈlʌvd ˌwʌnz] Angehörige; Nahestehende <IV U5, 108>
one-way [ˈwʌnweɪ] einfach <IV U3, 66>
onion [ˈʌnjən] Zwiebel II
onion rings [ˈʌnjən ˌrɪŋz] Zwiebelringe <IV U5, 112>
online [ˌɒnˈlaɪn] online II
only [ˈəʊnli] nur I; einzige III
to open [ˈəʊpn] öffnen; aufmachen I
open [ˈəʊpn] offen; geöffnet III
opening [ˈəʊpnɪŋ] Anfang; Eröffnung <IV U5, 111>
opening times [ˈəʊpnɪŋ ˌtaɪmz] Öffnungszeiten IV U5, 105
operation [ˌɒprˈeɪʃn] Operation III
operator [ˈɒpreɪtə] Vermittlung III
camera operator [ˈkæmrə ˌɒpreɪtə] Kameramann; Kamerafrau <III>
opinion [əˈpɪnjən] Meinung III
in my opinion [ɪn ˈmaɪ‿əˌpɪnjən] meiner Meinung nach III
opportunity [ˌɒpəˈtjuːnəti] Gelegenheit; Chance IV U1, 18
opposite [ˈɒpəzɪt] Gegenteil <II>
opposite [ˈɒpəzɪt] gegenüber I
optimistic [ˌɒptɪˈmɪstɪk] optimistisch III
option [ˈɒpʃn] Möglichkeit; Wahl; Option IV U2, 34
or [ɔː] oder I
oral [ˈɔːrl] mündlich <IV U1, 24>
orange [ˈɒrɪndʒ] Orange I
orange [ˈɒrɪndʒ] orange I
orchestra [ˈɔːkɪstrə] Orchester III
order [ˈɔːdə] Reihenfolge <III>
to order [ˈɔːdə] bestellen II
ordinal number [ˌɔːdɪnəl ˈnʌmbə] Ordinalzahl <I>
ordinary [ˈɔːdnri] gewöhnlich; normal <IV U5, 114>
organic [ɔːˈgænɪk] Bio-; organisch <IV U3, 72>
organization [ˌɔːgnaɪˈzeɪʃn] Organisation <IV U5, 106>
to organize [ˈɔːgənaɪz] organisieren II
origin [ˈɒrɪdʒɪn] Ursprung; Herkunft <IV U3, 70>
original [əˈrɪdʒnl] original; ursprünglich IV U3, 54
to originate [əˈrɪdʒneɪt] entstehen IV U5, 97
other [ˈʌðə] andere; weitere I
each other [ˌiːtʃ‿ˈʌðə] einander; sich; sich gegenseitig III
on the other (hand) [ɒn ði ˈʌðə (hænd)] andererseits IV U5, 107
others [ˈʌðəz] andere II
the others [ði‿ˈʌðəz] die anderen I
ounce [aʊns] Unze (Maßeinheit: 28,35 Gramm) <IV U5, 112>
our [aʊə] unser, unsere I
ours [aʊəz] unsere III
ourselves [ˌaʊəˈselvz] selber; selbst III
out [aʊt] heraus II; aus; draußen; außerhalb <IV U3, 68>
to ask sb out [ˌɑːsk … ˈaʊt] sich mit jmdm. verabreden IV U2, 42
to fall out of [ˌfɔːl‿ˈaʊt‿əv] herausfallen aus IV U2, 42
to go out [ˌgəʊ‿ˈaʊt] ausgehen III
to keep out [ˌkiːp‿ˈaʊt] draußen halten III
out and about [ˌaʊt‿ən‿əˈbaʊt] unterwegs I
out of [ˈaʊt‿əv] aus … heraus II; von <IV U2, 44>
out of fashion [ˌaʊt‿əv ˈfæʃn] altmodisch; nicht mehr aktuell IV U4, 81
outdated [ˌaʊtˈdeɪtɪd] veraltet IV U4, 81
outdoor [ˌaʊtˈdɔː] Freiluft-; Outdoor- III
the outdoors [ˌði ˈaʊtdɔːz] die freie Natur IV U5, 96

outfit ['aʊtfɪt] Outfit; Kleidung III
outnumbered [ˌaʊt'nʌmbəd] in der Unterzahl IV U5, 102
outside [ˌaʊt'saɪd] draußen; im Freien II; außerhalb IV U2, 38
outside world [ˌaʊtsaɪd 'wɜ:ld] Außenwelt IV U3, 58
oven ['ʌvn] Backofen II
over ['əʊvə] über III; vorbei IV U1, 22
over there [ˌəʊvə 'ðeə] da drüben; dort drüben II
to **owe** [əʊ] schulden III
to **own** [əʊn] besitzen II
own [əʊn] eigene II
owner ['əʊnə] Besitzer; Besitzerin IV U5, 101

P

p.m. [ˌpi:'em] nachmittags *(Uhrzeit)* II
to **pack** [pæk] packen; einpacken II
to pack up ['pæk‿ʌp] packen; einpacken II
package ['pækɪdʒ] Paket IV U5, 102
packed lunch [ˌpækt 'lʌnʃ] Lunchpaket; Vesper II
packet ['pækɪt] Packung; Tüte I
pad [pæd] Polster; Schutz <IV U2, 50>
paddle ['pædl] Paddel <IV U3, 72>
paddle steamer ['pædl ˌsti:mə] Raddampfer <IV U5, 144>
standup **paddleboarding** ['stændʌp ˌpædlbɔ:dɪŋ] Stehpaddeln <IV U3, 72>
paddlewheel ['pædlˌwi:l] Schaufelrad <IV U5, 144>
paella [paɪ'elə] Paella IV U5, 99
page [peɪdʒ] Seite I
paid [peɪd] simple past, past participle von *to pay* II
to **paint** [peɪnt] streichen; anmalen; malen IV U4, 75
pair [peə] Paar IV U2, 41
a pair of [ə 'peər‿əv] ein Paar II
to **pan** [pæn] schwenken <IV U4, 89>
pancake ['pænkeɪk] Pfannkuchen II
to **panic** ['pænɪk] panisch werden II

pantomime ['pæntəmaɪm] Weihnachtstheaterstück II
pants *(pl) (AE)* [pænts] Hose IV U2, 38
paper ['peɪpə] Papier III
paperboy ['peɪpəˌbɔɪ] Zeitungsausträger IV U2, 41
papergirl ['peɪpəˌgɜ:l] Zeitungsausträgerin IV U2, 41
parade [pə'reɪd] Parade; Umzug III
paradise ['pærədaɪs] Paradies IV ZI, 9
paragraph ['pærəgrɑ:f] Paragraf; Absatz <IV U2, 43>
pardon ['pɑ:dn] Begnadigung; Entschuldigung; Verzeihung IV U3, 67
to **pardon** ['pɑ:dn] begnadigen; entschuldigen; verzeihen IV U3, 53
Pardon? ['pɑ:dn] Wie bitte? I
parent ['peərnt] Elternteil <IV U1, 192>
parents *(pl)* ['peərnts] Eltern II
park [pɑ:k] Park I
amusement park [ə'mju:zmənt ˌpɑ:k] Freizeitpark <IV U4, 215>
national park [ˌnæʃnl 'pɑ:k] Nationalpark; Naturpark <IV U4, 89>
theme park ['θi:m ˌpɑ:k] Freizeitpark I; Themenpark II
parking lot *(AE)* ['pɑ:kɪŋ ˌlɒt] Parkplatz IV U1, 15
parrot ['pærət] Papagei I
part [pɑ:t] Rolle; Teil II
to take part (in) [ˌteɪk 'pɑ:t] teilnehmen (an) II
partner ['pɑ:tnə] Partnerin; Partner III
part-time [ˌpɑ:t'taɪm] Teilzeit-; Halbtags- IV U2, 33
party ['pɑ:ti] Party; Feier I
pass [pɑ:s] Ausweis; Pass IV U2, 34
to **pass** [pɑ:s] reichen II; vorbeigehen; durchgehen IV U4, 85
to pass by [ˌpɑ:s 'baɪ] vorbeigehen <IV U5, 114>
to pass on [ˌpɑ:s‿'ɒn] weitergeben <III>
passenger ['pæsndʒə] Passagier; Passagierin II
passive ['pæsɪv] Passiv; Passiv- <IV U5, 100>

passport ['pɑ:spɔ:t] Pass; Reisepass <IV U1, 22>
past [pɑ:st] Vergangenheit III
past perfect [ˌpɑ:st 'pɜ:fɪkt] Plusquamperfekt <IV U1, 20>
simple past [ˌsɪmpl 'pɑ:st] einfache Vergangenheit <III>
past [pɑ:st] nach *(bei Uhrzeitangaben)* II; vorbei (an) III
half past (two) [ˌhɑ:f 'pɑ:st] halb (drei) I
pasta ['pæstə] Pasta; Nudeln II
pasta bake [ˌpæstə 'beɪk] Nudelauflauf II
to **paste** [peɪst] einfügen II
pasty ['pæsti] Pastete II
path [pɑ:θ] Pfad; Weg <IV U1, 30>
patient ['peɪʃnt] Patient; Patientin II
patient ['peɪʃnt] geduldig III
to **patrol** [pə'trəʊl] patrouillieren; Streife gehen <IV U1, 29>
patterned ['pætənd] gemustert II
pause [pɔ:z] Pause <IV U2, 50>
pay [peɪ] Bezahlung; Lohn; Gehalt IV U2, 38
pay phone ['peɪ fəʊn] Münztelefon III
*to **pay** [peɪ] bezahlen II
to pay attention to [ˌpeɪ‿ə'tenʃn tʊ] beachten <III>
to pay back [ˌpeɪ 'bæk] zurückzahlen II
to pay the bill [ˌpeɪ ðə 'bɪl] die Rechnung bezahlen III
payment machine ['peɪmənt ˌməʃi:n] Bezahlautomat II
PE (Physical Education) [ˌpi:'i:, ˌfɪzɪkl edʒʊ'keɪʃn] Sportunterricht I
peace [pi:s] Frieden III
peaceful ['pi:sfl] friedlich IV U5, 96
peach [pi:tʃ] Pfirsich I
peanut butter [ˌpi:nʌt 'bʌtə] Erdnussbutter III
pecan ['pi:kæn] Pekannuss IV U3, 67
pen [pen] Füller; Stift I
pence *(pl)* [pens], **penny** *(sg)* ['peni] Pence *(brit. Währungseinheit)* I
… are 99p. [ɑ: 'naɪntinaɪn ˌpens] … kosten 99 Pence. I

pencil ['pensl] Bleistift; Buntstift I
pencil case ['pensl ˌkeɪs] Federmäppchen I
pencil sharpener ['pensl ˌʃɑːpnə] Anspitzer I
penguin ['peŋgwɪn] Pinguin I
people *(pl)* ['piːpl] Leute; Menschen I
pepper ['pepə] Pfeffer II
peppermint ['pepəmɪnt] Pfefferminz <IV U5, 113>
per [pɜː] pro IV U2, 33
percent (%) [pə'sent] Prozent IV U1, 22
past **perfect** [ˌpɑːst 'pɜːfɪkt] Plusquamperfekt <IV U1, 20>
present **perfect** [ˌpreznt 'pɜːfɪkt] das Perfekt <III>
perfect ['pɜːfɪkt] perfekt; vollkommen IV ZI, 9
to **perform** [pə'fɔːm] auftreten; aufführen III
performance [pə'fɔːməns] Aufführung; Vorstellung <IV U2, 50>
perfume ['pɜːfjuːm] Parfüm III
period ['pɪəriəd] Stunde; Unterrichtsstunde IV U2, 34; Periode; Zeitspanne <IV U2, 139>
period of time [ˌpɪəriəd‿əv 'taɪm] Zeitraum <IV U4, 86>
study hall period ['stʌdi hɔːl ˌpɪəriəd] Freistunde IV U2, 34
permanent ['pɜːmnənt] permanent; dauerhaft <IV U1, 24>
person ['pɜːsn] Person; Mensch II
personal ['pɜːsnl] persönlich III
personality [ˌpɜːsn'æləti] Persönlichkeit <III>
perspective [pə'spektɪv] Perspektive; Blickwinkel <IV U3, 68>
to **persuade** [pə'sweɪd] überreden <III>
pesticide ['pestɪsaɪd] Pestizid; Schädlingsbekämpfungsmittel <IV U4, 88>
pet [pet] Haustier I
pet shop ['pet ʃɒp] Tierhandlung III
phone [fəʊn] Telefon II
to answer the phone [ˌɑːnsə ðə 'fəʊn] ans Telefon gehen III
cell phone *(AE)* ['sel fəʊn] Mobiltelefon; Handy IV U3, 59
mobile (phone) ['məʊbaɪl (ˌfəʊn)] Handy; Mobiltelefon I
pay phone ['peɪ fəʊn] Münztelefon III
phone call ['fəʊn ˌkɔːl] Telefonanruf I
phone number ['fəʊn ˌnʌmbə] Telefonnummer III
to **phone** [fəʊn] anrufen; telefonieren II
photo ['fəʊtəʊ] Foto I
to take a photo [ˌteɪk‿ə 'fəʊtəʊ] ein Foto machen I
to take photos [ˌteɪk 'fəʊtəʊz] fotografieren; Fotos machen II
phrase [freɪz] Redewendung; Ausdruck; Satz <III>
PE (**Physical** Education) [ˌpiː'iː, ˌfɪzɪkl edʒʊ'keɪʃn] Sportunterricht I
physical ['fɪzɪkl] physisch; körperlich IV U1, 22
pic (picture) [pɪk ('pɪktʃə)] Foto IV U4, 80
to **pick** [pɪk] auswählen; aussuchen; nehmen <IV U1, 17>; pflücken; herauslesen <IV U4, 88>
to pick up [ˌpɪk‿'ʌp] aufheben II; aufgreifen <III>; abholen IV U2, 43
to pick up the pieces [ˌpɪk ˌʌp ðə 'piːsiːz] etw. wieder in den Griff bekommen <IV U2, 139>
Take your pick. ['teɪk jə ˌpɪk] Such dir was aus. <IV U1, 136>
mixed **pickles** [ˌmɪkst 'pɪklz] gemischtes Essiggemüse <IV U5, 112>
pick-up ['pɪkʌp] Abholung; Pick-up IV U5, 102
picnic ['pɪknɪk] Picknick I
picture ['pɪktʃə] Bild II; Film <IV U4, 142>
pie [paɪ] Kuchen; Pastete II
pie chart ['paɪ ˌtʃɑːt] Kuchendiagramm; Tortendiagramm <IV U1, 23>
piece [piːs] Stück II
a piece of [ə 'piːs‿əv] ein Stück <IV U1, 28>
bits and pieces *(pl only)* [ˌbɪts‿ən 'piːsɪz] Stückchen <IV U1, 136>
piece of cake [piːs‿əv keɪk] einfach <IV U3, 68>
pierogi [pjɜ'rɔgi] Pirogge II
guinea **pig** ['gɪni ˌpɪg] Meerschweinchen I
pile [paɪl] Stapel; Haufen <IV U4, 93>
Pilgrim ['pɪlgrɪm] Pilger- <IV U3, 70>
pilot ['paɪlət] Pilot; Pilotin IV U4, 79
pinch [pɪntʃ] Prise II
pineapple ['paɪnæpl] Ananas III
pinhead ['pɪnhed] Trottel IV U2, 38
pink [pɪŋk] pink; rosa I
pipe [paɪp] Rohr III
pirate ['paɪrət] Seeräuber; Seeräuberin; Pirat; Piratin I
it's a **pity** [ˌɪts‿ə 'pɪti] (es ist) schade IV U3, 63
pizza ['piːtsə] Pizza I
place [pleɪs] Platz; Stelle; Ort I
to take place [ˌteɪk 'pleɪs] stattfinden <III>
plain [pleɪn] Ebene <IV U2, 138>
plain [pleɪn] schlicht; einfach II
plan [plæn] Plan II
to **plan** [plæn] planen III
plane [pleɪn] Flugzeug II
planet ['plænɪt] Planet <IV U2, 48>
plank [plæŋk] Brett; Planke II
plant [plɑːnt] Pflanze I
plantain ['plæntеɪn] Kochbanane II
plantation [plæn'teɪʃn] Plantage IV U5, 97
plaster ['plɑːstə] Pflaster III
plastic ['plæstɪk] Plastik; Kunststoff III
plate [pleɪt] Teller II
play [pleɪ] Theaterstück II
role play ['rəʊl ˌpleɪ] Rollenspiel <II>
to **play** [pleɪ] spielen I
player ['pleɪə] Spieler; Spielerin II
playground ['pleɪgraʊnd] Schulhof; Pausenhof; Spielplatz I

playing card [ˈpleɪɪŋ ˌkɑːd] Spielkarte <IV U4, 92>
please [pliːz] bitte I
pledge [pledʒ] Versprechen IV U2, 34
pledge of allegiance [ˌpledʒ‿əv‿əˈliːdʒns] Treueeid IV U2, 34
plot [plɒt] Handlung <III>
plural [ˈplʊərl] Mehrzahl; Plural <IV U2, 41>
plus [plʌs] plus <IV U2, 50>
pocket [ˈpɒkɪt] Tasche; Hosentasche II
pocketful [ˈpɒkɪtfʊl] Tasche voll <IV U1, 19>
podcast [ˈpɒdkɑːst] Podcast IV U4, 94
poem [ˈpəʊɪm] Gedicht III
point [pɔɪnt] Punkt IV U5, 115
lookout point [ˈlʊkaʊt ˌpɔɪnt] Aussichtspunkt II
starting point [ˈstɑːtɪŋ ˌpɔɪnt] Ausgangspunkt <III>
turning point [ˈtɜːnɪŋ ˌpɔɪnt] Wendepunkt <III>
to point (at) [ˌpɔɪnt‿ˈət] zeigen (auf) I
to point out [ˌpɔɪnt‿ˈaʊt] zeigen; darauf hinweisen IV U1, 15
pointless [ˈpɔɪntləs] sinnlos IV U4, 77
police [pəˈliːs] Polizei III
police officer [pəˈliːs‿ɒfɪsə] Polizeibeamter; Polizeibeamtin I
Polish [ˈpəʊlɪʃ] polnisch; Polnisch; aus Polen IV U1, 22
polite [pəˈlaɪt] höflich II
political [pəˈlɪtɪkl] politisch IV U1, 23
polystyrene [ˌpɒlɪˈstaɪriːn] Styropor <IV U3, 71>
swimming **pool** [ˈswɪmɪŋ ˌpuːl] Schwimmbad I
poor [pɔː] arm IV U1, 18
pop [pɒp] Pop *(Musik)* III
popcorn [ˈpɒpkɔːn] Popcorn I
popular [ˈpɒpjələ] beliebt III
populated [ˈpɒpjəleɪtɪd] bevölkert; besiedelt IV U4, 74
population *(no pl)* [ˌpɒpjəˈleɪʃn] Bevölkerung; Einwohner; Einwohnerzahl III
pork [pɔːk] Schweinefleisch II
porridge [ˈpɒrɪdʒ] Haferbrei III
port [pɔːt] Hafen IV U5, 98
position [pəˈzɪʃn] Position <IV U3, 61>
positive [ˈpɒzətɪv] positiv III
possessive pronoun [pəˈsesɪv ˌprəʊnaʊn] Possessivpronomen <III>
possible [ˈpɒsəbl] möglich <IV U2, 50>
not **possibly** [nɒt ˈpɒsəbli] unmöglich III
post [pəʊst] Post *(online gestellte Nachricht)* IV U4, 80
post office [ˈpəʊst‿ɒfɪs] Postamt I
to post [pəʊst] aufgeben *(einen Brief)*; abschicken *(einen Brief)* III; online stellen; posten IV U4, 80
postcard [ˈpəʊstkɑːd] Postkarte I
poster [ˈpəʊstə] Poster I
pot [pɒt] Topf III; Becher <IV U3, 71>
potato *(sg)* [pəˈteɪtəʊ], **potatoes** *(pl)* [pəˈteɪtəʊz] Kartoffel II
jacket potato [ˌdʒækɪt pəˈteɪtəʊ] Ofenkartoffel II
mashed potatoes [ˌmæʃt pəˈteɪtəʊz] Kartoffelbrei II
pound [paʊnd] Pfund *(brit. Währungseinheit)* I
... is £1.25. [ɪz ˈwʌn paʊnd twentiˌfaɪv] ... kostet ein Pfund fünfundzwanzig. I
poverty [ˈpɒvəti] Armut IV U1, 23
power [ˈpaʊə] Energie; Kraft; Macht III
powerful [ˈpaʊəfl] stark; mächtig; bedeutend; beeindruckend IV U1, 22
practical [ˈpræktɪkl] praktisch IV U4, 89
practice [ˈpræktɪs] Training; Übung I
to practise [ˈpræktɪs] üben; trainieren III
prairie [ˈpreəri] Prärie <IV U2, 138>
prayer [preə] Gebet IV U4, 85
precise [prɪˈsaɪs] genau <IV U1, 31>
to prefer [prɪˈfɜː] vorziehen II
preparation [ˌprepərˈeɪʃn] Zubereitung <IV U5, 112>
to prepare [prɪˈpeə] zubereiten; (sich) vorbereiten III
preposition [ˌprepəˈzɪʃn] Präposition <III>
prerequisite [ˌpriːˈrekwɪzɪt] Voraussetzung <IV U2, 48>
present [ˈpreznt] Geschenk I; Gegenwart; Präsens <IV U3, 67>
simple present [ˌsɪmpl ˈpreznt] Gegenwart; Präsens <III>
present perfect [ˌpreznt ˈpɜːfɪkt] das Perfekt <III>
present progressive [ˌpreznt prəˈgresɪv] Verlaufsform der Gegenwart <III>
to present [prɪˈzent] vorstellen I; präsentieren IV U2, 33
presentation [ˌpreznˈteɪʃn] Präsentation; Vortrag IV U2, 51
presenter [prɪˈzentə] Moderator; Moderatorin <IV U4, 142>
president [ˈprezɪdnt] Präsident; Präsidentin IV U3, 53; Sprecher; Sprecherin <IV U2, 46>
pretty [ˈprɪti] hübsch II; ziemlich; ganz schön IV U2, 34
prewriting [priːˈraɪtɪŋ] vor dem Schreiben <III>
price [praɪs] Preis II
pride [praɪd] Stolz IV U5, 98
principal *(AE)* [ˈprɪnsɪpl] Schulleiter; Schulleiterin IV U2, 34
prison [ˈprɪzn] Gefängnis II
prize [praɪz] Preis II
pro and contra [ˌprəʊ ən ˈkɒntrə] für und wider <IV U5, 115>
probably [ˈprɒbəbli] wahrscheinlich III
problem [ˈprɒbləm] Problem I
process [ˈprəʊsəs] Prozess <IV U2, 48>
to produce [prəˈdjuːs] hervorbringen; produzieren III
dairy **product** [ˈdeəri ˌprɒdʌkt] Milchprodukt; Milcherzeugnis <IV U3, 72>
production [prəˈdʌkʃn] Produktion; Herstellung <III>
profile [ˈprəʊfaɪl] Profil; Steckbrief <III>

programme ['prəʊgræm] Programm; Sendung I

present **progressive** [ˌpreznt prə'gresɪv] Verlaufsform der Gegenwart <III>

project ['prɒdʒekt] Projekt III

to **promise** ['prɒmɪs] versprechen IV U2, 34

prompt card ['prɒmt ˌkɑːd] Stichwortkarte <IV U2, 51>

pronoun ['prəʊnaʊn] Pronomen; Fürwort <IV U5, 104>

possessive pronoun [pə'sesɪv ˌprəʊnaʊn] Possessivpronomen <III>

to **pronounce** [prə'naʊns] aussprechen <IV U2, 51>

pronunciation [prəˌnʌnsi'eɪʃn] Aussprache <IV U1, 15>

prop [prɒp] Requisit III

to **protect** [prə'tekt] schützen III

protective [prə'tektɪv] Schutz- <IV U2, 50>

protest ['prəʊtest] Protest; Demonstration IV U5, 96

to **protest** [prə'test] protestieren <IV U3, 140>

Protestant ['prɒtɪstnt] protestantisch; Protestant; Protestantin III

protester [prə'testə] Gegner; Gegnerin IV U5, 98

proud (of) [praʊd (əv)] stolz (auf) III

to **prove** [pruːv] beweisen IV U4, 84

pub [pʌb] Kneipe; Gasthaus III

the **public** [ðə 'pʌblɪk] die Öffentlichkeit <IV U5, 144>

public ['pʌblɪk] öffentlich <IV U3, 140>

public transport [ˌpʌblɪk 'trænspɔːt] öffentliche Verkehrsmittel III

published ['pʌblɪʃt] veröffentlicht <IV U3, 72>

pudding ['pʊdɪŋ] Nachspeise; Pudding II

Puerto Rican [ˌpwɜːtə‿'riːkən] puertorikanisch; aus Puerto Rico; Puertorikaner; Puertorikanerin <IV U1, 136>

to **puke** [pjuːk] erbrechen; sich übergeben IV U3, 62

to **pull** [pʊl] ziehen I

pumpkin ['pʌmpkɪn] Kürbis; Kürbis- <IV U3, 72>

punctuation [ˌpʌŋktʃu'eɪʃn] Zeichensetzung; Interpunktion <III>

purple ['pɜːpl] lila; violett I

on **purpose** [ɒn 'pɜːpəs] absichtlich II

to **push** [pʊʃ] schieben; drücken I; schubsen; drängeln III

*to **put** [pʊt] setzen; legen; stellen I

to put a comment [ˌpʊt‿ə 'kɒment] einen Kommentar schreiben <I>

to put in [ˌpʊt‿'ɪn] einsetzen I

to put in the right order [ˌpʊt‿ɪn ðə 'raɪt ɔːdə] in die richtige Reihenfolge bringen I

to put on [ˌpʊt‿'ɒn] anlegen; anziehen III

to put up [ˌpʊt‿'ʌp] aufstellen; errichten IV U3, 64

put [pʊt] simple past von *to put* I

puzzle ['pʌzl] Rätsel; Puzzle <I>

Q

qualification [ˌkwɒlɪfɪ'keɪʃn] Qualifikation; Abschluss; Schulabschluss <IV U4, 88>

better **quality** food [ˌbetə 'kwɒləti ˌfuːd] qualitativ besseres Essen <IV U3, 72>

quarter ['kwɔːtə] Viertel <IV U2, 50>

quarter past ['kwɔːtə pɑːst] Viertel nach I

quarter to ['kwɔːtə tə] Viertel vor I

queen [kwiːn] Königin III

question ['kwestʃən] Frage I

queue [kjuː] Warteschlange II

quick [kwɪk] schnell II

quiet ['kwaɪət] ruhig; leise; still III

to go quiet [ˌgəʊ 'kwaɪət] still werden III

to keep quiet [ˌkiːp 'kwaɪət] ruhig sein <III>

quite [kwaɪt] ziemlich III

quiz [kwɪz] Quiz; Rätsel <I>

quote [kwəʊt] Zitat <IV U3, 73>

R

raccoon [rə'kuːn] Waschbär I

race [reɪs] Wettrennen; Rennen I; Rasse <IV U5, 106>

racism ['reɪsɪzm] Rassismus IV U5, 98

radiator ['reɪdieɪtə] Heizkörper IV U3, 59

radio ['reɪdiəʊ] Radio II

rafting ['rɑːftɪŋ] Rafting III

from **rags** to riches [frəm ˌrægz tə‿'rɪtʃɪz] vom Tellerwäscher zum Millionär <IV U1, 28>

railroad *(AE)* ['reɪlrəʊd] Eisenbahn <IV U5, 144>

railway ['reɪlweɪ] Eisenbahn IV U4, 86

railway track ['reɪlweɪ ˌtræk] Gleis IV U3, 64

rain [reɪn] Regen III

to **rain** [reɪn] regnen I

rainbow ['reɪnbəʊ] Regenbogen III

raincoat ['reɪnkəʊt] Regenmantel III

rainy ['reɪni] regnerisch I

ran [ræn] simple past von *to run* III

rang [ræŋ] simple past von *to ring* III

ranger *(AE)* [reɪndʒə] Ranger, Rangerin <IV U1, 29>

to **rank** [ræŋk] einstufen <IV U3, 59>

ranking list ['ræŋkɪŋ lɪst] Rangliste; Rangfolge <IV U3, 59>

rap [ræp] Rap <I>

to **rap** [ræp] rappen II

rapper ['ræpə] Rapper; Rapperin III

raspberry ['rɑːzbri] Himbeere III

to **rate** [reɪt] bewerten; einstufen III

I'd **rather** [aɪd 'rɑːðə] ich würde lieber III

rating ['reɪtɪŋ] Bewertung <III>

razor ['reɪzə] Rasierer; Rasierapparat IV U3, 59

RE (Religious Education) [ɑː‿'riː, rɪˌlɪdʒəs‿edʒʊ'keɪʃn] Religionsunterricht I

to **reach** [riːtʃ] erreichen IV U3, 63

to **react** [ri'ækt] reagieren IV U2, 38

reaction [ri'ækʃn] Reaktion IV U2, 38
*to **read** [ri:d] lesen I
reader ['ri:də] Leser; Leserin IV U1, 21
reading ['ri:dɪŋ] Lesen <I>
ready ['redi] fertig; bereit I
to get ready [ˌget 'redi] sich vorbereiten; sich fertig machen IV U3, 54
real [rɪəl] echt; richtig; wirklich II
reality [ri'æləti] Realität; Wirklichkeit <IV U1, 28>
really ['rɪəli] wirklich I; echt II
reason ['ri:zn] Grund III
to give reasons [ˌgɪv 'ri:znz] Gründe nennen; Gründe angeben III
*to **rebuild** [ˌri:'bɪld] wiederaufbauen <IV U2, 139>
receipt [ri'si:t] Quittung II
recent ['ri:snt] kürzlich; neueste; letzte <IV U4, 88>
recess *(AE)* ['ri:ses] Pause IV U2, 35
recipe ['resɪpi] Rezept II
to **record** [rɪ'kɔ:d] aufnehmen <III>
recording [rɪ'kɔ:dɪŋ] Aufnahme <III>
recording studio [rɪ'kɔ:dɪŋ ˌstju:diəʊ] Tonstudio I
recyclable [ˌri:'saɪkləbl] wiederverwertbar; recycelbar <IV U3, 71>
to **recycle** [ˌri:'saɪkl] recyceln; wiederverwerten <IV U3, 71>
red [red] rot I
redwood (tree) ['redwʊd (tri:)] Mammutbaum IV U4, 74
to **refuse** [rɪ'fju:z] sich weigern; ablehnen IV U5, 107
region ['ri:dʒn] Region; Gegend IV U4, 86
registration [ˌredʒɪ'streɪʃn] Überprüfung der Anwesenheit I; Anmeldung II
to **regret** [rɪ'gret] bedauern IV U3, 58
regular ['regjələ] regelmäßig; normal; üblich; gleichmäßig IV U4, 89
regulation [ˌregjə'leɪʃn] Vorschrift; Regelung; Regulierung <IV U4, 88>
to **reject** [rɪ'dʒekt] zurückweisen; ablehnen IV U5, 99
relationship [rɪ'leɪʃnʃɪp] Beziehung <IV U2, 46>
to **relax** [rɪ'læks] sich entspannen <IV U2, 47>
relaxed [rɪ'lækst] entspannt; locker; gelassen IV U4, 74
relaxing [rɪ'læksɪŋ] entspannend; erholsam III
to **release** [rɪ'li:s] veröffentlichen; herausgeben; freigeben; freisetzen; loslassen IV U5, 97
reliable [rɪ'laɪəbl] verlässlich; zuverlässig; vertrauenswürdig IV U5, 109
religion [rɪ'lɪdʒn] Religion <IV U5, 106>
religious [rɪ'lɪdʒəs] religiös; gläubig IV U1, 23
RE (Religious Education) [ˌɑ:ˌ'ri:, rɪˌlɪdʒəs ˌedʒʊ'keɪʃn] Religionsunterricht I
religious freedom [ˌrɪlɪdʒəs 'fri:dəm] Religionsfreiheit <IV U3, 70>
to **remember** [rɪ'membə] sich merken; sich erinnern (an) II
to **remove** [rɪ'mu:v] entfernen IV U5, 98
rent [rent] Miete II
to **rent** [rent] mieten III
to **repair** [rɪ'peə] reparieren III
to **repeat** [rɪ'pi:t] wiederholen III
to **replace** [rɪ'pleɪs] ersetzen IV U1, 12
report [rɪ'pɔ:t] Bericht IV U4, 84
to **report** (on) [rɪ'pɔ:t (ɒn)] berichten (über) IV U2, 33
reported speech [rɪˌpɔ:tɪd 'spi:tʃ] indirekte Rede <IV U5, 104>
reporter [rɪ'pɔ:tə] Reporter; Reporterin III
republic [rɪ'pʌblɪk] Republik III
reputation [ˌrepjə'teɪʃn] Ruf; Ansehen IV U5, 107
request [rɪ'kwest] Anfrage IV U4, 81
required [rɪ'kwaɪəd] erforderlich; notwendig <IV U2, 48>
are required [rɪ'kwaɪəd] werden gebeten <IV U2, 48>
requirement [rɪ'kwaɪəmənt] Voraussetzung; Anforderung <IV U1, 24>
animal **rescue** shelter [ˌænɪml 'reskju: ˌʃeltə] Tierheim I
to **rescue** ['reskju:] retten <IV U5, 114>
to **resent** [rɪ'zent] übelnehmen; verübeln IV U5, 99
reservation [ˌrezə'veɪʃn] Reservierung IV U4, 76; Reservat IV U2, 32
to make a reservation [ˌmeɪk ə 'rezəveɪʃn] reservieren III
resident ['rezɪdnt] Bewohner; Bewohnerin; Anwohner; Anwohnerin; Einwohner; Einwohnerin <IV U1, 24>
to **respect** [rɪ'spekt] respektieren IV U4, 89
to **respond** [rɪ'spɒnd] reagieren; erwidern; antworten <IV U5, 108>
responsible [rɪs'pɒnsəbl] verantwortlich; verantwortungsvoll IV U2, 38
the **rest** [ðə 'rest] der Rest IV U1, 22
to **rest** [rest] rasten; ausruhen; liegen IV U4, 85
restaurant ['restrɒnt] Restaurant II
restroom *(AE)* ['restrʊm] Toilette IV U2, 41
result [rɪ'zʌlt] Ergebnis II
*to **retell** [ˌri:'tel] nacherzählen; nochmals erzählen <IV U2, 42>
return ticket [rɪ'tɜ:n ˌtɪkɪt] Hin- und Rückfahrkarte III
to **return** [rɪ'tɜ:n] zurückkehren; zurückgeben IV U1, 22
review [rɪ'vju:] Kritik III
revising [rɪ'vaɪzɪŋ] Überarbeitung <III>
Industrial **Revolution** [ɪnˌdʌstriəl revl'u:ʃn] industrielle Revolution III
rhyme [raɪm] Reim <IV U1, 136>
to **rhyme** [raɪm] (sich) reimen III
rhythm ['rɪðm] Rhythmus III
rice [raɪs] Reis II
rich [rɪtʃ] reich III
ridden ['rɪdn] past participle von *to ride* II
ride [raɪd] Fahrt; Ritt IV U1, 14
to take a ride [ˌteɪk ə 'raɪd] fahren IV U4, 74
*to **ride** [raɪd] fahren; reiten II
horse **riding** ['hɔ:s ˌraɪdɪŋ] Reiten I
right [raɪt] Recht IV U5, 96

civil rights *(pl)* [ˌsɪvl ˈraɪts] Bürgerrechte IV U5, 96
right [raɪt] richtig; korrekt I; also II; rechts III; gerade; genau; in dem Moment als IV U2, 42
right ahead [ˌraɪt‿əˈhed] geradeaus IV U1, 15
right away [ˌraɪt‿əˈweɪ] sofort; gleich IV U4, 80
right now [ˌraɪt ˈnaʊ] jetzt gerade III
right there [ˌraɪt ˈðeə] genau vor dir <III>
to be right [biː ˈraɪt] recht haben II
to do the right thing [ˌduː ðə ˈraɪt θɪŋ] das Richtige tun III
to turn right [ˌtɜːn ˈraɪt] (nach) rechts abbiegen I
all right [ˌɔːl ˈraɪt] in Ordnung; alles klar II
on the right [ɒn ðə ˈraɪt] auf der rechten Seite; rechts I
You're right. [jɔː‿ˈraɪt] Du hast recht. I
*to **ring** [rɪŋ] läuten; klingeln III
ice **rink** [ˈaɪs ˌrɪŋk] Eislaufbahn <IV U1, 25>
*to **rise** [raɪz] steigen <IV U5, 114>
to **risk** [rɪsk] riskieren <IV U5, 115>
river [ˈrɪvə] Fluss I
road [rəʊd] Straße I
roadwork *(AE)* [ˈrəʊdwɜːk] Straßenbauarbeiten IV U1, 14
roast [rəʊst] gebraten <IV U3, 72>
roast beef [ˌrəʊst ˈbiːf] Roastbeef; Rinderbraten <IV U5, 112>
robotic [rəˈbɒtɪk] roboterhaft <IV U1, 136>
rock [rɒk] Fels; Stein III
rock climbing [ˈrɒk ˌklaɪmɪŋ] Klettern I
rock [rɒk] Rock *(Musik)* III
rock'n'roll [ˌrɒk‿ən ˈrəʊl] Rock 'n' Roll *(Musikrichtung)* IV U5, 97
rode [rəʊd] simple past von *to ride* II
role [rəʊl] Rolle IV U5, 107
role play [ˈrəʊl ˌpleɪ] Rollenspiel <II>

to **roll up** [ˌrəʊl‿ˈʌp] zusammenrollen; aufrollen; aufkrempeln IV U3, 62
roller coaster [ˈrəʊlə ˌkəʊstə] Achterbahn II
the **Romans** [ðə ˈrəʊmənz] die Römer III
romance [ˈrəʊmæns] Liebesgeschichte III
Romanian [rʊˈmeɪniən] Rumäne; Rumänin; aus Rumänien; Rumänisch; rumänisch <IV U5, 222>
roof [ruːf] Dach II
room [ruːm] Zimmer; Raum I
root [ruːt] Wurzel IV U5, 97
root word [ˌruːt ˈwɜːd] Stammwort <III>
rope [rəʊp] Seil I
rose [rəʊz] Rose IV ZI, 8
roulade [rʊːˈlɑːd] Roulade <IV U3, 72>
round trip [ˌraʊnd ˈtrɪp] Hin- und Rückflug; Hin- und Rückfahrt <IV U3, 66>
routine [ruːˈtiːn] Routine; Ablauf <IV U2, 50>
royal [ˈrɔɪəl] königlich II
rubber [ˈrʌbə] Gummi III
rubbish [ˈrʌbɪʃ] Müll; Abfall II
rude [ruːd] unhöflich; unverschämt IV U2, 39
rugby [ˈrʌgbi] Rugby III
to **ruin** [ˈruːɪn] ruinieren; zerstören II
rule [ruːl] Regel III; Herrschaft IV U5, 98
ruler [ˈruːlə] Lineal I
*to **run** [rʌn] rennen; laufen I; betreiben; leiten; führen III
to run about [ˈrʌn‿əˌbaʊt] herumrennen II
to run away [ˌrʌn‿əˈweɪ] weglaufen III
to run out of [ˌrʌn‿ˈaʊt‿əv] ausgehen *(Ware)* III
run [rʌn] past participle von *to run* III
rung [rʌŋ] past participle von *to ring* III
gold **rush** [ˈgəʊld ˌrʌʃ] Goldrausch IV U4, 84

to **rush** [rʌʃ] eilen; sich beeilen; stürzen III
to rush down [rʌʃ ˈdaʊn] hinuntereilen II
rush hour [ˈrʌʃ ˌaʊə] Hauptverkehrszeit IV U1, 14
Russian [ˈrʌʃn] russisch; Russisch; aus Russland; Russe; Russin IV U5, 99
to **rust** [rʌst] rosten IV U4, 75

S

sad [sæd] traurig III
safe [seɪf] in Sicherheit; sicher III
to keep safe [ˌkiːp ˈseɪf] schützen III
safety [ˈseɪfti] Sicherheit IV U4, 75
safety measure [ˈseɪfti ˌmeʒə] Sicherheitsmaßnahme; Schutzmaßnahme <IV U2, 48>
safety net [ˈseɪfti ˌnet] Sicherheitsnetz IV U4, 75
said [sed] simple past von *to say* I
sail [seɪl] Segel <IV U3, 71>
to **sail** [seɪl] segeln IV U4, 85
sailing ship [ˈseɪlɪŋ ʃɪp] Segelboot <IV U3, 70>
saint [seɪnt] Heilige; Heiliger <IV U5, 108>
salad [ˈsæləd] Salat II
sale [seɪl] Schlussverkauf; Ausverkauf II
jumble sale [ˈdʒʌmbl ˌseɪl] Flohmarkt II
sales associate *(AE)* [ˌseɪlz əˈsəʊʃiət] Verkäufer; Verkäuferin IV U2, 38
saleswoman [ˈseɪlzˌwʊmən] Verkäuferin <IV U5, 110>
salsa [ˈsælsə] Salsasoße <IV U5, 112>
salt [sɔːlt] Salz II
the **same** [ðə ˈseɪm] derselbe; gleich II
sample [ˈsɑːmpl] Probe <IV U1, 24>
sandal [ˈsændl] Sandale <IV U4, 77>
sandwich [ˈsænwɪdʒ] Sandwich; belegtes Brot I
sang [sæŋ] simple past von *to sing* II
sank [sæŋk] simple past von *to sink* III

sat [sæt] simple past, past participle von *to sit* IV U3, 63
satnav ['sætnæv] Navi I
Saturday ['sætədeɪ] Samstag I
sauce [sɔ:s] Soße II
cocktail sauce ['kɒkteɪl ˌsɔ:s] Cocktailsoße <IV U5, 112>
sausage ['sɒsɪdʒ] Wurst; Bratwurst II
sausage roll [ˌsɒsɪdʒ 'rəʊl] Blätterteig mit Wurstfüllung II
to **save** [seɪv] speichern II; retten; bergen III; sparen IV U1, 22; aufheben IV U3, 54
saw [sɔ:] simple past von *to see* I
saxophone ['sæksəfəʊn] Saxofon I
*to **say** [seɪ] nachsprechen; nennen; sagen; sprechen I
to say hi to [ˌseɪ 'haɪ tə] grüßen; Grüße ausrichten I
to say sorry [ˌseɪ 'sɒri] sich entschuldigen II
It says … [ɪt 'sez] Hier steht …; Es heißt … <III>
to **scan** [skæn] scannen; nach Details durchsuchen <III>
to **scare** [skeə] erschrecken II
*to be **scared** [bi: 'skeəd] Angst haben; erschrocken sein II
scarf *(sg)* [skɑ:f], **scarves** *(pl)* [skɑ:vz] Schal; Tuch I
scary ['skeəri] gruselig; beängstigend I
scene [si:n] Szene II
to set the scene [ˌset ðə 'si:n] beste Voraussetzungen schaffen <IV U3, 69>
schedule *(AE)* ['skedʒu:l] Stundenplan; Fahrplan IV U2, 33
school [sku:l] Schule I
at school [ət 'sku:l] in der Schule I
boarding school ['bɔ:dɪŋ ˌsku:l] Internat <IV U2, 139>
driving school ['draɪvɪŋ ˌsku:l] Fahrschule <IV U2, 44>
high school ['haɪ ˌsku:l] Highschool *(weiterführende Schule, Oberstufe)* IV U1, 18
school life ['sku:‿laɪf] Schulalltag <I>
school trip [ˌsku:l 'trɪp] Klassenfahrt I
schoolyard ['sku:ljɑ:d] Schulhof <IV U1, 28>
Science [saɪəns] Wissenschaft; Naturwissenschaft I
computer science [kəmˌpju:tə 'saɪəns] Informatik <III>
science fiction [ˌsaɪəns 'fɪkʃn] Science-Fiction I
scientist ['saɪəntɪst] Wissenschaftler; Wissenschaftlerin <IV U2, 48>
scissors *(pl)* ['sɪzəz] Schere III
nail scissors *(pl)* ['neɪl ˌsɪzəz] Nagelschere III
scone [skɒn] Scone *(eine Art süßes Brötchen)* II
score [skɔ:] Punktestand II
Scot [skɒt] Schotte; Schottin III
Scottish ['skɒtɪʃ] schottisch III
scrambled egg [ˌskræmbld‿'eg] Rührei II
to **scream** [skri:m] schreien; kreischen III
script [skrɪpt] Drehbuch; Skript <III>
scriptwriter ['skrɪptˌraɪtə] Drehbuchautor; Drehbuchautorin <III>
sea [si:] Meer I
seal [si:l] Seehund; Robbe <III>
search [sɜ:tʃ] Suche <IV U1, 17>
search engine ['sɜ:tʃ‿endʒɪn] Suchmaschine <IV U1, 31>
to **search** [sɜ:tʃ] durchsuchen; suchen IV U1, 22
to search for ['sɜ:tʃ fə] suchen nach <III>
at the **seaside** [ət ðə 'si:saɪd] am Meer I
season ['si:zn] Saison; Jahreszeit IV U1, 18
seat [si:t] Sitz III; Sitzplatz; Platz IV U5, 102
Have a seat. [ˌhæv‿ə 'si:t] Setzen Sie sich.; Setz dich. IV U3, 54
second ['sekənd] Sekunde II
second ['sekənd] zweite I; zweitens IV U2, 51
secret ['si:krət] Geheimnis II
secret ['si:krət] geheim II
section ['sekʃn] Abschnitt <III>
security [sɪ'kjʊərəti] Sicherheit <IV U1, 31>
*to **see** [si:] sehen I
to see friends [si: 'frendz] Freunde treffen I
I see. [aɪ 'si:] Ich verstehe. IV U5, 103
See you. ['si: ju:] Tschüss.; Bis bald. I
See you later. [ˌsi: jə 'leɪtə] Tschüss.; Bis bald. I
See you soon! ['si: ju ˌsu:n] Bis bald! I
to **seem** [si:m] scheinen III
seen [si:n] past participle von *to see* II
segregated ['segrɪgeɪtɪd] getrennt IV U5, 106
segregation [ˌsegrɪ'geɪʃn] Rassentrennung; Trennung IV U5, 106
self [self] selbst; sich III
selfie ['selfi] Selfie *(Schnappschuss von sich selbst)* IV U4, 83
selfish ['selfɪʃ] selbstsüchtig IV U2, 39
*to **sell** [sel] verkaufen III
semester [sɪ'mestə] Halbjahr; Schulhalbjahr; Semester <IV U2, 48>
*to **send** [send] schicken; senden I
senior citizen [ˌsi:njə 'sɪtɪzn] Rentner; Rentnerin <IV U5, 223>
sensation [sen'seɪʃn] Sensation <IV U5, 145>
*to make **sense** [ˌmeɪk 'sens] Sinn ergeben; einleuchten <III>
sense of smell [ˌsens‿əv 'smel] Geruchssinn <IV U1, 30>
sent [sent] simple past von *to send* I; past participle von *to send* II
sentence ['sentəns] Satz <I>
separate ['seprət] getrennt; separat; verschieden IV U5, 106
September [sep'tembə] September I
sequence ['si:kwəns] Sequenz; Szene; Abfolge <IV U1, 25>

Serbian ['sɜːbiən] serbisch; Serbisch; aus Serbien; Serbe; Serbin <IV U5, 222>

serious ['sɪəriəs] schwer; ernst III
Are you serious? [ˌɑː ju 'sɪəriəs] Im Ernst? III
to take sth seriously [ˌteɪk 'sɪəriəsli] etw. ernst nehmen IV U1, 18

to **serve** [sɜːv] servieren IV U2, 33

service ['sɜːvɪs] Dienst III
emergency service [ɪ'mɜːdʒnsi ˌsɜːvɪs] Notdienst; Rettungsdienst III

set [set] Satz <IV U4, 92>

*to **set** off [ˌset_'ɒf] aufbrechen; sich aufmachen; auslösen IV U4, 84

*to **set** the scene [ˌset ðə 'siːn] beste Voraussetzungen schaffen <IV U3, 69>

setting ['setɪŋ] Schauplatz <III>

to **settle** ['setl] besiedeln; sich niederlassen (in) IV U4, 75

settler ['setlə] Siedler; Siedlerin IV U2, 32

seven ['sevn] sieben I

seventeen [ˌsevn'tiːn] siebzehn I

seventy ['sevnti] siebzig I

several ['sevrl] einige; mehrere; verschiedene IV U4, 80

shampoo [ʃæm'puː] Shampoo III

shamrock ['ʃæmrɒk] Kleeblatt III

to **share** [ʃeə] teilen III

shark [ʃɑːk] Hai I

pencil **sharpener** ['pensl ˌʃɑːpnə] Anspitzer I

she [ʃiː] sie I

sheep *(sg)* [ʃiːp], **sheep** *(pl)* [ʃiːp] Schaf I

sheet of paper ['ʃiːt_əv ˌpeɪpə] Blatt Papier <IV U4, 92>

shelf *(sg)* [ʃelf], **shelves** *(pl)* [ʃelvz] Regal; Regalbrett I
walnut **shell** ['wɔːlnʌt ˌʃel] Walnussschale <IV U3, 71>

shelter ['ʃeltə] Schutz; Obdach <IV U5, 114>
animal rescue shelter [ˌænɪml 'reskjuː ˌʃeltə] Tierheim I

*to **shine** [ʃaɪn] scheinen; glänzen IV ZI, 8

shiny ['ʃaɪni] glänzend IV U4, 85

ship [ʃɪp] Schiff I
sailing ship ['seɪlɪŋ ʃɪp] Segelboot <IV U3, 70>
ship builder ['ʃɪp ˌbɪldə] Schiffsbauer; Schiffsbauerin III

shipyard ['ʃɪpjɑːd] Werft III

shirt [ʃɜːt] Hemd; Shirt I

shock [ʃɒk] Schock <IV U5, 114>

shoe [ʃuː] Schuh I

shone [ʃɒn] simple past, past participle von *to shine* IV ZI, 8

*to **shoot** (a film) [ˌʃuːt (ə 'fɪlm)] (einen Film) drehen <III>
Oh shoot! [əʊ 'ʃuːt] Mensch! IV U2, 34
to shoot (at) [ʃuːt (ət)] schießen (auf) IV U3, 63

shop [ʃɒp] Laden; Geschäft I
corner shop ['kɔːnə ˌʃɒp] Tante-Emma-Laden I
shop assistant ['ʃɒp_əˌsɪstnt] Verkäufer; Verkäuferin II
sports shop ['spɔːts ˌʃɒp] Sportgeschäft I

shopping ['ʃɒpɪŋ] Einkaufen I
to do the shopping [ˌduː ðə 'ʃɒpɪŋ] Einkäufe machen; Besorgungen machen II
to go shopping [ˌgəʊ 'ʃɒpɪŋ] einkaufen gehen II
shopping centre ['ʃɒpɪŋ ˌsentə] Einkaufszentrum I
shopping list ['ʃɒpɪŋ ˌlɪst] Einkaufszettel I
shopping mall ['ʃɒpɪŋ ˌmɔːl] Einkaufszentrum IV U1, 15

short [ʃɔːt] kurz II

shortly ['ʃɔːtli] kurz III

shorts *(pl)* [ʃɔːts] Shorts; kurze Hose I

shot [ʃɒt] Schuss; Einstellung; Aufnahme <IV U2, 45>
establishing shot [ɪ'stæblɪʃɪŋ ˌʃɒt] Anfangsszene; Eingangsszene <IV U2, 45>

shot [ʃɒt] simple past, past participle von *to shoot* IV U3, 63

shotgun ['ʃɒtgʌn] Schrotflinte; Jagdgewehr IV U5, 107

should [ʃʊd] sollte III

shout [ʃaʊt] Schrei I

to **shout** [ʃaʊt] schreien; rufen II

show [ʃəʊ] Show; Wettbewerb I; Schau; Aufführung IV U5, 102
talent show ['tælənt ˌʃəʊ] Talentwettbewerb I
talk show ['tɔːk ˌʃəʊ] Talkshow <IV U3, 68>
TV show [ˌtiː 'viː ˌʃəʊ] Fernsehsendung II

*to **show** [ʃəʊ] zeigen II
to show up [ˌʃəʊ_'ʌp] auftauchen; erscheinen IV U2, 42

showboat ['ʃəʊˌbəʊt] Theaterschiff <IV U5, 144>

show-business ['ʃəʊˌbɪznɪs] Showbusiness; Showgeschäft; Unterhaltungsindustrie IV U4, 75

shower ['ʃaʊə] Dusche III
shower gel ['ʃaʊə ˌdʒel] Duschgel III

shredded ['ʃredɪd] gehackt; klein gemacht <IV U5, 112>

shrimp [ʃrɪmp] Krabbe; Garnele <IV U5, 112>

*to **shut** up [ˌʃʌt_'ʌp] die Klappe halten IV U3, 63

shy [ʃaɪ] schüchtern IV U2, 39

sick [sɪk] krank III
to be sick [biː 'sɪk] sich übergeben I
to feel sick [ˌfiːl 'sɪk] Übelkeit verspüren; sich schlecht fühlen IV U5, 103

side [saɪd] Seite I

sidewalk *(AE)* ['saɪdwɔːk] Gehweg; Bürgersteig IV U1, 15

sight [saɪt] Sehenswürdigkeit II

sightseeing ['saɪtsiːɪŋ] Besichtigungstour IV U1, 15
to go sightseeing [gəʊ 'saɪtsiːɪŋ] eine Besichtigungstour machen II

sign [saɪn] Schild; Zeichen III

sign language ['saɪn ˌlæŋgwɪdʒ] Gebärdensprache; Zeichensprache III
star sign ['stɑː ˌsaɪn] Sternzeichen IV U1, 14
to sign [saɪn] unterschreiben; unterzeichnen IV U3, 53
to sign autographs [ˌsaɪn 'ɔːtəgrɑːfs] Autogramme geben IV U3, 53
signal ['sɪgnl] Empfang; Signal; Zeichen III
signal word ['sɪgnl ˌwɜːd] Signalwort <III>
signature ['sɪgnətʃə] Unterschrift <IV U2, 44>
silence ['saɪləns] Stille; Schweigen; Ruhe III
silent ['saɪlənt] schweigsam; stumm III
silk [sɪlk] Seide III
silly ['sɪli] albern II; dumm; doof III
similar ['sɪmɪlə] ähnlich <III>
simple ['sɪmpl] einfach III
simple past [ˌsɪmpl 'pɑːst] einfache Vergangenheit <III>
simple present [ˌsɪmpl 'preznt] Gegenwart; Präsens <III>
simply ['sɪmpli] einfach nur IV U4, 84
since [sɪns] seit; seitdem IV U4, 80
***to sing** [sɪŋ] singen I
singer ['sɪŋə] Sänger; Sängerin I
singing ['sɪŋɪŋ] Gesangs- III
single ['sɪŋgl] einzeln <III>
single ticket ['sɪŋgl ˌtɪkɪt] einfache Fahrkarte III
sink [sɪŋk] Becken; Spülbecken <IV U3, 71>
***to sink** [sɪŋk] untergehen; sinken III
sinking ['sɪŋkɪŋ] Untergang III
siren ['saɪrən] Sirene; Martinshorn <IV U1, 19>
sister ['sɪstə] Schwester I
***to sit** [sɪt] sitzen I
site [saɪt] Seite *(im Internet)* IV U4, 80
construction site [kən'strʌkʃn ˌsaɪt] Baustelle IV U1, 15
situation [ˌsɪtju'eɪʃn] Situation II
six [sɪks] sechs I
sixteen [ˌsɪk'stiːn] sechzehn I
sixty ['sɪksti] sechzig I
size [saɪz] Größe II
skateboard ['skeɪtbɔːd] Skateboard III
sketch [sketʃ] Zeichnung; Skizze <IV U2, 51>
to ski [skiː] Ski fahren II
skiing ['skiːɪŋ] Skifahren III
skill [skɪl] Fertigkeit <I>
to skim [skɪm] überfliegen <III>
skirt [skɜːt] Rock I
sky [skaɪ] Himmel <IV U2, 48>
skyline ['skaɪlaɪn] Skyline IV U1, 12
skyscraper ['skaɪskreɪpə] Wolkenkratzer IV U1, 14
to slap [slæp] einen Klaps geben; schlagen IV U3, 64
slave [sleɪv] Sklave; Sklavin IV U4, 86
slavery ['sleɪvri] Sklaverei <IV U5, 98>
sled [sled] Schlitten <IV U1, 29>
sleep [sliːp] Schlaf III
***to sleep** [sliːp] schlafen I
sleepover ['sliːpˌəʊvə] Übernachtung I
slept [slept] simple past, past participle von *to sleep* II
slice [slaɪs] Scheibe; Stück <IV U5, 113>
sliced bread [ˌslaɪst 'bred] in Scheiben geschnittenes Brot III
slogan ['sləʊgən] Slogan; Werbespruch IV U4, 77
to slow to a walk [ˌsləʊ tʊ‿ə 'wɔːk] in Schritttempo verfallen IV U3, 63
slow [sləʊ] langsam III
small [smɔːl] klein I
small talk ['smɔːl ˌtɔːk] Smalltalk <IV U3, 54>
smart [smɑːt] schlau; klug; intelligent III
smartphone ['smɑːtˌfəʊn] Smartphone IV U4, 80
smell [smel] Geruch III
smelly [smeli] stinkend; übelriechend IV U3, 63
smile [smaɪl] Lächeln <IV U4, 95>
to smile [smaɪl] lächeln III
smoke [sməʊk] Rauch III
smoked tofu ['sməʊkt ˌtəʊfuː] geräucherter Tofu <IV U5, 112>
smoothie ['smuːði] Smoothie <IV U3, 72>
smuggler ['smʌglə] Schmuggler; Schmugglerin II
smurf [smɜːf] Schlumpf I
snack [snæk] Snack; Imbiss I
snake [sneɪk] Schlange I
snow [snəʊ] Schnee IV U1, 14
so [səʊ] deshalb; also I; so II
so far [ˌsəʊ 'fɑː] bis jetzt IV U1, 18
so much ['səʊ ˌmʌtʃ] so sehr III
so that [səʊ 'ðæt] damit; so dass IV U2, 34
soap [səʊp] Seife III
social ['səʊʃl] gesellschaftlich; sozial <IV U1, 136>
social media [ˌsəʊʃl 'miːdiə] soziale Medien IV U4, 80
Social Studies ['səʊʃl ˌstʌdiz] Gesellschaftslehre; Sozialkunde I
society [sə'saɪəti] Gesellschaft IV U5, 100
sock [sɒk] Socke I
sofa ['səʊfə] Sofa II
software ['sɒftweə] Software II
solar ['səʊlə] Sonnen-; Solar-; solar III
solar system ['səʊlə] Sonnensystem <IV U2, 48>
sold [səʊld] simple past, past participle von *to sell* III
soldier ['səʊldʒə] Soldat; Soldatin III
solid ['sɒlɪd] fest III
solution [sə'luːʃn] Lösung IV U5, 98
to solve [sɒlv] lösen I
some [sʌm] einige; ein paar I; etwas II
somebody ['sʌmbədi] jemand III
somebody else [ˌsʌmbədi 'els] jemand anderes II
something ['sʌmθɪŋ] etwas I
a little something [ə ˌlɪtl 'sʌmθɪŋ] eine Kleinigkeit IV U3, 54
sometimes ['sʌmtaɪmz] manchmal I
somewhere ['sʌmweə] irgendwo <III>
son [sʌn] Sohn III
song [sɒŋ] Lied I

soon [su:n] bald II
as soon as [əz 'su:n_əz] sobald IV U4, 89
See you soon! ['si: ju ˌsu:n] Bis bald! I
sore [sɔ:] schmerzhaft; wund II
sore throat [ˌsɔ: 'θrəʊt] Halsschmerzen II
Sorry. ['sɒri] Tut mir leid.; Entschuldigung. I
to be sorry [bi: 'sɒri] leidtun III
to feel sorry for [ˌfi:l 'sɒri fə] Mitleid haben mit; bedauern III
I'm sorry. [aɪm 'sɒrɪ] Es tut mir leid.; Entschuldigung. I
Sorry about … ['sɒri ˌəbaʊt] Es tut mir leid wegen … I
sort [sɔ:t] Sorte; Art II
to **sort** [sɔ:t] sortieren IV U2, 38
sound [saʊnd] Ton; Laut; Geräusch III
sounds [saʊndz] Laute <I>
to **sound** [saʊnd] klingen II
soup [su:p] Suppe II
sweet and **sour** [ˌswi:t_ən 'saʊə] süßsauer <IV U5, 222>
source [sɔ:s] Quelle IV U1, 23
south [saʊθ] Süden III
south of ['saʊθ_əv] südlich von IV ZI, 9
in the south of [ˌɪn ðə 'saʊθ_əv] im Süden von III
southern ['sʌðən] südlich IV U5, 96
Southerner ['sʌðnə] Südstaatler; Südstaatlerin IV U5, 97
southwest [ˌsaʊθ'west] Südwesten III
souvenir [ˌsu:vn'ɪə] Souvenir; Andenken III
souvenir shop ['su:vnɪə ˌʃɒp] Souvenirladen III
soy bean ['sɔɪ ˌbi:n] Sojabohne IV ZI, 9
space [speɪs] Ort; Stelle; Platz; Raum; Fläche IV U1, 22
spaghetti [spə'geti] Spaghetti II
Spanish ['spænɪʃ] spanisch; Spanisch; aus Spanien IV U5, 98
*to **speak** [spi:k] sprechen II
speaking ['spi:kɪŋ] Sprechen <I>
spear [spɪə] Speer <IV U2, 138>
special ['speʃl] besonders; speziell I
special effect [ˌspeʃl ɪ'fekt] Spezialeffekt <IV U4, 142>
special offer [ˌspeʃl_'ɒfə] Sonderangebot III
with special needs [wɪð ˌspeʃl 'ni:dz] mit Behinderung III
specific [spə'sɪfɪk] spezifisch; speziell <III>
spectacular [spek'tækjələ] spektakulär III
spectator [spek'teɪtə] Zuschauer; Zuschauerin <IV U2, 50>
speech [spi:tʃ] Sprache; Rede III
direct speech [dɪˌrekt 'spi:tʃ] direkte Rede <IV U3, 73>
farewell speech [feə'wel spi:tʃ] Abschiedsrede II
reported speech [rɪˌpɔ:tɪd 'spi:tʃ] indirekte Rede <IV U5, 104>
speech bubble ['spi:tʃ ˌbʌbl] Sprechblase <III>
speech impaired ['spi:tʃ ɪmˌpeəd] sprachbehindert IV U5, 102
*to **spell** [spel] buchstabieren I
spell check ['spel ˌtʃek] Rechtschreibprüfprogramm <III>
spell checker ['spel ˌtʃekə] Rechtschreibprüfprogramm <IV U2, 49>
spelling ['spelɪŋ] Rechtschreibung I
*to **spend** [spend] ausgeben *(Geld)*; verbringen *(Zeit)* II
spent [spent] simple past, past participle von *to spend* II
spice [spaɪs] Gewürz II
spicy ['spaɪsi] würzig; pikant II
spider ['spaɪdə] Spinne III
*to **spill** [spɪl] auslaufen; verschütten IV U3, 63
spilt [spɪlt] simple past, past participle von *to spill* IV U3, 63
spirit ['spɪrɪt] Stimmung; Geist IV U4, 85
splash [splæʃ] Platsch I
spoke [spəʊk] simple past von *to speak* II
spoken ['spəʊkn] past participle von *to speak* II
spoon [spu:n] Löffel II
sport [spɔ:t] Sport I; Sportart III
sports shop ['spɔ:ts ˌʃɒp] Sportgeschäft I
sporting event ['spɔ:tɪŋ ɪˌvent] Sportereignis; Sportveranstaltung <IV U2, 50>
to **sprain** [spreɪn] verstauchen; verrenken III
sprang up [ˌspræŋ_'ʌp] simple past von *to spring up* IV U4, 86
*to **spread** [spred] streichen <IV U5, 112>
spring roll [ˌsprɪŋ 'rəʊl] Frühlingsrolle II
*to **spring up** [ˌsprɪŋ_'ʌp] entstehen; entspringen IV U4, 86
sprung up [ˌsprʌŋ_'ʌp] past participle von *to spring up* IV U4, 86
squad [skwɒd] Gruppe; Team; Mannschaft IV U2, 34
square [skweə] Platz II
square mile (= sq. mi.) [ˌskweə 'maɪl] Quadratmeile IV ZI, 8
to **squeeze** [skwi:z] drücken; pressen; quetschen IV U3, 63
stadium ['steɪdiəm] Stadion II
staff *(no pl)* [stɑ:f] Personal; Belegschaft; Kollegium IV U2, 38
stage [steɪdʒ] Bühne II
at this stage [æt ðɪs 'steɪdʒ] zu diesem Zeitpunkt <IV U5, 108>
stairs *(pl)* [steəz] Treppe II
stall [stɔ:l] Stand; Bude <IV U5, 110>
food stall ['fu:d ˌstɔ:l] Essensstand II
market stall ['mɑ:kɪt ˌstɔ:l] Marktstand; Marktbude <IV U2, 200>
stallholder ['stɔ:lˌhəʊldə] Standinhaber; Standinhaberin II
stamp [stæmp] Briefmarke III
*to **stand** [stænd] stehen II; ertragen; ausstehen IV U5, 99
to stand out ['stænd_aʊt] auffallen; herausragen; herausstechen IV U1, 12
to stand up [stænd_'ʌp] aufstehen IV U3, 64

standup paddleboarding ['stændʌp ˌpædlbɔːdɪŋ] Stehpaddeln <IV U3, 72>
star [stɑː] Star I; Stern III
star sign ['stɑː ˌsaɪn] Sternzeichen IV U1, 14
to **stare** [steə] starren III
start [stɑːt] Start; Anfang III
for a start [ˌfɔːr‿ə 'stɑːt] zunächst III
to **start** [stɑːt] anfangen; beginnen; starten II; gründen III
to start a band [ˌstɑːt‿ə 'bænd] eine Band gründen II
starting point ['stɑːtɪŋ ˌpɔɪnt] Ausgangspunkt <III>
starter ['stɑːtə] Vorspeise II
state [steɪt] Staat; Bundesstaat; Land IV ZI, 8; Zustand IV U1, 22
state government ['steɪt ˌgʌvnmənt] Landesregierung IV U5, 98
State House *(AE)* ['steɪt ˌhaʊs] Regierungsgebäude IV U5, 98
statement ['steɪtmənt] Aussage; Behauptung; Erklärung IV U1, 22
station ['steɪʃn] Haltestelle; Station; Bahnhof III
statistical [stə'tɪstɪkl] statistisch <IV U1, 26>
statistics *(no pl)* [stə'tɪstɪks] Statistik IV U1, 22
status ['steɪtəs] Status IV U4, 81
to **stay** [steɪ] übernachten; bleiben II
to stay up [steɪ 'ʌp] aufbleiben IV U2, 36
*to **steal** [stiːl] stehlen IV U2, 38
steam engine ['stiːm‿endʒɪn] Dampfmaschine III
paddle **steamer** ['pædl ˌstiːmə] Raddampfer <IV U5, 144>
steamship ['stiːmʃɪp] Dampfschiff; Dampfer IV U1, 22
steel [stiːl] Stahl III
step [step] Schritt III; Stufe II
to **step** [step] treten; steigen IV U4, 86
stereotype ['steriəʊtaɪp] Stereotyp; Klischee <IV U2, 42>
stick [stɪk] Stock II
sticker ['stɪkə] Aufkleber II
still [stɪl] noch; immer noch; dennoch III
to **stir** [stɜː] rühren; umrühren II
stocks [stɒks] Pranger III
stole [stəʊl] simple past von *to steal* IV U2, 38
stolen ['stəʊlən] past participle von *to steal* IV U2, 38
stomach ['stʌmək] Magen; Bauch II
stomach ache ['stʌmək ˌeɪk] Bauchweh; Bauchschmerzen II
stone [stəʊn] Stein III
stood [stʊd] simple past, past participle von *to stand* II
stop [stɒp] Haltestelle; Halt II
bus stop ['bʌs ˌstɒp] Bushaltestelle II
full stop [ˌfʊl 'stɒp] Punkt <III>
one stop [ˌwʌn 'stɒp] einmal Umsteigen <IV U3, 66>
to **stop** [stɒp] aufhören I; verhindern <IV U5, 114>
store *(AE)* [stɔː] Laden; Geschäft IV U2, 33
department store [dɪ'pɑːtmənt ˌstɔː] Kaufhaus II
to **store** [stɔː] aufbewahren; lagern <IV U1, 30>
storm [stɔːm] Sturm IV U2, 32
story ['stɔːri] Geschichte I
feature story ['fiːtʃə ˌstɔːri] Leitartikel; Sonderbericht <IV U5, 110>
mystery story ['mɪstri ˌstɔːri] Krimi (= Kriminalgeschichte); Detektivgeschichte IV U3, 53
story *(AE)* ['stɔːri] Stock; Stockwerk; Etage IV U1, 14
story-telling ['stɔːriˌtelɪŋ] Geschichtenerzählen <IV U2, 42>
straight [streɪt] gerade <IV U2, 47>
straight ahead [ˌstreɪt ə'hed] geradeaus <IV U1, 191>
straight on [streɪt‿'ɒn] geradeaus I
hair **straightener** ['heə ˌstreɪtnə] Haarglätter IV U3, 59
straightforward [ˌstreɪt'fɔːwəd] aufrichtig; geradlinig III
strange [streɪndʒ] merkwürdig; seltsam II; fremd IV U1, 18
straw [strɔː] Trinkhalm II
drinking straw ['drɪŋkɪŋ ˌstrɔː] Trinkhalm <IV U3, 71>
strawberry ['strɔːbri] Erdbeere II
stream [striːm] Bach <IV U2, 138>
to **stream** [striːm] **streamen** *(im Internet)* IV U4, 80
street [striːt] Straße III
street art ['striːt ɑːt] Straßenkunst <IV U1, 28>
street gang ['striːt ˌgæŋ] Straßengang <IV U1, 136>
strength [streŋθ] Stärke; Kraft IV U2, 39
stress [stres] Stress IV U3, 57
to **stretch** [stretʃ] sich strecken; erstrecken; dehnen IV U3, 52
strict [strɪkt] streng; strikt IV U2, 34
striking ['straɪkɪŋ] bemerkenswert; auffallend III
comic **strip** ['kɒmɪk strɪp] Comic <III>
to **stroll** [strəʊl] schlendern; bummeln IV U4, 76
strong [strɒŋ] stark III
structure ['strʌktʃə] Struktur; Aufbau III
to **structure** ['strʌktʃə] strukturieren; gliedern <IV U2, 46>
stubborn ['stʌbən] eigensinnig; störrisch IV U2, 39
*to be **stuck** [biː 'stʌk] feststecken; nicht weg können; festsitzen; hängen bleiben IV U2, 34
*to get **stuck** [ˌget 'stʌk] stecken bleiben IV U3, 54
student ['stjuːdnt] Schüler; Schülerin; Student; Studentin I
studio ['stjuːdiəʊ] Studio IV U4, 75
recording studio [rɪ'kɔːdɪŋ ˌstjuːdiəʊ] Tonstudio I
TV studio [ˌtiː'viː ˌstjuːdiəʊ] Fernsehstudio II
study hall period ['stʌdi hɔːl ˌpɪəriəd] Freistunde IV U2, 34
study skills [ˌstʌdi 'skɪlz] Fertigkeit Lern- und Arbeitstechniken <I>

to study ['stʌdi] studieren; lernen IV U2, 34
stuff [stʌf] Zeug IV U2, 34
stunt [stʌnt] Stunt <IV U2, 50>
stuntman ['stʌntmæn] Stuntman IV U3, 53
style [staɪl] Stil III
subject ['sʌbdʒɪkt] Schulfach I
core subject [ˌkɔ: 'sʌbdʒɪkt] Pflichtfach IV U2, 35
submarine [ˌsʌbmr'i:n] U-Boot I
to subscribe [səb'skraɪb] abonnieren IV U4, 81
subtotal ['sʌbˌtəʊtl] Zwischensumme <IV U3, 66>
suburb ['sʌbɜ:b] Vorort IV U1, 15
subway *(AE)* ['sʌbweɪ] U-Bahn IV U1, 14
to succeed (in) [sək'si:d (ɪn)] Erfolg haben (mit/bei); nachfolgen IV U1, 19
success [sək'ses] Erfolg III
successful [sək'sesfl] erfolgreich III
such [sʌtʃ] solch IV U2, 38
suddenly ['sʌdnli] plötzlich; auf einmal II
sugar ['ʃʊgə] Zucker I
suggestion [sə'dʒestʃn] Vorschlag; Anregung <IV U3, 72>
to suit [su:t] stehen; passen II
suitable ['su:təbl] geeignet; passend <IV U2, 51>
suitcase ['su:tkeɪs] Koffer II
trolley suitcase ['trɒli ˌsu:tkeɪs] Rollkoffer III
to sum up [ˌsʌm‿'ʌp] zusammenfassen IV U3, 73
to summarise ['sʌmraɪz] zusammenfassen <IV U3, 73>
summary ['sʌmri] Zusammenfassung <III>
summer ['sʌmə] Sommer II
sun [sʌn] Sonne III
to sunbathe ['sʌnbeɪð] sonnenbaden II
Sunday ['sʌndeɪ] Sonntag I
sunglasses *(pl)* ['sʌnˌglɑ:sɪz] Sonnenbrille II
sunk [sʌŋk] past participle von *to sink* III
sunny ['sʌni] sonnig I
super ['su:pə] super II
superhero ['su:pəˌhɪərəʊ] *(sg)*, **superheroes** ['su:pəˌhɪərəʊz] *(pl)* Superheld IV U3, 61
supermarket ['su:pəˌmɑ:kɪt] Supermarkt II
supplies *(pl)* [sə'plaɪz] Vorräte <IV U1, 30>
support [sə'pɔ:t] Unterstützung; Hilfe IV U1, 19
to support [sə'pɔ:t] unterstützen IV U5, 100
supporter [sə'pɔ:tə] Anhänger; Anhängerin; Fan <IV U2, 50>
sure [ʃʊə] sicher I
to make sure [ˌmeɪk 'ʃɔ:] dafür sorgen; sich versichern III
sure of oneself ['ʃʊər‿əv ˌwʌnself] selbstsicher III
to surf [sɜ:f] surfen; wellenreiten II
to surf the internet [ˌsɜ:f ði 'ɪntənet] im Internet surfen II
surface ['sɜ:fɪs] Oberfläche IV U4, 86
surfer ['sɜ:fə] Wellenreiter; Wellenreiterin; Surfer; Surferin IV ZI, 9
surfing ['sɜ:fɪŋ] Surfen; Wellenreiten III
surprise [sə'praɪz] Überraschung I
to surprise [sə'praɪz] überraschen <III>
surprised [sə'praɪzd] überrascht II
survey ['sɜ:veɪ] Umfrage II
to survive [sə'vaɪv] überleben III
sushi ['su:ʃi] Sushi IV U5, 99
suspense [sə'spens] Spannung <III>
swam [swæm] simple past von *to swim* II
swamp [swɒmp] Sumpf IV ZI, 9
to swap [swɒp] tauschen <IV U4, 92>
*__to swear__ [sweə] schwören <IV U2, 45>
sweatshirt ['swetʃɜ:t] Sweatshirt I
*__to sweep__ [swi:p] fegen II
sweet [swi:t] Süßigkeit; Bonbon I
sweet [swi:t] süß III
sweet and sour [ˌswi:t‿ən 'saʊə] süßsauer <IV U5, 222>
swept [swept] simple past, past participle von *to sweep* II
*__to swim__ [swɪm] schwimmen II
swimmer ['swɪmə] Schwimmer; Schwimmerin IV U4, 78
*to go **swimming** [ˌgəʊ 'swɪmɪŋ] schwimmen gehen I
swimming pool ['swɪmɪŋ ˌpu:l] Schwimmbad I
Swiss [swɪs] schweizerisch; aus der Schweiz; Schweizer; Schweizerin IV U4, 84
sword [sɔ:d] Schwert III
swum [swʌm] past participle von *to swim* II
symbol ['sɪmbl] Symbol IV U1, 13
Syrian ['sɪriən] syrisch; aus Syrien; Syrer; Syrerin <IV U5, 222>
system ['sɪstəm] System IV U5, 107

T

table ['teɪbl] Tisch I; Tabelle <III>
table tennis ['teɪbl ˌtenɪs] Tischtennis II
tablespoon ['teɪblspu:n] Esslöffel <IV U5, 113>
tablet ['tæblət] Tablette II; Tablet IV U3, 58
tactic ['tæktɪk] Taktik; Vorgehensweise III
take [teɪk] Aufnahme <III>
*__to take__ [teɪk] nehmen; mitnehmen I; hinbringen II; dauern III
to take a break [ˌteɪk‿ə 'breɪk] Pause machen II
to take a photo [ˌteɪk‿ə 'fəʊtəʊ] ein Foto machen I
to take a ride [ˌteɪk‿ə 'raɪd] fahren IV U4, 74
to take a test [ˌteɪk‿ə 'test] eine Prüfung machen <IV U2, 44>
to take a trip [ˌteɪk‿ə 'trɪp] eine Fahrt machen III
to take action [teɪk‿'ækʃn] eingreifen <IV U5, 114>

to take care of sb [ˌteɪk ˈkeər‿əv] sich um jmdn. kümmern; für jmdn. sorgen IV U2, 41
to take notes [ˌteɪk ˈnəʊts] sich Notizen machen I
to take off [ˌteɪk‿ˈɒf] ausziehen III; durchstarten; abheben IV U1, 18
to take out [ˌteɪk‿ˈaʊt] herausnehmen I
to take part (in) [ˌteɪk ˈpɑːt] teilnehmen (an) II
to take photos [ˌteɪk ˈfəʊtəʊz] fotografieren; Fotos machen II
to take place [ˌteɪk ˈpleɪs] stattfinden <III>
to take sth seriously [ˌteɪk ˈsɪəriəsli] etw. ernst nehmen IV U1, 18
to take the dog for a walk [ˌteɪk ðə ˌdɒg fər‿ə ˈwɔːk] den Hund spazieren führen II
to take turns [ˌteɪk ˈtɜːnz] sich abwechseln <II>
Take care. [ˈteɪk ˌkeə] Macht's gut. I
Take your pick. [ˈteɪk jə ˌpɪk] Such dir was aus. <IV U1, 136>

takeaway [ˈteɪkəweɪ] Essen zum Mitnehmen II
takeaway [ˈteɪkəweɪ] zum Mitnehmen II
taken [ˈteɪkn] past participle von *to take* II
talent [ˈtælənt] Talent I
talent show [ˈtælənt ˌʃəʊ] Talentwettbewerb I
talented [ˈtæləntɪd] begabt; talentiert III
talk [tɔːk] Gerede II; Vortrag; Rede <III>
to give a talk [ˌgɪv‿ə ˈtɔːk] einen Vortrag halten <III>
small talk [ˈsmɔːl ˌtɔːk] Smalltalk <IV U3, 54>
talk show [ˈtɔːk ˌʃəʊ] Talkshow <IV U3, 68>
to **talk** (to) [ˈtɔːk tə] sprechen (mit); reden (mit) I
to talk about [ˈtɔːk‿əˌbaʊt] sprechen über II

tall [tɔːl] groß; hoch II
tape [teɪp] Klebeband <IV U3, 71>
task [tɑːsk] Aufgabe; Auftrag <I>
taste [teɪst] Geschmack <IV U5, 112>
to **taste** [teɪst] schmecken <IV U3, 72>
tasty [ˈteɪsti] lecker; schmackhaft III
taught [tɔːt] simple past, past participle von *to teach* III
tax [tæks] Steuer <IV U3, 66>
taxi [ˈtæksi] Taxi II
tea [tiː] Tee; (frühes) Abendessen I
tea bag [ˈtiː ˌbæg] Teebeutel <IV U5, 113>
tea light [ˈtiː ˌlaɪt] Teelicht <IV U3, 71>
*to **teach** [tiːtʃ] beibringen; unterrichten; lehren III
teacher [ˈtiːtʃə] Lehrer; Lehrerin I
team [tiːm] Team; Mannschaft I
teamwork [ˈtiːmwɜːk] Teamwork II
*to **tear** (up) [teər (ʌp)] kaputt machen; reißen; zerreißen IV U2, 33
to **tease** [tiːz] hänseln; sticheln; reizen IV U2, 38
teaspoon *(tsp)* [ˈtiːspuːn] Teelöffel *(TL)* II
technology [tekˈnɒlədʒi] Technologie <IV U4, 90>
Design Technology (DT) [dɪˌzaɪn tekˈnɒlədʒi, ˌdiːˈtiː] Technik I
Welding Technology [ˈweldɪŋ ˌteknɒlədʒi] Schweißtechnik <IV U2, 48>
teen [tiːn] Jugend-; Teenager; Jugendliche; Jugendlicher II
teenage [ˈtiːneɪdʒ] jugendlich IV U3, 54
teenager [ˈtiːneɪdʒə] Teenager; Jugendliche; Jugendlicher; III
telephone [ˈtelɪfəʊn] Telefon III
telephone box [ˈtelɪfəʊn ˌbɒks] Telefonzelle II
*to **tell** [tel] erzählen; sagen I
temperature [ˈtemprətʃə] Temperatur; Fieber <IV U4, 88>
ten [ten] zehn I
tennis [ˈtenɪs] Tennis I
tense [tens] Zeit; Zeitform <III>
tent [tent] Zelt II

tepee [ˈtiːpiː] Tipi <IV U2, 138>
terrible [ˈterəbl] schrecklich; schlimm; furchtbar I
terrifying [ˈterəfaɪɪŋ] furchterregend; erschreckend IV U2, 32
territory [ˈterɪtri] Gebiet; Revier; Territorium <IV U5, 144>
test [test] Test; Klassenarbeit I
to take a test [ˌteɪk‿ə ˈtest] eine Prüfung machen <IV U2, 44>
to **test** [test] testen; prüfen II
text [tekst] Text II
advertising text [ˈædvətaɪzɪŋ ˌtekst] Werbetext <IV U4, 78>
text message [ˈtekst ˌmesɪdʒ] SMS II
to **text** [tekst] eine SMS schreiben II
texter [ˈtekstə] SMS-Schreiber; SMS-Schreiberin II
than [ðæn] als II
thank God [ˌθæŋk‿ˈgɒd] Gott sei Dank <IV U3, 70>
Thank you. [ˈθæŋk ju] Danke. I
thankful [ˈθæŋkfl] dankbar IV U3, 54
thanks [θæŋks] danke I
Thanks so much. [ˌθæŋk‿səʊ ˈmʌtʃ] Vielen Dank.; Herzlichen Dank. IV U4, 94
Thanksgiving [ˌθæŋksˈgɪvɪŋ] Erntedankfest IV U3, 53
that [ðæt] das I; dass III; so *(Betonung)* III
after that [ˈɑːftə ðət] danach I
so that [səʊ ˈðæt] damit; so dass IV U2, 34
that night [ˌðæt ˈnaɪt] an jenem Abend; in jener Nacht II
That's £2.24. [ðæts ˈtuː paʊndz ˌtwenti fɔː] Das macht zwei Pfund und 24 Pence. I
That's because … [ˌðæts bɪˈkɒz] Das liegt daran, dass … III
that's why [ˈðæts waɪ] deswegen III
the [ðə] der; die *(auch Pl.)*; das I
the same [ðə ˈseɪm] derselbe; gleich II
theater *(AE)* [ˈθɪətə] Theater IV U1, 13

movie theater *(AE)* ['mu:vi ˌθi:ətə] Kino IV U5, 106
theatre ['θɪətə] Theater II
their [ðeə] ihr, ihre *(Pl.)* I
theirs [ðeəz] ihre III
them [ðem; ðəm] sie *(Pl.)*; ihnen I
theme [θi:m] Thema; Motto <IV U5, 107>
theme park ['θi:m ˌpɑ:k] Freizeitpark I; Themenpark II
themselves [ðəm'selvz] selber; sie selbst; sich selbst; selbst III
then [ðen] dann; danach I; damals III
then again [ˌðen ə'gen] andererseits III
there [ðeə] da; dort I
down there [ˌdaʊn 'ðeə] dahin; da unten IV U5, 98
over there [ˌəʊvə 'ðeə] da drüben; dort drüben II
there are [ðeər‿'ɑ:] da sind; es gibt I
there is [ðeə 'ɪz] da ist; dort ist; es gibt I
these [ði:z] diese (hier) II
they [ðeɪ] sie *(Pl.)* I
thing [θɪŋ] Sache; Ding I
*to **think** [θɪŋk] denken; glauben I
to think of ['θɪŋk‿əv] sich ausdenken; sich etwas einfallen lassen <III>
third [θɜ:d] dritte I
thirsty ['θɜ:sti] durstig II
thirteen [θɜ:'ti:n] dreizehn I
thirty ['θɜ:ti] dreißig I
this [ðɪs] das; dies I
like this [laɪk 'ðɪs] ähnlich; so <III>
this way [ðɪs 'weɪ] in diese Richtung II; auf diese Weise <III>
those [ðəʊz] jene II
though [ðəʊ] jedoch III
thought [θɔ:t] Gedanke IV U3, 62
thought bubble ['θɔ:t ˌbʌbl] Denkblase; Gedankenblase <IV U1, 19>
thought [θɔ:t] simple past, past participle von *to think* II
a/one **thousand** [ə/wʌn 'θaʊznd] eintausend; tausend II

three [θri:] drei I
threw [θru:] simple past von *to throw* IV U2, 38
throat [θrəʊt] Hals II
sore throat [ˌsɔ: 'θrəʊt] Halsschmerzen II
through [θru:] durch II
throughout [θru'aʊt] überall in <IV U5, 114>
*to **throw** [θrəʊ] werfen IV U2, 38
thrown [θrəʊn] past participle von *to throw* IV U2, 38
Thursday ['θɜ:zdeɪ] Donnerstag I
ticket ['tɪkɪt] Karte II; Fahrschein; Eintrittskarte III
return ticket [rɪ'tɜ:n ˌtɪkɪt] Hin- und Rückfahrkarte III
single ticket ['sɪŋgl ˌtɪkɪt] einfache Fahrkarte III
to **tidy (up)** [ˌtaɪdi 'ʌp] aufräumen; in Ordnung bringen II
to **tie** [taɪ] binden; zubinden; fesseln IV U3, 62
tiger ['taɪgə] Tiger I
tight [taɪt] eng; fest II
time [taɪm] Zeit; Uhrzeit I; Mal III
all the time [ˌɔ:l ðə 'taɪm] die ganze Zeit III
brewing time ['bru:ɪŋ ˌtaɪm] Brühzeit <IV U5, 113>
free time [ˌfri: 'taɪm] Freizeit I
in time [ɪn 'taɪm] rechtzeitig I
on time [ɒn 'taɪm] pünktlich III
opening times ['əʊpnɪŋ ˌtaɪmz] Öffnungszeiten IV U5, 105
period of time [ˌpɪəriəd‿əv 'taɪm] Zeitraum <IV U4, 86>
time travel ['taɪm ˌtrævl] Zeitreise III
time zone ['taɪm ˌzəʊn] Zeitzone IV ZI, 8
timeline ['taɪmˌlaɪn] Zeitstrahl <III>
timetable ['taɪmˌteɪbl] Stundenplan I; Fahrplan III
tin [tɪn] Dose; Büchse; Mülleimer IV U3, 63
tiny ['taɪni] klein; winzig III
tip [tɪp] Tipp; Ratschlag II

tired [taɪəd] müde I
to get tired of sth [ˌget 'taɪəd‿əv] etw. sattbekommen; etw. satthaben IV U1, 14
tissue ['tɪʃu:] Taschentuch III
title ['taɪtl] Titel; Überschrift <II>
job title ['dʒɒb ˌtaɪtl] Stellenbezeichnung; Berufsbezeichnung IV U2, 38
to [tʊ] in; nach; zu; vor *(bei Uhrzeitangaben)* I; bis II
to the north of [ˌtə ðə 'nɔ:θ‿əv] nördlich von III
toast [təʊst] Toast II
tobacco *(no pl)* [tə'bækəʊ] Tabak <IV U5, 144>
today [tə'deɪ] heute I
together [tə'geðə] zusammen; gemeinsam I
to get together [ˌge‿tə'gəðə] zusammenkommen; zusammenfinden IV U3, 52
toilet ['tɔɪlət] Toilette I
told [təʊld] simple past von *to tell* I
to **tolerate** ['tɒlreɪt] tolerieren; dulden IV U5, 98
tomato *(sg)* [tə'mɑ:təʊ], **tomatoes** *(pl)* [tə'mɑ:təʊz] Tomate II
tomorrow [tə'mɒrəʊ] morgen II
ton [tʌn] Tonne *(Gewicht)* IV U4, 80
tone [təʊn] Ton <IV U4, 95>
tongue twister ['tʌŋ ˌtwɪstə] Zungenbrecher <III>
tonight [tə'naɪt] heute Abend; heute Nacht II
tonne [tʌn] Tonne II
too [tu:] auch I; zu II
too much [ˌtu: 'mʌtʃ] zu sehr II
took [tʊk] simple past von *to take* II
tool [tu:l] Werkzeug; Gerät II
tooth *(sg)* [tu:θ], **teeth** *(pl)* [ti:θ] Zahn III
toothbrush ['tu:θbrʌʃ] Zahnbürste III
toothpaste ['tu:θpeɪst] Zahnpasta III
toothpick ['tu:θpɪk] Zahnstocher II
top [tɒp] Top; Oberteil II; oberer Teil; oberes Ende III; Spitze IV U1, 13
at the top [æt ðə 'tɒp] oben III

topic [ˈtɒpɪk] Thema IV U2, 51
torch [tɔːtʃ] Taschenlampe I
tore (up) [tɔːr (ʌp)] simple past von *to tear up* IV U2, 33
torn (up) [tɔːn (ʌp)] past participle von *to tear up* IV U2, 33
torn [tɔːn] zerrissen; aufgerissen IV U4, 83
tornado [tɔːˈneɪdəʊ] Tornado; Wirbelsturm IV U2, 32
total [ˈtəʊtl] Summe <IV U3, 66>
total [ˈtəʊtl] Gesamt-; gesamt IV ZI, 8; komplett <IV U3, 68>
*to keep in **touch** [ˌkiːp ɪn ˈtʌtʃ] in Verbindung bleiben II
to **touch** [tʌtʃ] berühren III
touchdown [ˈtʌtʃdaʊn] Touchdown <IV U2, 50>
tough [tʌf] hart III
tour [tʊə] Tour; Fahrt; Reise IV U4, 76
guided tour [ˈgaɪdɪd ˌtɔː] Führung <IV U1, 13>
tourism [ˈtʊərɪzm] Tourismus IV U1, 18
tourist [ˈtʊərɪst] Tourist; Touristin I
Tourist Information Centre [ˈtʊərɪst ɪnfəˈmeɪʃn ˌsentə] Touristeninformation I
in **tow** [ɪn ˈtəʊ] im Schlepptau IV U2, 42
towards [təˈwɔːdz] in Richtung; auf … zu IV U3, 62
towel [ˈtaʊəl] Handtuch III
tower [ˈtaʊə] Turm II
clock tower [ˈklɒk ˌtaʊə] Uhrenturm II
town [taʊn] Stadt I
ghost town [ˈgəʊst ˌtaʊn] Geisterstadt IV U4, 86
town hall [ˌtaʊn ˈhɔːl] Rathaus II
toy [tɔɪ] Spielzeug III
cuddly toy [ˈkʌdli ˌtɔɪ] Kuscheltier III
track [træk] Strecke IV U5, 102
railway track [ˈreɪlweɪ ˌtræk] Gleis IV U3, 64
tractor [ˈtræktə] Traktor I
trader [ˈtreɪdə] Händler; Händlerin <IV U2, 138>
tradition [trəˈdɪʃn] Tradition III
traditional [trəˈdɪʃnl] traditionell III
traffic [ˈtræfɪk] Verkehr III
traffic jam [ˈtræfɪk ˌdʒæm] Stau IV U1, 14
tragic [ˈtrædʒɪk] tragisch <IV U2, 138>
trail [treɪl] Wanderweg; Spur IV U5, 102
train [treɪn] Zug I
trainer [ˈtreɪnə] Turnschuh I; Trainer; Trainerin IV U5, 103
training [ˈtreɪnɪŋ] Training III
tram [træm] Straßenbahn III
transcontinental [ˌtrænsˌkɒntɪˈnentl] transkontinental *(über den Kontinent hinweg)* IV U4, 86
transfer [trænsˈfɜː] Transport; Transfer IV U5, 102
to **translate** [trænzˈleɪt] übersetzen IV U5, 102
translation [trænzˈleɪʃn] Übersetzung <III>
transparency [trænˈspærnsi] Folie <IV U2, 51>
transport [ˈtrænspɔːt] Transport <IV U1, 29>
public transport [ˌpʌblɪk ˈtrænspɔːt] öffentliche Verkehrsmittel III
to **transport** [trænˈspɔːt] transportieren; befördern <IV U1, 30>
transport [ˈtrænspɔːt] Verkehrs- IV U4, 86
trash (AE) [træʃ] Abfall; Müll IV U3, 62
travel [ˈtrævl] (das) Reisen <IV U1, 29>
time travel [ˈtaɪm ˌtrævl] Zeitreise III
to **travel** [ˈtrævl] reisen II; fahren III
travelling [ˈtrævlɪŋ] (das) Reisen <IV U3, 52>
tray [treɪ] Tablett II
treasure [ˈtreʒə] Schatz II
tree [triː] Baum I
trend [trend] Trend; Entwicklung; Richtung IV U4, 80
trending [ˈtrendɪŋ] trendsetzend IV U4, 81
trendy [ˈtrendi] trendy; modisch IV U4, 81
tribe [traɪb] Stamm; Volksstamm <IV U1, 24>
trick [trɪk] Trick; Streich I; Kunststück III
Trick or treat! [ˌtrɪk‿ə ˈtriːt] Süßes, sonst gibt's Saures! I
tricky [ˈtrɪki] schwierig; knifflig IV U2, 38
trip [trɪp] Ausflug I; Trip; Fahrt; Reise III
boat trip [ˈbəʊt ˌtrɪp] Bootsfahrt; Schiffsfahrt II
field trip [ˈfiːld ˌtrɪp] Schulausflug <IV U2, 46>
outgoing trip [ˌaʊtgəʊɪŋ ˈtrɪp] Hinfahrt <IV U3, 66>
return trip [ˌrɪtɜːn ˈtrɪp] Rückfahrt <IV U3, 66>
round trip [ˌraʊnd ˈtrɪp] Hin- und Rückflug; Hin- und Rückfahrt <IV U3, 66>
school trip [ˌskuːl ˈtrɪp] Klassenfahrt I
to take a trip [ˌteɪk‿ə ˈtrɪp] eine Fahrt machen III
trolley suitcase [ˈtrɒli ˌsuːtkeɪs] Rollkoffer III
trouble [ˈtrʌbl] Schwierigkeiten; Problem; Ärger III
trousers *(pl)* [ˈtraʊzəz] Hose I
truck [trʌk] Wagen; Karre III; Truck; Lastwagen <IV U1, 30>
true [truː] wahr II; treu IV U2, 34
to come true [ˌkʌm ˈtruː] wahr werden; in Erfüllung gehen IV U1, 18
to **trust** [trʌst] vertrauen IV U5, 109
to **try** [traɪ] probieren; versuchen II
to try on [traɪ‿ˈɒn] anprobieren II
to try out [traɪ‿ˈaʊt] ausprobieren III
T-shirt [ˈtiːʃɜːt] T-Shirt I
tube [tjuːb] Schlauch; Rohr III
Tuesday [ˈtjuːzdeɪ] Dienstag I
on Tuesday [ˌɒn ˈtjuːzdeɪ] am Dienstag I
tuna [ˈtjuːnə] Thunfisch II
tunnel [ˈtʌnl] Tunnel III

(wind) **turbine** [(wɪnd) 'tɜːbaɪn] Windrad III
turkey ['tɜːki] Truthahn; Pute IV U3, 53
Turkish ['tɜːkɪʃ] türkisch; Türkisch; aus der Türkei IV U5, 99
Turkish bath [ˌtɜːkɪʃ 'bɑːθ] Dampfbad III
turn [tɜːn] Drehung IV U5, 102
to take turns [ˌteɪk 'tɜːnz] sich abwechseln <II>
to wait one's turn [ˌweɪt wʌnz 'tɜːn] warten, bis man an der Reihe ist <IV U5, 110>
to **turn** [tɜːn] abbiegen III
to turn around [ˌtɜːn‿ə'raʊnd] (sich) umdrehen III
to turn into [ˌtɜːn‿'ɪntə] umwandeln in; verwandeln in <IV U1, 28>
to turn left [ˌtɜːn 'left] (nach) links abbiegen I
to turn off [ˌtɜːn‿'ɒf] abschalten; ausschalten <IV U1, 25>
to turn on [ˌtɜːn‿'ɒn] einschalten IV U3, 64
to turn right [ˌtɜːn 'raɪt] (nach) rechts abbiegen I
turning point ['tɜːnɪŋ ˌpɔɪnt] Wendepunkt <III>
tutor ['tjuːtə] Klassenlehrer; Klassenlehrerin I
tutor group ['tjuːtə ˌɡruːp] Klasse *(in einer englischen Schule)* I
tutorial [tjuː'tɔːriəl] Anleitung; Tutorial IV U4, 80
TV [ˌtiː'viː] Fernseher; Fernsehen I
TV show [ˌtiː 'viː ˌʃəʊ] Fernsehsendung II
TV studio [ˌtiː'viː ˌstjuːdiəʊ] Fernsehstudio II
to watch TV [ˌwɒtʃ tiː'viː] fernsehen I
on TV [ɒn ˌtiː'viː] im Fernsehen IV U1, 13
twelve [twelv] zwölf I
twenty ['twenti] zwanzig I
twenty-one [ˌtwenti'wʌn] einundzwanzig I
twice [twaɪs] zweimal; doppelt IV U2, 38
to **twist** [twɪst] verdrehen; verzerren II
two [tuː] zwei I
type [taɪp] Sorte; Typ; Art III
to **type** [taɪp] tippen <III>
typical ['tɪpɪkl] typisch <IV U2, 35>
tyre [taɪə] Reifen III

U

umbrella [ʌm'brelə] Regenschirm II
umpire ['ʌmpaɪə] Schiedsrichter; Schiedsrichterin <III>
unable [ʌn'eɪbl] unfähig <IV U1, 24>
unappealing [ˌʌnə'piːlɪŋ] uninteressant IV U4, 77
uncle ['ʌŋkl] Onkel I
uncomfortable [ʌn'kʌmftəbl] unbequem; unangenehm II
under ['ʌndə] unter I
underground ['ʌndəɡraʊnd] U-Bahn II
underlined [ˌʌndə'laɪnd] unterstrichen <III>
*to **understand** [ˌʌndə'stænd] verstehen II
understood [ˌʌndə'stʊd] simple past von *to understand* II
unemployed [ˌʌnɪm'plɔɪd] arbeitslos IV U1, 18
unemployment *(no pl)* [ˌʌnɪm'plɔɪmənt] Arbeitslosigkeit <IV U2, 139>
unexpected [ˌʌnɪk'spektɪd] unerwartet <III>
unfair [ʌn'feə] unfair III
unfashionable [ʌn'fæʃnəbl] unmodisch II
to **unfriend** [ʌn'frend] entfreunden *(jmdn. von seiner Freundesliste streichen)* IV U4, 81
unfriendly [ʌn'frendli] unfreundlich III
unhappy [ʌn'hæpi] unglücklich II
uniform ['juːnɪfɔːm] Uniform I
unit ['juːnɪt] Lektion; Kapitel <I>
imperial unit [ɪm'pɪəriəl ˌjuːnɪt] englische Maßeinheit <IV U5, 112>
university [ˌjuːnɪ'vɜːsəti] Universität III
unjust [ʌn'dʒʌst] ungerecht IV U5, 106
unlike [ʌn'laɪk] anders als; im Gegensatz zu III
*to be **unlucky** [biː ʌn'lʌki] Pech haben <IV U5, 114>
unmotivated [ˌʌn'məʊtɪveɪtɪd] unmotiviert IV U2, 39
unofficial [ˌʌnə'fɪʃl] inoffiziell <IV U2, 50>
unpleasant [ʌn'pleznt] unangenehm; unerfreulich IV U1, 22
unpopular [ʌn'pɒpjələ] unpopulär; unbeliebt III
until [ʌn'tɪl] bis I
unusual [ʌn'juːʒl] ungewöhnlich <II>; außergewöhnlich IV U4, 77
up [ʌp] hinauf; oben II
to end up [ˌend‿'ʌp] enden; landen <IV U5, 114>
to make up [ˌmeɪk‿'ʌp] erfinden; sich ausdenken <III>
to pick up [ˌpɪk‿'ʌp] abholen IV U2, 43
to put up [ˌpʊt‿'ʌp] aufstellen; errichten IV U3, 64
to show up [ˌʃəʊ‿'ʌp] auftauchen; erscheinen IV U2, 42
to shut up [ˌʃʌt‿'ʌp] die Klappe halten IV U3, 63
to stand up [ˌstænd‿'ʌp] aufstehen IV U3, 64
to wash up [ˌwɒʃ‿'ʌp] abwaschen; abspülen <IV U2, 200>
update [ʌp'deɪt] Aktualisierung <IV U1, 31>
to **update** ['ʌpdeɪt] updaten; auf den neuesten Stand bringen IV U4, 81
updated [ʌp'deɪtɪd] aktualisiert <IV U1, 30>
to **upload** ['ʌpləʊd] hochladen; ins Internet stellen II
upper ['ʌpə] obere III
upset [ʌp'set] aufgebracht; bestürzt I
upside-down [ˌʌpsaɪd 'daʊn] umgedreht; auf den Kopf gestellt <IV U4, 92>

US [ˌju:ˈes] US-amerikanisch IV U1, 18
us [ʌs] wir; uns I
to use [ju:z] benutzen; verwenden II
to get used to (sth) [ˌget ˈju:zd tə] sich an (etw.) gewöhnen IV U1, 19
used to (live) [ˈju:st tə] (wohnte) früher III
useful [ˈju:sfl] nützlich; hilfreich III
usually [ˈju:ʒli] normalerweise; gewöhnlich II

V

vacation *(AE)* [vəˈkeɪʃn] Ferien; Urlaub IV U5, 104
vacuum cleaner [ˈvækju:m ˌkli:nə] Staubsauger IV U3, 59
valid [ˈvælɪd] gültig III
van [væn] Lieferwagen; Transporter III
variety [vəˈraɪəti] Auswahl <IV U3, 72>
veganism *(no pl)* [ˈvi:gənɪzm] Veganismus IV U4, 83
vegetable (veg) [ˈvedʒtəbl] Gemüse II
vegetarian [ˌvedʒɪˈteəriən] Vegetarier; Vegetarierin I
veggie bean cake [ˌvedʒi ˈbi:n keɪk] *vegetarisches Bohnengericht* II
verb [vɜ:b] Verb <III>
verse [vɜ:s] Vers; Strophe <III>
version [ˈvɜ:ʃn] Version <III>
very [ˈveri] sehr I
very first [ˈveri fɜ:st] allererste III
vet [vet] Tierarzt; Tierärztin III
via [vaɪə] über; per <IV U5, 114>
victim [ˈvɪktɪm] Opfer <IV U5, 108>
Victorian era [vɪkˌtɔ:riən ˈɪərə] viktorianisches Zeitalter III
video [ˈvɪdiəʊ] Video IV U3, 54
video chat [ˈvɪdiəʊ ˌtʃæt] Video-Chat III
Vietnamese [ˌvjetnəˈmi:z] vietnamesisch; Vietnamesisch; aus Vietnam; Vietnamese; Vietnamesin IV U5, 98
view [vju:] Aussicht; Sicht; Ausblick; Blick IV U1, 14
viewing [ˈvju:ɪŋ] Hör-/Sehverstehen <I>
Viking [ˈvaɪkɪŋ] Wikinger- III
village [ˈvɪlɪdʒ] Dorf III
violent [ˈvaɪəlnt] gewaltsam; gewalttätig; brutal <IV U5, 114>
visit [ˈvɪzɪt] Besuch III
to visit [ˈvɪzɪt] besuchen II
visitor [ˈvɪzɪtə] Besucher; Besucherin II
vocabulary [vəˈkæbjəlri] Vokabular; Wortschatz II
voice [vɔɪs] Stimme III
volleyball [ˈvɒlibɔ:l] Volleyball IV U4, 74
volume [ˈvɒlju:m] Inhalt <IV U5, 112>
volunteer [ˌvɒlənˈtɪə] Freiwilliger; Freiwillige; ehrenamtlicher Helfer; ehrenamtliche Helferin III
to vote [vəʊt] abstimmen; wählen <IV U2, 49>
to vote for [ˈvəʊt fə] abstimmen über; wählen IV U2, 33
voyage [ˈvɔɪɪdʒ] Reise; Fahrt III

W

wage [weɪdʒ] Lohn IV U2, 38
wagon [ˈwægən] Waggon; Planwagen IV U4, 85
to wait [weɪt] warten II
to wait for [ˈweɪt fɔ:] warten auf II
to wait one's turn [ˌweɪt wʌnz ˈtɜ:n] warten, bis man an der Reihe ist <IV U5, 110>
waiter [ˈweɪtə] Kellner II
waitress [ˈweɪtrəs] Kellnerin; Bedienung IV U4, 89
*to **wake** up [weɪk‿ˈʌp] aufwachen II
walk [wɔ:k] Spaziergang III
night walk [ˌnaɪt ˈwɔ:k] Nachtwanderung I
to slow to a walk [ˌsləʊ tʊ‿ə ˈwɔ:k] in Schritttempo verfallen IV U3, 63
to take the dog for a walk [ˌteɪk ðə ˌdɒg fər‿ə ˈwɔ:k] den Hund spazieren führen II
a five minute walk [ə ˈfaɪv mɪnɪt ˌwɔ:k] fünf Minuten zu Fuß III
to walk [wɔ:k] gehen I; laufen II
dog **walker** [ˈdɒg ˌwɔ:kə] Hundeausführer; Hundeausführerin IV U2, 41
walking [ˈwɔ:kɪŋ] Wandern III
wall [wɔ:l] Mauer; Wand II
wallet [ˈwɒlɪt] Brieftasche; Geldbörse III
walnut shell [ˈwɔ:lnʌt ˌʃel] Walnussschale <IV U3, 71>
to want (to) [wɒnt (tə)] wollen I
war [wɔ:] Krieg <IV U1, 192>
Civil War [ˌsɪvl ˈwɔ:] Bürgerkrieg IV U3, 140
wardrobe [ˈwɔ:drəʊb] Kleiderschrank I
warm [wɔ:m] warm I
to warn [wɔ:n] warnen III
was [wɒz] simple past von *to be* I
to wash [wɒʃ] (sich) waschen; spülen III
to wash up [ˌwɒʃ‿ˈʌp] abwaschen; abspülen <IV U2, 200>
*to do the **washing** up [ˌdu: ðə ˈwɒʃɪŋ‿ʌp] abspülen II
waste [weɪst] Abfall <IV U1, 30>
to waste [weɪst] verschwenden IV U2, 38
to watch [wɒtʃ] anschauen; ansehen I; aufpassen auf; zuschauen; beobachten II
to watch TV [ˌwɒtʃ ti:ˈvi:] fernsehen I
bird **watching** [ˈbɜ:d ˌwɒtʃɪŋ] Vogelbeobachtung III
whale **watching** [ˈweɪl ˌwɒtʃɪŋ] Walbeobachtung IV U3, 52
water [ˈwɔ:tə] Wasser I
bucket of water [ˈbʌkɪt‿əv ˌwɔ:tə] Eimer Wasser I
mineral water [ˈmɪnrl ˌwɔ:tə] Mineralwasser III
water level [ˈwɔ:tə ˌlevl] Wasserpegel; Wasserstand <IV U5, 144>
waterproof [ˈwɔ:təpru:f] wasserfest <IV U3, 71>
waters *(pl only)* [ˈwɔ:təz] Gewässer <IV U5, 114>
wave [weɪv] Welle IV ZI, 9
to wave [weɪv] winken II

way [weɪ] Weg; Art und Weise III
way in [ˌweɪ ˈɪn] Einstieg <I>
way of life [ˌweɪ əv ˈlaɪf] Lebensart; Lebensweise IV U5, 96
way to go [ˈweɪ tə ˌɡəʊ] super II
asking the way [ˈɑːskɪŋ ðə ˌweɪ] nach dem Weg fragen I
either way [ˈaɪðə ˌweɪ] ganz egal; so oder so <IV U1, 137>
No way! [ˌnəʊ ˈweɪ] Auf keinen Fall!; Was?!; Echt?! III
on the way [ˌɒn ðə ˈweɪ] auf dem Weg; unterwegs I
this way [ðɪs ˈweɪ] in diese Richtung II; auf diese Weise <III>
way [weɪ] weit <IV U4, 142>
we [wiː; wi] wir I
weak [wiːk] schwach III
weakness [ˈwiːknəs] Schwäche IV U2, 39
wealth [welθ] Reichtum III
*to **wear** [weə] tragen *(Kleidung)* I
weather [ˈweðə] Wetter I
web [web] Spinnennetz; Netz III
website [ˈwebsaɪt] Website II
wedding [ˈwedɪŋ] Hochzeit II
Wednesday [ˈwenzdeɪ] Mittwoch I
on Wednesdays [ɒn ˈwenzdeɪz] mittwochs I
week [wiːk] Woche I
on **weekdays** [ɒn ˈwiːkdeɪz] unter der Woche; an Werktagen III
weekend [ˈwiːkend] Wochenende I
at the weekend [ˌət ðə ˈwiːkend] am Wochenende I
weekly [ˈwiːkli] wöchentlich III
to **weigh** [weɪ] wiegen II
weight [weɪt] Gewicht <IV U1, 31>
to **welcome** [ˈwelkəm] begrüßen; willkommen heißen IV U4, 80
welcome (to) [ˈwelkəm (tʊ)] willkommen (bei/in) I
You're **welcome**. [jɔː ˈwelkəm] Gern geschehen. I
Welding Technology [ˈweldɪŋ ˌteknɒlədʒi] Schweißtechnik <IV U2, 48>
well [wel] na ja I; gut II
Well done! [ˌwel ˈdʌn] Gut gemacht! I
well-informed [ˌwelɪnˈfɔːmd] gut informiert <IV U3, 68>
well-known [ˌwelˈnəʊn] wohl bekannt <IV U4, 142>
well-organized [ˈwel‿ɔːɡnaɪzd] gut organisiert <IV U1, 27>
welly [ˈweli] Gummistiefel I
Welsh [welʃ] walisisch; Walisisch; Waliser; Waliserin III
went [went] simple past von *to go* I
were [wɜː] simple past von *to be* I
west [west] Westen III
west of [ˈwest‿əv] westlich von IV ZI, 9
western [ˈwestən] Western *(Filmart)* <IV U4, 142>
country and **western** music [ˌkʌntri ənd ˈwestən ˌmjuːzɪk] Countrymusik <IV U5, 145>
wet [wet] nass I
whale [weɪl] Wal IV U3, 52
whale watching [ˈweɪl ˌwɒtʃɪŋ] Walbeobachtung IV U3, 52
what [wɒt] was I; welche II; wie III
What a ... [ˈwɒt‿ə] Was für ein/eine ... I
What about ...? [ˈwɒt‿əˌbaʊt] Was ist mit ...? I
What about you? [ˌwɒt‿əbaʊt ˈjuː] Und du? II
what else [ˌwɒt‿ˈels] was sonst; was noch III
What else can you ...? [ˌwɒt‿ˈels kæn juː] Was kannst du noch ...? <I>
What have you been up to? [ˌwɒt‿əv juː biːn ˈʌp tə] Was hast du (in letzter Zeit) gemacht?; Wie läuft's bei dir? IV U3, 55
What time is it? [ˌwɒt ˈtaɪm‿ɪz‿ɪt] Wie spät ist es?; Wie viel Uhr ist es? I
What to ... [ˈwɒt tə] Was man ... II
What's up? [ˌwɒts‿ˈʌp] Wie geht's? IV U3, 54
What's wrong? [ˌwɒts ˈrɒŋ] Was ist los?; Was stimmt nicht? II
What's your name? [ˌwɒts jə ˈneɪm] Wie heißt du? I
wheel [wiːl] Rad II
big wheel [ˌbɪɡ ˈwiːl] Riesenrad II
wheelchair [ˈwiːltʃeə] Rollstuhl III
when [wen] wann I; wenn; als II
where [weə] wo; wohin; woher I
Where are you from? [ˌweər‿ə ju ˈfrɒm] Woher kommst du? I
wherever [weəˈrevə] wo(hin) auch immer; egal wo(hin); überall wo(hin) III
which [wɪtʃ] welche II; die; der; dem; den; das III
a **while** [ə ˈwaɪl] eine Weile IV U2, 34
while [waɪl] während II
to **whisper** [ˈwɪspə] flüstern <IV U5, 104>
white [waɪt] weiß I
who [huː] wer I; die; welche II; der; dem; den III
whole [həʊl] ganz III
whom [huːm] wen; wem III
whose [huːz] dessen; deren III
why [waɪ] warum I
that's why [ˈðæts waɪ] deswegen III
wide [waɪd] breit IV U5, 96
widely [waɪd] weitgehend <IV U5, 108>
wife *(sg)* [waɪf], **wives** *(pl)* [waɪvz] Ehefrau III
the **wild** [ðə ˈwaɪld] Wildnis; freie Wildbahn IV U5, 102
wild [waɪld] wild III
wilderness [ˈwɪldənəs] Wildnis IV U4, 85
wildlife [ˈwaɪldlaɪf] Tierwelt *(in freier Wildbahn)* IV U5, 102
will [wɪl] werden II
willing [ˈwɪlɪŋ] bereitwillig IV U2, 39
*to **win** [wɪn] gewinnen; siegen I
wind [wɪnd] Wind I
wind farm [ˈwɪnd fɑːm] Windpark III
window [ˈwɪndəʊ] Fenster I
windscreen wiper [ˈwɪnskriːn ˌwaɪpə] Scheibenwischer III
windy [ˈwɪndi] windig I

wine [waɪn] Wein IV U3, 62
winner ['wɪnə] Sieger; Siegerin; Gewinner; Gewinnerin I
winter ['wɪntə] Winter I
windscreen **wiper** ['wɪnskri:n ˌwaɪpə] Scheibenwischer III
wire ['waɪə] Draht; Kabel III
wish [wɪʃ] Wunsch <IV U1, 19>
Best wishes, [ˌbest 'wɪʃɪz] Viele Grüße, I
to **wish** [wɪʃ] wünschen III
witch [wɪtʃ] Hexe I
with [wɪð] mit I
within [wɪ'ðɪn] innerhalb <IV U2, 138>
without [wɪ'ðaʊt] ohne III
witness ['wɪtnəs] Zeuge; Zeugin IV U5, 107
woke up [ˌwəʊk‿'ʌp] simple past von *to wake up* II
woman *(sg)* ['wʊmən], **women** *(pl)* ['wɪmɪn] Frau I
won [wʌn] simple past von *to win* I; past participle von *to win* II
won't (= will not) [wəʊnt] nicht werden II
wonderful ['wʌndəfl] wunderbar III
wood [wʊd] Holz; Wald III
wool [wʊl] Wolle I
word [wɜ:d] Wort IV U1, 22
linking word [ˌlɪŋkɪŋ 'wɜ:d] Verbindungswort <IV U3, 73>
root word [ˌru:t 'wɜ:d] Stammwort <III>
signal word ['sɪgnl ˌwɜ:d] Signalwort <III>
work [wɜ:k] Arbeit I
to **work** [wɜ:k] arbeiten I; funktionieren II
to work off [ˌwɜ:k‿'ɒf] abarbeiten IV U1, 22
workbook ['wɜ:kbʊk] Arbeitsheft I
worker ['wɜ:kə] Arbeiter; Arbeiterin II
working conditions *(pl only)* ['wɜ:kɪŋ kənˌdɪʃnz] Arbeitsbedingungen <IV U4, 88>
working hours *(pl)* ['wɜ:kɪŋ ˌaʊəz] Arbeitszeit IV U2, 38
workshop ['wɜ:kʃɒp] Workshop II
acting workshop ['æktɪŋ ˌwɜ:kʃɒp] Schauspielworkshop II
world [wɜ:ld] Welt II
all around the world [ɔ:l‿əˌraʊnd ðə 'wɜ:ld] in aller Welt III
in the world [ɪn ðə 'wɜ:ld] auf der Welt II
outside world [ˌaʊtsaɪd 'wɜ:ld] Außenwelt IV U3, 58
world-class ['wɜ:ldˌklɑ:s] weltklasse <IV U1, 136>
worn [wɔ:n] past participle von *to wear* II
worried ['wʌrid] beunruhigt; besorgt II
worry ['wʌri] Sorge <IV U5, 114>
to **worry** ['wʌri] sich Sorgen machen I
worst [wɜ:st] schlimmste; schlechteste III
*to be **worth** [bi: 'wɜ:θ] wert sein III
would [wʊd] würde(n) II
would like [wʊd 'laɪk] würde(n) gern; hätte(n) gern II
I wouldn't like (to) ... [aɪ 'wʊdnt laɪk (tə)] Ich möchte nicht ...; Ich würde nicht gerne ... I
I'd love to ... (= I would love to) [aɪd 'lʌv tə] Ich würde sehr gern ... III
Would you like (to) ...? [ˌwʊd jə 'laɪk (tə)] Möchtest du? I
wrap [ræp] Wrap II
bubble wrap ['bʌbl ˌræp] Luftpolsterfolie <IV U3, 71>
wrist [rɪst] Handgelenk IV U3, 63
*to **write** [raɪt] schreiben I
writer ['raɪtə] Schriftsteller; Schriftstellerin II; Verfasser; Verfasserin; Autor; Autorin III
writing ['raɪtɪŋ] Schreiben <I>
written ['rɪtn] past participle von *to write* <IV U3, 72>; schriftlich <IV U2, 44>
wrong [rɒŋ] falsch I
to be wrong [bi: 'rɒŋ] unrecht haben; sich irren III
wrote [rəʊt] simple past von *to write* I

Y

year [jɪə] Jahr; Jahrgangsstufe; Klasse I
boom years ['bu:m ˌjɪəz] Blütezeit; fette Jahre *(ugs.)* IV U4, 86
yearbook ['jɪəbʊk] Jahrbuch <IV U2, 49>
year-old [ˌjɪər‿'əʊld] jährig; Jahre alt IV U2, 38
to **yell** [jel] brüllen; laut schreien <IV U2, 50>
yellow ['jeləʊ] gelb I
yes [jes] ja I
yesterday ['jestədeɪ] gestern I
yet [jet] schon II
not ... yet [nɒt ... 'jet] noch nicht II
yogurt ['jɒgət] Joghurt II
you [ju:] du; Sie; ihr; euch; dich; dir; Ihnen I
You're right. [jɔ:‿'raɪt] Du hast recht. I
You're welcome. [jɔ: 'welkəm] Gern geschehen. I
young [jʌŋ] jung II
your [jɔ:] dein, deine; euer, eure; Ihr, Ihre I
yours [jɔ:z] deine; eure; Ihre I
Yours, [jɔ:z] Eure *(als Briefabschluss)* I
yourself [jɔ:'self] dich selbst II
by yourself [baɪ 'jɔ:self] allein II
yourselves [jɔ:'selvz] selber; ihr/euch/Sie/sich (selbst) III
youth hostel ['ju:θ ˌhɒstl] Jugendherberge III
youth *(no pl)* [ju:θ] Jugend-; Jugend III

Z

zebra ['zebrə] Zebra I
zero ['zɪərəʊ] null I
zip line ['zɪp ˌlaɪn] Seilrutsche III
ZIP Code ['zɪp kəʊd] Postleitzahl <IV U2, 44>
time **zone** ['taɪm ˌzəʊn] Zeitzone IV ZI, 8
zoo [zu:] Zoo; Tierpark I

zookeeper [ˌzuːˈkiːpə] Tierpfleger; Tierpflegerin I
to **zoom in** [ˈzuːm‿ɪn] heranzoomen <I>

Boys' names

Al [æl] IV U5, 105
Alaqua [ˈælækwə] <IV U2, 139>
Chris [krɪs] IV U3, 62
CJ [ˈsiːˌdʒeɪ] IV U2, 45
Daniel [ˈdænjəl] <IV U4, 76>
David [ˈdeɪvɪd] IV U1, 14
Derek [ˈderɪk] IV U4, 80
Donald [ˈdɒnld] IV U1, 16
Edward [ˈedwəd] IV U4, 85
Ethan [ˈiːθn] IV U5, 102
Finn [fɪn] <IV U3, 72>
Gordie [ˈgɔːdi] IV U3, 62
Henry [ˈhenri] IV U1, 16
Jacob [ˈdʒeɪkəb] IV U3, 54
José [həʊˈzeɪ] IV U1, 18
Matt [mæt] IV U5, 102
Matteo [məˈtɪəʊ] <IV U4, 88>
Michael [ˈmaɪkl] IV U2, 38
Ramon [rəˈmɒn] <IV U4, 88>
Robert [ˈrɒbət] IV U3, 54
Ronan [ˈrəʊnən] IV U1, 25
Scott [skɒt] IV U1, 16
Teddy [ˈtedi] IV U3, 63
Vern [vɜːn] IV U3, 63
Warren [ˈwɒrn] IV U2, 33
Wesley [ˈwezli] IV U1, 25

Girls' names

Amy [ˈeɪmi] IV U1, 16
Angela [ˈændʒlə] IV U1, 19
Anna [ˈænə] IV U5, 98
Becky [ˈbeki] IV U4, 78
Brenda [ˈbrendə] IV U3, 54
Caitlin [ˈkeɪtlɪn] <IV U2, 44>
Claudette [klɔːˈdet] IV U5, 106
Emma [ˈemə] <IV U3, 72>
Jennifer [ˈdʒenɪfə] IV U3, 58
Jessica [ˈdʒesɪkə] IV U1, 25
Julia [ˈdʒuːliə] IV U3, 54
Lily [ˈlɪli] IV U3, 54
Linda [ˈlɪndə] IV U1, 16
Marie [məˈriː] IV U2, 39
Nancy [ˈnænsi] IV U1, 16
Pam [pæm] <IV U3, 72>
Pat [pæt] <IV U2, 139>
Ruby [ˈruːbi] IV U2, 45
Ruth [ruːθ] IV U3, 58
Sandy [ˈsændi] IV U4, 78
Stacey [ˈsteɪsi] IV U2, 39
Susan [ˈsuːzn] IV U1, 16

Surnames

Beeman [ˈbiːmən] IV U3, 64
Blanco [ˈblæŋkəʊ] IV U1, 18
Colvin [ˈkɒlvɪn] IV U5, 106
DeSpain [dəˈspeɪn] IV U3, 62
Lachance [ˈlæʃɑːns] IV U3, 62
Lane [leɪn] IV U5, 105
Lee [liː] IV U4, 80
Miller [ˈmɪlə] IV U3, 54
Singh [sɪŋ] IV U1, 14
Sutter [ˈsʌtə] IV U4, 84
Turino [tjʊˈriːnəʊ] <IV U5, 114>
Warner [ˈwɔːnə] <IV U3, 72>
Williams [ˈwɪljəmz] IV U5, 98

Place names

Africa [ˈæfrɪkə] Afrika II
Alabama (AL) [æləˈbæmə] *Bundesstaat in den USA* IV ZI, 9
Alaska (AK) [əˈlæskə] Alaska IV ZI, 8
America [əˈmerɪkə] Amerika II
Arkansas (AR) [ˈɑːkənsɔː] *Fluss und Bundesstaat in den USA* <IV U2, 138>
Asia [ˈeɪʒə] Asien IV U4, 74
Australia [ɒsˈtreɪliə] Australien I
Bishop [ˈbɪʃəp] *Ortsname* IV U4, 76
Bodie [ˈbəʊdi] *Ortsname* IV U4, 86
Boston [ˈbɒstən] *Stadt in den USA* III
The **British Isles** [ðə ˌbrɪtɪʃ ˈaɪlz] die Britischen Inseln III
the **Bronx** [ðə ˈbrɒŋks] *Stadtteil von NYC* IV U1, 12
Brooklyn [ˈbrʊklɪn] *Stadtteil von NYC* IV U1, 12
California (CA) [ˌkælɪˈfɔːniə] Kalifornien IV ZI, 9
Canada [ˈkænədə] Kanada III
Cape Cod [ˌkeɪp ˈkɒd] *Ortsname* <IV U3, 70>
Castle Rock [ˌkɑːsl ˈrɒk] *Stadt in den USA* IV U3, 63
Central Valley [ˌsentrl ˈvæli] *Tal in Kalifornien* <IV U4, 88>
Chicago [ʃɪˈkɑːgəʊ] *Stadt in den USA* <IV U2, 44>
China [ˈtʃaɪnə] China IV U1, 23
Cleveland [ˈkliːvlənd] *Stadt in den USA* <IV U3, 72>
Coloma [kəˈləʊmə] *Ortsname* IV U4, 84
Colorado (CO) [ˌkɒlərˈɑːdəʊ] *Bundesstaat in den USA* IV ZI, 10
Cuba [ˈkjuːbə] Kuba IV U1, 18
The **Czech Republic** [ðə ˌtʃek rɪˈpʌblɪk] Tschechien II
Daytona [deɪˈtəʊnə] *Stadt in den USA* IV U5, 102
Del Mar [ˌdel ˈmɑː] *Ortsname* <IV U4, 77>
Denmark [ˈdenmɑːk] Dänemark III
Doheny [dəˈhiːni] *Strand in Kalifornien* <IV U4, 77>
The **Dominican Republic** [ðə dəˌmɪnɪkn rɪˈpʌblɪk] Dominikanische Republik IV U1, 23
Eastern Europe [ˈiːstn ˌjʊərəp] Osteuropa IV U1, 23
England [ˈɪŋglənd] England I
Europe [ˈjʊərəp] Europa II
Florida (FL) [ˈflɒrɪdə] *Bundesstaat in den USA* IV U5, 96
Florida Keys [ˈflɒrɪdə ˌkiːz] *Inselkette in den USA* IV U5, 145
France [frɑːns] Frankreich II
Germany [ˈdʒɜːməni] Deutschland I
Great Britain [ˌgreɪt ˈbrɪtn] Großbritannien III
Greece [griːs] Griechenland IV U1, 23
Hangtown [ˈhæŋtaʊn] *Ortsname* IV U4, 85
Harlow [ˈhɑːləʊ] *Stadt in den USA* IV U3, 64

Hawaii [hə'waɪiː] *Inselkette im Pazifischen Ozean* IV ZI, 9
Huntsville ['hʌntsvɪl] *Ort in den USA* IV ZI, 10
Illinois (IL) [ˌɪlɪ'nɔɪ] *Bundesstaat in den USA* <IV U2, 44>
India ['ɪndiə] Indien I
Indiana (IN) [ˌɪndi'ænə] *Bundesstaat in den USA* IV ZI, 10
Italy ['ɪtəli] Italien II
Jamaica [dʒə'meɪkə] Jamaika II
Japan [dʒə'pæn] Japan <IV U4, 90>
Kentucky (KY) [ken'tʌki] *Bundesstaat in den USA* IV ZI, 10
Las Vegas [ˌlæs 'veɪgəs] *Großstadt in den USA* IV ZI, 10
Latin America [ˌlætɪn ə'merɪkə] Lateinamerika IV U1, 18
Lincoln ['lɪŋkən] *Ortsname* IV U2, 38
Little Italy [ˌlɪtl 'ɪtli] *Stadtteil von NYC* IV U1, 25
London ['lʌndən] *Hauptstadt von England* I
Los Angeles [lɒs‿'ændʒɪliːz] *Stadt in den USA* IV U3, 52
Louisiana (LA) [luˌiːzi'ænə] *Bundesstaat in den USA* IV ZI, 9
Maine (ME) [meɪn] *Bundesstaat in den USA* IV U3, 53
Manhattan [mæn'hætn] *Stadtteil von NYC* IV U1, 12
Massachusetts [ˌmæsə'tʃuːsɪts] *Bundesstaat in den USA* <IV U3, 66>
Mexico ['meksɪkəʊ] Mexiko IV U1, 23
Miami [maɪ'æmi] *Stadt in den USA* IV U3, 54
The **Midwest** [ˌðə 'mɪdwest] der Mittlere Westen IV ZI, 9
Mississippi (MS) [ˌmɪsɪ'sɪpi] *Bundesstaat in den USA* IV ZI, 9
Montgomery [mɑːnt'gʌmri] *Stadt in den USA* IV U5, 106
Narrabeen ['nærəbiːn] *Strand in Australien* <IV U4, 77>
Nashville ['næʃvɪl] *Ort in den USA* IV U5, 97
Nebraska (NE) [nɪ'bræskə] *Bundesstaat in den USA* IV U2, 38
The **Netherlands** [ðə 'neðələndz] die Niederlande II
Nevada (NV) [nə'vɑːdə] *Bundesstaat in den USA* IV ZI, 10
New England [ˌnjuː‿'ɪŋglənd] Neuengland IV ZI, 8
New Mexico (NM) [njuː 'meksɪkəʊ] *Bundesstaat in den USA* IV ZI, 10
New Orleans [ˌnjuː‿ɔː'liənz] *Stadt in den USA* IV U5, 97
New York City (NYC) [ˌnjuː jɔːk 'sɪti] *Großstadt in den USA* IV U1, 12
North America [ˌnɔːθ‿ə'merɪkə] Nordamerika IV ZI, 8
North Carolina (NC) [ˌnɔːθ kær'laɪnə] *Bundestaat in den USA* IV U5, 101
North Dakota (ND) [ˌnɔːθ də'kəʊtə] *Bundesstaat in den USA* IV ZI, 10
Northern Ireland [ˌnɔːðn‿'aɪələnd] Nordirland III
Norway ['nɔːweɪ] Norwegen III
Oklahoma (OK) [ˌəʊklə'həʊmə] *Bundesstaat in den USA* <IV U2, 139>
Panama [ˌpænə'mɑː] *Ortsname* IV U4, 85
Park Ridge ['pɑːk ˌrɪdʒ] *Ortsname* <IV U2, 44>
Pennsylvania (PA) [ˌpensɪl'veɪniə] *Bundesstaat in den USA* IV ZI, 10
Philadelphia [ˌfɪlə'delfiə] *Stadt in den USA* <IV U3, 66>
The **Philippines** [ˌðə 'fɪlɪpiːnz] die Philippinen IV U1, 21
Plymouth ['plɪməθ] *Ortsname* <IV U3, 70>
Poland ['pəʊlənd] Polen II
Queens [kwiːnz] *Stadtteil von NYC* IV U1, 12
Raleigh ['rɑːli] *Ort in den USA* IV U5, 101
The **Republic of Ireland** [ðə rɪˌpʌblɪk‿əv‿'aɪələnd] Irland III
Russia ['rʌʃə] Russland IV U1, 23
Sacramento [ˌsækrə'mentəʊ] *Ortsname* IV U4, 84
San Francisco [ˌsæn frən'sɪskəʊ] *Stadt in den USA* IV U4, 74
Santa Cruz [ˌsæntə 'kruːz] *Stadt in den USA* <IV U4, 77>
Scandinavia [ˌskændɪ'neɪviə] Skandinavien IV U1, 23
Scotland ['skɒtlənd] Schottland III
Seattle [si'ætl] *Großstadt in den USA* IV ZI, 10
Siberia [saɪ'bɪəriə] Sibirien <IV U2, 138>
South Carolina (SC) [ˌsaʊθ kær'laɪnə] *Bundesstaat in den USA* IV U5, 98
South Dakota (SD) [ˌsaʊθ də'kəʊtə] *Bundesstaat in den USA* IV U2, 34
Spain [speɪn] Spanien II
Spartanburg [ˌspɑːtn'bɜːg] *Ort in den USA* <IV U5, 114>
Staten Island [ˌstætn‿'aɪlənd] *Stadtteil von NYC* IV U1, 12
Trestles ['treslz] *Strand in Kalifornien* <IV U4, 77>
Turkey ['tɜːki] Türkei II
The **United Kingdom (UK)** [ðə juːˌnaɪtɪd 'kɪŋdəm] Vereinigtes Königreich von Großbritannien und Nordirland III
USA (United States of America) [ˌjuːes'eɪ (juːˌnaɪtɪd ˌsteɪts‿əv ə'merɪkə)] USA (Vereinigte Staaten von Amerika) III
Venice Beach [ˌvenɪs 'biːtʃ] *Stadtteil von Los Angeles* <IV U1, 26>
Vietnam [ˌvjet'næm] Vietnam IV U1, 23
Virginia (VA) [və'dʒɪnjə] *Bundesstaat in den USA* IV U3, 53
Wales [weɪlz] Wales III
Washington (WA) ['wɒʃɪŋtən] *Bundesstaat in den USA* IV ZI, 10
Washington, D.C. [ˌwɒʃɪŋtən ˌdiː'siː] *Hauptstadt der USA* IV ZI, 8
West Africa [ˌwest 'æfrɪkə] Westafrika IV U5, 98
West Coast [ˌwest 'kəʊst] Westküste <IV U1, 24>

Other names

Academy Award [əˌkædəmi‿ə'wɔːd] *Filmpreis* <IV U4, 142>

American Dream [əˌmerɪkən ˈdriːm] der amerikanische Traum IV U1, 18

The **Appalachian Mountains** [ðə ˌæpəleɪʃən ˈmaʊntɪnz] Die Appalachen IV ZI, 8

the **Atlantic** [ətˈlæntɪk] Atlantischer Ozean IV U1, 13

Avatar [ˌævəˈtɑː] *Filmtitel* <IV U4, 142>

Batman [ˈbætmæn] *Filmtitel* <IV U1, 137>

Baxendale Road [ˈbæksndeɪl ˌrəʊd] *Straßenname* <IV U2, 44>

bento [ˈbentəʊ] *Kästchen für Speisen* <IV U4, 90>

Big Apple [ˌbɪg‿ˈæpl] *Spitzname für NYC* IV U1, 12

Bird Highway [ˌbɜːd ˈhaɪweɪ] *Straßenname* <IV U2, 44>

Bollywood [ˈbɒliwʊd] *indische Filmindustrie: Bombay + Hollywood* II

Broadway [ˈbrɔːdweɪ] *Straße in NYC* IV U1, 14

Brooklyn Bridge [ˌbrʊklɪn ˈbrɪdʒ] *Brücke in NYC* IV U1, 14

California Star [ˌkælɪfɔːniə‿ˈstɑː] *Name einer Zeitung* IV U4, 84

Carbine Street [ˌkɑːbaɪn ˈstriːt] *Straßenname* IV U3, 62

Census Bureau [ˈsensəs ˌbjʊərəʊ] Statistisches Bundesamt <IV U1, 26>

Central Park [ˌsentrl ˈpɑːk] *Park in NYC* IV U1, 14

Chief Ten Bears [ˌtʃiːf ˈten beəz] Häuptling Zehn Bären <IV U2, 138>

Chinatown [ˈtʃaɪnətaʊn] *chinesisches Stadtviertel* IV U4, 74

Colorado River [ˌkɒlərɑːdəʊ ˈrɪvə] *Fluss in den USA* IV ZI, 8

Christopher **Columbus** [ˌkrɪstəfə kəˈlʌmbəs] *Entdecker* <IV U2, 138>

Columbus Day [kəˌlʌmbəs ˈdeɪ] *Feiertag in den USA* <IV U3, 141>

The **Confederate Flag** [ðə kənˈfedrət ˌflæg] Konföderiertenflagge IV U5, 98

cookie [ˈkʊki] *Spitzname* <IV U4, 90>

Curtiss-Wright Flying Field [ˌkɜːtɪsraɪt ˈflaɪɪŋ fiːld] *Flughafenname* IV U5, 101

Declaration of Independence [ˌdekləreɪʃn‿əv‿ɪndɪˈpendəns] Unabhängigkeitserklärung IV ZI, 10

Denali [dəˈnɑːli] *höchster Berg in Nordamerika (neuer Name)* IV ZI, 8

Department of Homeland Security [dɪˌpɑːtmənt‿əv ˌhəʊmlænd sɪˈkjʊərəti] Heimatschutzbehörde IV U1, 23

Steve **Ditko** [ˌstiːv ˈdɪtkəʊ] *Künstler* <IV U1, 137>

Ellis Island [ˌelɪs‿ˈaɪlənd] *Insel vor NYC* IV U1, 20

Empire State Building [ˌempaɪə steɪt ˈbɪldɪŋ] *Gebäude in NYC* IV U1, 14

Empire State of Mind (Part II) Broken Down [ˌempaɪə ˌsteɪt‿əv ˈmaɪnd (pɑːt ˈtuː) ˌbrəʊkn ˈdaʊn] *Liedname* <IV U1, 19>

European Union [ˌjʊərəpiːən ˈjuːnjən] Europäische Union III

The **Everglades** [ði ˈevəgleɪdz] *Nationalpark in den USA* IV U5, 102

Executive Mansion [ˌɪgzekjətɪv ˈmænʃn] *Wohnsitz des Gouverneurs* IV U5, 101

Family History Center [ˌfæmli ˈhɪstri ˌsentə] Familiengeschichtezentrum IV U1, 22

Fifth Avenue [ˌfɪfθ‿ˈævənjuː] *Straße in NYC* <IV U1, 136>

First World War [ˈfɜːst ˌwɜːld ˌwɔː] Erster Weltkrieg <IV U2, 138>

Fort Knox [ˌfɔːt ˈnɒks] *Lager für die Goldreserven des Schatzamtes der USA* IV ZI, 10

Fruit4U [ˌfruːtfəˈjuː] *Firmenname* <IV U2, 39>

Mahatma **Gandhi** [məˌhɑːtmə ˈgændi] *Personenname* IV U5, 107

George Washington [ˌdʒɔːdʒ ˈwɒʃɪŋtən] *1. Präsident der USA (1789–1797)* <IV U3, 140>

Gold Rush [ˈgəʊld ˌrʌʃ] Goldrausch in Kalifornien IV U4, 75

The **Golden Gate Bridge** [ðə ˌgəʊldn ˌgeɪt ˈbrɪdʒ] *berühmte Brücke in San Francisco* IV U4, 74

Gone with the Wind [ˌgɒn wɪð ðə ˈwɪnd] Vom Winde verweht <IV U4, 142>

Gotham City [ˌgɒθəm ˈsɪti] *fiktiver Ort im Film Batman* <IV U1, 137>

Grand Canyon [ˌgrænd ˈkænjən] *Sehenswürdigkeit in den USA* IV U4, 76

Grand Central Station [ˌgrænd sentrl ˈsteɪʃn] *Hauptbahnhof in NYC* IV U1, 14

Grand Central Terminal [ˈgrænd ˌsentrl ˌtɜːmɪnl] *alter Name des Hauptbahnhofs in NYC* IV U1, 16

The **Great Plains** [ðə ˌgreɪt ˈpleɪnz] *Flachland in den USA* <IV U2, 138>

Gulf Coast [ˈgʌlf ˌkəʊst] Golfküste IV U5, 96

Gulf of Mexico [ˌgʌlf‿əv ˈmeksɪkəʊ] Golf von Mexiko <IV U5, 144>

The **Hobbit** [ðə ˈhɒbɪt] Der Hobbit <IV U4, 142>

Hollywood [ˈhɒliwʊd] *Zentrum der amerikanischen Filmindustrie (in Los Angeles)* II

Huarache [ˌhuːəˈrɑːtʃə] *Name einer Schuhfirma* <IV U4, 77>

Hurricane Katrina [ˌhʌrɪkən kəˈtriːnə] *Name eines Wirbelsturms* <IV U5, 108>

Independence Day [ˌɪndɪˈpendəns ˌdeɪ] amerikanischer Unabhängigkeitstag <IV U3, 141>

Indy 500 [ˌɪndi faɪvˈhʌndred] *Name eines Autorennens* IV ZI, 10

Iron Man [ˈaɪən ˌmæn] *Filmtitel* <IV U1, 137>

Jaws [dʒɔːz] Der weiße Hai <IV U4, 142>

John F. Kennedy Airport [ˌdʒɒn‿ef kenədi ˈeəpɔːt] *Flughafen in NYC* IV U1, 16

Jurassic World [dʒʊˈræsɪk ˌwɜːld] *Filmtitel* <IV U4, 142>

Martin Luther **King** [ˌmɑːtɪn ˌluːθə ˈkɪŋ] *Personenname* IV U5, 107

Stephen **King** [ˌstiːvn ˈkɪŋ] *US-amerik. Schriftsteller* IV U3, 62

Jack **Kirby** [ˌdʒæk ˈkɜːbi] *Künstler* <IV U1, 137>

Ku Klux Klan [ˌkuː klʌks ˈklæn] *ein rassistischer Geheimbund in den Südstaaten der USA* IV U5, 107

Stan **Lee** [ˌstæn ˈliː] *Schriftsteller* <IV U1, 137>

Lexington Avenue [ˈleksɪŋtn ˌævənjuː] *Straße in NYC* IV U1, 14

Abraham **Lincoln** [ˌeɪbrəhæm ˈlɪŋkən] *16. Präsident der USA (1861-1865)* <IV U3, 140>

Long Island [ˌlɒŋ‿ˈaɪlənd] *Teilort von NYC* <IV U1, 137>

Malcolm X [ˌmælkəm ˈeks] *Personenname* IV U5, 107

Mardi Gras [ˌmɑːdi ˈgrɑː] Faschingsdienstag IV U5, 98

Martin Luther King Day [ˌmɑːtɪn ˌluːθə ˌkɪŋ ˈdeɪ] *Feiertag in den USA zu Ehren Martin Luther Kings* <IV U3, 140>

Mayflower [ˈmeɪflaʊə] *Schiffsname* <IV U3, 70>

Tim **McGraw** [ˌtɪm məˈgrɔː] *Liedtitel* IV U5, 97

Memorial Day [məˌmɔːriəl ˈdeɪ] *Feiertag in den USA* <IV U3, 140>

Mesa Verde [ˌmeɪsə ˈvɜːdi] *US-Nationalpark* IV ZI, 10

Metropolitan Museum of Art [metrəˌpɒlətn mjuːˌziːəm‿əv‿ˈɑːt] *Museum in NYC* IV U1, 14

Mississippi River [ˌmɪsɪsɪpi ˈrɪvə] *Fluss in den USA* IV ZI, 8

Missouri River [mɪˌzʊəri ˈrɪvə] *Fluss in den USA* IV ZI, 8

Mt. McKinley [ˌmaʊnt məˈkɪnli] *höchster Berg in Nordamerika (alter Name)* IV ZI, 8

NASCAR (National Association for Stock Car Racing) [ˈnæzkɑː] *amerikanischer Motorsportverband* IV U5, 102

New World [ˌnjuː ˈwɜːld] *alter Name für Amerika* <IV U3, 70>

Niagara Falls [naɪˌægrə ˈfɔːlz] Niagarafälle IV U3, 52

One World Trade Center [ˌwʌn ˈwɜːld ˌtreɪd ˌsentə] *Gebäude in NYC* IV U1, 12

Oscar [ˈɒskə] *Filmpreis* <IV U4, 142>

Pacific Ocean [pəˌsɪfɪk‿ˈəʊʃn] Pazifischer Ozean IV ZI, 9

Rosa **Parks** [ˌrəʊzə ˈpɑːks] *amerikanische Bürgerrechtlerin* IV U5, 107

PNC Plaza [ˌpiːensiː ˈplɑːzə] *Name eines Wolkenkratzers* IV U5, 101

Presidents' Day [ˌprezɪdnts ˈdeɪ] *Feiertag in den USA* <IV U3, 140>

Sir Walter **Raleigh** [sɜː ˌwɒltə ˈrɔːli] *englischer Schriftsteller* IV U5, 101

Research Triangle Park [ˌrɪsɜːtʃ ˈtraɪæŋgl pɑːk] *Forschungszentrum in North Carolina* IV U5, 101

Rio Grande [ˌriːəʊˈgrænd] *Fluss in den USA* <IV U2, 138>

River Thames [ˌrɪvə ˈtemz] *Fluss in London* II

Rockefeller Center [ˈrɒkəfelə ˌsentə] *Gebäude in NYC* IV U1, 14

the **Rockies** (= the Rocky Mountains) [ðə ˈrɒkiz] *Gebirge in Nordamerika* <IV U4, 89>

Rocky Mountains [ˌrɒki ˈmaʊntɪnz] *Gebirge in Nordamerika* IV ZI, 9

Silicon Valley [ˌsɪlɪkən ˈvæli] *Ort, wo viele Computerfirmen ihren Sitz haben* IV U4, 75

Silverley [ˌsɪlvəˈli] *Firmenname* IV U5, 109

Sitting Bull [ˌsɪtɪŋ ˈbʊl] *Name des Häuptlings eines Indianerstammes* IV ZI, 10

Sydney **Smith** [ˌsɪdni ˈsmɪθ] *Personenname* IV U5, 107

Snow White and the Seven Dwarfs [ˌsneʊ waɪt‿ən ðə ˌsevn ˈdwɔːfs] Schneewittchen und die sieben Zwerge <IV U4, 142>

Space Needle [ˈspeɪs ˌniːdl] *Sehenswürdigkeit in Seattle* IV ZI, 10

Star Wars [ˈstɑː ˌwɔːz] Krieg der Sterne <IV U4, 142>

Statue of Liberty [ˌstætʃuː‿əv ˈlɪbəti] *Freiheitsstatue in NYC* IV U1, 13

Joseph **Strauss** [ˌdʒəʊzɪf ˈstraʊs] *Architekt* IV U4, 75

SummerStage Festival [ˈsʌməsteɪdʒ ˌfestɪvl] *jährliches Fest in NYC* <IV U1, 136>

Super Bowl [ˈsuːpə bəʊl] *Meisterschaftsendspiel des NFL* <IV U2, 50>

Surfin' USA [ˈsɜːfɪn ˌjuːesˈeɪ] *Liedtitel* <IV U4, 77>

Taylor **Swift** [ˌteɪlə ˈswɪft] *Personenname* IV U5, 97

Times Square [ˈtaɪm‿ˌskweə] *Platz in NYC* IV U1, 14

US Space & Rocket Center [ˌjuːes ˌspeɪs‿ən ˈrɒkɪt ˌsentə] *Raumfahrtmuseum in den USA* IV ZI, 10

Ventura County Line [venˌtʊərə ˌkaʊnti ˈlaɪn] *Name einer Bahnlinie* <IV U4, 77>

Very Large Array [ˌveri lɑːdʒ‿əˈreɪ] *Radioteleskop in den USA* IV ZI, 10

Walk of Fame [ˌwɔːk‿əv ˈfeɪm] *Straße in Hollywood mit Sternen für bekannte Leute* IV U4, 75

Wall Street [ˈwɔːl ˌstriːt] *Straße in NYC* IV U1, 14

The **White House** [ðə ˈwaɪt ˌhaʊs] das Weiße Haus IV U3, 53

The **Wizard of Oz** [ðə ˌwɪzəd‿əv ˈɒz] Der Zauberer von Oz <IV U4, 142>

World Trade Center [ˌwɜːld ˈtreɪd ˌsentə] *Gebäude in NYC bis 2001* IV U1, 12

World Wide Web [ˌwɜːld waɪd ˈweb] *ein über das Internet abrufbares System* IV U4, 80

Yosemite [jəʊˈsemɪti] *Nationalpark in den USA* IV U4, 76

Malala **Yousafzai** [ˌməlælæ ˈjuːsæfzaɪ] *Personenname* IV U5, 107

A

abarbeiten to work off IV U1, 22
abbiegen to turn III
abdecken to cover IV U3, 58
Abend evening I
an jenem Abend that night II
heute Abend tonight II
Abendessen dinner II
(frühes) Abendessen tea I
abends in the evenings III
Abenteuer adventure I
Abenteurer adventurer IV U5, 101
Abenteurerin adventurer IV U5, 101
aber but I
abfahren to leave II
Abfall rubbish II; trash (AE) IV U3, 62
abheben to take off IV U1, 18
abholen to pick up IV U2, 43
Abholung pick-up IV U5, 102
Abkömmling descendant IV U1, 22
ablehnen to reject IV U5, 99; to refuse IV U5, 107
abonnieren to subscribe IV U4, 81
abräumen to clear IV U2, 33
den Tisch abräumen to clear the table II
abschaffen to abolish IV U5, 107
abschicken *(einen Brief)* to post III
Abschieds- leaving II
Abschiedsrede farewell speech II
abschließen to lock I
sich abseilen to abseil II
absichtlich on purpose II
absolut absolutely IV U3, 59
abspülen to do the washing up II
abstauben to dust IV U2, 38
abstimmen über to vote for IV U2, 33
Abteilung department II
acht eight I
Achterbahn roller coaster II
achtzehn eighteen I
achtzig eighty I
Ackerbau farming IV U4, 84
Ackerboden farmland IV U2, 32
Ackerland farmland IV U2, 32
Action action IV U5, 107
Adapter adaptor III
addieren to add IV U5, 101
Adjektiv adjective III
Adresse address II
Affe monkey I
Afrikaner African IV U5, 97
Afrikanerin African IV U5, 97
afrikanisch African IV U5, 97
Afroamerikaner African American IV U5, 96
Afroamerikanerin African American IV U5, 96
afroamerikanisch African-American IV U5, 101
Ahnung idea I
keine Ahnung haben to have no idea IV U1, 14
Aktenkoffer briefcase III
Aktentasche briefcase III
Aktivität activity I
nicht mehr aktuell out of fashion IV U4, 81
akzeptieren to accept IV U5, 99
albern silly II
Alkohol alcohol *(no pl)* IV U3, 58
alle all I; everyone II; everybody IV U2, 43
Allee avenue IV U1, 14
allein alone I; by yourself II
ganz allein all alone I
allerdings certainly IV U1, 18
allererste very first III
Allergie allergy II
allergisch gegen allergic to II
alles everything II
alles in allem all in all IV U3, 61
alles klar all right II
allgemein in general IV U3, 73
Alligator alligator IV ZI, 9
Alphabet alphabet I
als than II; when II; as III
also so I; right II
alt old I; ancient IV U4, 76
Alter age I
älter elderly IV U3, 54
altertümlich ancient IV U4, 76
Altglascontainer bottle bank II
altmodisch old-fashioned IV U4, 74; out of fashion IV U4, 81
Aluminium aluminium III
am Dienstag on Tuesday I
am Schluss by the end II
am Wochenende at the weekend I
Amerikaner American IV ZI, 9
Amerikanerin American IV ZI, 9
Amerikanisch American IV ZI, 9
amerikanisch American IV ZI, 9
amisch Amish IV U3, 58
die Amischen the Amish IV U3, 53
Ampel lights IV U1, 14
sich amüsieren to enjoy oneself III
amüsiert amused IV U3, 63
an on; at I; by IV U3, 63
an Bord on board III
an der Spitze (von) at the front of II
Ananas pineapple III
anbauen to grow IV U3, 58
anbieten to offer IV U2, 38
andauern to last IV U4, 79; to continue IV U4, 86
Andenken souvenir III
andere other I; others II
ein anderer another II
die anderen the others I
anderer Meinung sein to disagree II
andererseits then again III; on the other (hand) IV U5, 107
seine Meinung ändern to change one's mind III
(sich) ändern to change III
anders different I
anders als unlike III
andocken to dock IV U1, 22
anerkennen to appreciate IV U5, 99
Anfang start; beginning III
anfangen to start II
Anfrage request IV U4, 81
anführen to lead IV U3, 58
Anführer leader III
Anführerin leader III
Angeln fishing IV U5, 104
angenehm comfortable III
angezogen dressed III
angreifen to attack IV U2, 42
Angriff attack IV U1, 12

Angst haben to be scared; to be afraid II
ängstlich afraid II
Anhänger follower IV U4, 81
Anhängerin follower IV U4, 81
anheuern to hire IV U4, 85
anhören to listen (to) I
ankommen to arrive II
Ankömmling arrival IV U1, 22
Ankündigung announcement II
anlegen to put on III
Anleitung tutorial IV U4, 80
anmalen to paint IV U4, 75
Anmeldeformular entry form II
Anmeldung registration II
annähernd nearly IV U3, 64
annehmen to guess IV U3, 59; to accept IV U5, 99
Annonce ad(vert) (= advertisement) IV U2, 38
Anordnung layout IV U4, 77
sich **anpassen** to adapt (to) IV U1, 19
anprobieren to try on II
Anruf call III
anrufen to call I; to phone II
Anrufer caller II
Anruferin caller II
anschauen to watch; to look at I; to have a look II; to check out IV U1, 14
sich **anschließen** to join III
Ansehen reputation IV U5, 107
ansehen to watch I
Anspitzer pencil sharpener I
morgendliche **Ansprache** morning message IV U2, 34
ansprechend appealing IV U4, 77
anstoßen to hit III
Antenne antenna III
Antwort answer II
antworten to answer I
Anzahl number IV U4, 75
Anzeige ad(vert); advertisement II
anziehen to put on III; to attract IV U5, 98
sich anziehen to get dressed II
April April I
Arbeit work I; job II
arbeiten to work I
Arbeiter worker II
Arbeiterin worker II
Arbeitsheft workbook I
Arbeitskollege co-worker IV U2, 38
Arbeitskollegin co-worker IV U2, 38
arbeitslos unemployed IV U1, 18
arbeitsreich busy I
Arbeitszeit working hours *(pl)* IV U2, 38
Architekt architect IV U4, 75
Architektin architect IV U4, 75
Archiv archive II
Areal area III
Ärger trouble III
Arm arm I
arm poor IV U1, 18
Armee army III
armselig miserable III
Armut poverty IV U1, 23
Art sort II; type; kind III
Art und Weise way III
Arzt doctor II
Ärztin doctor II
ärztlich medical IV U1, 22
Astronomie astronomy IV U2, 34
atmen to breathe III
Attacke attack IV U1, 12
auch too; also I
auch nicht not … either III
auf on; at I
auf dem Weg on the way I
auf der linken Seite on the left I
auf der rechten Seite on the right I
auf einmal suddenly II
Auf Wiedersehen! Goodbye. I
auf … zu towards IV U3, 62
auf dem Land in the country I
auf der Welt in the world II
Auf keinen Fall! No way! III
Aufbau structure III
aufbewahren to keep IV U2, 34
aufbleiben to stay up IV U2, 36
aufbrechen to set off IV U4, 84
auffallen to stand out IV U1, 12
auffallend striking III
aufführen to perform III
Aufführung show IV U5, 102
Aufgabe job II
aufgeben to give up III
aufgeben *(einen Brief)* to post III
aufgebracht upset I
aufgeregt excited; nervous II
aufgerissen torn IV U4, 83
aufheben to pick up II; to save IV U3, 54
jmdn. **aufheitern** to cheer sb up III
aufhören to stop I; to finish II; to end IV U2, 34
Aufkleber sticker II
aufkrempeln to roll up IV U3, 62
Auflage edition IV U4, 84
aufmachen to open I
sich aufmachen to set off IV U4, 84
jmdn. **aufmuntern** to cheer sb up III
aufpassen to look after II
aufpassen auf to watch II
aufräumen to tidy (up) II
aufregend exciting I
Aufregung excitement IV U4, 75
aufrichtig straightforward III
aufrollen to roll up IV U3, 62
aufschauen to look up II
aufstehen to get up I; to stand up IV U3, 64
aufstellen to put up IV U3, 64
auftauchen to appear III; to show up IV U2, 42
auftreten to perform III
aufwachen to wake up II
aufwachsen to grow up III
Aufzug elevator *(AE)* IV U1, 13
Auge eye II
Augenblick moment II
August August I
im August in August I
aus from I
aus dem Weg gehen to avoid IV U3, 62
aus … heraus out of II
Ausbildung education IV U2, 38
Ausblick view IV U1, 14
auschecken to check out III
auseinander apart IV U3, 52
Auseinandersetzung argument II
ausfallen to fail IV U1, 19

Ausflug trip I
Ausgabe edition IV U4, 84
ausgeben *(Geld)* to spend II
ein ausgefüllter Tag a busy day I
ausgehen to go out III
ausgehen *(Ware)* to run out of III
im Ausland abroad IV U4, 86
ins Ausland abroad IV U4, 86
ausländisch foreign IV U1, 19
auslaufen to spill IV U3, 63
ausleihen to borrow II
auslösen to set off IV U4, 84
ausprobieren to try out III; to check out IV U1, 14
ausräumen to clear IV U2, 33
ausruhen to rest IV U4, 85
Ausrüstung equipment III
Aussage statement IV U1, 22
Ausschnitt clip IV U4, 80
aussehen to look II
Außenwelt outside IV U3, 58
außer except III
außergewöhnlich unusual IV U4, 77
außerhalb outside IV U2, 38
außerhalb des Lehrplans extracurricular IV U2, 34
Außerirdische alien I
Außerirdischer alien I
äußerst extremely IV U4, 80
außerunterrichtlich *(Zusatzunterricht)* extracurricular IV U2, 34
Aussicht view IV U1, 14
Aussichtspunkt lookout point II
ausstehen to stand IV U5, 99
aussteigen to get off II
Ausstellung exhibition III
Austausch exchange IV U2, 34
Ausverkauf sale II
Auswahl choice IV U5, 102
auswählen to choose II
auswandern to emigrate IV U1, 19
ausweichen to avoid IV U3, 62
Ausweis ID III; pass IV U2, 34
Auswirkung impact IV U4, 80
ausziehen to take off III
Auto car I
Autogramm autograph IV U3, 53
Autogramme geben to sign autographs IV U3, 53
Automat machine II
Autor writer III
Autorin writer III

B

Baby baby II
Babysitter babysitter IV U2, 41
Babysitterin babysitter IV U2, 41
einen Kuchen backen to make a cake I
Bäcker baker III
Bäckerei baker's III
Bäckerin baker III
Backofen oven II
Bad bathroom I
Badezimmer bathroom I; bathroom *(AE)* IV U2, 34
Bahnhof station I
bald soon II
Ball ball II; dance IV U2, 33
Banane banana I
Band band II
Bank bench III
Bär bear I
Bargeld cash II
Baseball baseball IV U1, 13
Basketball basketball II
Bauarbeiter builder II
Bauarbeiterin builder II
Bauch stomach II
Bauchschmerzen stomach ache II
Bauchweh stomach ache II
bauen to build II
Bauer farmer I
Bäuerin farmer I
Bauernhof farm I
Baum tree I
Baumwolle cotton III
Baustelle construction site IV U1, 15
beängstigend scary I
beantworten to answer I
bedauern to feel sorry for III; to regret IV U3, 58
bedecken to cover IV U3, 58
bedeuten to mean III
bedeutend major IV ZI, 8; powerful IV U1, 22
sich bedienen to help oneself III
Bedienung waitress IV U4, 89
Bedingung condition IV U1, 22
sich beeilen to hurry II; to rush III
beeindrucken to impress III
beeindruckend powerful IV U1, 22
beeinflussen to influence IV U4, 80
beenden to finish II; to end IV U2, 34
sich befassen (mit) to deal (with) IV U3, 73
sich befinden to be located IV U1, 13
befördern to carry II
befragen to interview I
Befrager interviewer IV U1, 18
Befragerin interviewer IV U1, 18
Befragung interview II
befreunden *(jmdn. zu seiner Freundesliste hinzufügen)* to friend IV U4, 81
begabt talented III
begeistert excited II
Beginn beginning III
beginnen to start II; to begin IV U1, 18
begnadigen to pardon IV U3, 53
Begnadigung pardon IV U3, 67
begrüßen to welcome IV U4, 80
behalten to keep IV U2, 34
Behauptung statement IV U1, 22
mit Behinderung with special needs III
behutsam cautious III
bei at I
bei Bewusstsein awake III
beibringen to teach III
beide both III
Bein leg II
beinahe almost III; nearly IV U3, 64
beinhalten to include IV U5, 102
Beispiel example IV U1, 18
zum Beispiel for example IV U2, 34
bekannt familiar IV U2, 34
sich beklagen to complain III
Bekleidungsvorschriften dress code IV U2, 36
bekommen to get I
bekräftigen to confirm IV U4, 84

belästigen to bother IV U5, 107
Belegschaft staff *(no pl)* IV U2, 38
beliebt popular III
bellen to bark III
bemerken to notice III
bemerkenswert striking III
sich **benehmen** to behave IV U2, 38
benennen to name IV ZI, 9
benutzen to use II
beobachten to watch II
bequem comfortable III
Bereich area IV U1, 22
bereit ready I
bereits already II
bereitwillig willing IV U2, 39
Berg mountain III; hill IV U4, 74
  in den Bergen in the mountains III
Bergarbeiter miner III
Bergarbeiterin miner III
bergen to save III
Bergwerk mine III
Bericht report IV U4, 84
berichten (über) to report (on) IV U2, 33
Beruf job II; career IV U1, 18
Berufsbezeichnung job title IV U2, 38
berühmt famous I
  berühmte Person celebrity IV U5, 97
berühren to touch III
Besatzung crew III
beschäftigt busy I
beschreiben to describe IV U3, 73
Beschwerde complaint III
sich **beschweren** to complain III
Besichtigungstour sightseeing IV U1, 15
  eine Besichtigungstour machen to go sightseeing II
besiedeln to settle IV U4, 75
besiedelt populated IV U4, 74
besitzen to own; to have got II
Besitzer owner IV U5, 101
Besitzerin owner IV U5, 101
besonders special I; especially IV U1, 13
besorgt worried II
Besorgungen machen to do the shopping II
besser better I
bestätigen to confirm IV U4, 84
bestbezahlt best-paid IV U1, 13; best-paying IV U2, 39
beste best II
  die besten the best II
besteigen to climb III
bestellen to order II
bestimmte certain IV U1, 22
bestürzt upset I
Besuch visit III
besuchen to visit II
Besucher visitor II
Besucherin visitor II
Beton concrete III
betreiben to run III
betreten to enter IV U3, 54
betrunken drunk IV U3, 62
Bett bed I
  ins Bett gehen to go to bed I
Bettdecke blanket IV U3, 62
beunruhigt worried II
bevölkert populated IV U4, 74
Bevölkerung population *(no pl)* III
bevor before II
bevorstehen to come up III
(sich) **bewegen** to move III
beweglich mobile IV U4, 80
Bewegung move III; movement IV U1, 13
beweisen to prove IV U4, 84
sich **bewerben** (für/um) to apply (for) IV U2, 38
bewerten to rate III
Bewohner inhabitant III
Bewohnerin inhabitant III
bei **Bewusstsein** awake III
Bezahlautomat payment machine II
bezahlen to pay II
Bezahlung pay IV U2, 38
Bezirk borough IV U1, 12
bezweifeln to doubt IV U3, 59
Bibliothek library III
Bier beer IV U3, 62
bieten to offer IV U2, 38
Bild picture II
bilden to make I
Bildung education IV U2, 38
billig cheap II
binden to tie IV U3, 62
Biologie Biology I
bis to II; until I
  bis jetzt so far IV U1, 18
  bis zu before II
  Bis bald! See you soon! I
  Bis bald. See you later.; See you. I
  bis (spätestens) by III
ein **bisschen** a little; a bit II
bitte please I
  Bitte schön. Here you are. I
bitten um to ask for II
Blatt leaf IV U3, 52
blau blue I
bleiben to stay II
  etw. bleiben lassen to give sth a miss III
  hängen bleiben to be stuck IV U2, 34
  in Verbindung bleiben to keep in touch II
Bleistift pencil I
Blick view IV U1, 14
Block block IV U1, 14
Blog blog II
Blogger blogger IV U4, 81
Bloggerin blogger IV U4, 81
Blume flower III
Bluse blouse I
bluten to bleed III
Blütezeit boom years IV U4, 86
Boden ground; bottom III; earth IV U4, 76
Bonbon sweet I
Bonus bonus IV U2, 39
Boomtown *(eine Stadt, die sehr schnell wächst)* boomtown IV U4, 86
Boot boat II
Bootsfahrt boat trip II
an **Bord** on board III
böse angry II; naughty III; evil IV U3, 63
Boss boss II
Botschaft message II
Boulevard avenue IV U1, 14
Bowlen bowling IV U3, 58
Box box I

Branche business IV U5, 97
braten to fry IV U5, 98
Bratwurst sausage II
Brauch custom IV U5, 97
brauchen to need I
nicht **brauchen** needn't I
braun brown I
brechen to break II
breit wide IV U5, 96
brennen to be on fire II; to burn III
Brett plank II
Brief letter III
Briefmarke stamp III
Brieftasche wallet III
bringen to bring II
britisch British II
Broschüre brochure III; booklet IV U5, 102
Brot bread II
belegtes **Brot** sandwich I
Brotlaib loaf III
Brücke bridge II
Bruder brother I
Buch book I
buchen to book IV U4, 76
Bücherei library III
Büchse tin IV U3, 63
Buchstabe letter III
buchstabieren to spell I
Bucht bay IV U4, 75
Büfett buffet III
bügeln to iron IV U3, 58
Bühne stage II
bummeln to stroll IV U4, 76
Bundesstaat state IV ZI, 8
bunt colourful II
Buntstift pencil I
Burg castle II
Bürgerkrieg Civil War IV U3, 140
Bürgerrechte civil rights *(pl)* IV U5, 96
Bürgersteig sidewalk *(AE)* IV U1, 15
Büro office II
Bus bus I
im **Bus** on the bus II
Bushaltestelle bus stop II
Butter butter I

C

Café café I
Cafeteria cafeteria I
Camp camp II
campen gehen to go camping II
Camping camping III
Campingplatz campsite III
Campus campus IV U2, 35
Cent *(Währung)* cent III
Center centre III; center *(AE)* IV U1, 13
Chance chance II; opportunity IV U1, 18
chatten to chat II
Cheerleader *(Mädchen, das in einer Gruppe eine Sportmannschaft anfeuert)* cheerleader IV U2, 34
Cheerleading *(Aktivitäten der Cheerleader)* cheerleading IV U2, 34
Chef boss II
Chefin boss II
Chefkoch head chef II
Chili chilli II
chillen to chill out IV U4, 76
Chinese Chinese IV U5, 99
Chinesin Chinese IV U5, 99
Chinesisch Chinese IV U5, 99
chinesisch Chinese IV U5, 99
christlich Christian IV U3, 53
nach **Christus** AD (= Anno Domini) III
circa about II
Clip clip IV U4, 80
Cola coke I
College college *(AE)* IV U5, 101
Comic(heft) comic II
Computer computer I
Computerspiele- gaming IV U4, 80
Cornflakes cereal III
Courage courage IV U5, 107
Cousin cousin II
Cousine cousin II
Crew crew III
Curry curry II
Cyber-Mobbing cyberbullying IV U4, 80

D

da there I
da drüben over there II
da unten down there IV U5, 98
da ist there is I
da sind there are I
da because I
Dach roof II
Dachboden attic I
dahin down there IV U5, 98
damals then III; back then IV U1, 14
Dame lady II
damit so that IV U2, 34
Dampfbad Turkish bath III
Dampfer steamship IV U1, 22
Dampfmaschine steam engine III
Dampfschiff steamship IV U1, 22
danach then; after that I; after III
Herzlichen **Dank**. Thanks so much. IV U4, 94
Vielen **Dank**. Thanks so much. IV U4, 94
dankbar thankful IV U3, 54
danke thanks I
Danke. Thank you. I
dann then I
das the I; this; that I; which III
dass that III
Datei file II
Datum date I
Dauer length IV U4, 75
dauern to take III; to last IV U4, 79
davor before that III; in front of II
Debatte debate IV U5, 98
Decke blanket IV U3, 62
decken to lay II
dehnen to stretch IV U3, 52
dein your I
deine yours I; your I
dem who; which III
Demonstration protest IV U5, 96
den who; which III
denken to think I
Denkmal monument II
dennoch still III
deprimiert down III
der the I; who II; which III

deren whose III
derselbe the same II
Desaster disaster III
deshalb so I
Design design IV U4, 77
dessen whose III
deswegen that's why III
Detail detail IV U5, 102
Detektivgeschichte mystery story IV U3, 53
Detektor detector III
deutlich clear IV U4, 77
Deutsch German I
deutsch German III
Dezember December I
dich you I
dich selbst yourself II
dicht dense IV U4, 74
die *(auch Pl.)* the I; who II; which III
Diele hall IV U2, 34
Dienst service III
Dienstag Tuesday I
am Dienstag on Tuesday I
dies this I
diese (hier) these II
Ding thing I
vor allen Dingen above all IV U1, 18
dir you I
Diskriminierung discrimination IV U5, 96
Diskussion debate IV U5, 98
Distanz distance IV ZI, 9
Dollar *(amer. Währungseinheit)* dollar IV ZI, 8
Donnerstag Thursday I
doof silly III
doppelt twice IV U2, 38
Dorf village III
dort there I
dort drüben over there II
dort ist there is I
Dose can I; tin IV U3, 63
Dr. *(Anrede)* Dr III
Draht wire III
Drama drama III
drängeln to push III
Draufgänger daredevil IV U3, 53
Draufgängerin daredevil IV U3, 53
draußen outside II
draußen halten to keep out III
dreckig dirty I
Drehort location III
Drehung turn IV U5, 102
drei three I
dreißig thirty I
dreizehn thirteen I
dringend badly IV U2, 38; desperately IV U4, 85
drinnen in II; inside IV U1, 25
dritte third I
da **drüben** over there III
drücken to push I; to squeeze IV U3, 63
Dschungel jungle IV U4, 85
du you I
Dudelsack bagpipes *(pl)* III
dulden to tolerate IV U5, 98
dumm silly III
dunkel dark I
Dunkelheit the dark III
durch through II
quer durch across IV U3, 54
Durcheinander mess I
durchgehen to pass IV U4, 85
Durchsage announcement II
durchschnittlich average IV U3, 58
durchstarten to take off IV U1, 18
durchsuchen to search IV U1, 22
dürfen may II; to be able to; to be allowed to IV U2, 34
nicht dürfen mustn't III
nicht/nie dürfen must not/never III
Darf es sonst noch etwas sein? Anything else? I
durstig thirsty II
Dusche shower III
Duschgel shower gel III

E

echt real II; really II
Echt?! No way! III
Ecke corner III
Edition edition IV U4, 84
Es ist **egal**. It doesn't matter. II
egal wo(hin) wherever III
Ehefrau wife III
ehemalige former IV U2, 33
Ehemaligentreffen Homecoming *(AE)* IV U2, 33
Ehemann husband IV U3, 54
Ehre honor *(AE)* IV U1, 25
ehrenamtliche Helferin volunteer III
ehrenamtlicher Helfer volunteer III
ehrgeizig ambitious IV U1, 18
ehrlich honest III; honestly IV U3, 63
Ei egg I
eifersüchtig jealous II
eigene own II
Eigenschaftswort adjective III
eigensinnig stubborn IV U2, 39
eigentlich actually; in fact III; anyway IV U1, 14; basically IV U4, 80
Eigentümer landlord II
eilen to rush III
Eimer Wasser bucket of water I
ein a; an I
ein bisschen a bit II
ein paar a few III
ein wenig a bit II
einander each other III
Einbrecher burglar I
Einbrecherin burglar I
einchecken to check in III
eindeutig clear IV U4, 77
eindringen (in) to invade III
einerseits on the one hand IV U5, 115
einfach easy I; plain II; simple III; just IV U2, 38
einfach nur simply IV U4, 84
einfache Fahrkarte single ticket III
Einfluss impact IV U4, 80; influence IV U5, 98
einflussreich important II
einfügen to paste II
einführen to introduce IV U5, 98
Einführung introduction III
eingängig catchy IV U4, 77
Eingangstor gateway IV U1, 12
eingeboren native IV U4, 86
einheimisch native IV U4, 86
einholen to catch up with IV U3, 62
einhundert a/one hundred I

einige some I; a few III; several IV U4, 80; a number of IV U5, 98
sich **einigen** to compromise IV U5, 98
Einkäufe machen to do the shopping II
Einkaufen shopping I
einkaufen gehen to go shopping II
Einkaufszentrum shopping centre I; shopping mall IV U1, 15
Einkaufszettel shopping list I
einladen to invite I
Einladung invitation I
einleiten to introduce IV U5, 98
Einleitung introduction III
einmal once IV U1, 25
noch einmal once more II
einmarschieren (in) to invade III
einpacken to pack; to pack up II
einprägsam catchy IV U4, 77
eins one I
einsam lonely III
einschalten to turn on IV U3, 64
einschlafen to fall asleep III
einsetzen to put in I
einst once IV U1, 25
einsteigen to get on III
einstellen to hire IV U4, 85
Einstellung attitude IV U4, 89
einstufen to rate III
Eintrag entry IV U4, 86
eintreten to enter IV U3, 54
Eintrittskarte ticket III
nicht **einverstanden** sein to disagree II
Einwanderer immigrant IV U1, 13
Einwandererin immigrant IV U1, 13
einwandern to immigrate IV U1, 18
Einwohner inhabitant; population *(no pl)* III
Einwohnerin inhabitant III
Einwohnerzahl population *(no pl)* III
Einzelheit detail IV U5, 102
einzige only III
Eis ice cream I; ice IV U4, 85
Eisberg iceberg III
Eiscreme ice cream I
Eisenbahn railway IV U4, 86
eiskalt freezing IV U3, 54; ice-cold IV U4, 85
Elefant elephant I
elegant chic I
elektrisch electric IV U3, 59
Elektrizität electricity III
elend miserable III
elf eleven I
Eltern parents *(pl)* II
E-Mail e-mail I
emigrieren to emigrate IV U1, 19
Empfang signal III
Ende end II; ending III
am Ende at the back IV U5, 106
ganz am Ende at the bottom IV U3, 62
oberes Ende top III
enden to finish II; to end IV U2, 34
endlich at last II; finally IV U4, 85
Energie power III
eng tight II
die **Engländer** the English III
Englisch English I
englisch English I
Entdeckung discovery IV U4, 84
entfernen to remove IV U5, 98
entfernt away II; apart IV U3, 52
Entfernung distance IV ZI, 9
entfliehen to escape IV U1, 23
entfreunden *(jmdn. von seiner Freundesliste streichen)* to unfriend IV U4, 81
entgegentreten to confront IV U5, 98
enthalten to include IV U5, 102
enthalten sein to be included III
entkommen to escape IV U1, 23
entlang along I; down III
(sich) **entscheiden** to decide III
Entscheidung decision IV U1, 18
entschuldigen to pardon IV U3, 53
sich entschuldigen to say sorry II
Entschuldigung pardon IV U3, 67
Entschuldigung! Excuse me! I
Entschuldigung. Sorry.; I'm sorry. I
sich **entspannen** to chill out IV U4, 76
entspannend relaxing III
entspannt relaxed IV U4, 74
entspringen to spring up IV U4, 86
entstehen to spring up IV U4, 86; to originate IV U5, 97
(sich) **entwickeln** to develop IV U1, 18
Entwicklung trend IV U4, 80
Enzyklopädie encyclopedia IV U4, 86
er he I
erbrechen to puke IV U3, 62
Erdbeere strawberry II
Erdboden ground III; earth IV U4, 76
Erde earth IV U4, 76
die Erde earth IV U4, 76
Erdkunde Geography I
Erdnussbutter peanut butter III
Ereignis event IV U1, 13
erfahren to learn IV U3, 62; to experience IV U5, 98
etwas erfahren über to learn about sth III
Erfahrung experience IV U4, 79
erfinden to invent III
Erfinder inventor III
Erfinderin inventor III
Erfindung invention III
Erfolg success III
Erfolg haben (mit/bei) to succeed (in) IV U1, 19
erfolgreich successful III
erforschen to explore II
erfüllt sein von … to be alive with … IV U5, 97
in **Erfüllung** gehen to come true IV U1, 18
Ergebnis result II
ergreifen to grab III
erhängen to hang IV U4, 85
erholsam relaxing III
sich **erinnern** (an) to remember II
erklären to explain III
Erklärung statement IV U1, 22
erkunden to explore II
sich **erkundigen** nach to ask about II
erlauben to allow IV U4, 84
erleben to experience IV U5, 98
Erlebnis experience IV U4, 79
Ermordung killing IV U5, 98
ernst serious III
Im Ernst? Are you serious? III

etw. ernst nehmen to take sth seriously IV U1, 18
Erntedankfest Thanksgiving IV U3, 53
erraten to guess II
erreichen to reach IV U3, 63
errichten to put up IV U3, 64
erscheinen to appear III; to show up IV U2, 42
erschöpft exhausted III
erschrecken to scare II; to jump III
erschreckend terrifying IV U2, 32
erschrocken sein to be scared II
ersetzen to replace IV U1, 12
erstaunlich amazing II
erste first I
erste Stunde *(in der Schule)* homeroom IV U2, 45
erstellen to make I
als **Erstes** first I
erstrecken to stretch IV U3, 52
ertragen to stand IV U5, 99
Erwachsene adult III
Erwachsener adult III
erwarten to expect III
erzählen to tell I
Erzähler narrator I
Erzählerin narrator I
Erziehung education IV U2, 38
es it I
es gibt there are; there is I
Es tut mir leid wegen … Sorry about … I
Es tut mir leid. I'm sorry. I
Essen food I; meal II; dinner IV U3, 53
Essen zum Mitnehmen takeaway II
essen to eat I; to have II
Essensstand food stall II
Esszimmer dining room I
Etage story *(AE)* IV U1, 14
etwa about II
etwas something I; some II
euch you I
euer your I
eure yours I; your I
Eure *(als Briefabschluss)* Yours, I
Euro *(Währung)* euro III
Europäisch European IV U2, 32
europäisch European IV U2, 32
ewig forever II
exakt exact III
Exemplar copy IV U5, 97
existieren to be around IV U4, 80
Experte expert IV U4, 77
Expertin expert IV U4, 77
explodieren to explode III
Explosion explosion III
exzellent excellent IV U5, 102

F

Fabel fable III
Fabrik factory III
(zu etw.) **fähig** sein to be able to (do sth) IV U2, 34
Fahne flag II
fahren to go I; to ride II; to travel III; to drive IV U2, 33; to take a ride IV U4, 74
gegen etw. fahren to hit III
Ski fahren to ski II
Fahrer driver III
Fahrerin driver III
einfache **Fahrkarte** single ticket III
Fahrplan timetable III; schedule *(AE)* IV U2, 33
Fahrpreis fare III
Fahrrad bike I
Fahrschein ticket III
Fahrspur lane IV U4, 75
Fahrt trip; voyage; journey III; ride IV U1, 14; tour IV U4, 76
eine Fahrt machen to take a trip III
Fakt fact II
Fall case IV U5, 98
fallen to fall I; to fall (over); to fall off III
falls if II
falsch wrong I
Faltblatt flyer II
falten to fold IV U2, 38
Familie family I
Fan fan I
fangen to catch II
Fantasie fantasy II
fantastisch fantastic II
Fantasy fantasy II
Farbe colour I; color *(AE)* IV ZI, 8
Fasching carnival IV U5, 98
Fass barrel IV U3, 53
fast almost III; nearly IV U3, 64
Fastfood fast food I
faszinierend fascinating IV U4, 77
faul lazy IV U2, 39
Februar February I
Federmäppchen pencil case I
fegen to sweep II
fehlschlagen to fail IV U1, 19
Feier party I; celebration IV U3, 52
feiern to celebrate I
Feiertag holiday III
Feind enemy III
Feindin enemy III
Feld field IV ZI, 9
Fels rock III
Fenster window I
Ferien holiday I; vacation *(AE)* IV U5, 104
in der **Ferne** in the distance IV U1, 14
Fernsehen TV I
im Fernsehen on TV IV U1, 13
fernsehen to watch TV I
Fernseher TV I
Fernsehsendung TV show II
Fernsehstudio TV studio II
fertig ready I
sich fertig machen to get ready IV U3, 54
fertigstellen to finish II; to complete IV U5, 101
fesseln to tie IV U3, 62
Fest festival III
fest tight II; solid III
festhalten to hold III
Festival festival III
festnehmen to arrest IV U5, 107
festsitzen to be stuck IV U2, 34
feststecken to be stuck IV U2, 34
fette Jahre *(ugs.)* boom years IV U4, 86
Feuer fire I
Feuerwehrauto fire engine II
Fieber fever IV U4, 84
Film film; movie I
Filzstift felt-tip I

Finanz- financial IV U1, 14
finanziell financial IV U1, 14
finden to find I
Finger finger III
Fingerabdruck fingerprint II
Firma company II
Fisch fish I
Fischen fishing IV U5, 104
fit fit III
Fitnessraum gymnasium III
flach flat IV U2, 32
Fläche area IV ZI, 9; space IV U1, 22
Flagge flag II
Flamingo flamingo I
Flamme flame III
Flasche bottle I
Fledermaus bat I
Fleisch meat I
fleißig hard-working IV U2, 39
fliegen to fly II
fliehen to escape IV U1, 23
fließend fluent III
Flohmarkt jumble sale II
flüchten to escape IV U1, 23
Flug flight II
Flughafen airport II
Flugzeug plane II
Flur hall IV U2, 34; corridor II
Fluss river I
flüssig fluent III
Flyer flyer II
folgen to follow IV U5, 98
Follower follower IV U4, 81
Followerin follower IV U4, 81
Fön hairdryer III
in **Form** fit III
fortfahren to go ahead IV U1, 18
fortsetzen to continue IV U4, 86
Foto photo I
  ein Foto machen to take a photo I
  Fotos machen to take photos II
fotografieren to take photos II
Frage question I
fragen to ask I
  fragen nach to ask about II
  nach dem Weg fragen asking the way I
die **Franzosen** the French IV U5, 98
Französisch French I
Frau woman I; lady II
Frau *(Anrede)* Mrs; Ms I
frech cheeky; naughty III
frei free IV U1, 22
  ein freier Tag a day off III
  freie Wildbahn the wild IV U5, 102
  die freie Natur the outdoors IV U5, 96
  Land der Freien land of the free IV U3, 53
freigeben to release IV U5, 97
Freiheit freedom *(no pl)* IV U1, 23
Freiland- free range II
Freiluft- outdoor III
freisetzen to release IV U5, 97
Freistunde study hall period IV U2, 34
Freitag Friday I
Freiwillige volunteer III
Freiwilliger volunteer III
Freizeit free time I
Freizeitpark theme park I
fremd strange IV U1, 18; foreign IV U1, 19
Freude fun I
Freund friend I
  Freunde treffen to see friends I
Freund *(in einer Paarbeziehung)* boyfriend IV U2, 42
Freundin friend I
Freundin *(in einer Paarbeziehung)* girlfriend IV U2, 38
freundlich kind II; friendly III
Freundschaften schließen to make friends I
Frieden peace III
friedlich peaceful IV U5, 96
frieren to freeze; to get cold III
Frisbee frisbee I
Frisbeescheibe frisbee I
frisch fresh II
Friseur hairdresser II
Friseurin hairdresser II
frittieren to fry IV U5, 98
froh glad IV U3, 54
Frucht fruit I
früh early I
  früher earlier I
  früher in the old days III
  (wohnte) früher used to (live) III
frühere former IV U2, 33
Frühlingsrolle spring roll II
Frühstück breakfast I
frühstücken to have breakfast I
Frühstückspension bed and breakfast (B & B) III
(sich) **fühlen** to feel II
  sich schlecht fühlen to feel sick IV U5, 103
  sich wie zu Hause fühlen to make oneself at home III
führen to run III; to lead IV U3, 58
Führer guide II; leader III
Führerin guide II; leader III
Führerschein driver's license *(AE)* IV U2, 38
(sich) **füllen** to fill III
Füller pen I
fünf five I
fünfzehn fifteen I
fünfzig fifty I
funktionieren to work II
für for I
  für immer forever II
furchtbar awful; terrible I; horrible; dreadful III
sich **fürchten** to be afraid II
furchterregend terrifying IV U2, 32; frightening IV U3, 63
Fuß foot I
  zu Fuß on foot I
Fuß *(Längenmaß: 30,48 cm)* foot IV U1, 12
Fußball football I
Fußboden floor I
Fußgelenk ankle II
Fußknöchel ankle II
füttern to feed I

G

Gabel fork II
Gang corridor II
ganz all II; whole III
  ganz allein all alone I

ganz am Ende at the bottom IV U3, 62
den ganzen Tag all day III
gar nicht not at all II
Garten garden I
Gas gas III
Gasse alley IV U2, 32; lane IV U4, 75
Gast guest III
Gastfamilie host family IV U2, 34
Gasthaus pub III
Gebärdensprache sign language III
Gebäude building II
geben to give I; to be around IV U4, 80
Autogramme geben to sign autographs IV U3, 53
einen Klaps geben to slap IV U3, 64
jmdm. das Gefühl geben etw. zu sein to make sb feel like sth III
es gibt there are; there is I
Gebet prayer IV U4, 85
Gebiet area III; grounds *(pl)* IV U1, 13
geboren werden to be born III
(in der Pfanne) **gebraten** fried II
gebrochen broken IV U2, 41
Geburtstag birthday I
Alles Gute zum Geburtstag! Happy birthday! I
Gedanke thought IV U3, 62
Gedicht poem III
geduldig patient III
gefährlich dangerous III
Gefängnis prison II; jail IV U5, 107
gefeuert fired III
gefrieren to freeze III
gefrierend freezing IV U3, 54
jmdm. das **Gefühl** geben etw. zu sein to make sb feel like sth III
gegen against II; around III
gegen etw. fahren to hit III
Gegend area III; region IV U4, 86
im **Gegensatz** zu unlike III
sich **gegenseitig** each other III
gegenüber opposite I
Gegner protester IV U5, 98
Gegnerin protester IV U5, 98
Gehalt pay IV U2, 38
geheim secret II
Geheimnis mystery I; secret II
gehen to go; to walk I
aus dem Weg gehen to avoid IV U3, 62
gehen um to be about III
ins Bett gehen to go to bed I
über die Grenze gehen to cross the border IV U1, 19
gehören (zu) to belong (to) IV U1, 14
gehörlos deaf III
Gehweg sidewalk *(AE)* IV U1, 15
Geist ghost II; spirit IV U4, 85
Geisterstadt ghost town IV U4, 86
geistig mental IV U1, 22
Gel gel III
Gelände grounds *(pl)* IV U1, 13
gelangweilt bored IV U3, 57
gelassen relaxed IV U4, 74
gelb yellow I
Geld money I
Geldbörse wallet III
Geldschein note II
gelegen sein to be located IV U1, 13
Gelegenheit chance II; opportunity IV U1, 18
geliebt beloved IV U4, 85
gemäß according to III
gemein mean IV U3, 63
Gemeinde community IV U1, 18
gemeinsam together I
Gemeinschaft community IV U1, 18
Gemüse vegetable (veg) II
Obst- und **Gemüseladen** greengrocer's III
gemustert patterned II
gemütlich cosy III
genannt werden to be called II
genau exact III; right IV U2, 42; exactly IV U3, 59
genau genommen in fact III
generell in general IV U3, 73
genießen to enjoy II
genug enough III
genügend enough III
Geocaching geocaching I
geöffnet open III
Geografie Geography I
gerade right IV U2, 42
gerade (eben) just II
geradeaus straight on I; right ahead IV U1, 15
geradlinig straightforward III
Gerät tool II; device IV U3, 58
Geräusch noise I; sound III
Gerede talk II; gossip IV U3, 58
Gericht dish II; court IV U5, 107
Gerichtsverhandlung court case IV U5, 107
Gern geschehen. You're welcome. I
gern mögen to love I
hätte(n) gern would like II
Ich würde nicht gerne … I wouldn't like (to) … I
Ich würde sehr gern … I'd love to … (= I would love to) III
würde(n) gern would like II
Geruch smell III
gesamt total IV ZI, 8
Gesamt- total IV ZI, 8
Gesangs- singing III
Geschäft shop I; store *(AE)* IV U2, 33; business IV U5, 97
Geschäftsführer manager IV U2, 38
Geschäftsführerin manager IV U2, 38
Geschäftsmann businessman IV U4, 84
geschehen to happen II
Geschenk present I
Geschichte History; story I; history III
Geschoss bullet IV U3, 63
Gesellschaft company II; society IV U5, 100
Gesellschaftslehre Social Studies I
Gesetz law III
Gesicht face IV U3, 63
Gespräch conversation III
Gestaltung design IV U4, 77
gestatten to allow IV U4, 84
gestern yesterday I
gesund healthy III
Getränk drink II
Getreide corn IV ZI, 9
getrennt segregated; separate IV U5, 106
gewinnen to win I

Gewinner winner I
Gewinnerin winner I
sich an (etw.) **gewöhnen** to get used to (sth) IV U1, 19
gewöhnlich usually II
Gewürz spice II
Gips cast III
Giraffe giraffe I
Gitarre guitar III
Gitter grid IV U5, 101
Glanz glamor *(AE)* IV U4, 75
glänzen to shine IV ZI, 8
glänzend shiny IV U4, 85
Glas glass II; jar III
glauben to think I; to believe II
gläubig religious IV U1, 23
gleich the same II; right away IV U4, 80
gleichmäßig regular IV U4, 89
Gleis railway track IV U3, 64
Glocke bell II
Glück haben to be lucky III
viel **Glück** good luck II
glücklich happy I
glücklicherweise luckily IV U2, 38
Glückstag lucky day II
Glückszahl lucky number I
Glückwunsch! Congratulations! II
Glühbirne light bulb III
Gold gold III
Gold- gold III; golden IV U4, 75
golden gold III; golden IV U4, 75
Goldrausch gold rush IV U4, 84
Göttin goddess IV U1, 22
Grab grave III
graben to dig IV U4, 85
Grad degree IV U5, 102
Gras grass I
grau grey I
greifen to grab III
Grenze border III
die Grenze überschreiten to cross the border IV U1, 19
über die Grenze gehen to cross the border IV U1, 19
Griechisch Greek IV U5, 99
griechisch Greek IV U5, 99
Grill barbecue I
Grillparty barbecue I
grinsen to grin IV U3, 64
groß big; high I; tall; large II
großartig great I; fantastic II; grand III
Größe size II
Großeltern grandparents *(pl)* II
Großmutter grandmother III
Großstadt city II
Großvater grandfather II
großzügig generous IV U2, 39
grün green I
Grund reason; bottom III
Gründe angeben to give reasons III
Gründe nennen to give reasons III
im Grunde genommen basically IV U4, 80
Grundbesitzer landowner IV U4, 84
Grundbesitzerin landowner IV U4, 84
gründen to start III; to found IV U5, 98
grundsätzlich basically IV U4, 80
Gruppe group I; squad IV U2, 34
gruselig scary I; creepy IV U3, 53
Grüß dich. Hello there. I
Grüße ausrichten to say hi to I
Viele **Grüße**, Best wishes, I
grüßen to say hi to I
gültig valid III
Gummi rubber III
Gummistiefel welly I
Gürtel belt IV U3, 62
gut good I; fine II; nice III; well II
gut sein in/bei to be good at I
Guten Morgen. Good morning. II
Gut gemacht! Well done! I
Güter goods *(no pl)* IV U1, 18

H

Haar hair III
Haarbürste hairbrush III
Haare hair III
sich die Haare schneiden lassen to have a haircut II
Haargel hair gel III
Haarglätter hair straightener IV U3, 59
Haarschnitt haircut II
haben to have I
hätte(n) gern would like II
keine Ahnung haben to have no idea IV U1, 14
Spaß haben to enjoy oneself III
Du hast recht. You're right. I
Hafen harbour II; harbor *(AE)* IV U1, 22; port IV U5, 98
Hafer oat III
Haferbrei porridge III
Hähnchen chicken IV U5, 98
Hai shark I
halb half III
halb (drei) half past (two) I
eine halbe Million half a million III
Halbtags- part-time IV U2, 33
(die) **Hälfte** half IV U4, 80
Hallen- indoor III
Hallo. Hello.; Hi.; Hello there. I
Hals throat II
Halsband collar I
Halsschmerzen sore throat II
Halt stop II
halten to keep II; to hold III
die Klappe halten to shut up IV U3, 63
Haltestelle stop II
Haltung attitude IV U4, 89
Hamburger burger II
Hand hand I
handeln von to be about III
Handgelenk wrist IV U3, 63
Handlung action IV U5, 107
Handtuch towel III
Handy mobile (phone) I; cell phone *(AE)* IV U3, 59
hängen to hang II
hängen bleiben to be stuck IV U2, 34
hänseln to tease IV U2, 38
hart hard II; tough III
hassen to hate I
häufig often I
Haupt- major IV ZI, 8
Hauptgericht main course II
hauptsächlich mostly IV U2, 41
Hauptstadt capital (city) III
Hauptverkehrszeit rush hour IV U1, 14

Haus house I
im Haus around the house I
nach Hause home I
sich wie zu Hause fühlen to make oneself at home III
zu Hause at home I
Hausaufgabe(n) homework I
Hausaufgabe(n) machen to do homework I
Häuschen cottage III
Häuserblock block IV U1, 14
Hausmeister caretaker I
Hausmeisterin caretaker I
Haustier pet I
Heer army III
Heft book I; booklet IV U5, 102
Heim home I
Heimat home country IV U1, 19
Heimatland home country IV U1, 19
Heimweh haben to be homesick III
heiraten to get married II
heiß hot I
heißen to be called II
willkommen heißen to welcome IV U4, 80
Heizkörper radiator IV U3, 59
Held hero III
helfen to help I
Helfer helper IV U4, 89
Helferin helper IV U4, 89
Helikopter helicopter IV U4, 79
hell bright IV ZI, 8
Helm helmet III
Hemd shirt I
heraus out II
aus … heraus out of II
herausfallen aus to fall out of IV U2, 42
herausfinden to find; to find out I; to learn IV U3, 62
herausgeben to release IV U5, 97
herauskommen to get out III
herausnehmen to take out I
herausragen to stand out IV U1, 12
herausstechen to stand out IV U1, 12
Herbst fall *(AE)* IV ZI, 8
hereinkommen to get in I; to enter IV U3, 54
hergestellt sein aus to be made of III
Herr *(Anrede)* Mr I
herrlich lovely II
Herrschaft rule IV U5, 98
herüber across IV U3, 54
herum around I
herumkommen to get around III
herumrennen to run about II
sich **herumtreiben** (mit) to hang out (with) IV U3, 58
herunter down III
herunterfallen to fall off III
herunterladen to download II
hervorbringen to produce III
hervorragend excellent IV U5, 102
Herz heart III
Herzlichen Dank. Thanks so much. IV U4, 94
heute today I
heute Abend tonight II
heute Nacht tonight II
heutzutage now II; nowadays IV U5, 115
Hexe witch I
Hi. Hi. I
hier here I
hiesig local III
Highschool *(weiterführende Schule, Oberstufe)* high school IV U1, 18
Hightech- high-tech IV U4, 75
Hilfe help II; support IV U1, 19
hilfreich useful; helpful III
hilfsbereit cooperative; helpful IV U2, 38
Himbeere raspberry III
Hin- und Rückfahrkarte return ticket III
hinauf up II
hinausgeworfen fired III
hinbringen to take II
hinein into IV U3, 62
in … hinein inside II
hineingehen to go on II; to enter IV U3, 54
hineingelangen to get into IV U1, 14
hineinkommen to get into IV U1, 14
hinfallen to fall (over) III
hinkommen to get there III
hinkommen zu to get to IV U1, 14
hinnehmen to accept IV U5, 99
hinten at the back IV U5, 106
im hinteren Teil at the back IV U5, 106
hinter behind II
Hinter- back IV U3, 62
Hintergrund background III
im Hintergrund in the background III
hinüber across IV U3, 54
hinunter down III
hinuntereilen to rush down II
Hinweis clue I
darauf **hinweisen** to point out IV U1, 15
hinzufügen to add IV U5, 101
zu … hinzufügen to bookmark II
Hip-Hop *(Musik)* hip hop III
historisch historic IV U5, 98
Hit hit IV U5, 97
Hitparade charts *(pl only)* IV U5, 97
Hitze heat IV U5, 102
Hobby hobby III
hoch high I; tall II
hochladen to upload II
Hochzeit wedding II
hoffen to hope I
Hoffnung hope IV U1, 13
hoffnungsvoll hopeful III
höflich polite II
Höhe height II
Höhle cave II
holen to get II
Holz wood III
Homepage homepage III
hören to listen (to); to hear I
Hose trousers *(pl)* I; pants *(pl) (AE)* IV U2, 38
kurze Hose shorts *(pl)* I
Hosentasche pocket II
Hospital hospital I
Hot Dog *(Würstchen im Brötchen)* hot dog IV U1, 14
Hotel hotel II
Hotelfachschule catering college II
hübsch beautiful I; pretty; lovely II
Hubschrauber helicopter IV U4, 79

Hügel hill IV U4, 74
Huhn chicken I
Hühnchen chicken II
Hummer lobster IV U3, 52
Hund dog I
Hundeausführer dog walker IV U2, 41
Hundeausführerin dog walker IV U2, 41
Hundekeks dog biscuit II
hundert a/one hundred I
hungrig hungry I
husten to cough III
Hut hat II
hüten to look after II

I

ich I; me I
Ich heiße ... My name is ... I
Ich komme aus ... I'm from ... I
Ich weiß (es) nicht! I don't know! I
ich würde lieber I'd rather III
Idee idea I
Identität identity IV U5, 98
ihm him I
ihn him I
Ihnen you I
ihnen them I
ihr you I; its III; her I
ihr *(Pl.)* their I
Ihr your I
Ihre yours I; your I
ihre hers II; theirs III; her I; their I
im August in August I
im Bus on the bus II
Im Ernst? Are you serious? III
im Freien outside II
im Haus around the house I
im Schlepptau in tow IV U2, 42
im Stadtzentrum downtown *(AE)* IV U1, 14
im Süden von in the south of III
im vorderen Bereich at the front of II
Imbiss snack I
immer always I
für immer forever II
immer noch still III
immerhin after all IV U5, 115
Immigrant immigrant IV U1, 13
Immigrantin immigrant IV U1, 13
Immigration immigration IV U1, 22
immigrieren to immigrate IV U1, 18
in in; to; at I; inside III; into IV U3, 62
in der Ferne in the distance IV U1, 14
in der Pause at break I
in der Schule at school I
in der Mitte von in the centre of III
in der Unterzahl outnumbered IV U5, 102
in Form fit III
in Ordnung fine; all right II
in Richtung towards IV U3, 62
in ... hinein inside II
Indianer Native American IV U1, 16
Indianerin Native American IV U1, 16
indianisch Native American IV U1, 16
indisch Indian II
Industrie industry III
industrielle Revolution Industrial Revolution III
Informatik IT (Information Technology) I
Information information *(no pl)* I; information desk II
Informationen information *(no pl)* I
informativ informative IV U4, 77
Ingenieur engineer II
Ingenieurin engineer II
Inhalt content III
inmitten among III
innen in inside III
innen inside IV U1, 25
Innen- indoor III
im **Innern** inside III
Innovation innovation IV U4, 80
Insekt insect III
Insel island II
insgesamt all in all IV U3, 61
Inspektion inspection IV U1, 22
Institut college *(AE)* IV U5, 101
intelligent clever I; smart; intelligent III
interessant interesting I
sich **interessieren** für to be interested in III; to care about IV U3, 58
interessiert sein an to be interested in III
Internet internet II
im Internet surfen to surf the internet II
ins Internet stellen to upload II
Internettagebuch blog II
Interview interview II
interviewen to interview I
Interviewer interviewer IV U1, 18
Interviewerin interviewer IV U1, 18
die **Iren** the Irish III
irgendein any II
irgendetwas anything II
irgendwelche any II
Irisch Irish III
irisch Irish III
sich **irren** to be wrong III
Italiener Italian II
Italienerin Italian II
Italienisch Italian II
italienisch Italian II

J

ja yes I
na ja well I
Jacke coat I; jacket II
Jagdgewehr shotgun IV U5, 107
Jäger chaser IV U2, 33; hunter IV U4, 85
Jägerin chaser IV U2, 33; hunter IV U4, 85
Jahr year I
Jahre alt year-old IV U2, 38
fette Jahre *(ugs.)* boom years IV U4, 86
Jahreszeit season IV U1, 18
Jahrgangsstufe year I
Jahrhundert century III
jährig year-old IV U2, 38
jährlich annual III
jamaikanisch Jamaican II
jämmerlich miserable III
Januar January I
Japaner Japanese IV U5, 99
Japanerin Japanese IV U5, 99
Japanisch Japanese IV U5, 99
japanisch Japanese IV U5, 99

Jeans jeans *(pl)* I
jede any III
jedenfalls anyway III
jeder every; everyone I; everybody IV U2, 43
jedoch however; though III
jemals ever II
jemand somebody III
jemand anderes somebody else II
jene those II
jetzt now I
jetzt gerade right now III
Job job I
Joghurt yogurt II
Journalismus journalism IV U2, 34
Journalistik journalism IV U2, 34
Jugend youth *(no pl)* III
Jugend- teen II; youth *(no pl)* III
Jugendherberge youth hostel III
jugendlich teenage IV U3, 54
Jugendliche teen II; teenager III
Jugendlicher teen II; teenager III
Jugendzentrum activity centre III
Juli July I
jung young II
Junge boy I
Juni June I
Juror judge II
Jurorin judge II
Juwelierladen jeweller's III

K

Kabel wire III
Kaffee coffee IV U1, 14
Käfig cage I
Kaiserreich empire III
Kalender calendar IV U5, 102
kalt cold I
Kamel camel I
Kamm comb III
Kampf battle; fight III
kämpfen to fight III
Kanarienvogel canary III
Kanone cannon II
Kanonenkugel cannon ball II
Kanufahren canoeing I
Kapitän captain I
Kapitänin captain I
Kappe cap I
kaputt broken IV U2, 41
kaputt machen to tear (up) IV U2, 33
Karneval carnival IV U5, 98
Karotte carrot II
Karre truck III
Karriere career IV U1, 18
Karte card I; ticket II; map IV U4, 80
Kartoffel potato II
Kartoffelbrei mashed potatoes II
Kartoffelchip crisp I
Karton cardboard III
Käse cheese I
Käsekuchen cheesecake II
Katastrophe disaster III
Katholik Catholic III
Katholikin Catholic III
katholisch Catholic III
Katze cat I
kaufen to buy I
Kaufhaus department store II
Kaugummi chewing gum I
kaum little IV U1, 22
kein no I; not … any II
keine Ahnung haben to have no idea IV U1, 14
Keks biscuit II
Kellner waiter II
Kellnerin waitress IV U4, 89
kennen to know I
kennen lernen to meet I; to get to know II
kennzeichnen to mark III
Kerl guy IV U2, 42
Kerze candle I
Ketchup ketchup II
Kidneybohne kidney bean II
Kilogramm (kg) kilogram (kg) I
sieben Kilogramm täglich 7 kilograms a day I
Kilometer (km) kilometre (km) I
40 Kilometer pro Stunde 40 kilometres an hour I
Kilt kilt III
Kind child; kid II
Kinder children *(pl)* II
Kinderzimmer bedroom I
Kino cinema I; the movies *(AE)* IV U3, 58; movie theater *(AE)* IV U5, 106
Kirche church II
Kiste box I
die **Klappe** halten to shut up IV U3, 63
klappen to fold IV U2, 38
einen **Klaps** geben to slap IV U3, 64
klar clear IV U4, 77
alles klar all right II
Klasse year I; class III; grade *(AE)* IV U2, 33
Klasse *(in einer englischen Schule)* tutor group I
Klassenarbeit test I
Klassenfahrt school trip I
Klassenlehrer tutor I
Klassenlehrerin tutor I
Klassenzimmer classroom I
klassisch *(Musik)* classical III
Klatsch gossip IV U3, 58
Klebstoff glue I
Kleeblatt shamrock III
Kleid dress I
Kleider *(Pl.)* clothes *(pl)* I
Kleiderordnung dress code IV U2, 36
Kleiderschrank wardrobe I
Kleidung clothes *(pl)* I; outfit III
klein small I; little II; tiny III
eine **Kleinigkeit** a little something IV U3, 54
Kletter- climbing IV U4, 78
Klettern rock climbing I
klettern to climb III
klicken to click I
klingeln to ring III
klingen to sound II
Kloß dumpling II
Klub club II
Klubhaus clubhouse IV U3, 62
klug clever I; smart; intelligent III
Kneipe pub III
Knie knee III
knifflig tricky IV U2, 38
Knoblauch garlic II
knuddelig cuddly III
Koch chef II

Kochbanane plantain II
Kochen cooking II
kochen to cook II
Köchin chef II
Koffer suitcase II
Kohl cabbage II
Kohle coal III
Kokosnuss coconut II
Kollegium staff *(no pl)* IV U2, 38
Kollektion collection IV U1, 13
Kombination combination II
kommen to come I
Komm schon! Come on! III
Kommentar comment IV U4, 80
kommunizieren to communicate IV U4, 80
Komödie comedy III
Kompromisse schließen to compromise IV U5, 98
Konfitüre jam III
konfrontieren to confront IV U5, 98
König king III
Königin queen III
königlich royal II
Konkurrenz competition IV U2, 34
können can I; may II; to be able to IV U2, 34
nicht können can't I; cannot III
nicht weg können to be stuck IV U2, 34
konnte could III
Ich konnte nicht anders als ... I couldn't help but ... III
könnte could III; might IV U3, 63
Kontakt contact IV U1, 18
Konto account IV U4, 80
Kontrolle inspection; check IV U1, 22; control IV U3, 53
kontrollieren to check III
Konversation conversation III
(sich) **konzentrieren** to concentrate IV U3, 58
Konzert concert II
kooperativ cooperative IV U2, 38
Kopf head II
Kopfhörer headphones *(pl)* IV U3, 59
Kopfsalat lettuce II
Kopfschmerzen headache II
kopfüber head first III
Kopfweh headache II
Kopie copy II
kopieren to copy II
Korbball netball I
Korn corn IV ZI, 9
Körper body III
körperlich physical IV U1, 22
Körperlotion body lotion III
korrekt right I; correct IV U1, 14
Korridor hall IV U2, 34
kosten to cost III
... kosten 99 Pence. ... are 99p. I
... kostet ein Pfund fünfundzwanzig. ... is £1.25. I
kostenlos free III
köstlich delicious II
Kostüm costume; fancy dress I
Kraft power III; strength IV U2, 39
krank ill II; sick III
Krankenhaus hospital I
Krankenpfleger nurse II
Krankenschwester nurse II
Krankenwagen ambulance III
Krankheit disease IV U1, 22
Kraut cabbage II
Kreis circle III
kreischen to scream III
Kreuzung intersection *(AE)* IV U1, 15
Kricket cricket II
Krimi (= Kriminalgeschichte) mystery story IV U3, 53
Kritik review III
Krokodil crocodile I
Kubaner Cuban IV U1, 18
Kubanerin Cuban IV U1, 18
kubanisch Cuban IV U1, 18
Küche kitchen I
Kuchen cake I; pie II
einen Kuchen backen to make a cake I
Kugel bullet IV U3, 63
Kuh cow III
kühl cool I
kühlen to cool III
Kühlschrank fridge III
Kultur culture IV U1, 18
Kulturbewegung cultural movement IV U1, 13
kulturell cultural IV U1, 13
sich **kümmern** (um) to care (for) III
sich kümmern um to care about IV U3, 58
sich um jmdn. kümmern to take care of sb IV U2, 41
Kumpel buddy *(infml)* IV U2, 45
Kunde customer III
Kundin customer III
Kunst Art I
Kunststoff plastic III
Kunststück trick III
Kuppel dome II
Kurs course III; class IV U2, 34
kurz short II; shortly III
kurze Hose shorts *(pl)* I
Kurzfilm clip IV U4, 80
Kuscheltier cuddly toy III
Kuss kiss II
küssen to kiss III
Küste coast III
an der Küste on the coast III

L

lächeln to smile III
Lachen laugh IV U3, 63
lachen to laugh II
Ladegerät charger III
Laden shop I; store *(AE)* IV U2, 33
Tante-Emma-Laden corner shop I
Lage location III
Lager camp II
lahm lame IV U2, 38
Lamm lamb II
Lampe lamp I
Land country I; land II; countryside III; state IV ZI, 8
auf dem Land in the country I
Land der Freien land of the free IV U3, 53
landen to land IV U3, 54
Landesregierung state government IV U5, 98
Landkarte map III
ländliche Gegend country I

Landschaft countryside III; landscape IV ZI, 9
Landwirt farmer I
Landwirtin farmer I
Landwirtschaft farming IV U4, 84
Landwirtschaftsflächen farmland IV U2, 32
lang long I
Länge length IV U4, 75
langsam slow III
langweilig boring I; dull IV U4, 77
Laptop laptop I
Lasagne lasagne II
lassen to leave II; to let III
lass uns let's I
Laufbahn career IV U1, 18
laufen to run I; to walk II
Wie läuft's? How's it going? IV U3, 54
jmdn. auf dem **Laufenden** halten to keep sb informed IV U4, 84
Laut sound III
laut noisy; loud III; according to III
läuten to ring III
Layout layout IV U4, 77
Leben life I; lifetime IV U4, 76
am Leben alive III
zum Leben erwecken to bring life IV U1, 22
leben to live I
Lebensart lifestyle IV U4, 74; way of life IV U5, 96
Lebensmittel food I; groceries *(pl)* IV U4, 89
Lebensweise way of life IV U5, 96
Lebenszeit lifetime IV U4, 76
lecker nice; tasty III
Leder leather III
leer empty IV U4, 86
legen to put I; to lay II
Lehre lesson IV U2, 38
lehren to teach III
Lehrer teacher I; instructor III
Lehrerin teacher I; instructor III
Leiche body IV U3, 62
leicht easy I
Es tut mir **leid** wegen … Sorry about … I
Es tut mir **leid**. I'm sorry. I
Tut mir **leid**. Sorry. I
leidtun to be sorry III
leihen to lend II
Leine lead I
leise quiet III
leistungsorientiert competitive III
leiten to run III
Leiter ladder I
Lektion lesson IV U2, 38
lernen to learn II; to study IV U2, 34
kennen lernen to meet I; to get to know II
lesen to read I
Leser reader IV U1, 21
Leserin reader IV U1, 21
zu guter **Letzt** at last II
letzte last I
letztlich finally IV U4, 85
leuchtend bright IV ZI, 8
Leute people *(pl)* I; guys II
Lexikon encyclopedia IV U4, 86
Licht light IV U1, 13
Liebe/Lieber …, *(Anrede in Briefen)* Dear …, I
Liebe love IV U4, 85
lieben to love I
liebend loving IV U4, 85
lieber even IV U1, 14
ich würde lieber I'd rather III
Liebesgeschichte romance III
liebevoll loving IV U4, 85
Lieblings- favourite I; favorite *(AE)* IV U4, 80
Lied song I
Lieferwagen van III
liegen to be located III; to rest IV U4, 85
Lifestyle lifestyle IV U4, 74
Lift elevator *(AE)* IV U1, 13
Liga league IV U1, 18
lila purple I
Limonade lemonade II
Lineal ruler I
Linie line II
in erster Linie above all IV U1, 18
Link link IV U4, 80
links on the left I; left III
Liste list II
LKW-Fahrer lorry driver II
LKW-Fahrerin lorry driver II
Loch hole I
locker relaxed IV U4, 74; loose II
Löffel spoon II
Lohn wage; pay IV U2, 38
lokal local III
lose loose II
lösen to solve I
loslassen to release IV U5, 97
loslegen to go ahead IV U1, 18
Lösung solution IV U5, 98
Löwe lion I
Luft air IV U1, 22
Luftballon balloon I
Lunchpaket packed lunch II
lustig funny I
Luxus- deluxe IV U5, 102

M

machen to do; to make I
ein Foto machen to take a photo I
Hausaufgabe(n) machen to do homework I
kaputt machen to tear (up) IV U2, 33
sich Notizen machen to take notes I
Gut gemacht! Well done! I
Mach dir nichts draus. Never mind. II
Macht nichts. Never mind. II
Macht's gut. Take care. I
sie machte she was making II
Macht power III
mächtig powerful IV U1, 22
Mädchen girl I
Magen stomach II
Magie magic II
Magier magician IV U3, 63
Magierin magician IV U3, 63
magisch magic II
Mahlzeit meal II
Mai May I
Mais corn IV ZI, 9
Make-up make-up IV U3, 58

Mal time III
malen to paint IV U4, 75
Mama mum I; mama II;
mom *(AE)* IV U1, 18
Mammutbaum redwood (tree)
IV U4, 74
Manager manager IV U2, 38
Managerin manager IV U2, 38
manchmal sometimes I
Mann man I
Mannschaft team I; crew III; squad
IV U2, 34
Märchen fable III
Marke brand III
markieren to mark III
Markt market II
Marmelade jam III
März March I
Maschine machine II
Material material III
Mathe Maths I; Math *(AE)* IV U2, 34
Mathematik Maths I; Math *(AE)*
IV U2, 34
Matsch mud III
matt dull IV U4, 77
Mauer wall II
Maus mouse I
Mayonnaise mayonnaise II
meckern to nag III
Medien media IV U5, 98
soziale Medien social media
IV U4, 80
Medikamente medicine III
Medizin medicine III
medizinisch medical IV U1, 22
Meer sea I; ocean IV ZI, 9
am Meer at the seaside I
Meerschweinchen guinea pig I
Mehl flour II
in Mehl wenden to cover in flour
IV U5, 98
mehr more I
nicht mehr not ... any more III
mehrere several IV U4, 80; a number
of IV U5, 98
Mehrheit majority IV U1, 22
die Mehrheit most I
Mehrzahl majority IV U1, 22
meiden to avoid IV U3, 62
Meile mile II
mein my I
meine my I; mine II
meiner Meinung nach in my
opinion III
meinen to mean III
Meinung opinion III
einer Meinung sein (mit) to agree
(with) III
seine Meinung ändern to change
one's mind III
anderer Meinung sein to disagree
II
meiner Meinung nach in my
opinion III
am **meisten** most II
die **meisten** most I
meistens mostly IV U2, 41
melken to milk III
eine **Menge** a lot of I
jede **Menge** lots of I; lots III
Mensa cafeteria I
Mensch person II
Menschen people *(pl)* I
Menschenmenge crowd II
menschlich human III
sich **merken** to remember II
merkwürdig strange; funny II
Messer knife II
Metall metal III
Meter metre I
Methode method II
Metzgerei butcher's III
mich me I
Miete rent II
mieten to rent III; to hire IV U4, 85
Mikrowelle microwave IV U3, 59
Milch milk I
Milchmischgetränk milkshake III
Milchshake milkshake III
mild mild I
Milliarde billion IV U1, 13
Million million III
eine halbe Million half a million
III
Minderheit minority IV U1, 22
Mindest- minimum IV U2, 38
mindestens at least III
Mineralwasser mineral water III
minimal minimum IV U2, 38
Minimum minimum IV U2, 38
Minute minute II
mir me I
von mir of mine II
mischen to mix IV U5, 98
mit with I
mit *(dem Zug)* by *(train)* I
mitbringen to bring II
Mitglied member IV U3, 52
Mitleid haben mit to feel sorry for III
zum **Mitnehmen** takeaway II
mitnehmen to take I
Mittagessen lunch I
Mittagspause lunchtime I
Mittagszeit lunchtime I
Mitte centre; middle III; center *(AE)*
IV U1, 13
in der Mitte in the middle III
in der Mitte von in the centre of III
Mitternacht midnight III
Mittwoch Wednesday I
mittwochs on Wednesdays I
mixen to mix IV U5, 98
mobil mobile IV U4, 80
Mobiltelefon mobile (phone) I; cell
phone *(AE)* IV U3, 59
Mode fashion *(no pl)* IV U3, 58
modern modern I
modisch fashionable II; trendy
IV U4, 81
mögen to like I; to enjoy III
am liebsten mögen to like ...
best I
am meisten mögen to like ...
best I
gern mögen to love I
nicht mögen to hate I; to dislike
IV U4, 81
Ich möchte nicht ... I wouldn't like
(to) ... I
Ich möchte ... I'd like (to) ... (= I
would like to) I
Möchtest du? Would you like
(to) ...? I

Möglichkeit chance IV U1, 18; option IV U2, 34
Moment moment II
in dem Moment als right IV U2, 42
Monat month I
monatlich monthly III
Monster monster III
Montag Monday I
Mörder murderer III
Mörderin murderer III
Morgen morning I
Guten Morgen. Good morning. II
morgen tomorrow II
morgendliche Ansprache morning message IV U2, 34
Moschee mosque II
motiviert motivated IV U1, 18
Motor engine IV U3, 54
Motorrad motorbike I
Moussaka moussaka II
müde tired I
Müll rubbish II; trash (AE) IV U3, 62
Mülleimer tin IV U3, 63
multikulturell multicultural IV U5, 98
Mund mouth II
Münze coin III
Münzgeld change II
Münztelefon pay phone III
Museum museum II
Musik music I
Musik- musical III
musikalisch musical III
Musikgruppe band II
Müsli cereal III
Muslim Muslim I
Muslimin Muslim I
müssen must I; to have to II
nicht müssen needn't I
Mut courage IV U5, 107
mutig brave III
Mutter mother I
Mütze cap I

N

Na schön. Fair enough. III
nach to; after I
nach Hause home I
nach dem Weg fragen asking the way I
nach *(bei Uhrzeitangaben)* past II
Nachbar neighbour III
Nachbarin neighbour III
Nachfahre descendant IV U1, 22
Nachfahrin descendant IV U1, 22
nachfolgen to succeed (in) IV U1, 19
Nachmittag afternoon I
nachmittags in the afternoon I
nachmittags *(Uhrzeit)* p.m. II
Nachricht message II
Nachricht(en) news II
nachschauen to look I; to look up II
Nachsitzen detention IV U2, 35
Nachspeise dessert; pudding II
nachsprechen to say I
nächste next I
als **Nächstes** next II
Nacht night I
heute Nacht tonight II
in jener Nacht that night II
Nachtwanderung night walk I
Nagel nail III
Nagelschere nail scissors *(pl)* III
nah near III
in der **Nähe** von near I
Nahrung food I
Name name I
Nase nose I
die Nase voll haben (von) to be fed up (with) III
nass wet I
national national III
National- national III
Natur nature III
die freie Natur the outdoors IV U5, 96
natürlich of course I
Naturwissenschaft Science I
Navi satnav I
Nebel fog IV U4, 75
neben next to I
neblig foggy I
negativ negative IV U5, 99
nehmen to take I
etw. ernst nehmen to take sth seriously IV U1, 18
neidisch jealous II
nein no I
nennen to say I; to call III
auf die **Nerven** gehen to get on one's nerves III
nerven to bother IV U5, 107
nervös nervous II
nett nice I; kind II; friendly III
Netz web III; net IV U4, 75
neu new I
auf den neuesten Stand bringen to update IV U4, 81
Neuheit innovation IV U4, 80
Neuigkeit(en) news II
neun nine I
Neuntklässler freshman *(AE)* IV U2, 34
Neuntklässlerin freshman *(AE)* IV U2, 34
neunzehn nineteen I
neunzig ninety I
nicht not I
auch nicht not … either III
nicht brauchen needn't I
nicht dürfen mustn't III
nicht einverstanden sein to disagree II
nicht können can't I; cannot III
nicht mehr not … any more III
nicht mögen to hate I; to dislike IV U4, 81
nicht müssen needn't I
nicht wahr? isn't it? II
nicht weg können to be stuck IV U2, 34
nicht werden won't (= will not) II
nicht- non- IV U4, 86
Nichte niece III
Nichts wie weg. Off we went. III
nichts nothing IV U5, 99
nie never I
niederbrennen to burn down II
sich **niederlassen** (in) to settle IV U4, 75
niedlich cute I
niedrig low II
niemals never I
niemand nobody III; no one I

nirgendwo nowhere IV U2, 34
nirgendwohin nowhere IV U2, 34
noch still III; even II
noch ein another II
noch einmal again; once more II
noch nicht not … yet II
Norden north III
nördlich northern III
nördlich von to the north of III; north of IV ZI, 9
Nordosten northeast III
Nordwesten northwest III
nordwestlich northwest of III
nörgeln to nag III
normal regular IV U4, 89
normalerweise usually II
die **Normannen** the Normans III
Notdienst emergency service III
Note grade *(AE)* IV U2, 33
Notfall emergency III
sich **Notizen** machen to take notes I
Notruf emergency call III
November November I
Nudelauflauf pasta bake II
Nudeln pasta II
null zero I
null *(bei Uhrzeiten und Telefonnummern)* oh I
Nummer number I
nun now I
nur only I; just II
Nuss nut I
nützlich useful; helpful III

O

oben up II; at the top III
obere upper III
oberer Teil top III
oberes Ende top III
Oberfläche surface IV U4, 86
Oberteil top II
Obst fruit I
Obst- und Gemüseladen greengrocer's III
obwohl although IV U5, 107
oder or I
Ofenkartoffel jacket potato II
offen open III
öffentliche Verkehrsmittel public transport III
offiziell official IV U4, 84
öffnen to open I
Öffnungszeiten opening times IV U5, 105
oft often I
ohne without III
Ohr ear II
okay OK I; alright IV U3, 58
Oktober October I
Öl oil IV U5, 98
Oma grandma II
Onkel uncle I
online online II
online stellen to post IV U4, 80
Opa grandad III
Operation operation III
optimistisch optimistic III
Option option IV U2, 34
Orange orange I
orange orange I
Orchester orchestra III
in **Ordnung** fine; all right II
in Ordnung bringen to tidy (up) II
organisieren to organize II
original original IV U3, 54
Ort place I; space IV U1, 22
örtlich local III
Osten east III
östlich von east of IV ZI, 9
Outdoor- outdoor III
Outfit outfit III
Ozean ocean IV ZI, 9

P

Paar pair IV U2, 41
ein Paar a pair of II
ein **paar** some I; a few III
(ein) paar (a) couple of IV U2, 34
packen to pack; to pack up II
Packung packet I
Paella paella IV U5, 99
Paket package IV U5, 102
panisch werden to panic II
Papa dad I
Papagei parrot I
Papier paper III
Pappe cardboard III
Parade parade III
Paradies paradise IV ZI, 9
Parfüm perfume III
Park park I
Parkplatz parking lot *(AE)* IV U1, 15
Partner partner III
Partnerin partner III
Party party I
Pass pass IV U2, 34
Passagier passenger II
Passagierin passenger II
passen to suit; to fit II
passieren to happen II
Pasta pasta II
Pastete pasty; pie II
Patient patient II
Patientin patient II
Pause break I; recess *(AE)* IV U2, 35
in der Pause at break I
Pause machen to take a break II
Pausenhof playground I
peinlich embarrassing IV U2, 42
Pekannuss pecan IV U3, 67
Pence *(brit. Währungseinheit)* pence I
Das macht zwei Pfund und 24 Pence. That's £2.24. I
… kosten 99 Pence. … are 99p. I
Pendler commuter IV U1, 15
Pendlerin commuter IV U1, 15
perfekt perfect IV ZI, 9
Person person II
berühmte Person celebrity IV U5, 97
Personal staff *(no pl)* IV U2, 38
Personalausweis ID III
persönlich personal III
Pfannkuchen pancake II
Pfeffer pepper II
Pferd horse I
Pfirsich peach I
Pflanze plant I
Pflaster plaster III
Pflichtfach core subject IV U2, 35
Pfund *(brit. Währungseinheit)* pound I

Das macht 2 Pfund und 24 Pence. That's £2.24. I
... kostet ein Pfund fünfundzwanzig. ... is £1.25. I
physisch physical IV U1, 22
Picknick picnic I
Pick-up pick-up IV U5, 102
pikant spicy II
Pilot pilot IV U4, 79
Pilotin pilot IV U4, 79
Pinguin penguin I
pink pink I
Pirat pirate I
Piratin pirate I
Pirogge pierogi II
Pizza pizza I
Plan plan II; map IV U4, 80
planen to plan III
Planke plank II
Plantage plantation IV U5, 97
Planwagen wagon IV U4, 85
Plastik plastic III
Platsch splash I
platt flat IV U2, 32
Platz place I; square II; space IV U1, 22; seat IV U5, 102
plaudern to chat II
plötzlich suddenly II
Podcast podcast IV U4, 94
politisch political IV U1, 23
Polizei police III
Polizeibeamter police officer I
Polizeibeamtin police officer I
Polnisch Polish IV U1, 22
polnisch Polish IV U1, 22
Pommes frites chips *(pl)* I
Pop *(Musik)* pop III
Popcorn popcorn I
Porzellan china III
positiv positive III
Post *(online gestellte Nachricht)* post IV U4, 80
Postamt post office I
Poster poster I
Postkarte postcard I
praktisch practical IV U4, 89
Praline chocolate IV U3, 54
Prämie bonus IV U2, 39
Pranger stocks III
Präsentation presentation IV U2, 51
präsentieren to present IV U2, 33
Präsident president IV U3, 53
Präsidentin president IV U3, 53
Preis prize; price II
pressen to squeeze IV U3, 63
Prise pinch II
pro per IV U2, 33
pro Stück each II
probieren to try II
Problem problem I; trouble III
produzieren to produce III
Programm programme I
Projekt project III
Prominente celebrity IV U5, 97
Prominenter celebrity IV U5, 97
Propellerboot airboat IV U5, 102
Prospekt brochure III
Protest protest IV U5, 96
Protestant Protestant III
Protestantin Protestant III
protestantisch Protestant III
Prozent percent (%) IV U1, 22
prüfen to test II
Pudding pudding II
Punkt point IV U5, 115
Punktestand score II
pünktlich on time III
Pute turkey IV U3, 53
putzen to clean I

Q

Quadratmeile square mile (= sq. mi.) IV ZI, 8
Quelle source IV U1, 23
quer durch across IV U3, 54
quetschen to squeeze IV U3, 63
Quittung receipt II

R

Rad wheel II
Radfahren cycling III
Radiergummi eraser I
Radio radio II
Rafting rafting III
rappen to rap II
Rapper rapper III
Rapperin rapper III
Rasierapparat razor IV U3, 59
Rasierer razor IV U3, 59
Rassentrennung segregation IV U5, 106
Rassismus racism IV U5, 98
rasten to rest IV U4, 85
Raster grid IV U5, 101
Rat advice III
raten to guess II
Rathaus town hall II
Ratschlag advice III; tip II
Rätsel mystery I
Rauch smoke III
Raum room I; space IV U1, 22
reagieren to react IV U2, 38
Reaktion reaction IV U2, 38
Rechner calculator I
Rechnung bill III
Recht right IV U5, 96
recht haben to be right II
Du hast recht. You're right. I
rechthaberisch bossy IV U2, 39
rechts on the right I; right III
Rechtschreibung spelling I
Rechtsfall court case IV U5, 107
rechtzeitig in time I
Rede speech III
reden (mit) to talk (to) I
Regal shelf I
Regalbrett shelf I
Regel rule III
regelmäßig regular IV U4, 89
Regen rain III
Regenbogen rainbow III
Regenmantel raincoat III
Regenschirm umbrella II
Regierung government IV U2, 32
Regierungsgebäude State House *(AE)* IV U5, 98
Region region IV U4, 86
Regisseur director II
Regisseurin director II
regnen to rain I
regnerisch rainy I
Reich empire III

reich rich III
reichen to pass II
Reichtum wealth III; fortune IV U4, 85
Reifen tyre III
in die richtige **Reihenfolge** bringen to put in the right order I
(sich) **reimen** to rhyme III
Reis rice II
Reise trip; voyage; journey III; tour IV U4, 76
reisen to travel II
Reiseziel destination IV U5, 96
reißen to tear (up) IV U2, 33
Reiten horse riding I
reiten to ride II
reizen to tease IV U2, 38
Religionsunterricht RE (Religious Education) I
religiös religious IV U1, 23
rennen to run I
reparieren to repair III
Reporter reporter III
Reporterin reporter III
Republik republic III
Requisit prop III
Reservat reservation IV U2, 32
reservieren to make a reservation III; to book IV U4, 76
Reservierung reservation IV U4, 76
respektieren to respect IV U4, 89
der **Rest** the rest IV U1, 22
Restaurant restaurant II
retten to save III
Rettungsboot lifeboat III
Rettungsdienst emergency service III
industrielle **Revolution** Industrial Revolution III
Rezept recipe II
Rhythmus rhythm III
richtig right I; real II; correct IV U1, 14
das **Richtige** tun to do the right thing III
Richtung direction IV U2, 33; trend IV U4, 80
in Richtung towards IV U3, 62
in diese Richtung this way II
Riese giant III
Riesen- giant III
riesengroß huge IV ZI, 9
Riesenrad big wheel II
riesig huge IV ZI, 9; giant III
Rindfleisch beef II
Ring circle III
Ritt ride IV U1, 14
Ritter knight III
Rock skirt I
Rock *(Musik)* rock III
Rohr tube; pipe III
Rolle part II; role IV U5, 107
Rollkoffer trolley suitcase III
Rollstuhl wheelchair III
Rolltreppe escalator II
Roman novel IV U3, 53
die **Römer** the Romans III
rosa pink I
Rose rose IV ZI, 8
rosten to rust IV U4, 75
rot red I
Rücken back IV U3, 64
Hin- und **Rückfahrkarte** return ticket III
Rucksack backpack IV U3, 62
Rückseite back IV U3, 64
Ruf call III; reputation IV U5, 107
rufen to call I; to shout II
Rugby rugby III
Ruhe silence III
ruhig quiet III
Rührei scrambled egg II
rühren to stir II
ruinieren to ruin II
rumhängen (mit) to hang out (with) IV U3, 58
Russe Russian IV U5, 99
Russin Russian IV U5, 99
Russisch Russian IV U5, 99
russisch Russian IV U5, 99
Rüstung armour III

S

Sache thing I
Sack bag I
Saft juice II
sagen to say; to tell I
Saison season IV U1, 18
Salat salad II
Salz salt II
sammeln to collect I
(sich) sammeln to gather IV U3, 64
Sammlung collection IV U1, 13
Samstag Saturday I
Sandwich sandwich I
Sänger singer I
Sängerin singer I
etw. **sattbekommen** to get tired of sth IV U1, 14
etw. **satthaben** to get tired of sth IV U1, 14
sauber clean I
sauber machen to clean I
sauer sein to be fed up (with) III
Saxofon saxophone I
Schachtel box I
(es ist) **schade** it's a pity IV U3, 63
Schaf sheep I
es **schaffen** to make it IV U3, 54
Schal scarf I
Schälchen bowl II
Schale bowl II
Schatz treasure II
schätzen to guess IV U3, 58; to appreciate IV U5, 99
Schau show IV U5, 102
schauen to look I
Schauspielen acting III
Schauspieler actor II
Schauspielerei acting III
Schauspielerin actor II
Schauspielworkshop acting workshop II
Scheibenwischer windscreen wiper III
scheinen to seem III; to shine IV ZI, 8
Schere scissors *(pl)* III
scherzen to joke III
schick chic I
schicken to send I
schieben to push I
schießen to kick III
schießen (auf) to shoot (at) IV U3, 63
Schiff ship I

Schiffsbauer ship builder III
Schiffsbauerin ship builder III
Schiffsdeck deck IV U1, 22
Schiffsfahrt boat trip II
Schild sign III
Schimmelkäse blue cheese II
Schinken ham II
Schlacht battle III
Schlaf sleep III
schlafen to sleep I; to be asleep III
Schlafzimmer bedroom I
schlagen to hit II; to beat III; to slap IV U3, 64
Schlagzeile headline IV U4, 77
Schlamm mud III
schlammig muddy I
Schlange snake I
schlau clever I; smart III
Schlauch tube III
schlecht bad I; ill II; evil IV U3, 63
sich schlecht fühlen to feel sick IV U5, 103
schlechteste worst III
schleifen to drag IV U5, 107
schlendern to stroll IV U4, 76
schleppen to drag IV U5, 107
im **Schlepptau** in tow IV U2, 42
schlicht plain II
schließen to close I
Kompromisse schließen to compromise IV U5, 98
Schließfach locker IV U2, 34
schließlich in the end; finally II; after all IV U5, 115
schlimm terrible I
schlimmste worst III
Schloss castle II
Schlumpf smurf I
Schluss end II; ending; conclusion III
am Schluss by the end II
zum Schluss in the end; finally II
Schlussfolgerung conclusion III
Schlussverkauf sale II
schmackhaft tasty III
schmerzhaft sore II
Schminke make-up IV U3, 58
Schmuck jewellery II
Schmuggler smuggler II
Schmugglerin smuggler II
schmutzig dirty I
Schnäppchen bargain II
schnappen to grab III
Schnee snow IV U1, 14
(sich) **schneiden** to cut II
sich die Haare schneiden lassen to have a haircut II
schnell fast; quick II
der/die/das schnellste the fastest I
Schokolade chocolate I
Tafel Schokolade bar of chocolate I
schon already; yet II
schon einmal before III
Schon gut. Never mind. II
schön nice; beautiful I; fine; lovely II
ganz schön pretty IV U2, 34
Schotte Scot III
Schottenrock kilt III
Schottin Scot III
schottisch Scottish III
Schrank cupboard III
schrecklich awful; terrible I; horrible III
Schrei shout I
schreiben to write I
eine SMS schreiben to text II
Schreibtisch desk IV U3, 62
schreien to shout II; to scream III
Schriftsteller writer II
Schriftstellerin writer II
Schritt step III
in **Schritttempo** verfallen to slow to a walk IV U3, 63
Schrotflinte shotgun IV U5, 107
schubsen to push III
schüchtern shy IV U2, 39
Schuh shoe I
schulden to owe III
Schule school I
in der Schule at school I
Schüler student I
Schülerin student I
Schulfach subject I
Schulgelände campus IV U2, 35
Schulhof playground I
Schulleiter principal *(AE)* IV U2, 34
Schulleiterin principal *(AE)* IV U2, 34
Schulstunde lesson I
schürfen to dig IV U4, 85
Schüssel bowl II
Schusswaffe gun IV U3, 62
schützen to keep safe; to protect III
schwach weak III; lame IV U2, 38
Schwäche weakness IV U2, 39
schwarz black I
Schweigen silence III
schweigsam silent III
Schweinefleisch pork II
Schweizer Swiss IV U4, 84
Schweizerin Swiss IV U4, 84
schweizerisch Swiss IV U4, 84
schwer heavy; hard II; serious III; badly III
schwerhörig deaf III
Schwert sword III
Schwester sister I
schwierig difficult III; hard II; tricky IV U2, 38
Schwierigkeiten trouble III
Schwimmbad swimming pool I
schwimmen to swim II
schwimmen gehen to go swimming I
Schwimmer swimmer IV U4, 78
Schwimmerin swimmer IV U4, 78
Science-Fiction science fiction I
Scone *(eine Art süßes Brötchen)* scone II
sechs six I
sechzehn sixteen I
sechzig sixty I
See lake III
Seeräuber pirate I
Seeräuberin pirate I
segeln to sail IV U4, 85
sehen to see I; to look II
Sehenswürdigkeit sight II
sehr very I; a lot II; badly III; extremely IV U4, 80
so sehr so much III
zu sehr too much II
Seide silk III
Seife soap III

Seil rope I
Seilrutsche zip line III
sein to be I
erfüllt sein von ... to be alive with ... IV U5, 97
sein his I; its III
seit for IV U4, 80; since IV U4, 80
seitdem since IV U4, 80
Seite page; side I
Seite *(im Internet)* site IV U4, 80
Sekunde second II
selber myself; ourselves; yourselves; themselves III
selbst myself; self III
dich selbst yourself II
er selbst himself III
ihr/euch/Sie/sich (selbst) yourselves III
sie selbst herself; themselves III
selbstbewusst confident III
selbstsicher confident; sure of oneself III
selbstsüchtig selfish IV U2, 39
selbstverständlich of course I
Selfie *(Schnappschuss von sich selbst)* selfie IV U4, 83
seltsam strange; funny II
senden to send I
Sendung programme I
Senf mustard II
separat separate IV U5, 106
September September I
servieren to serve IV U2, 33
Serviette napkin II
setzen to put I
Setz dich. Have a seat. IV U3, 54
Setzen Sie sich. Have a seat. IV U3, 54
Shampoo shampoo III
Shirt shirt I
Shorts shorts *(pl)* I
Show show I
Showbusiness show-business IV U4, 75
Showgeschäft show-business IV U4, 75
sich each other; self III
sich gegenseitig each other III
sich kümmern (um) to care (for) III
sicher sure I; safe III
Sicherheit safety IV U4, 75
in Sicherheit safe III
Sicherheitsnetz safety net IV U4, 75
Sicht view IV U1, 14
Sie you I
sie her; she I
sie *(Pl.)* they; them I
sieben seven I
siebzehn seventeen I
siebzig seventy I
Siedler settler IV U2, 32
Siedlerin settler IV U2, 32
siegen to win I
Sieger winner I
Siegerin winner I
Signal signal III
singen to sing I
sinken to sink III
sinnlos pointless IV U4, 77
Sitte custom IV U5, 97
Situation situation II
Sitz seat III
Sitzbank bench III
sitzen to sit I
Sitzplatz seat IV U5, 102
Skateboard skateboard III
Ski fahren to ski II
Skifahren skiing III
Sklave slave IV U4, 86
Sklavin slave IV U4, 86
Skyline skyline IV U1, 12
Slogan slogan IV U4, 77
Smartphone smartphone IV U4, 80
SMS message; text message II
eine SMS schreiben to text II
SMS-Schreiber texter II
SMS-Schreiberin texter II
Snack snack I
so like this I; so II
so dass so that IV U2, 34
so sehr so much III
so ... wie as ... as II
sobald as soon as IV U4, 89
Socke sock I
soeben just II
Sofa sofa II
sofort right away IV U4, 80
Software software II
sogar even II
Sohn son III
Sojabohne soy bean IV ZI, 9
solar solar III
Solar- solar III
solch such IV U2, 38
Soldat soldier III
Soldatin soldier III
sollte should III
Sommer summer II
Sonderangebot special offer III
Sonne sun III
Sonnen- solar III
sonnenbaden to sunbathe II
Sonnenbrille sunglasses *(pl)* II
sonnig sunny I
Sonntag Sunday I
sich **Sorgen** machen to worry I
dafür **sorgen** to make sure III
für jmdn. **sorgen** to take care of sb IV U2, 41
sorgfältig careful II
Sorte sort II; type; kind III
sortieren to sort IV U2, 38
Soße sauce II
Souvenir souvenir III
Souvenirladen souvenir shop III
soweit as far as IV U3, 59
sowohl ... als auch ... both ... and ... IV U5, 97
soziale Medien social media IV U4, 80
Sozialkunde Social Studies I
Spaghetti spaghetti II
spanisch Spanish IV U5, 98
Spanisch Spanish IV U5, 98
spannend exciting I
sparen to save IV U1, 22
Spaß fun I
Spaß haben to enjoy oneself III
zum Spaß for fun III
(zu) **spät** late I
später later I; after III
den Hund **spazieren** führen to take the dog for a walk II
Spaziergang walk III
speichern to save II

Speise dish II
Speisekarte menu II
spektakulär spectacular III
sperren to ban IV U5, 99
speziell special I
Spiegel mirror III
Spiel match; game I
spielen to play I; to act II
Spieler player II; gamer II
Spielerin player II; gamer II
Spielfeld court III
Spielkarte card I
Spielplatz playground I
Spielzeug toy III
Spind locker IV U2, 34
Spinne spider III
Spinnennetz web III
Spitze top IV U1, 13
an der Spitze (von) at the front of II
spitze awesome IV U2, 34
Spitzname nickname IV U1, 12
Sport sport I
Sportart sport III
Sportgeschäft sports shop I
Sportunterricht PE (Physical Education) I
sprachbehindert speech impaired IV U5, 102
Sprache language II; speech III
sprechen to say I; to speak II
sprechen (mit) to talk (to) I
sprechen über to talk about II
springen to jump IV U3, 63
Spritze injection III
spülen to wash III
Spülmaschine dishwasher IV U3, 59
Spur clue I; trail IV U5, 102
Staat state IV ZI, 8
Staatsangehörige citizen IV U1, 18
Staatsangehöriger citizen IV U1, 18
Staatsbürger citizen IV U1, 18
Staatsbürgerin citizen IV U1, 18
Stadion stadium II
Stadt town I; city II
Stadtmitte city centre III
Stadtplan map III
Stadtteil borough IV U1, 12
Stadtzentrum city centre III
im Stadtzentrum downtown *(AE)* IV U1, 14
Stahl steel III
Stand cart IV U1, 14
auf den neuesten Stand bringen to update IV U4, 81
Standinhaber stallholder II
Standinhaberin stallholder II
Star star I
stark heavy II; powerful IV U1, 22
Stärke strength IV U2, 39
starren to stare III
Start start III
starten to start II
Statistik statistics *(no pl)* IV U1, 22
stattdessen instead IV U2, 34
Status status IV U4, 81
Stau traffic jam IV U1, 14
Staub wischen to dust IV U2, 38
staubsaugen to hoover II
Staubsauger vacuum cleaner IV U3, 59
stecken bleiben to get stuck IV U3, 54
stehen to suit; to stand II
stehlen to steal IV U2, 38
steigen to climb III; to step IV U4, 86
Stein brick II; rock; stone III
Stelle place I; space IV U1, 22
stellen to put I
online stellen to post IV U4, 80
sich stellen to confront IV U5, 98
Stellenbezeichnung job title IV U2, 38
sterben to die III
Stern star III
Sternzeichen star sign IV U1, 14
Steuerung control IV U3, 53
sticheln to tease IV U2, 38
Stiefel boot II
Stift pen I
Stil style III
still quiet III
still werden to go quiet III
Stille silence III
Stimme voice III
stimmt's? isn't it? II
Stimmung spirit IV U4, 85
stinkend smelly IV U3, 63
Stock stick II; story *(AE)* IV U1, 14
Stockwerk floor II; story *(AE)* IV U1, 14
Stoff material III
Stolz pride IV U5, 98
stolz (auf) proud (of) III
stören to bother IV U5, 107
störrisch stubborn IV U2, 39
(sich) **stoßen** to hit III
strahlend bright IV ZI, 8
Strand beach I
den Strand nach Strandgut absuchen to go beach combing II
Straße road I; street III
Straßenbahn tram III
Straßenbauarbeiten roadwork IV U1, 14
streamen *(im Internet)* to stream IV U4, 80
Strecke track IV U5, 102
sich **strecken** to stretch IV U3, 52
Streich trick I
streichen to paint IV U4, 75
Streit argument II; fight III
(sich) **streiten** to fight III
streng strict IV U2, 34
Stress stress IV U3, 57
strikt strict IV U2, 34
Strom electricity III
Struktur structure III
Stück piece II
pro Stück each II
Student student I
Studentin student I
studieren to study IV U2, 34
Studio studio IV U4, 75
Stufe step II
Stuhl chair I
stumm silent III
Stunde hour I; period IV U2, 34
erste Stunde *(in der Schule)* homeroom IV U2, 45
40 Kilometer pro Stunde 40 kilometres an hour I
Stundenplan timetable I; schedule *(AE)* IV U2, 33
Stuntman stuntman IV U3, 53
Sturm storm IV U2, 32
suchen to search IV U1, 22
suchen nach to look for II

Süden south III
im Süden von in the south of III
südlich southern IV U5, 96
südlich von south of IV ZI, 9
Südstaatler Southerner IV U5, 97
Südstaatlerin Southerner IV U5, 97
Südwesten southwest III
Sumpf swamp IV ZI, 9
super cool I; super; way to go II; awesome IV U2, 34
Superheld superhero IV U3, 61
Supermarkt supermarket II
Suppe soup II
Surfen surfing III
surfen to surf II
im Internet surfen to surf the internet II
Surfer surfer IV ZI, 9
Surferin surfer IV ZI, 9
Sushi sushi IV U5, 99
süß sweet III; cute I
Süßes, sonst gibt's Saures! Trick or treat! I
Süßigkeit sweet I
Sweatshirt sweatshirt I
Symbol symbol IV U1, 13
System system IV U5, 107
Szene scene II

T

Tablet tablet IV U3, 58
Tablett tray II
Tablette tablet II
Tafel board I
Tafel Schokolade bar of chocolate I
Tag day I
ein freier Tag a day off III
eines Tages one day III
den ganzen Tag all day III
ein ausgefüllter Tag a busy day I
Tagebuch diary I
täglich daily IV U4, 80
vier Stunden täglich four hours a day I
Taktik tactic III
Talent talent I
talentiert talented III
Talentwettbewerb talent show I
Tante aunt II
Tanz dance III
Tanz- dancing IV U2, 43
Tanzen dancing IV U2, 43
tanzen to dance I
Tänzer dancer III
Tänzerin dancer III
Tanzveranstaltung dance IV U2, 33
tapfer brave III
Tapferkeit courage IV U5, 107
Tasche bag I; pocket II
Taschengeld allowance *(AE)* IV U2, 38
Taschenlampe torch I
Taschenrechner calculator I
Taschentuch tissue III
Tasse cup II
Tätigkeit job II
tatkräftig energetic IV U4, 89
Tatsache fact II
tatsächlich actually; in fact III
taub deaf III
tausend a/one thousand II
Taxi taxi II
Team team I; squad IV U2, 34
Teamwork teamwork II
Technik Design Technology (DT) I
Techniker engineer II
Technikerin engineer II
Tee tea I
Teelöffel *(TL)* teaspoon *(tsp)* II
Teenager teen II; teenager III
Teil part II
oberer Teil top III
unterer Teil bottom III
teilen to share III
teilnehmen (an) to take part (in) II
Telefon phone II; telephone III
ans Telefon gehen to answer the phone III
Telefonanruf phone call I
telefonieren to phone II
Telefonnummer phone number III
Telefonzelle telephone box II
Teller plate II
Tennis tennis I
Teppich carpet I
Test test I
testen to test II
teuer expensive II
Text lines *(pl)*; text II
Theater theatre; drama II
Theaterstück play II
Thema topic IV U2, 51
Themenpark theme park II
Thunfisch tuna II
tief deep IV U5, 102
Tier animal I
Tierarzt vet III
Tierärztin vet III
Tierhandlung pet shop III
Tierheim animal rescue shelter I
Tierpark zoo I
Tierpfleger zookeeper I
Tierpflegerin zookeeper I
Tierwelt *(in freier Wildbahn)* wildlife IV U5, 102
Tiger tiger I
Tipp tip II
Tisch table I
den Tisch decken to lay the table II
Tischler carpenter II
Tischlerin carpenter II
Tischtennis table tennis II
Toast toast II
Tochter daughter I
tod- deadly III
tödlich deadly III
Toilette toilet I; bathroom *(AE)* IV U2, 34; restroom *(AE)* IV U2, 41
tolerieren to tolerate IV U5, 98
toll great; brilliant I; amazing II
Tomate tomato II
Ton sound III
Tonne tonne II; barrel IV U3, 53
Tonne *(Gewicht)* ton IV U4, 80
Tonstudio recording studio I
Top top II
Topf pot III
Tor gate III; gateway IV U1, 12
Tornado tornado IV U2, 32
tot dead III
töten to kill III

Tötung killing IV U5, 98
Tour tour IV U4, 76
Tourismus tourism IV U1, 18
Tourist tourist I
Touristin tourist I
Touristeninformation Tourist Information Centre I
Tradition tradition III
traditionell traditional III
tragbar mobile IV U4, 80
tragen to carry II
tragen *(Kleidung)* to wear I
Trainer trainer IV U5, 103
Trainerin trainer IV U5, 103
trainieren to practise III
Training practice I; training III
Traktor tractor I
Transfer transfer IV U5, 102
transkontinental *(über den Kontinent hinweg)* transcontinental IV U4, 86
Transport transfer IV U5, 102
Transporter van III
Tratsch gossip IV U3, 58
Traum dream I
träumen to dream III
traurig sad III
treffen to meet I; to hit II
Freunde treffen to see friends I
sich treffen (mit) to hang out (with) IV U3, 58
treiben to drive IV U2, 33
Trend trend IV U4, 80
trendsetzend trending IV U4, 81
trendy trendy IV U4, 81
Trennung segregation IV U5, 106
Treppe stairs *(pl)* II
treten to kick III; to step IV U4, 86
treu true IV U2, 34
Treue allegiance IV U2, 34
Treueeid pledge of allegiance IV U2, 34
Trick trick I
trinken to drink II
Trinkhalm straw II
Trip trip III
trocken dry III
trocknen to dry IV U5, 98
Trommel- drumming III
Trottel pinhead IV U2, 38
trotzdem anyway III
Truthahn turkey IV U3, 53
Tschüss. See you later.; Bye.; See you. I
T-Shirt T-shirt I
Tuch scarf I
tun to do; to make I
Tut mir leid. Sorry. I
Tunnel tunnel III
Tür door I
Türkisch Turkish IV U5, 99
türkisch Turkish IV U5, 99
Türklingel doorbell IV U3, 54
Turm tower II
Turnhalle gym(nasium) IV U2, 42
turnieren to joust III
Turnierzweikampf jousting III
Turnschuh trainer I
Tüte bag; packet I
Tutorial tutorial IV U4, 80
Typ type III; guy IV U2, 42

U

U-Bahn underground II; subway *(AE)* IV U1, 14
U-Boot submarine I
Übelkeit verspüren to feel sick IV U5, 103
übelnehmen to resent IV U5, 99
übelriechend smelly IV U3, 63
üben to practise III
über about I; over; across III
über die Grenze gehen to cross the border IV U1, 19
überall all over I
überall wo(hin) wherever III
Überfahrt crossing IV U1, 22
überfüllt crowded IV U1, 22
sich **übergeben** to be sick I; to puke IV U3, 62
überhaupt nicht not at all II
überleben to survive III
überlegen to guess II
übernachten to stay II
Übernachtung sleepover I
überprüfen to check III
Überprüfung inspection IV U1, 22
Überprüfung der Anwesenheit registration I
überqueren to cross III
Überquerung crossing IV U1, 22
überrascht surprised II
Überraschung surprise I
die Grenze **überschreiten** to cross the border IV U1, 19
Überschrift headline IV U4, 77
übersetzen to translate IV U5, 102
überzeugend convincing III
überzeugt convinced IV U3, 59
üblich regular IV U4, 89
übrig left III
Übung exercise; practice I
Übungsheft exercise book I
Uhr clock II
Uhr *(Zeitangabe bei vollen Stunden)* o'clock I
Uhrenturm clock tower II
Uhrzeit time I
um at I
um … herum around IV U1, 14
(sich) **umdrehen** to turn around III
umfallen to fall (over) III
Umfrage survey II
umgehen (mit) to deal (with) IV U3, 73
umher around I
umrühren to stir II
umsteigen to change III
umziehen to move (house) II
Umzug parade III
Unabhängigkeit independence IV U1, 13; freedom *(no pl)* IV U1, 23
unangenehm uncomfortable II; unpleasant IV U1, 22
unbeliebt unpopular III
unbequem uncomfortable II
und and I
unerfreulich unpleasant IV U1, 22
unfair unfair III
Unfall accident III
unfreundlich unfriendly III
ungefähr about II
ungefähr um around III
Ungeheuer monster III

ungeordnet disorganized IV U2, 39
ungerecht unjust IV U5, 106
ungewöhnlich unusual IV U4, 77
unglaublich amazing II
Unglück disaster III
unglücklich unhappy II
unhöflich rude IV U2, 39
Uniform uniform I
uninteressant unappealing IV U4, 77
Universität university III; college *(AE)* IV U5, 101
unmodisch unfashionable II
unmöglich impossible; not possibly III
unmotiviert unmotivated IV U2, 39
Unordnung mess I
unorganisiert disorganized IV U2, 39
unpopulär unpopular III
unrecht haben to be wrong III
uns us I
unschuldig innocent IV U3, 63
unser our I
unsere our I; ours III
unten at the bottom III
  da unten down there IV U5, 98
unter under I; among III
unterbrechen to interrupt IV U4, 94
untere lower III
  unterer Teil bottom III
Untergang sinking III
untergehen to sink III
Unterhaltsgeld allowance *(AE)* IV U2, 38
Unterhaltung conversation III
Unterhaltungsindustrie show-business IV U4, 75
Unterricht class; lesson I
unterrichten to teach III
Unterrichtsstunde class; period IV U2, 34
unterschiedlich different I
unterschreiben to sign IV U3, 53
unterstützen to support IV U5, 100
Unterstützung support IV U1, 19
unterwegs on the way; out and about I
in der **Unterzahl** outnumbered IV U5, 102
unterzeichnen to sign IV U3, 53
unverschämt rude IV U2, 39
updaten to update IV U4, 81
Ureinwohner Amerikas Native American IV U1, 16
Ureinwohnerin Amerikas Native American IV U1, 16
Urgroßeltern great-grandparents IV U1, 25
Urlaub holiday I; vacation *(AE)* IV U5, 104
ursprünglich original IV U3, 54
Ururopa great-great-grandad I
US-amerikanisch US IV U1, 18

V

Vanillesauce custard II
Vater father I
Veganismus veganism *(no pl)* IV U4, 83
Vegetarier vegetarian I
Vegetarierin vegetarian I
Ventilator fan IV U3, 59
sich mit jmdm. **verabreden** to ask sb out IV U2, 42
Verabredung date IV U2, 42
veraltet outdated IV U4, 81
verändern to change III
veranschaulichen to bring life IV U1, 22
Veranstaltung event IV U1, 13
verantwortlich responsible IV U2, 38
verantwortungsvoll responsible IV U2, 38
verärgert angry II; annoyed III
Verband bandage III
verbannen to ban IV U5, 99
verbessern to correct I
verbieten to ban IV U5, 99
verbinden to attach; to connect III; to link IV U5, 107
Verbindung link IV U4, 80
  in Verbindung bleiben to keep in touch II
verblüfft amazed IV U3, 53
verboten forbidden IV U3, 58
verbrennen to burn down II; to burn III
verbringen *(Zeit)* to spend II
verdienen to deserve IV U4, 80
verdrehen to twist II
Verein club II
Vereinsheim clubhouse IV U3, 62
Verfasser writer III
Verfasserin writer III
Verfolger chaser IV U2, 33
Verfolgerin chaser IV U2, 33
Vergangenheit past III
vergessen to forget I
vergleichen to compare I
vergnügt amused IV U3, 63
vergrößern to increase IV U4, 84
verhaften to arrest IV U5, 107
Verhalten behavior *(AE)* IV U2, 38
sich **verhalten** to behave IV U2, 38
Verhandlung case IV U5, 98
sich **verirren** to get lost I
verkaufen to sell III
Verkäufer shop assistant II; assistant III; sales associate *(AE)* IV U2, 38
Verkäuferin shop assistant II; assistant III; sales associate *(AE)* IV U2, 38
Verkehr traffic III
Verkehrs- transport IV U4, 86
öffentliche **Verkehrsmittel** public transport III
verkleidet dressed III
Verkleidung fancy dress I
verlassen to leave II
verlässlich reliable IV U5, 109
verlegen embarrassed II
verletzen to hurt II
verletzt hurt II
Verletzung injury III
sich **verlieben** (in) to fall in love (with) III
verlieren to lose II
vermeiden to avoid IV U3, 62
vermischen to mix IV U5, 98
vermissen to miss II
Vermittlung operator III
Vermögen fortune IV U4, 85

vermuten to guess IV U3, 58
vernünftig intelligent III
veröffentlichen to release IV U5, 97
verpassen to miss II
verrenken to sprain III
verrückt crazy I
jmdn. verrückt machen to drive sb crazy III
versagen (in/bei) to fail (at) IV U1, 19
verschieden separate IV U5, 106
verschiedene several IV U4, 80
verschwenden to waste IV U2, 38
verschwinden to disappear IV U3, 62
sich **versichern** to make sure III
versprechen to promise IV U2, 34
sich **verständigen** to communicate IV U4, 80
verstauchen to sprain III
(sich) **verstecken** to hide III
verstehen to understand II; to get III; to know IV U5, 103
etw. verstehen to get sth IV U5, 102
Versuch experiment II
versuchen to try II
vertrauen to trust IV U5, 109
vertrauenswürdig reliable IV U5, 109
vertraut familiar IV U2, 34
verübeln to resent IV U5, 99
verursachen to cause IV U4, 86
vervollständigen to complete I; to finish II
verwenden to use II
verwirrt confused III
verzeihen to pardon IV U3, 53
Verzeihung pardon IV U3, 67
verzerren to twist II
auf etw. **verzichten** to give sth a miss III
verzweifelt desperately IV U4, 85
Vesper packed lunch II
Video video IV U3, 54
Video-Chat video chat III
viel a lot; much; lots of I; lots III; a lot of I
viel Glück good luck II
viele many II
Viele Grüße, Best wishes, I
Vielen Dank. Thanks so much. IV U4, 94
wie viele how many II
vielleicht maybe I; may II
vier four I
vierte fourth I
Viertel nach quarter past I
Viertel vor quarter to I
vierzehn fourteen I
vierzig forty I
Vietnamese Vietnamese IV U5, 98
Vietnamesin Vietnamese IV U5, 98
vietnamesisch Vietnamese IV U5, 98
Vietnamesisch Vietnamese IV U5, 98
viktorianisches Zeitalter Victorian era III
violett purple I
Vogel bird I
Vogelbeobachtung bird watching III
Vokabular vocabulary II
voll full III
Volleyball volleyball IV U4, 74
völlig completely III; absolutely IV U3, 59
vollkommen perfect IV ZI, 9
vollständig complete IV U5, 106
von from; of I; by II
von hinten from behind I
von ... weg off IV U5, 107
vor ago; in front of II; ahead of IV U1, 22; before IV U3, 61
vor allem especially IV U1, 13
vor ... wimmeln to be alive with ... IV U5, 97
vor *(bei Uhrzeitangaben)* to I
vorangehen to go ahead IV U1, 18
vorbei over IV U1, 22
vorbei (an) past III
vorbeigehen to pass IV U4, 85
(sich) **vorbereiten** to prepare III
sich vorbereiten to get ready IV U3, 54
Vordergrund foreground III
im Vordergrund in the foreground III
Vorgehensweise tactic III
vorhaben to be up to III
vorher before II
vorhersagen to foretell III
Vormittag morning I
vormittags *(Uhrzeit)* a.m. II
Vorort suburb IV U1, 15
Vorrichtung device IV U3, 58
vorsichtig careful II; cautious; guarded III
Sei vorsichtig! Be careful! I
Vorsingen audition II
Vorspeise starter II
Vorspielen audition II
Vorsprechen audition II
vorstellen to present I; to introduce III
sich (etw.) vorstellen to imagine (sth) IV U4, 85
Vorstellungsgespräch interview IV U2, 38
Vortanzen audition II
Vortrag presentation IV U2, 51
vorziehen to prefer II

W

wach awake III
wachsen to grow IV U3, 58
Wagen truck III
Waggon wagon IV U4, 85
Wahl option IV U2, 34; choice IV U5, 102
wählen to choose II; to vote for IV U2, 33
Wahlfach elective IV U2, 34
Wahnsinnsspaß blast IV U2, 34
wahr true II
wahr werden to come true IV U1, 18
während while II; during III
wahrnehmen to notice III
wahrscheinlich probably III
Währung currency IV ZI, 8
Wahrzeichen landmark IV U1, 14
Wal whale IV U3, 52
Walbeobachtung whale watching IV U3, 52
Wald wood III; forest IV U3, 53
Waliser Welsh III
Waliserin Welsh III
Walisisch Welsh III

walisisch Welsh III
Wand wall II
Wandern hiking; walking III
wandern to hike II
Wanderweg trail IV U5, 102
Wandgemälde mural III
wann when I
Waren goods *(no pl)* IV U1, 18
warm warm I
warnen to warn III
warten to wait II
warten auf to wait for II
Warteschlange queue II
warum why I
was what I
Was?! No way! III
Was für ein/eine ... What a ... I
Was hast du (in letzter Zeit) gemacht? What have you been up to? IV U3, 55
Was ist los? What's wrong? II
Was ist mit ...? What about ...? I
Was man ... What to ... II
was noch what else III
was sonst what else III
Was stimmt nicht? What's wrong? II
Waschbär raccoon I
(sich) **waschen** to wash III
Wäschetrockner dryer IV U3, 58
Wasser water I
Eimer Wasser bucket of water I
Website website II
Wechselgeld change II
wechseln to change II
Wecker alarm clock I
Weg way III; alley IV U2, 32; lane IV U4, 75
auf dem Weg on the way I
aus dem Weg gehen to avoid IV U3, 62
weg away II
nicht weg können to be stuck I
wegen because of III
weglaufen to run away III
weh tun to hurt II
Weide field IV ZI, 9
sich **weigern** to refuse IV U5, 107
Weihnachten Christmas I
Weihnachtstheaterstück pantomime II
weil because I
eine **Weile** a while IV U2, 34
Wein wine IV U3, 62
Art und **Weise** way III
auf diese **Weise** like this I
weiß white I
Weißkopfseeadler bald eagle IV ZI, 8
weit far III
weitere other I
weitergehen to keep going IV U4, 85
weitermachen to keep going IV U4, 85; to continue IV U4, 86
welche which; what; who II
Welle wave IV ZI, 9
Wellenreiten surfing III
wellenreiten to surf II
Wellenreiter surfer IV ZI, 9
Wellenreiterin surfer IV ZI, 9
Welt world II
auf der Welt in the world II
in aller Welt all around the world III
weltberühmt best known IV U2, 32
wem whom III
wen whom III
in Mehl **wenden** to cover in flour IV U5, 98
wenig little IV U1, 22
ein wenig a bit II
wenige a few III; few IV U3, 53
weniger less III
wenigstens at least III
wenn when; if II
wer who I
Werbespot ad(vert); advertisement II
Werbespruch slogan IV U4, 77
werden to get I; will; to become II
genannt werden to be called II
nicht werden won't (= will not) II
wahr werden to come true IV U1, 18
werfen to throw IV U2, 38
Werft shipyard III
Werk factory III
an **Werktagen** on weekdays III
Werkzeug tool II
wert sein to be worth III
Westen west III
westlich von west of IV ZI, 9
Wettbewerb show I; competition II
wetten (auf) to bet III
Wetter weather I
wettkampforientiert competitive III
wichtig important II; major IV ZI, 8
wichtig nehmen to care about IV U3, 58
wie like I; how I; as II; what III
Wie alt bist du? How old are you? I
Wie bitte? Pardon? I
Wie geht es dir? How are you? I
Wie geht's? What's up?; How's it going? IV U3, 54
Wie geht's dir? How are you doing? IV U3, 55
Wie heißt du? What's your name? I
Wie läuft's? How's it going? IV U3, 54
Wie läuft's bei dir? What have you been up to? IV U3, 55
Wie man ... How to ... II
wie sehr how much III
Wie spät ist es? What time is it? I
Wie viel (kostet/kosten) ...? How much (is/are) ...? I
Wie viel Uhr ist es? What time is it? I
wie viele how many II
Wie wäre es mit ...? How about ...? II
so ... wie as ... as II
wieder again II
wiederholen to repeat III
Auf **Wiedersehen**. Goodbye. I
wiegen to weigh II
Wiese field IV ZI, 9
Wikinger- Viking III
wild wild III
freie **Wildbahn** the wild IV U5, 102
Wildnis wilderness IV U4, 85; the wild IV U5, 102
willkommen (bei/in) welcome (to) I
willkommen heißen to welcome IV U4, 80

vor … **wimmeln** to be alive with … IV U5, 97
Wind wind I
windig windy I
Windpark wind farm III
Windrad (wind) turbine III
winken to wave II
Winter winter I
winzig tiny III
wir we; us I
Wirbelsturm tornado IV U2, 32
wirklich really I; real II; actually III
wirr confused III
Staub **wischen** to dust IV U2, 38
wissen to know I
Ich weiß (es) nicht! I don't know! I
Wissenschaft Science I
Witz joke I
Witze machen to joke III
witzig funny I
wo where I
wo(hin) auch immer wherever III
Woche week I
unter der Woche on weekdays III
Wochenende weekend I
am Wochenende at the weekend I
wöchentlich weekly III
woher where I
Woher kommst du? Where are you from? I
wohin where I
wohnen to live I
Wohnung flat I
Wohnwagen caravan III
Wohnzimmer living room I
Wolke cloud IV U2, 33
Wolkenkratzer skyscraper IV U1, 14
wolkig cloudy I
Wolldecke blanket IV U3, 62
Wolle wool I
wollen to want (to) I
Workshop workshop II
Wort word IV U1, 22
Wortschatz vocabulary II
Wrap wrap II
wund sore II
wunderbar wonderful III
wünschen to wish III
würde(n) would II
würde(n) gern would like II
Ich würde gerne … I'd like (to) … (= I would like to) I
Ich würde nicht gerne … I wouldn't like (to) … I
würdigen to appreciate IV U5, 99
Wurst sausage II
Wurzel root IV U5, 97
würzig spicy II
wütend angry II; furious III

Z

Zahl number I
zählen to count IV U1, 18
Zahn tooth III
Zahnbürste toothbrush III
Zahnpasta toothpaste III
Zahnstocher toothpick II
Zauber glamor *(AE)* IV U4, 75
Zauber- magic II
Zauberei magic II
Zauberer magician IV U3, 63
Zauberin magician IV U3, 63
Zebra zebra I
zehn ten I
Zeichen sign; signal III
Zeichensprache sign language III
zeichnen to draw II
zeigen to show II; to point out IV U1, 15
Zeile line II
Zeit time I
die ganze Zeit all the time III
viktorianisches **Zeitalter** Victorian era III
Zeitreise time travel III
Zeitschrift magazine I
Zeitschriftenladen newsagent's III
Zeitung newspaper II
Zeitungsausträger paperboy IV U2, 41
Zeitungsausträgerin papergirl IV U2, 41
Zeitzone time zone IV ZI, 8
Zelt tent II
Zelten camping III
zelten to go camping II
Zeltplatz campsite III
Zentimeter (cm) centimetre (cm) I
Zentrum centre III; center *(AE)* IV U1, 13
zerbrechen to break II
zerreißen to tear (up) IV U2, 33
zerrissen torn IV U4, 83
zerstören to ruin II
Zeug stuff IV U2, 34
Zeuge witness IV U5, 107
Zeugin witness IV U5, 107
Ziege goat III
Ziegelstein brick II
ziehen to pull I; to grow IV U3, 58; to drag IV U5, 107
Ziel ambition III; destination IV U5, 96
ziemlich quite III; pretty IV U2, 34
Zimmer room I
Zimmerdecke ceiling IV U1, 14
Zimmerin carpenter II
Zimmermann carpenter II
Zitrone lemon II
Zoo zoo I
zornig angry II
zu to I; too II
auf … zu towards IV U3, 62
zu Fuß on foot I
zu Hause at home I; back home II
zu sehr too much II
zubereiten to prepare III
zubinden to tie IV U3, 62
züchten to grow IV U3, 58
Zucker sugar I
zuerst first I; at first IV U4, 84
Zug train I
Zuhause home I
zuhören to listen (to) I
Zuhörer listener II
Zuhörerin listener II
Zukunft future III
zuletzt finally IV U4, 85
zum Schluss finally II
zum Spaß for fun III
zumachen to close I
zunächst for a start III; at first IV U4, 84
zunehmen to increase IV U4, 84
zuordnen to match I

V

zurück back I
zurückgeben to return IV U1, 22
zurückhaltend guarded III
zurückkehren to return IV U1, 22
zurückweisen to reject IV U5, 99
zurückzahlen to pay back II
zusammen together I, everyone II
zusammenfassen to sum up IV U3, 73
zusammenfinden to get together IV U3, 52
zusammenkommen to get together IV U3, 52
zusammenrollen to roll up IV U3, 62
zusammenzucken to jump III
Zusatz- extra II
zusätzlich extra II
zuschauen to watch II
Zustand condition; state IV U1, 22
zustimmen to agree II
Zutat ingredient II
zuverlässig reliable IV U5, 109
zuvor before II
Zuwanderung immigration IV U1, 22
zwanzig twenty I
zwei two I
zweimal twice IV U2, 38
zweite second I
zweitens second IV U2, 51
Zwiebel onion II
zwingen to force IV U2, 32
zwischen between II
zwölf twelve I

Lösungen

Lösungen Mediation

1. It said that the United States is free (from Great Britain).
2. President …
3. November
4. political, religious, economic reasons
5. Africans; people from Africa
6. New Hampshire, Massachusetts, Rhode Island, Connecticut, New York, New Jersey, Pennsylvania, Delaware, Maryland, Virginia, North Carolina, South Carolina, Georgia
7. Cherokee, Navajo, Sioux, Chippewa, Choctaw, Pueblo, Apache, Iroquois, Creek, Blackfeet, Seminole, Cheyenne, Arawak, Shawnee, Mohegan, Huron, Oneida, Lakota, Crow, Teton, Hopi, Inuit
8. Pacific (Ocean)
9. because there are 50 states
10. New Year's Day, Martin Luther King, Jr. Day, Presidents' Day, Memorial Day, Independence Day, Labor Day, Columbus Day, Veterans Day, Thanksgiving, Christmas

Lösungen Grammatik – TEST YOURSELF

G1
1. had
2. liked
3. did not / didn't take
4. did … do
5. Were
6. was not / wasn't

G2
1. had left
2. had not / hadn't done
3. had … started
4. had … done
5. had lived
6. had not / hadn't seen

G3
1. could not / couldn't / was not allowed to / wasn't allowed to
2. had to
3. could / was able to / was allowed to
4. did not / didn't have to
5. could / were allowed to
6. could not / couldn't / was not able to / wasn't able to

G4
1. need; will / 'll help
2. do not / don't phone; will / 'll be
3. does not / doesn't come; will / 'll lose
4. will not / won't find; does not / doesn't read
5. will / 'll talk; meet
6. will not / won't sleep; read

G5
1. ones
2. one
3. ones
4. ones
5. one
6. one

G6
1. aren't you?
2. isn't it?
3. weren't you?
4. don't you?
5. didn't you?
6. does he?

G7
1. Do
2. does
3. will
4. Did
5. –
6. did

G8
1. visited; would be
2. had; would not / wouldn't meet
3. was / were; would like
4. would … miss; did not / didn't come
5. would not / wouldn't worry; lived
6. would be; did not / didn't phone

G9
1. goes
2. is not / isn't surfing
3. Are … listening
4. do not / don't like
5. do … do
6. meet

G10
1. fast; slowly
2. well; easily
3. pretty
4. good; hard
5. heavily
6. unhappy

G11
1. has … met
2. have not / haven't seen
3. has … not called / hasn't … called
4. Have … forgotten
5. have not / haven't been
6. Have … watched

G12
1. was introduced
2. is made
3. are not / aren't cooked
4. were founded
5. is celebrated
6. was not / wasn't built

G13
1. Anna says (that) they prefer the Everglades.
2. She says (that) she wants to go on a boat tour.
3. She says (that) she doesn't like all those crowds.
4. She says (that) she doesn't want to feed the alligators.
5. She asks Ethan if he knows Florida.
6. She asks Ethan what he thinks.

G14
1. Al Lane said (that) he often worked with the alligators.
2. He said (that) some tourists didn't like alligators.
3. He said (that) they fed the animals at 10 o'clock.
4. He said (that) it was too late to feed the alligators.
5. He said (that) he didn't speak German.
6. He said (that) the visitors loved the warm weather.

Bildquellennachweis

Cover.1 plainpicture GmbH & Co. KG (BHarman), Hamburg; **Cover.2** Getty Images (Derek Von Briesen), München; **2.1** Getty Images (Photolibrary/Maremagnum), München; **3.1** Alamy Stock Photo (World History Archive), Abingdon, Oxon; **3.2** plainpicture GmbH & Co. KG (Michael Runkel), Hamburg; **4.1** Getty Images (Lonely Planet/jean pierre lescourret), München; **5.1** Getty Images (Stockbyte), München; **5.2** Getty Images (Daniel Zuchnik), München; **8.7** Getty Images (The Image Bank), München; **8.6** Getty Images (Corbis), München; **8.3** Getty Images (Perspectives), München; **8.4** Getty Images (First Light), München; **8.5** Getty Images (National Geographic Magazines), München; **8.8** plainpicture GmbH & Co. KG (Ableimages/David Harrigan), Hamburg; **8.1** Getty Images (Iconica), München; **8.2** Getty Images (E+/Ron Thomas), München; **8.9** plainpicture GmbH & Co. KG (Aurora Photos/Josh Miller), Hamburg; **10.6** Getty Images (The Image Bank), München; **10.12** Getty Images (Lonely Planet), München; **10.3** Getty Images (Bettmann), München; **10.11** Getty Images (Lonely Planet), München; **10.13** Getty Images (Universal Images Group), München; **10.1** Getty Images (DigitalGlobe), München; **10.2** Getty Images (The Image Bank), München; **10.9** Getty Images (Tim Fitzharris), München; **10.10** By Orlando Scott Goff, Bismarck, Dakota Territory - Heritage Auctions, Public Domain, https://commons.wikimedia.org/w/index.php?curid=27530348; **10.14** Getty Images (Science Source), München; **10.15** Getty Images (Photodisc), München; **10.16** Getty Images (Alan Copson), München; **10.17** Getty Images (David Sucsy), München; **10.4** plainpicture GmbH & Co. KG (Fancy Images/Whisson/Jordan), Hamburg; **10.5** By John Dunlap, text by Thomas Jefferson et al. - http://lcweb2.loc.gov/cgi-bin/ampage?collId=rbc3&fileName=rbc0001_2004pe76546page.db, Public Domain, https://commons.wikimedia.org/w/index.php?curid=33408334; **10.7** plainpicture GmbH & Co. KG (Image Source/Gu), Hamburg; **10.8** Getty Images (Corbis Documentary), München; **10.18** Getty Images (Cameron Davidson), München; **12.1** Getty Images (Photolibrary/Maremagnum), München; **12.2** plainpicture GmbH & Co. KG (Gine Seitz), Hamburg; **13.1** Avenue Images GmbH (ponton), Hamburg; **13.2** Getty Images (Lonely Planet/Michael Marquand), München; **13.3** Getty Images (Moment/© 2014 Noppon Umnajwannaphan), München; **14.2** Alamy Stock Photo (Etcheverry Images), Abingdon, Oxon; **14.1** Thinkstock (LUNAMARINA), München; **15.1** Thinkstock (pattilabelle), München; **18.1** Corbis (Duane Osborn/Somos Images), Berlin; **19** Song: Empire State of Mind, Text: CARTER, SHAWN/HUNTE, ANGELA/KEYES, BERT/Keys, Alicia/Robinson, Sylvia/SEWELL, JANET ANDREA/SHUCKBURGH, ALEXANDER WILLIAM, Verlag: Carter Boys Music / EMI April Music / Foray Music / Gambi Music Inc / Global Talent Publishing / J Sewell Publishing / Lellow Productions Inc / Masani El Shabazz EMI Music Publishing Germany GmbH, Berlin / Rolf Budde Musikverlag GmbH, Berlin / Neue Welt Musikverlag GmbH, Hamburg; **19.1** plainpicture GmbH & Co. KG (mia takahara), Hamburg; **22.1** Alamy Stock Photo (The Print Collector), Abingdon, Oxon; **25.1** shutterstock (Vacclav), New York, NY; **25.3** Thinkstock (stu99), München; **25.2** Alamy Stock Photo (Michael Dwyer), Abingdon, Oxon; **25.4** Thinkstock (iStockphoto), München; **26.1** Getty Images (Lonely Planet/jean pierre lescourret), München; **27.1** Reis, Axel, Oberderdingen; **28.1** Getty Images (Hulton Archive), München; **29.4** Fotolia.com (tharun15), New York; **29.3** Fotolia.com (gguy), New York; **29.2** Fotolia.com (Robert Wilson), New York; **29.1** Alamy Stock Photo (Randy Duchaine), Abingdon, Oxon; **30.1** Getty Images (First Light), München; **30.2** Getty Images (Gallo Images), München; **30.3** Thinkstock (mlharing), München; **32.1** Thinkstock (welcomia), München; **32.2** Alamy Stock Photo (World History Archive), Abingdon, Oxon; **33.1** Thinkstock (IPGGutenbergUKLtd), München; **33.3** Getty Images (J. Meric), München; **33.2** Alamy Stock Photo (Martin Shields), Abingdon, Oxon; **34.5** Getty Images, München; **34.3** Alamy Stock Photo (Marjorie Kamys Cotera/Bob Daemmrich Photography /), Abingdon, Oxon; **34.4** Getty Images (Universal Images Group), München; **34.1** Thinkstock (LivingImages), München; **34.2** plainpicture GmbH & Co. KG (Fancy Images/Hero), Hamburg; **35** Song: Cool Kids, Text: Dzwonek, Jesiah/Sierota, Graham/Sierota, Jamie/Sierota, Jefery/Sierota, Noah/Sierota Sydney, Verlag: Echosmith Songs/WB Music Corp./Jeffery David Songs/Upcast Music D/A/CH Neue Welt Musikverlag GmbH, Hamburg/Roba Music Verlag GmbH, Hamburg, Reach Music Publishing, Burbank CA; **36.2** Thinkstock (Wylius), München; **36.4** Thinkstock (John_Kasawa), München; **36.5** Thinkstock (Ramsey), München; **36.1** Thinkstock (xantuanx), München; **36.3** Thinkstock (Antonius_), München; **36.6** Thinkstock (Jupiterimages), München; **37.1** Alamy Stock Photo (ZUMA Press, Inc.), Abingdon, Oxon; **41.1** Thinkstock (Creatas), München; **45.1** JDM Productions Inc, New York; **47.1** Getty Images (E+/Steve Debenport), München; **48.1** Thinkstock (Digital Vision.), München; **48.2** Thinkstock (michal-rojek), München; **49.1** Getty Images (Roger Lecuyer), München; **50.1** Thinkstock (Mike Watson Images), München; **50.2** Thinkstock (Enterline Design Services LLC), München; **50.3** plainpicture GmbH & Co. KG (Image Source), Hamburg; **52.1** plainpicture GmbH & Co. KG (Michael Runkel), Hamburg; **52.2** Getty Images (Corbis), München; **53.3** f1 online digitale Bildagentur, Frankfurt; **53.2** Getty Images (Aurora), München; **53.1** plainpicture GmbH & Co. KG (NaturePL/Edwin Giesbers), Hamburg; **56.1** Getty Images (Thomas M. Barwick INC), München; **58.2** Thinkstock (Flying Colours Ltd), München; **58.1** Alamy Stock Photo (brt PHOTO), Abingdon, Oxon; **59.4** shutterstock (Maxx-Studio), New York, NY; **59.6** shutterstock (Zorandim), New York, NY; **59.2** Avenue Images GmbH (stock disc), Hamburg; **59.3** Thinkstock (Oleksiy Mark), München; **59.5** MEV Verlag GmbH, Augsburg; **59.1** iStockphoto (RF/Sascha Burkard), Calgary, Alberta; **61.1** Getty Images (Taxi/Troy Aossey), München; **62** From: The body, Stephen King, retold by Robin Waterfield; **62.1** Ullstein Bild GmbH (United Archives / KPA), Berlin; **63.1** Ullstein Bild GmbH (United Archives), Berlin; **67.3** JDM Productions Inc, New York; **67.2** JDM Productions Inc, New York; **67.1** JDM Productions Inc, New York; **67.4** JDM Productions Inc, New York; **70.1** Alamy Stock Photo (North Wind Picture Archives), Abingdon, Oxon; **74.1** shutterstock (mariakraynova), New York, NY; **74.2** plainpicture GmbH & Co. KG (CI2/Joel Bear Studios), Hamburg; **75.1** Getty Images (E+/Johnny Greig), München; **75.2** Getty Images (Kiyoshi Ota/Bloomberg), München; **75.3** Getty Images (Lonely Planet/jean pierre lescourret), München; **76.6** Getty Images (Blend Images), München; **76.1** shutterstock (bikeriderlondon), New York, NY; **76.2** Thinkstock (1001Love), München; **76.4** Alamy Stock Photo (Russ Bishop), Abingdon, Oxon; **76.5** Getty Images (Universal Images Group), München; **76.3** Thinkstock (somchaij), München; **77** Song: Surfin' U.S.A., Text: Brian Wilson, Verlag: ARC Music Corp. Good Tunes Music AG; **77.1** Ullstein Bild GmbH (Rolf Schulten), Berlin; **79.3** Beutel, Ulrike, Stuttgart; **79.4** Beutel, Ulrike, Stuttgart; **79.2** Beutel, Ulrike, Stuttgart; **79.1** Reis, Axel, Oberderdingen; **80.1** Getty Images (Hero Images), München; **81.1** Getty Images (South_agency), München; **83.1** Thinkstock (McIninch), München; **85.1** Alamy Stock Photo (Granger Historical Picture Archive), Abingdon, Oxon; **86.1** Alamy Stock Photo (Russ Bishop), Abingdon, Oxon; **87.1** Getty Images (E+/Steve Debenport), München; **88.1** Alamy Stock Photo (nik wheeler), Abingdon, Oxon; **89.1** JDM Productions Inc, New York; **91.1** Thinkstock (littlewormy), München; **93.1** Reis, Axel, Oberderdingen; **94.2** Reis, Axel, Oberderdingen; **94.1** Reis, Axel, Oberderdingen; **96.2** Alamy Stock Photo (World History Archive), Abingdon, Oxon; **96.1** Getty Images (Stockbyte), München; **97.2** Getty Images (Blend Images), München; **97.3** Getty Images (2013 Kevin Mazur), München; **97.1** Getty Images (Hulton Archive/The Print Collector), München; **98.1** shutterstock (Michael Rosebrock), New York, NY; **98.2** Thinkstock (emarto), München; **99.6** Thinkstock (Monkey Business Images), München; **99.7** Thinkstock (silviacrisman), München; **99.8** Thinkstock (bubu45), München; **99.2** Klett-Archiv-RF-HF, Stuttgart; **99.3** Klett-Archiv-RF-HF, Stuttgart; **99.4** Geoatlas, Hendaye; **99.1** Klett-Archiv-RF-HF, Stuttgart; **99.5** Geoatlas, Hendaye; **102.2** Getty Images (Stocktrek Images), München; **102.1** Getty Images (Jon Feingersh Photography 2011), München; **104.1** Getty Images (kristian sekulic), München; **106.1** laif (Richard Harbus/Polaris), Köln; **106.2** Picture-Alliance (Everett Collection), Frankfurt; **108.1** Getty Images (Sean Gardner), München; **109.3** February Films, London; **109.2** JDM Productions Inc, New York; **109.4** JDM Productions Inc, New York; **109.1** JDM Productions Inc, New York; **112.1** Fotolia.com (lubashi), New York; **113.5** shutterstock (jultud), New York, NY; **113.^6; "shutterstock (Suslik1983), New York, NY; 113.7** Thinkstock (pilipphoto), München; **113.3** Corbis (Matthias Kulka), Berlin; **113.4** shutterstock (George W. Bailey), New York, NY; **113.2** iStockphoto (sspopov), Calgary, Alberta; **113.1** iStockphoto (RF/Dmitry Bezkorovayny), Calgary, Alberta; **114.1** Alamy Stock Photo (US Coast Guard Photo), Abingdon, Oxon; **116.1** Thinkstock (pattilabelle), München; **124.1** Getty Images (Thomas M. Barwick INC), München; **126.3** Thinkstock (Oleksiy Mark), München; **126.4** shutterstock (Maxx-Studio), New York, NY; **126.6** shutterstock (Zorandim), New York, NY; **126.5** MEV Verlag GmbH, Augsburg; **126.1** iStockphoto (RF/Sascha Burkard), Calgary, Alberta; **126.2** Avenue Images GmbH (stock disc), Hamburg; **127.7** Getty Images (Blend Images), München; **127.6** Thinkstock (somchaij), München; **127.5** Thinkstock (1001Love), München; **127.4** Getty Images (Universal Images Group), München; **127.3** Alamy Stock Photo (Russ Bishop), Abingdon, Oxon; **127.2** shutterstock (bikeriderlondon), New York, NY; **127.1** Getty Images (Taxi/Troy Aossey), München; **129.1** Getty Images (Hero Images), München; **131.4** Geoatlas, Hendaye; **131.5** Geoatlas, Hendaye; **131.2** Klett-Archiv-RF-HF, Stuttgart; **131.1** Klett-Archiv-RF-HF, Stuttgart; **131.3** Klett-Archiv-RF-HF, Stuttgart; **132.1** Getty Images (Erika Goldring), München; **136.1** Getty Images (The Image Bank), München; **136.6** Getty Images (WireImage), München; **136.5** Alamy Stock Photo (PYMCA), Abingdon, Oxon; **136.4** Getty Images (Hulton Archive), München; **136.3** Getty Images (Michael Ochs Archives), München; **136.2** Corbis (Owaki - Kulla), Berlin; **137.2** Getty Images (Daniel Zuchnik), München; **137.1** Corbis (Bo Zaunders), Berlin; **138.1** Getty Images RF (The Image Bank), München; **138.3** Getty Images (Dorling Kindersley RF), München; **138.2** Kansas Historical Society, Topeka; **139.1** Getty Images (The Image Bank), München; **140.1** Getty Images RF (The Image Bank), München; **140.4** Thinkstock (JoeGough), München; **140.3** Getty Images (National Geographic Magazines), München; **140.2** Getty Images (Popperfoto), München; **141.2** Getty Images (De Agostini Picture Library), München; **141.3** iStockphoto (circlePS), Calgary, Alberta; **141.1** Getty Images (M_a_y_a), München; **142.1** Getty Images RF (The Image Bank), München; **142.4** Getty Images (Jemal Countess), München; **142.3** Getty Images (Kevin Winter), München; **142.2** Getty Images (Corbis Documentary), München; **143.2** Getty Images (DreamPictures), München; **143.1** Getty Images (Albert L. Ortega), München; **144.1** Getty Images RF (The Image Bank), München; **144.3** Getty Images (Corbis Documentary), München; **144.2** Getty Images (Lonely Planet), München; **145.2** Getty Images (Corbis Documentary), München; **145.1** Getty Images (Photographer's Choice), München; **146.1** Getty Images (Spencer Sutton), München; **146.4** Getty Images (Jiji Press / AFP), München; **146.2** Getty Images (Photolibrary), München; **146.3** Getty Images (Lonely Planet), München; **147.1** Getty Images (Gary S. Chapman), München; **149.1** Getty Images (Blend Images), München; **150.1** The Absolutely True Diary of a Part-Time Indian, Author: Sherman Alexie, Illustrator: Ellen Forney, Andersen Press.; **150-153; "The Absolutely True Diary of a Part-Time Indian, Sherman Alexie, Andersen Press; 151.1** The Absolutely True Diary of a Part-Time Indian, Author: Sherman Alexie, Illustrator: Ellen Forney, Andersen Press.; **152.2** The Absolutely True Diary of a Part-Time Indian, Author: Sherman Alexie, Illustrator: Ellen Forney, Andersen Press.; **152.1** The Absolutely True Diary of a Part-Time Indian, Author: Sherman Alexie, Illustrator: Ellen Forney, Andersen Press.; **190.4** iStockphoto (Marcel Pfost), Calgary, Alberta; **190.9** Fotolia.com (naughtynut), New York; **190.8** Fotolia.com (blondsteve), New York; **190.7** iStockphoto (Dominic Burke RF), Calgary, Alberta; **190.6** Fotolia.com (thorabeti), New York; **190.5** Fotolia.com (Pavel Losevsky), New York; **190.3** Fotolia.com (axeldrosta), New York; **190.2** iStockphoto (Michael Utech), Calgary, Alberta; **190.1** iStockphoto (stockcam), Calgary, Alberta; **191.3** Bananastock, Watlington / Oxon; **191.2** Das Fotoarchiv RF (RF), Essen; **191.1** Thinkstock (Owat Tasai), München; **198.11** iStockphoto (Alejandro Rivera), Calgary, Alberta; **198.10** Klett-Archiv (Weccard), Stuttgart; **198.9** Avenue Images GmbH (StockDisc), Hamburg; **198.8** shutterstock (igor.stevanovic), New York, NY; **198.7** Thinkstock (Stockbyte), München; **198.6** Avenue Images GmbH (Digital Vision), Hamburg; **198.5** Fotolia.com (Michael Shake), New York; **198.4** iStockphoto (Steve Debenport), Calgary, Alberta; **198.3** iStockphoto (herreid), Calgary, Alberta; **198.2** shutterstock (bikeriderlondon), New York, NY; **198.1** Fotosearch Stock Photography (Digital Vision), Waukesha, WI; **213.14** iStockphoto (Linda Steward), Calgary, Alberta; **213.13** Fotolia.com (Markus Mainka), New York; **213.12** iStockphoto (kodachrome25), Calgary, Alberta; **213.11** shutterstock (AXL), New York, NY; **213.10** iStockphoto (RF/Lukasz Janicki), Calgary, Alberta; **213.9** Thinkstock (iStock/Wojciech Gajda), München; **213.8** shutterstock (hadot 760), New York, NY; **213.7** Fotolia.com

(Angela Jones), New York; **213.6** iStockphoto (David Mathies), Calgary, Alberta; **213.5** Fotolia.com (pondchao), New York; **213.4** shutterstock (Alex Melnick), New York, NY; **213.3** iStockphoto (Marcel Pfost), Calgary, Alberta; **213.2** Fotolia.com (Sharpshot), New York; **213.1** Fotolia.com (Achim Thomae), New York; **220.27** shutterstock (Campre83), New York, NY; **220.26** shutterstock (Various-Everythings), New York, NY; **220.25** shutterstock (Niyazz), New York, NY; **220.24** shutterstock (Steve Allen), New York, NY; **220.23** shutterstock (argus), New York, NY; **220.22** shutterstock (Anchiy), New York, NY; **220.21** shutterstock (NAN SKYBLACK), New York, NY; **220.20** shutterstock (Various-Everythings), New York, NY; **220.19** shutterstock (Various-Everythings), New York, NY; **220.18** shutterstock (Various-Everythings), New York, NY; **220.17** shutterstock (Daboost), New York, NY; **220.16** shutterstock (Niyazz), New York, NY; **220.15** shutterstock (Various-Everythings), New York, NY; **220.14** shutterstock (PhotoStockImage), New York, NY; **220.13** shutterstock (Irina Rumyantseva), New York, NY; **220.12** shutterstock (ArpornSeemaroj), New York, NY; **220.11** shutterstock (Various-Everythings), New York, NY; **220.10** shutterstock (Aleksandar Mijatovic), New York, NY; **220.9** shutterstock (Visionsi), New York, NY; **220.8** shutterstock (stockcreations), New York, NY; **220.7** shutterstock (hlphoto), New York, NY; **220.6** shutterstock (rj lerich), New York, NY; **220.5** shutterstock (Aleksandra Duda), New York, NY; **220.4** shutterstock (Troscha), New York, NY; **220.3** shutterstock (stocksolutions), New York, NY; **220.2** shutterstock (Anna Mandrikyan), New York, NY; **220.1** shutterstock (Iryna Denysova), New York, NY; **221.16** Fotolia.com (Stefano Gasparotto), New York; **221.15** Fotolia.com (Kzenon), New York; **221.14** iStockphoto (Lya_Cattel), Calgary, Alberta; **221.13** shutterstock (Kzenon), New York, NY; **221.12** Fotolia.com (Iuliia Sokolovska), New York; **221.11** shutterstock (Scott Sanders), New York, NY; **221.10** Thinkstock (Jupiterimages), München; **221.9** iStockphoto (Linda Steward), Calgary, Alberta; **221.8** shutterstock (gorillaimages), New York, NY; **221.7** Fotolia.com (Thaut Images), New York; **221.6** Fotolia.com (Robert Pernell), New York; **221.5** Fotolia.com (Sharpshot), New York; **221.4** shutterstock (AXL), New York, NY; **221.3** shutterstock (Alex Melnick), New York, NY; **221.2** Fotolia.com (pondchao), New York; **221.1** iStockphoto (Marcel Pfost), Calgary, Alberta;

Textquellennachweis

S. 19: Song: Empire State of Mind, Text: CARTER, SHAWN/HUNTE, ANGELA/KEYES, BERT/Keys, Alicia/Robinson, Sylvia/SEWELL, JANET ANDREA/SHUCKBURGH, ALEXANDER WILLIAM, Verlag: Carter Boys Music / EMI April Music / Foray Music / Gambi Music Inc / Global Talent Publishing / J Sewell Publishing / Lellow Productions Inc / Masani El Shabazz EMI Music Publishing Germany GmbH, Berlin / Rolf Budde Musikverlag GmbH, Berlin / Neue Welt Musikverlag GmbH, Hamburg

S. 35: Song: Cool Kids, Text: Dzwonek, Jesiah/Sierota, Graham/Sierota, Jamie/Sierota, Jefery/Sierota, Noah/Sierota Sydney, Verlag: Echosmith Songs/WB Music Corp./Jeffery David Songs/Upcast Music D/A/CH Neue Welt Musikverlag GmbH, Hamburg/ Roba Music Verlag GmbH, Hamburg, Reach Music Publishing, Burbank CA

S. 62: From: The body, Stephen King, retold by Robin Waterfield

S. 77: Song: Surfin' U.S.A., Text: Brian Wilson, Verlag: ARC Music Corp. Good Tunes Music AG

S. 150–153: The Absolutely True Diary of a Part-Time Indian, Sherman Alexie, Andersen Press

Sollte es in einem Einzelfall nicht gelungen sein, den korrekten Rechteinhaber ausfindig zu machen, so werden berechtigte Ansprüche selbstverständlich im Rahmen der üblichen Regelungen abgegolten.

ALASKA
Denali
CANADA
CANADA
Seattle
Portland
WASHINGTON
OREGON
IDAHO
MONTANA
NORTH DAKOTA
SOUTH DAKO
WYOMING
NEBRASKA
Rocky Mountains
NEVADA
UTAH
San Francisco
Denver
COLORADO
CALIFORNIA
Las Vegas
HOLLYWOOD
Los Angeles
ARIZONA
OKLA
Pacific Ocean
San Diego
Phoenix
NEW MEXICO
TEXAS
HAWAII
MEXICO